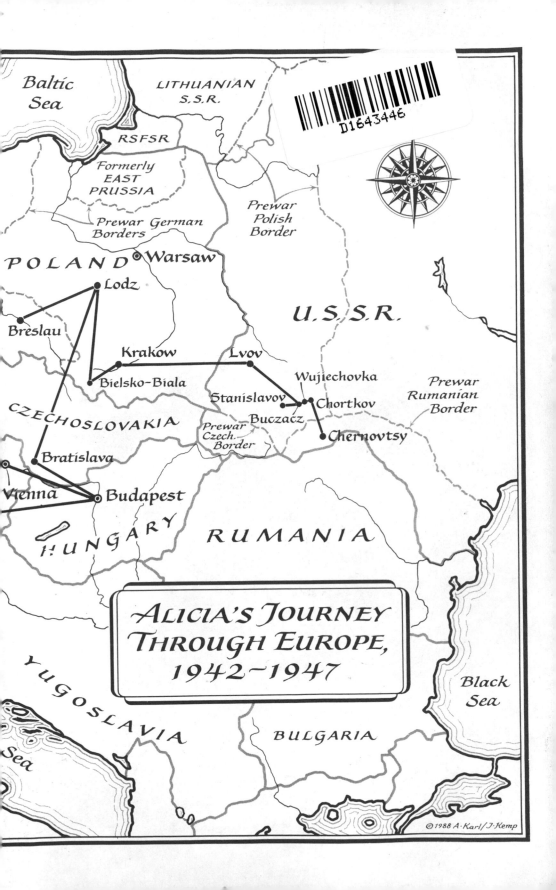

Baltic
Sea

LITHUANIAN
S.S.R.

RSFSR

Formerly
EAST
PRUSSIA

Prewar German
Borders

Prewar
Polish
Border

P O L A N D   ○ Warsaw

Lodz

Breslau

U. S. S. R.

Krakow   Lvov

Bielsko-Biala   Wujiechovka

CZECHOSLOVAKIA   Stanislavov   Chortkov   Prewar
Rumanian
Border

Buczacz

Prewar
Czech.
Border   Chernovtsy

Bratislava

Vienna   ○ Budapest

H U N G A R Y

R U M A N I A

ALICIA'S JOURNEY THROUGH EUROPE, 1942–1947

Y U G O S L A V I A

BULGARIA

Black
Sea

Sea

ALICIA

Alicia Appleman-Jurman

BANTAM PRESS

LONDON · NEW YORK · TORONTO · SYDNEY · AUCKLAND

*This book is dedicated to the children
of the ghettos who were cruelly murdered
by the Nazis and their collaborators.*

*May their memory live on forever, and
may children never again suffer such
anguish and despair.*

TRANSWORLD PUBLISHERS LTD
61-63 Uxbridge Road, London W5 5SA

TRANSWORLD PUBLISHERS (AUSTRALIA) PTY LTD
15-23 Helles Avenue, Moorebank, NSW 2170

TRANSWORLD PUBLISHERS (NZ) LTD
Cnr Moselle and Waipareira Aves,
Henderson, Auckland

Published 1989 by Bantam Press
a division of Transworld Publishers Ltd
Copyright © Alicia A. Appleman 1988
Endpaper map copyright © 1988 Anita Karl and Jim Kemp

British Library Cataloguing in Publication Data

Appleman-Jurman, Alicia, *1930–*
Alicia.
1. Poland. Jews. Appleman-Jurman, Alicia,
1930–
I. Title
940.53'15'03924

ISBN 0-593-01593-2

Printed and bound in Great Britain
by Mackays of Chatham plc, Chatham, Kent.

ACKNOWLEDGMENTS

This book is the story of an important and painful part of my life. I wish it were possible to express my thanks to every friend who believed in Alicia, many of whom read and provided constructive comments on the early drafts of my manuscript. I would, however, like to take this opportunity to acknowledge the contributions of the following friends: first, my gratitude to Janet Pack, who interviewed me for a newspaper article in 1978, encouraged me to write my story, and suffered with me as I relived the experiences of the war years.

The friendship of Margot Van Geffen, herself a survivor of a Japanese prison camp in Indonesia, and that of the wonderful family of Lou and Eve Sanders who gave me the courage to continue during the years I worked on the manuscript in Haarlem, Holland, where my husband was temporarily assigned. I owe much as well to the support of my friends at Beth Shalom in Whittier, California, to the members of the Shoah survivors organization, and to the students of Adat Noar.

I want to acknowledge the contribution of Sara J. Mitchell, whose constructive analysis and comments were invaluable in preparing the manuscript for submission to the publishing industry. I am grateful to my teacher at Fullerton College, James Blaylock, from whom I learned much about writing and for the advice and encouragement given me by Larry Belin. I thank Amy Roland for finding George M. Greenfield and George for agreeing to become my agent and for his efforts, which culminated in the decision by Bantam Books to publish my story.

I was very impressed by the quality of the editing of my manuscript by Bantam's Linda Loewenthal, whose comments, painted with a fine brush, have added greatly to the readability of the work, and I thank

Nessa Rapoport, who, with Linda, recognized a story that needed to be told and offered her support and encouragement. I wish to express my appreciation to Linda Biagi of Bantam Books for her efforts to place the book in foreign markets, since it is very important to me that my story be heard everywhere.

I am grateful for the support and understanding of my children, Daniel, Ronit, and Zachary, and Ronit's husband, Eric. Last but not least, I wish to acknowledge the contribution of my husband, Gabriel, whose native language is English and whose knowledge of grammar and usage was invaluable. Gabriel patiently edited my text without changing either my style or the meanings I wished to express.

CONTENTS

FOREWORD

I met Alicia in Israel in 1949. She was Ada then, and I was a volunteer, one of many who came to help defend that fledgling state. I was an assimilated, English-speaking American Jew with little knowledge of what had happened in Hitler's Europe other than what I had seen from a line of foxholes stretching from Omaha Beach in France to Paderborn, Germany, as an enlisted man in the United States Third and Ninth armies. Perhaps I was in Israel to appease my conscience, my feeling of guilt that I had not known enough, my illogical feeling that I could have done more to help my fellow Jews in Europe.

One day in early spring Alicia walked into my Hebrew class. There she was, tall, slender, dressed in the British style battle dress that was the uniform of the Israel defense forces, and wearing the big smile that is still her trademark—by anyone's standard a beauty. There was some chemistry. We became friends, then fell in love and married. Yes, I married Ada. I didn't know that I had also married Alicia.

In those first years of our marriage I spoke only a few words of Hebrew, a smattering of German from school and combat, and no Yiddish. Ada spoke some English, German, and the Slavic languages: Polish, Ukrainian, and Russian. Whenever we met anyone from what seemed to me to be an endless roster of Ada's friends, I would feel isolated in a sea of alien syllables. Yet Ada and I managed to communicate, and as I started to understand what she was saying, I began to realize, slowly, that there was a part of her life that I could never share. There was a bond of mutual experience between Alicia and her friends, Heniek, Beniek, and Tunia—and in those days, in my ignorance, I was jealous.

When Ada (Alicia) would cry and scream in her dreams at night, I

ix

would try to comfort her. I was not completely stupid; I simply didn't understand. Like most American Jews, I didn't know. We had been aware that Jews were being persecuted, beaten, put into camps. But a holocaust? furnaces? mass graves? It was only when the Allied forces entered the Nazi death camps that the full truth began to impact the world, and most forcibly the Jewish communities outside Europe. Even then, reading about the Holocaust did not have the same impact as living with someone who had been part of it.

It is not easy. It hurts. To this American husband it was devastating. There are multiple impacts: first I reacted with "There but for the grace of God go I." Then I questioned: Can human beings really do such things? Can it happen again? Could it happen to us? Should we have known? We owe them. Guilt. Guilt. Guilt.

Jews who survived the war in Europe are driven. They cannot forget, and they cannot bear the thought that the world will not remember. As they grow older, it becomes more and more important to them that no one be permitted to forget. This is what survivors owe the dead. It is the means by which survivors hope to prevent history from repeating itself.

For those who have not shared their experience, the stories of the Holocaust years can be wearing. They are hard to read, to hear. After thirty-six years of marriage they are still difficult for me to bear, and I must close my ears and my mind occasionally to preserve my sanity. Yet there are still important stories to be told and facts to be recorded, especially today, when there are those who would like to rewrite history.

Not all Jews died in the death camps. Not all Jews went to their deaths helplessly . . . many did not defend themselves in the mistaken belief that to do so would endanger the lives of others. Few have told the story of those who did fight back and survived and of their lives in Europe during the early postwar years. Alicia's experiences as told in this book make up such a story.

Alicia, whose name I Americanized from Ada to Alice in the United States and who now, with this book, is at peace with herself and wishes to resume her real name, has devoted over three years to the writing of *Alicia*. It has been an agonizing task. To write this book she has had to relive experiences that had been buried, mercifully, in her subconscious memories. She has had to reopen all her old wounds.

Yet I feel that the finished book has justified her work and pain. It is an autobiography. It is factual. It has not been embellished. All that has been changed are some of the names of people she wanted to save the anguish of remembering. And it tells the story of a young girl who managed to survive in a hostile world. It describes the actions of real people in a very unreal environment. The Nazis could not have almost completely destroyed the Jews of Poland had there been resistance to this by their neighbors, the Poles and Ukrainians. Actively, or by not acting, these people cooperated with the Germans. Yet Alicia tells of instances of kindness by individuals.

Can we say that all Germans, Poles, and Ukrainians were evil? Can we understand the rationalizations that Jews were not "one of us," or "had it coming," or were "Christ killers" and were being punished by God? To what extent did nice people close their hearts and minds to what was happening? To what extent was this dictated by personal fears or by self-interest? There are insights contained within this book which, as I discuss them with her, surprise even Alicia.

The real world is not black or white but many shades and colors. The story of Alicia covers the range of human experience. There are moments of tragedy and despair, true, but there are also moments of sweetness and even humor. Above all, Alicia has described a young girl who faced a terrifying and violent world and managed to retain her faith in humanity, in God, and in her people.

—Gabriel Appleman
California, June 1986

CHAPTER 1

Before the War

First they killed my brother Moshe. . . .
Then they killed my father. . . .
Then they killed my brother Bunio. . . .
Then they killed my brother Zachary. . . .
Then they killed my last brother, Herzl.
Only my mother and I were left. I vowed that I would never let them kill her, that I would protect my mother from the Nazis and their collaborators for as long as I lived.
Love and hate were what motivated my young mind and heart. Love for my dear, gentle mother—and hate for the cruel murderers.
And this is my story.

In 1938, there were eighteen thousand Jewish people in our Polish city of Buczacz, nearly one-third of the total population. Some of the more orthodox Jews wore the classic black frock coats and fur hats, while others dressed just like the rest of the residents and were largely well-integrated into the community.
We had many things to be proud of: the Hebrew schools, the Talmud Torah house, and our joy and pride, the Great Synagogue. It was a very impressive large structure with tall stained-glass windows. It had a small synagogue attached to one side, giving the impression of a father and son standing there proudly. The small synagogue was used for daily prayers, and the large synagogue for the Sabbath and the rest of the holidays.

I was quite familiar with the synagogue, since my older brother Bunio sang in the choir. We had a handsome young rabbi with a beautiful wife, and both were accomplished violinists. The rabbi chose his choir from among the students with good voices who attended Mr. Kofler's Hebrew school. My brother Bunio, who was an alto, was selected, and so was his friend David, who was a soprano. They were both soloists during the High Holiday prayers. I often listened to their rehearsals, sitting in the semi-darkness of the balcony, where the ladies prayed. My brother's voice would reach into the depth of my soul and carry me off into the beauty of its words and melody.

It was in this synagogue that Bunio had his Bar Mitzvah. Bunio's beautiful voice was a sensation. Of course Mama and I had to watch from upstairs, but we could see and hear everything. My youngest brother, Herzl, saved us some of the candies that were thrown at the Bar Mitzvah boy. We had a kiddush at the synagogue, a reception at home, and my mother prepared the midday meal for the students of the Beth Hamidrash—the house of Jewish studies. It was a beautiful day.

Part of being Jewish in Poland was learning to live with anti-Semitism. As a young child I had not encountered Jew-haters, partly because I was born in the remote mountains and also because my parents and older brothers were so protective. I didn't classify my friends as Jewish or Gentile, although I knew there was a difference between Judaism and Christianity. Life was pretty good, and we were happy—until the first shocking act of anti-Semitism hit our family.

It happened to my oldest brother, Zachary, in May of 1938. He was a student at the conservatory of music in Lvov and was on his way to school, violin case in hand, when a gang of five Polish boys began following him. They were Polish university students. "How about a little music, Jew-boy?" one of them asked. The others laughed. Zachary kept on walking, his eyes looking straight ahead, his fist clenching tighter around the handle of the case.

"What's the matter, Zhid [Jew]," another boy said. "Are you deaf or something?"

"How can he play the violin if he is deaf?" said another.

"Come on, Zhid, let's hear you play."

At that point my brother stopped. Turning around, he appraised the situation. Two of the boys were as tall as he; the others were shorter but stockier. They were all students in school uniforms. "Please, let me go in peace," Zachary said to them.

The boys surrounded him. "Not until you play us a song." One of the boys pushed him back roughly; another reached out and snatched away the violin case. My brother lunged toward him, but two others caught him and threw him against a wall, holding his arms firmly. A boy opened the case, took out the violin and bow, and began to make sawing noises on the instrument while the others laughed. "Well, it's no wonder you wouldn't play for us," he said. "This thing isn't worth anything." With that he bent over and smashed the violin against the pavement. With a cry Zachary broke free and threw himself forward, nearly reaching the boy. He was stopped by a swift kick in the stomach, which doubled him over with pain and took away his breath. That was when the boys fell upon him, kicking and punching. They held him by the hair and slammed his head against the pavement. They kicked him in the ribs, took turns holding his arms so the others could beat him, and finally left him there in the street, his broken violin a few feet away. He was helped by a Jewish music student who brought him back to his room.

Zachary came home to Buczacz by train with his wounds still fresh. I will never forget how my father paced back and forth as my mother examined Zachary and bandaged him. We were all there in the kitchen, all except for Bunio, who had choir practice and would be home later. I thought of him there at the synagogue, singing his heart out, not knowing his older brother had been beaten and humiliated.

The first time I really became aware of Germany and what was going on in Europe was when I went to get my father at Horovitz's candy store, where he was engaged in a game of billiards in the back room. I was waiting for him while sitting in a chair and eating an ice cream cone. Nearby, two men were smoking and talking. I did not pay much attention at first, but the word "war" caught my attention. I knew from history books about wars, and I had seen Papa's medal for bravery, which he had earned as an Austrian officer in the First World War. I also knew that wars could be terrible. One of the men insisted that Germany was going to move east no matter what, and there was going to be a war. Austria had already been invaded and Poland was going to be next, he continued. But the other man was more optimistic, saying that England was not going to let this happen. They kept mentioning other countries I had studied in my geography class, and suddenly the maps I had drawn seemed more real and threatening. I was loyal to my country and did not want anything to happen to it.

On the way home I mentioned this conversation to my father and his face became very sad. I knew his parents were in Austria and so were many of his friends. I realized suddenly that there was a lot going on that we children did not know and that I, at the age of eight, was too young to understand. Yet, from that day on I kept asking questions, and the answers I got frightened me.

But life had to go on, including school and Hebrew classes, and homework and friends, so I let things go; but the seed of worry was planted in my mind, and it grew. During the summer of 1938, which I spent at my uncle's home in Stanislavov where he practiced medicine, I tried to find out what was going on from my friend Milek, but he could not explain things to me. He did not know too much himself. My uncle was very busy that summer caring for his sick patients, and, as usual, he was very loving and wanted me to have a good time. He probably knew in his heart that the war would soon begin.

CHAPTER 2

Life Under the Russians

Poland will never forget the year 1939. Hitler had annexed Austria in 1938 and part of Czechoslovakia in March of 1939, without encountering resistance. Then, on September 1, Germany attacked Poland. The Poles fought bravely but were no match for the Germans, and within a couple of weeks the Polish army was defeated. Germany signed a peace treaty with Russia, and Hitler and Stalin divided Poland between them. East Poland, where we lived, was invaded by the Russians on September 17, 1939.

Before the Russians actually entered our city, cars carrying Polish army officers and their families traveled through our city for days on their way to the Romanian border. They were fleeing from the Germans, whose air force was bombing cities and civilians. Sometimes they would stop their cars for a rest, and I would have a chance to watch them. They looked very tired and sad, but the Polish pride and carriage was still there; even defeat could not take that away.

And then one day the traffic stopped, and an unusual hush fell over the city. There was an expectancy in the air and a general nervousness generated by the adults. We children were acutely aware that something very important was going to happen. We knew from the radio that Poland was losing the war with Germany, and the word "Russia" was heard often in our parents' conversations.

5

Strangers dressed in unfamiliar styles of clothing appeared on the streets. They were refugees from Germany, the majority of them Jewish. My parents were busy trying to find homes for them. My older brothers stayed home most of the time, and they explained the political situation to me. I heard about the Russian revolution and what Red Russia stood for. Before I had a chance to digest this information, the Russians entered Buczacz. A small group of people from our city came down the main street carrying red flags. Behind them was a cannon pulled by two horses followed by several soldiers.

I had expected a tremendous invasion. Surely, I thought, such a small army could not hurt us badly. But the following day the army trucks came, and within a few days the streets were filled with soldiers. They were everywhere, and to my surprise they were friendly.

The stores reopened and the soldiers flooded them. They bought everything in sight and paid with rubles (Russian currency). The soldiers were most interested in leather goods. My friend's father had a shoestore on the Hala Targova, and within two days his store was completely empty. What puzzled me most was how the soldiers bought the boots without trying them on. One day my friend and I watched in amazement as they left the shops carrying piles of big boxes that almost completely covered their faces. When they saw us, they put down their purchases and gave us each a small red enamel star, the same as the larger stars they wore pinned to their hats. They smiled and seemed quite likable. From their behavior it was clear that they intended to stay for a long time, if not forever, and they were working very hard to win the people's approval—especially that of the children.

School reopened for a new academic year. Russian teachers came to teach, and the major languages became Russian and Ukrainian. German was also taught, perhaps in honor of the Russian-German treaty. Our Polish teachers now had to learn Russian and Ukrainian in order to teach.

I will never forget our first day at school. I had my first shock when I entered our classroom and saw that the Madonna and Child were removed from their customary spot, replaced with pictures of two men. One, we were told, was Lenin and the other Stalin. They looked down on us very sternly, which I didn't like at all. I was deeply offended and hurt by this turn of events. Even though I was Jewish, I had a deep respect for the religion of my friends and felt their pain and disappointment. Luckily though, the churches and the synagogues remained open. Had they been closed, the people would have been enraged, and I don't know what would have happened.

So far we had not suffered from religious deprivation. However, we soon suffered from being classified as capitalists. A businessman was considered an enemy of the Soviet Union and was very soon relieved of his business and merchandise. Those who did not have businesses but were known as businessmen were asked to donate merchandise—clothing mainly—because the Russians assumed that their merchandise was kept at home. My father's fabric business in Bielsko, now under German occupation, was lost. He was asked to donate his samples, which he did.

Most of us, with the exception of a few, returned to our classrooms. Among the missing was a very fine boy and good student, Jezek Janowski, whose father had been head of the Polish police. What upset us the most was the absence of a lovely girl and my good friend, Wisia Urbanska. Both her parents were teachers. Her mother taught in our school, and her father was a high school math teacher.

One day I came home from school very upset. I couldn't eat my dinner, and instead of doing my homework I just sat staring at the pages. My mother noticed my mood and, gently taking my hands, pulled me to my feet and asked me to follow her. We sat down on the grass in the backyard and Mama, looking straight into my eyes, asked, "Alicia, dear, what is bothering you?"

I lowered my eyes, not wanting my mother to see the tears that were gathering there.

"I am frightened, Mama. My school friends are disappearing. Jezek Janowski has been missing for several days, and now Wisia and her mother have not come to school. There is a rumor going around that they have been taken away. Are they going to take us away too? Please tell me, Mama."

"Alicia, please look at me. I will try to explain the situation to you," my mother said softly.

"The rumors you have heard are true. The Russians are deporting former Polish government officials, Jewish refugees from Germany, and both Jewish and Gentile businessmen.

"Yes, we could be deported too," Mama added almost in a whisper. "But your uncle in Stanislavov, whose medical specialty is important to the Russians, is taking care of our safety, and the rest is up to God."

"But where are they being deported to, and when will they return to their homes?" I asked.

"We have heard that they are being taken to Siberia, and I don't know if they will ever return. We have to hope that they will."

＊　＊　＊

Even though my schoolmates and I worried over who would be missing next, we soon found ourselves very busy with little time to think. We had challenges before us. We had to learn new languages— Russian, Ukrainian, Latin, and German—in order to read the hundreds of handwritten pages the teachers gave us instead of books.

In addition to school we continued with our Hebrew lessons. We had to hide our teacher, Dr. Ferenhoff. Although he was given the title of rabbi and was considered a man of religion by the Russian authorities, he was not permitted to keep his school open to teach. Therefore, the Jewish parents ran an underground school, moving Dr. Ferenhoff from home to home. Even though we had to crowd around one table, hitting one another's elbows as we wrote, we enjoyed our studies and tried hard to please our teacher. We knew instinctively that he would be in danger if he were found to be teaching us.

My fears lessened somewhat when Zachary was given a permit to return to the conservatory in Lvov. Then to my great surprise my father was assigned to manage a chinaware store. I was very happy to see my father working, and I hoped this meant that we would not be sent to Siberia.

Bunio, Moshe, and Herzl attended the boys' school on Kolejova Street. As we began to understand the Russian language, the teachers and the government officials started a serious campaign to indoctrinate us into the Soviet system. The Russian-language teacher was always quoting things that Stalin had said. He, the teacher said, was the father of all children, and he commanded us to learn, and learn, and learn. I did not believe such stories. I had a father at home; besides, I did not like this man hanging in the place of the Madonna.

Actually life under Russian rule was not unpleasant. As the end of the school year approached, I was expecting all A's on my report card, which pleased me greatly. I brought my drawings to the art exhibit in the high school and won several prizes for my watercolors of mountain people and their surroundings. My notebook of flowers and leaves was also exhibited and was greatly admired by my classmates.

I was looking forward to the summer vacation with great anticipation. Zachary would be home and I would be able to follow him around again. I would go swimming in the river Stripa and explore the Fador, the meadowland that adjoined our city. Part of the time I promised to spend with a new classmate, Tunia, who had moved to Buczacz from nearby Tlusty. I had promised to help her with her Russian studies. When summer finally came, it met all my expectations and the time passed quickly.

*   *   *

The Russians were very interested in promoting their educational system and, at the beginning of the second school year, they began to encourage local students to attend school in the Soviet Union. This could be done now because all of us had become sufficiently fluent in the Russian language.

My second oldest brother, Moshe, had always been a good student and, lured by the opportunity for a better education, asked my parents if he might be allowed to study in Leningrad. Since Moshe had already studied away from home before the war had started, he knew how to take care of himself. Because of this and his persistence, he was granted permission.

So Moshe went off to Leningrad. Months went by. We sent him mail constantly, and my mother was forever going down to the post with packages of home-baked goodies. Moshe wrote back frequently at first; then his letters began arriving monthly, almost as though on a regular schedule. Something was strange about those later letters. While they were written in his hand, they didn't sound like my brother. They were cold, almost robotlike, and every letter praised the Soviet school system.

My parents became increasingly alarmed with each new letter. What was happening to their son? They wrote, asking questions that were never answered. There was no mention of his ever getting the cookies Mother had sent. Suddenly it was as though she had a stranger for a son.

Finally they began suggesting he come home, but he scorned the idea and insisted on staying in Leningrad. My father would have loved to go to Russia and personally bring Moshe home, but because our own situation was tenuous at best and traveling restrictions were rigid, it was impossible.

And then it happened! Moshe came home. I remember the night well. It was early morning, about two or three A.M. I did not hear the pounding on the front door, although others did. I awoke to footsteps running past my room and down the stairs. Then I heard my mother cry out. For a moment I remained under my covers, but then curiosity and concern for my mother drove me out. As I reached the top of the stairs, I saw all of my family gathered around my father, who held Moshe in a tight embrace.

My brother looked ghastly. Always a slender boy, he was now gaunt and pale. Dark circles ringed his eyes, giving his face a ghoulish, almost skeletal appearance. He was sobbing, as was my mother. But it was the look on my father's face that struck me the most. He looked as though he were in terrible pain but dared not let it show. Although he did not weep, his eyes were red as he cradled his son's head against his chest and stroked Moshe's rumpled hair. Because my father had been unable to act, his son had had to suffer in this way. Poor father, he loved us so much.

What Moshe told us about his experience in Russia explained all too well the bizarre contents of his letters. He had written them, it was true, but he and all the other students had been told what to say. Letters to and from home were screened carefully. Students were punished for any disparaging remarks made and were instructed to ignore inquiries about their living conditions.

He had been at school outside of Leningrad, where he and the other students were always hungry. Because of war preparations, there wasn't enough food; but the Russians didn't want the outside world to know. None of the students had had proper winter clothing, and packages from home were confiscated. The students were told that the packages would be distributed among the more needy Russians. All of Moshe's clothes were in tatters. In addition to their studies, which were grueling, all students had to work in nearby farms for the benefit of the state.

Finally my brother could bear it no longer. He had reached a point, he said, where if he didn't leave, he felt he would die. And so he schemed for weeks, waiting for the proper moment. When it came, out he went. For days he traveled, sometimes hitching a ride but mostly walking through woods and fields by night. He barely slept, so frightened was he of detection. And he had been able to bring only a little food along. The boy was near collapse; it was a miracle that he had been able to make it home.

Just before we went to sleep, Father told us to keep Moshe's return a secret until he could settle into life with us again. During those days Moshe slept a lot and ate ravenously. His color began to improve, and the circles under his eyes were starting to fade; but he was different from the boy who had left. He was jumpy and nervous. He didn't want to talk much, not even to Bunio, with whom he was very close.

Moshe had been home for about three weeks, when the Russian secret police came. I remember that they came late at night. The sound of their banging on the front door rang through the quiet house and awakened everyone. My mother told us children, Moshe as well, to stay upstairs; my father went down to talk to the police. They told him there was no real problem; they only wanted to talk to Moshe and hear his complaints about the school. They had received a notice from Leningrad that Moshe was missing. If students are unhappy in Russian schools, they said, they wanted to know why.

I couldn't judge how much time my father spent with the men, but after a while he came upstairs, had my brother get dressed, and the two of them went away with the police. I heard my father tell my mother, "We will be there only a few hours," as they left for the police station. She sent us all back to bed but waited up for Father's return.

I saw my father in the morning, and from his face and the look in his eyes I immediately knew that Moshe had not returned with him. I had to go to school even though I would rather have stayed home. I remembered what Father had said when Moshe got home—to keep everything normal. So reluctantly I left for school. When I got home I found out that Moshe had been taken to the Chortkov prison and that Father had followed him to Chortkov to wait until he was released.

Father was gone for four days, and when he came back Moshe was not with him. At the prison he had been told that Moshe was being kept until it could be decided how his case should be handled, whether or not he would be returned to the school in Leningrad, whether he would be allowed to remain in Buczacz, and what disciplinary action, if any, would be taken.

"Why are they holding him?" I asked Bunio.

"It's because they don't want him talking," he said. "They don't want word to get around about how bad it is in Russia."

A month went by, then two, then three. My father was allowed to go to the prison about once a month to see my brother. After these visits he would report that Moshe looked well, that his spirits were high, and that he would be coming home soon, hopefully very soon. But after we children had gone to bed, he would tell my mother the truth about their son; that they were trying to make an example of him on orders from Leningrad, and that the local authorities couldn't change the orders.

Then one early morning a policeman came to our home. It was bad news, he said. Moshe had died suddenly. It looked as though food poisoning was the cause. Our family was in shock. We had been hoping for his release from prison every day, and now he was dead.

Father left immediately for Chortkov. We stayed home from school waiting for his return with my brother's body, but he came home alone. They wouldn't let him bring his son home. Moshe was buried in the prison cemetery. Father brought back the only possession my brother was allowed to have in prison—a chess set he had made from bread. As my father fingered the little nubs of dried bread that had served as my brother's pawns and rooks, his eyes grew teary. "The commandant told me how very sorry he was," he said, his voice filled with pain. "He said that had our son lived, he could have become a champion chess player."

A kind of darkness descended upon our home. It felt as though the sun had stopped shining and the world stood frozen. We followed the traditional seven days of mourning, the shiva. We sat on low stools. Papa and my brothers had their garments torn at the lapels. People came to visit and sit with us.

Zachary came home, but even his presence could not stop me from crying for my brother. I felt very guilty. Perhaps I should have loved him more. But I did truly love him. I remembered how he had once told me that he wanted to become a tree doctor.

"You mean a doctor like Uncle Kurtz?" I had asked.

Moshe burst out laughing. "Not like Uncle Kurtz; a tree doctor, a little like Grandpa Kurtz."

"Grandpa is going to be surrounded by doctors, since I, too, want to be a doctor," I said. Moshe patted my hand gently and smiled.

Now he was dead. I would never see him again. An emotion I couldn't even understand gripped me, and I couldn't stop crying.

My brother's death brought changes in my parents. Mama was very pale and was constantly wiping her eyes. She moved in kind of a trance and didn't answer us when we were talking to her. My heart ached for her, and I was very worried that she might get ill.

Papa looked thinner. He was not attentive to us the way he used to be, and the light in his beautiful blue eyes, the joyous sparkle that went with his laughter, disappeared. Moshe's death meant more than the loss of a son—it also made my parents realize that their lives were not their own to control, that they no longer had the power to protect their children. We had found out, as had many others, what life under Russian occupation could really mean.

CHAPTER 3

The German
Occupation

As quickly as they had entered, the Russians disappeared from Buczacz. It was at the beginning of the fall of 1941. School had closed for the summer and classes had not yet resumed when the sound of guns were heard outside the city. Word had it that the Germans were close by. Then one morning all the Russians were gone, and with them some of our own townspeople, who, because they had supported the Russians, now feared reprisals from the Germans.

After the Russians left, there was wild looting in town. Windows were smashed, stores ransacked—even my father's china shop fell victim to the mobs. Then it became quiet, and the townspeople waited for their new captors. Our Jewish community was particularly concerned. Would the Germans treat us as they did their own Jews? Many families had fled to Poland from Germany when the war began in 1939. My father had in fact worked to bring over a German Jewish doctor and his two children—their mother had already died.

Then the Germans came. Mostly I remember the motorcycles. To this day I shudder when I hear the roaring sound of a motorcycle outside my house. No one really knew what would happen, and everyone was in shock. I was mostly wondering if school would start on time and whether Jewish children would be allowed to attend.

One day when I came down to breakfast my father was not there.

"Where is Papa?" I asked.

"Oh, he left early," said my mother as she served me my porridge. "He has gone to register."

"Register? Register for what?"

My brother Bunio reached across me for a piece of bread.

"Haven't you heard that all men between the ages of eighteen and fifty are to register at the police station?"

"No."

"Well, there you are," he said between bites.

"When will he be home?" I asked as my mother placed a glass of milk before me.

"By midday, most likely," she said. "Now, Alicia, eat your breakfast."

Midday came, and my father did not return. The sky had clouded over, and at two o'clock we heard a sound like thunder outside the town, coming from the direction of the Fador.

By nightfall Papa still had not returned, and Bunio was sent to the police station to find out what was happening. "Go back home," he was told. "Your father will get home in due time."

It was obvious that Papa would not be coming home that night. My mother did not sleep, and we children took turns sitting up with her. She was very troubled. Although she tried not to show it, the tightly gripped handkerchief in her hand revealed her anguish.

In the early morning my mother left the house to meet with the men who had formed a committee to represent the Jewish people to the German authorities. They were later to be known as the Judenrat, but then they were an unofficial committee consisting of a number of well-known Jewish men. Mother was gone only a short while and, upon her return, went straight into her bedroom. She was there a short time, then hastily left the house again. I wanted to ask her where she was going, but she was in such a hurry I decided not to; instead, I followed her. She went into a building near our big synagogue. As I waited for her to come out, I saw more women enter the building, and a terrible fear gripped my heart. Was this some kind of registration of mothers now? Would my mama be gone the way Papa was? Then the door opened and mother appeared. Walking very stiffly, looking neither to the left nor to the right, she went straight home. I waited a little while longer and followed her.

Now, with Mother safely home, I thought once more of my father.

Maybe he had returned home during my absence and I would find him there.

I saw my brother Bunio leave the house, and, fearing that he might reprimand me for being out so early, I set upon him first.

"Bunio, where are you going so early and why are you leaving us alone? Does Mama know you are going out?"

"She sent me to the police station to ask for news about Papa," he said.

"May I come with you? Please, Bunio."

"Not now. You help Mama; she is very nervous right now."

Bunio was right. Mother was nervous but did not seem particularly sad. She was lost in thought and did not even ask me where I had been when I entered the kitchen. Bunio came home shortly with the same answer. "Papa will return in time."

But Papa did not return. Three days passed, and we had not heard from him. By this time the families who had had their men taken were frantic. The realization that they had completely disappeared began to sink in, followed by anger and desperation.

Both Bunio and Zachary made discreet inquiries of their Christian friends. No one had seen anything. If they knew something, they were not going to tell. One of them mentioned the Fador; that was all. The search for the missing men started. Bunio went to the Fador fearing the worst, but could find nothing, not so much as a trace. About six hundred leading citizens of our Jewish community had just vanished.

His news angered me. "You couldn't have looked very hard," I accused him.

"Alicia, I looked everywhere."

"You couldn't have. You couldn't have."

"Alicia"—his voice was gentle—"I looked everywhere I could think of."

My mother, listening to our argument, sat quietly, holding my brother Herzl on her lap, looking drained of all strength. The ordeal was clearly showing on her now.

Zachary spoke. "Do you remember the thunder we heard the other day? Don't you remember how odd we thought it?"

Suddenly I realized what he was hinting at. "It *was* thunder!" I cried. "Don't tell me it wasn't."

"It could have been thunder, sweetheart, but I didn't think so then. I think"—he looked at my mother, and with a choked voice added—"we should start preparing ourselves for the worst."

"No," I cried. "No! He is still somewhere, our father is still . . . I tell you!"

My mother did not speak up. Did she believe this nonsense too?

"Well," I said, "if you can't find him, I will."

"Alicia, you won't find him," said Bunio, shaking his head.

"Yes, I will," I cried hotly. "And don't you try to stop me!"

I ran over the Fador into the woods. I went back and forth, calling and calling. "Papa! It's Alicia! Papa, where are you?"

I must have walked for miles and miles, from the woods to the Fador, crossing the river and back into the woods, calling, calling. I looked for anything—a scrap of clothing, anything that might suggest that a large group of people had been in the area. Several times I found something—a matchstick here, a broken cup there—but there was no sign of the people anywhere. Hours went by, and my throat was beginning to feel sore from all the calling, but I continued walking and calling, walking and calling. Suddenly I felt very tired and sat down on a log.

I don't know how long I sat there, when suddenly I heard a voice calling my name. I sprang to my feet. "Papa!" I cried. "Papa, I am here!"

"Stay where you are," the voice called back. "I am coming." Then the figure of my brother Zachary came into sight. Tears of disappointment welled in my eyes as I sat heavily back on the log. I didn't look up as he approached.

He reached out and stroked my hair.

"You are a mess," he said. I didn't raise my head. He sat down beside me.

"It's time to go home now," he said softly. "Mama is worrying."

I looked over at him. There was so much of our father in Zachary—the blond hair, the gray-blue eyes, the way he laughed, the sense of strength. I saw all those things now, and the resemblance was comforting.

"Zachary," I asked, "do you think Papa is dead?"

He looked at me with eyes brimming with tears, then reached over and pulled me close to him, saying, "I just don't know, sweetheart. I just don't know." I rested my head against his chest and felt his strong arms holding me close. "I looked everywhere," I told him. "I could not find him. I could not find anything."

"I know."

"Zachary, what will we do without Papa?"

He kissed the top of my head. "We must hope for the best. You know how our people think; we must hope. We will miss him very much, but we must continue living."

"Are they going to kill us all?"

He smiled. "No, sweetheart, not even if they tried." He stood up and pulled me to my feet. "Come on now. Let's go home and tell Mama that we are hungry and we want our dinner right away."

And so we walked home together, Zachary's strong arm around my shoulder. We never saw our father again. None of the families of the six hundred men ever did. Only one man escaped, and he immediately went into hiding. It would be almost three years before I would find him and learn what had really happened to my father. Not until 1967, when the German SS officer in charge of the mass murder was found and brought to trial, did I learn how the Germans had asked the Jewish community to pay ransom for the release of the captives—after they had already been murdered. My mother had given away all her remaining jewelry and money to ransom my father, leaving us with no means of support.

CHAPTER 4

My First Escape

It was soon frighteningly clear to the Jewish people in Buczacz that the elimination of the six hundred men was only the first step in a methodical German plan. First the Germans removed all young and influential men—civic, business and religious leaders—anyone who could sway public opinion or who could inspire the people to resist. The next step was to move the people out of their homes into one special area, a ghetto. To do this, the Germans enlisted the help of the Ukrainian police. Rumors were circulating that this was about to happen, and some families were already looking for a place to live in the selected area before the actual expulsion from their homes.

We had friends who owned a small home in the new ghetto near the Bashte meadow, not far from the river Stripa in the northern part of Buczacz. They agreed to let us have one room that we could use should the rumors prove true, in exchange for a monthly rent payment. Quietly we started moving some of our linens and dishes at night to what might become our new home. We were careful not to be obvious, since we did not want to be stopped by the Ukrainian police who were constantly patrolling our neighborhood.

What we feared happened one early morning in September. The Ukrainian police came into our house and ordered us out. They stood there in their blue uniforms, guns pointing at us, watching every move we made. My mother had told us what might happen and had begged my brothers not to say anything and not to give the police a reason to arrest or shoot us. Even though we were somewhat prepared for the move, when it actually came it was a very painful experience. We took what we could carry. Anger and frustration brought tears to my eyes, but I did not let the policemen see them. Zachary noticed them and whispered to me in Hebrew, "*Chavivati*, my dear, we'll return to our home someday when the war is over; things don't last forever." Squeezing my hand, he smiled at me.

The anger that gripped my whole being lessened, and a wave of tremendous love for my brother overcame me. Helping me carry my bundle with one hand while carrying his with the other, Zachary pulled me out of the house. I did turn my head for a last look at my home, but I knew that in the future I would try to avoid passing it.

On the way to our new neighborhood we met people who were also being driven from their homes. They carried bundles, and some were crying openly.

We settled quickly into our new place. The first thing we did was buy a small round iron stove with a plate on top to heat one pot: We were lucky to get it. We all doubled up in our beds. My youngest brother, Herzl, liked to sleep with his favorite brother, Bunio. At least Herzl was one member of our family who was young enough not to fully understand our situation.

New regulations followed our resettlement. All of the Jews had to wear a white armband with a yellow Star of David on it. We were to stay home after sunset and were absolutely forbidden in most public places, such as parks, marketplaces, movies, schools, and main streets. Our center of civic life became the building that housed the Jewish council known in German as the Judenrat. It was located near the big synagogue, which had been closed. The punishment promised to anyone who dared enter the synagogue was death.

We avoided all public places except the marketplace. We went there not to buy, but to sell. My mother took her linens to trade with the farmers—linens that had been handed down from her mother and grandmother. My little brother Herzl, now nine, bought and sold lighter flints. Mama did not allow my older brothers to go to the market for fear they might be arrested by the Ukrainian police and shot.

I was now eleven years old and my specialty was soap, an item that was beginning to become very scarce. I would buy a bar of soap for ten zlotys from a Jewish family who made it in their home and would try to sell it for twelve zlotys, or ten zlotys and a piece of bread. My customers were farmers who came to the city to trade their produce for clothing, soap, matches, flints, and other items. I would crouch among the wagons that gathered in the bustling marketplace on Thursdays. I had to keep low to avoid the Ukrainian policemen, who now regularly patrolled our city, especially on market day. If caught, you would lose your merchandise, be taken to the police station, and eventually shot. It was a very dangerous way to earn money, but I had to do it. I had a responsibility, my first of many yet to come.

One day in November, Bunio disappeared while on the way to get some wood for our stove. We could not sleep during the night for worrying about him. Early in the morning Mama went to the Judenrat. She was told that the German and Ukrainian police had taken about one hundred boys to a work camp in Borki Wielki, about one hundred miles from Buczacz. But the Judenrat would be allowed to contact the boys, and they would be allowed to receive food packages, one every two weeks. About their eventual return, the Judenrat did not know but would work hard for their release. Mama came home very unhappy. Losing Bunio, that handsome, athletic boy, filled us with terrible anguish. Herzl grieved deeply for Bunio. Since Papa's disappearance, Bunio had been both brother and father to Herzl. I caught him crying silently several times, crying and rocking his small body back and forth. A poor, miserable nine-year-old boy.

We put all our energies into sending Bunio food packages. Every two weeks a wagon with packages left from the Judenrat grounds for Borki Wielki. The driver who owned the wagon was a Gentile. He traveled with two Jewish men who held special travel permits. I was always there to see the wagon off, to make sure that the package to Bunio was safely in place. I always carried it there myself, hugging it close to my heart. There were pieces of bread tenderly packed by my mother: Not a crumb was missing from the pieces I carried back from the market in my apron. I was tempted at times to break off a little corner to satisfy my continuous hunger, but my love for my brother was greater than the temptation, and I was proud of myself.

Two days after the wagon left we had news from my brother. He was not allowed to write, but he sent oral messages. He was well, was working hard in a stone quarry, and sent his love to us. I would wait to see one of the men who traveled with the packages and beg him to tell me more about Bunio. How does he look, how does he feel? Once the man replied, "Oh, he is well. He, too, is asking many questions about his family. I can see you are very close." Then he added gently, "You miss your brother very much, don't you?" I just nodded and hurried away, not wanting the man to see the tears that were suddenly blinding me.

Detaining Jewish people for forced labor was a common practice with the Germans, and the Ukrainians had adopted the custom with relish. I myself had been caught twice; the first time to polish furniture and floors at the German police station. Most of the furniture was looted from Jewish homes after the owners were thrown out. As I worked my way through the massive wooden pieces, one item caught my eye. It was my father's nightstand. Tears of anger sprang to my eyes as I began to recognize the pieces of our furniture—chairs, tables—all from our lovely home. I wiped away the tears and began to polish my furniture. I remembered that there was a hidden compartment inside the nightstand. My father showed it to me once when I was in his bedroom. Quietly, so that I would not be noticed, I tried to find it, but I couldn't. It gave me some measure of satisfaction to believe that the Germans had not found it either.

The second time, I was caught in the afternoon and ordered to clean the floors in my old school—and in my very own classroom. The room had changed. Gone were the pictures of Stalin and Lenin. The Madonna and Child were back in their former place. My armband with the Star of David was slipping as I worked, so I took it off and placed it near the Madonna. Shouldn't she, too, be wearing an armband like mine? Wasn't she missing the Jewish children?

I remember watching as the Christian children walked to school, dressed in their pretty dresses and bright ribbons. They were lovely, and I envied not only their clothes but their freedom to be educated. It was a bitter experience.

I also remember that at one point the desire to learn overcame the warnings I had received about staying away. One day I climbed a tree outside the window of my classroom and watched. Through the window I could see my former classmates sitting at their desks. One of these was my friend Slavka, whom I had known since we first came to Buczacz. She was a Gentile, but then, so were many of my friends.

It didn't take long for my presence to become known to those inside the classroom. One by one heads turned, and I could see the children whispering together. When Slavka turned to look, our eyes met; she couldn't wave, of course, for fear of reprimand from the teacher. I was holding fast to the tree. Our exchange was bittersweet—my misery at not being allowed in the school, her sympathy mingled with helplessness to correct the situation. In a moment she looked away and didn't turn around again.

I think the teacher also knew I was there, but she said nothing— perhaps the sight of a lonely child desperate for knowledge touched her heart. I stayed up in that tree for quite a while, listening to the lesson, trying to memorize what was being said. It was so frustrating, so utterly maddening, I couldn't stand it. I absolutely could not stand it. So when the teacher asked the next question, a dozen hands shot up, including mine. Zip! I was out of that tree and flat on my back among the leaves on the ground, the breath completely knocked out of me. Looking straight up as I struggled to breathe, I could see a sea of faces at the window, all small, round little faces with noses pressed against the glass and mouths agape. Slavka's face was among them. She peered down unhappily as the teacher rushed down the stairs and out the door to me.

"Are you all right?" she asked, helping me into a sitting position.

I nodded shakily. My breath was coming back in gasps. The teacher rubbed my back until I could breathe normally, then she said, "Alicia, you know you can't come back here anymore."

I looked up at her forlornly. "But I don't mind the tree," I said.

She smiled, a smile I remembered so well from the times when she taught our class geography. "It is too dangerous, Alicia, and I don't mean the tree. Do you understand?" She wiped the dirt from my sweater, and, in doing so, her fingers brushed over the yellow Star of David on my armband.

"Alicia," she said, "you understand, don't you?"

I did.

Our lives had suddenly taken on a routine that was as monotonous as it was frightening. I peddled soap at the marketplace together with my brother Herzl, making sure not to be seen by the Germans or the Ukrainian police. My mother and her friend Ruth found a place near the river over the Bashte meadow near where we lived. Some of the village farm women passed there on the way to the city market to sell their produce. It was a relatively safe place, but it was difficult to sell anything to those women; they were convinced that they could get a better deal in the city. Yet my mother and her friend managed to get some potatoes, some grain, and sometimes a small bottle of sunflower oil.

Several weeks later Bunio was still in the work camp. We missed him desperately and continued to send him packages. During this time Zachary had not been content to sit. He and some friends began patrolling our neighborhood, trying to organize some kind of resistance group. But people were afraid to raise a hand against the Germans for fear of retaliation. For my proud brother, whose father had taught him to fight so well, this was an extremely maddening situation.

In his quiet way he kept a watchful eye on us and his friends and their families. He came to be loved by the people he visited, both old Buczacz families and new arrivals from neighboring towns and villages. Our town had become the center for all the Jewish people within hundreds of miles.

And they adored him, this handsome young man who made his rounds almost daily through the streets of the crowded ghetto. The young people even began singing songs Zachary had written. One I remember was a plaintive song about a grandfather holding his grandson on his lap and telling the young child to always honor and remember his father, who had been killed by the Nazi Germans, by saying the memorial Kaddish for him.

Some of Zachary's songs, and many others, were sung by the young people when they gathered one evening at a friend's home. I had gone there with Zachary and sat quietly listening to songs of love, brotherhood, and yearning for life. Some songs were in Hebrew about Eretz Israel, the land of Israel. Sometimes a girl's sweet voice would start with a joyous tune, only to be interrupted in the middle by a heartbreaking sob. Life seemed so vigorous in these young people. I was moved by the beauty of the music, yet I was pained by the knowledge that death was so near.

Those thoughts were to haunt me again the following day. I had been visiting two of my friends in their home. One of the boys was my own age and he was teaching me how to play chess. Their father was a physician whom my father had helped to escape from Germany. On the other side of the door we could hear the sound of boots tramping on the pavement, but there was always marching going on those days in Buczacz, and we had grown accustomed to it. Suddenly the front door was kicked open and several German policemen entered the house. Everyone inside—the doctor, his two children, and I—was ordered out.

The doctor pleaded with the policemen to let me go, pointing out that I was not his child but was just visiting his children. "Please let her go home," he added with tears in his voice.

"Silence, damned Jew!" was the reply he received as the policemen pushed us roughly toward the door. We had no choice but to go.

With guns pointing at us, we walked up Kolejova Street to the train station. For a moment I thought we might be taken to the police station or the Fador, but we were not. In an hour we were at the farthest end of the train station. There were other Jewish people sitting on the ground; SS troops were standing over them with pointed guns. We were in a state of shock. All of this had happened very quickly. Homes attacked, people marched out, and here we were at the station facing a freight train. We were to go somewhere in this train, but where? Where could they be taking women and children? Certainly not to a work camp. This is crazy, I thought; this is a crazy nightmare.

The herd of human captives grew larger and larger as more people were added. We were kept there for a long time; at least two hours, it seemed. Fortunately we were allowed to sit. All the time, sitting and waiting, I wondered what was to become of us. After being chased out of our homes we were now being taken away from our city.

Oddly enough, my mind was not so much on my predicament as it was on my mother. How could I get a message to her? All this had happened swiftly and, it seemed, only in one section of the ghetto. The rest of the people in the ghetto were probably just beginning to realize what had happened. I worried about my mother—one son dead, her husband probably dead, one son imprisoned in a work camp, and her only daughter taken without a chance to say good-bye. I would be gone, there was no telling how long, maybe forever. And she would not know how I had disappeared.

Suddenly the locomotive of the waiting freight train started up and a shrill whistle like a shriek of agony, pierced the air. A loud German voice commanded us to get into the boxcars. I held the hand of one of the boys, who in turn held his father's hand. We pulled each other up into the boxcars. There was crying and moaning because one of the SS brutes was using a whip to speed up the loading of the cars.

The cars were very tightly packed, so most of the people were forced to stand. Some of the smaller children were able to sit at their parent's feet, but I was older and quite tall for my eleven years. I stood.

After the last person had been packed aboard the train, the doors were shut, and the car was plunged into near darkness, prompting cries from the people within.

We soon realized that the car was not entirely dark. Light could be seen through cracks between the boards, and better still, there were small barred windows, open and without glass, which let enough light in so that once our eyes had adjusted, we could see fairly clearly.

The train started with a lurch that threw several people off their feet. It pulled slowly out of the station. Several men concentrated to see if they could tell what direction it would take; one man said north, another east, another southeast—they could not be sure.

As the train picked up speed, cold wind began to whistle through the barred openings. It was November, and many people had been forced from their homes without a coat. I was wearing a sweater. I had left my coat at the doctor's home.

There was a young woman standing very near me, holding a baby. She had wrapped it in her shawl to keep it warm, and I noticed that she kept shifting the child from arm to arm, trying to ease the strain of its weight on her shoulders. I reached over and touched her arm. She started, looking at me in surprise.

"Shall I hold the baby a little while?" I asked. "It would give you a chance to rest."

She smiled. "Thank you, but no. I want to hold him as long as I can."

The trip wore on and on. One hour, two hours; it became quite late in the afternoon. Some people had even fallen asleep standing up, leaning on the shoulders of their loved ones. Some tried to lie down on the floor between the legs of those standing. But this worked best for the small children.

I saw a man reach up and shake the bars on one of the windows. "Hey!" he cried. "This bar is loose. Look!"

Another man reached over and tried the bar. It was true. Several men worked their way through the mass of people to the window, taking turns wrenching at the steel bar. They pounded at it with the palms of their hands, wrapped shawls around it and pulled—anything to work it free.

Finally, after much effort, the bar pulled away from its bottom bolt and could be twisted up and away from the window. But this still left too small an opening for anyone to squeeze through, so they continued working.

More time passed, and we could feel the train slowing down.

Someone was lifted to the window to see what was happening. "We are entering a mountain range," he said. "The incline is forcing the train to slow down."

With renewed vigor they pounded at the remaining bars until a second one was pried free and could be twisted back. This left an opening large enough for children to escape. The man closest to the window kissed his eight-year-old son, told him to go to his grand-mother's home, where his mother was, lifted him up, and pushed him through the opening into the bushes alongside the railway tracks. With tears in his eyes he turned and said, "Who is next?" There was silence. Most parents kept their children close and would not allow them to be pushed through the window. Only two more kissed their children and moved them toward the men at the window.

My father's friend, the doctor, was one of those helping pass the children out of the train window. He reached down for me. "Come, Alicia," he said. "The train is traveling as slowly as it ever will. There is a slope covered with bushes with a stream at the bottom. Remember to roll when you hit the ground. Run and hide until the train leaves; then just follow the railroad tracks back home."

"But wait," I said, stepping back. "Help your own children first."

"No," he said. "They are staying with me."

"But why?"

"Alicia"—he squeezed my shoulder and looked at me sadly—"Alicia, the world has gone insane when people do this kind of thing to other people."

His voice became husky, and he cleared his throat before continuing. I could see that his eyes had become very wet. "I don't want to be a part of the human race anymore," he said. "And anyway, what would my children do without a father? Their mother is dead. Where would they go? How could they live?

"No, they will go with me. We will suffer our fate together. But you, Alicia, you have a mother; you have brothers. You have to try to return to them. Do you hear me?" He gripped my arms tightly. "You must live, Alicia. You must live." And with that he lifted me up and handed me over to another of the men. "She goes next," he said.

It was the most terrifying thing that had ever happened to me— more terrifying than the time I met a wild boar in the forest in Rosulna. As I was pushed through the window I could see the slope far below me. To be pushed from a moving train . . . but I no longer had a say in the matter. I was going out that window and in a hurry.

In a moment I was flying through the air, and then crash! I hit a bush. A big branch gave way under me, forming a kind of cradle for my body. "Roll, Alicia, roll." I kept hearing the doctor's instructions, and I rolled off the branch and down the hill, gaining speed as I went. I could hear what sounded like guns near me. Apparently the Germans had discovered our escape and were shooting at us.

But the train kept moving and I heard no more gunfire. After a while I eased into a sitting position. I checked myself for damage. I was certainly banged up—my legs and face were scratched, my sweater torn, and my elbows and knees were bleeding. I was sore all over. Later I would find that my shoulders, back, and hips were covered with bruises. But nothing seemed to be broken. The bushes had cushioned my fall. The men in the train had known what they were doing.

I thought of my mother and brothers, and new strength flowed into my battered body. I had to get home quickly. All I had to do, the doctor told me, was to follow the railway tracks.

But where was home? How far away? How long to get there?

CHAPTER 5

My Brother Bunio

I was running over the railroad tracks, frantic to escape from the train. I had just jumped out of a boxcar window and I thought I had escaped to safety but, to my great horror, the train was chasing after me and was trying to catch me. It was getting closer and closer. I could hear its loud whistle and the voice of the doctor who helped me escape urging me to run, run faster. Suddenly out of nowhere there was a river in front of me and I felt myself falling into the cold water. Somewhere in midair my fall had become a graceful dive and, when I finally hit the water, it was with a feeling of great relief.

The water was blue, and there were many fish swimming around. It was so peaceful, and I let the current carry me. Slowly, very slowly, I surfaced and I could hear voices from far away, as though from a long tunnel. Then one voice became clearer.

"Her fever has broken. She will be all right now. Just keep her covered."

I felt myself being lifted gently and put down again. I felt a spoon in my mouth. I tried to swallow the warm liquid, but it hurt my throat. The pain made me fully awake.

I was in bed, my head cradled in my mother's arm while she was trying to spoon-feed me tea. I looked up at Mama, and I could see the tears in her eyes. I turned my head to the right, and there stood my brothers. Zachary had a big smile on his face—a smile that did not reach his eyes, which were looking at me with great concern. Herzl

28

stood there with his mouth open, as though he were trying to say something but the words would not come out.

I took another painful swallow, and then another, and just closed my eyes. I was very tired. Suddenly it dawned on me that I was home. I wanted to shout out loud. I am home! I am home again! But I didn't have the strength.

A week passed before I was strong enough to be out of bed. I returned to selling soap and getting bread to send to Bunio in the labor camp. But when I slept, the nightmares took over again, and I relived my escape from the train, the return home, the fever, and the pain. I woke up in the mornings drenched in perspiration and shaking with fear. My nightmares did not go unnoticed by my family. One morning I found Zachary standing near my bed.

"Alicia, I would like us to take a little walk. We will go over the Bashte down the river, and just walk and talk."

"Zachary, do you think it is safe?" I asked.

"Oh, come on, you sleepyhead, get dressed."

He started pulling at my blanket. I threw my pillow at him and got dressed quickly.

It was wonderful to walk with Zachary. When we reached the top of the hill he spread a blanket on the ground and we sat down. I leaned my head on his shoulder, and we just sat there looking at the river. After a while I started talking. I told Zachary about my experience on the train. I repeated the words the doctor had told me when I asked him to save his children and explained how I followed the railroad tracks, how ill I had felt. Finally, choking on tears, I told him that if I hadn't loved and worried about my family so much, I would never have made it home. Then my tears came and I cried and cried.

I don't know how long we sat there when Zachary said, "Here, Alicia, take this. It's time to get back."

He handed me a handkerchief with a red apple in it. I used the handkerchief but kept the apple. I couldn't eat it just then. How wonderful of Zachary, I thought. He knew how much I loved apples.

When we were close to home Zachary stopped me and, taking my hand, looked at me.

"Alicia, sweetheart, I know how painful this might be for you, but could you repeat what you just told me to some people at the Judenrat? They should know exactly what happened. It is very important."

"Zachary, I would do anything for you, you know that. You are the best brother in the world, and I love you," I added in a whisper.

In a small room at the Judenrat we met two men. Zachary had apparently arranged it, and they were waiting for us. They knew what had happened, they said. There were two survivors: me and another girl who was hurt and still in bed.

I did not look at the men as I told them my story, but when I finished I glanced at them and saw that they were shaken and had tears in their eyes.

"Please, Zachary, take your sister home and then come back," the older of the men said.

"I will go home by myself," I said, and headed for the door. I had just closed the door when I heard an angry voice coming from the room. I recognized my brother's voice. He was very angry. For some reason he was speaking in Hebrew. "*Lo!* [No!]" he kept saying, "we can't just sit and wait. We will all be killed." And then, like thunder, a voice answered him—also in Hebrew. "You want to fight? Then fight. But when the Germans retaliate by killing hundreds of women and children, how will you feel then? Can you bear the thought of such a mass murder? Do you want this on your conscience? Do you? Speak up, Zachary!"

As the argument continued, I was afraid that this shouting was going to get out of control, so I quickly opened the door and entered the room. My heart turned over with pain when I saw my brother. He just stood there with his head lowered and his fists clenched. He looked completely defeated. I took his hand in mine and pulled him out of the room. We walked home in silence.

I looked at Zachary just before we entered our home. He was his old self again, but there was a certain look of determination about him that I couldn't understand.

The winter of 1941 started with a snowstorm. For several days we were unable to leave our room. I was very worried, and not only because we had so little food, but because we couldn't get enough water for bathing. My mother insisted that we wash our bodies every day even though we had only a small basin. She said that keeping our bodies and our clothing clean was very important for our health, and we wanted to please her. Melting the snow gave us some water but not enough.

Then one day the storm stopped. The sun began to shine, melting some of the snow, which then froze into a slippery ice at night.

We could get outside now. The market was filled with farmers' sleighs again, and I returned to selling soap in order to get bread for Bunio. I had always been on time to deliver Bunio's package. I couldn't understand why I had almost missed the sleigh the last two times; I just barely caught them as they were turning into the main street. One day I literally ran into the horses trying to stop them. I was very angry with the men in charge. I knew I was on time; why did they leave earlier? I finally got the package under the straw that covered them and, giving my letter to Bunio to the Jewish man in charge, let them ride on. I was so upset, I forgot to tell the man to tell my brother that we loved him and missed him very much.

I was still thinking about what just happened and did not notice my friend Slavka until she called my name.

"Alicia, can we go somewhere and talk?"

"Talk?" I asked, surprised. "You want to talk with me? All right, we will talk," I said brusquely.

I was very disappointed in Slavka. I hadn't seen her for some time now and had to admit I missed her very much. At least she could have come to say hello. I imagined that her mother didn't let her visit me anymore, so I was really surprised to see her now. She must have been waiting for me. She knew about Bunio and what day packages left for Borki Wielki. Her cousin was one of the Ukrainians riding the sleigh. What could have brought her out to see me so early in the morning? Wasn't she supposed to go to school? She looked so distressed, I forgot my anger and disappointment.

"What is it, dear Slavka? What happened to you?" I asked, taking her hand in mine.

"Don't you know, Alicia? Your brother Bunio was shot in the camp. I heard it from my cousin."

"Bunio shot? What are you talking about? How can Bunio be shot when I just delivered a package for him? You must be mistaken! He can't be shot!" I screamed as I pushed her hand away.

"Yes, he was. Everybody knows it. One of the boys in camp escaped, so the Germans lined up everybody and shot every tenth boy. He was one of them."

As I stood there, my body started to tremble, and a fear that Slavka might be telling the truth stabbed at my heart. Was Bunio already dead when I delivered the last two packages for him? Had the sleigh left early to avoid me? This was all crazy, a ridiculous nightmare. Slavka was going to disappear, and I would be on my way home.

I closed my eyes for a moment, and when I opened them, Slavka was still standing near me. I felt a flood of anger spreading through my whole being, and suddenly it was all directed at Slavka.

"So now my brother Bunio is dead. If it were not for you Ukrainians helping the Germans capture our boys, my brother would still be alive. It wasn't enough that you took my father and probably murdered him. You, our neighbors, betrayed us and joined the murdering Gestapo. I saw all of you when the police threw us out of our home. Yes, I know why you are doing this. Hitler promised you a free Ukraine. Well, it will be a Ukraine soaked with Jewish blood, but it will never be free. When Hitler finishes with us, he will kill you too. Just mark my words. And your policeman uncle will be the first to hang one way or another."

I had lost control of myself in my grief and was screaming at her.

"And tell your priest, who preaches hatred of the Jews every Sunday, that he will pay for it someday!"

Slavka got hold of my arm and was pulling me away. "Stop it, Alicia!" she screamed at me. "A Ukrainian policeman may hear you."

But I couldn't stop it. Finally I turned and, shaking with sobs, I ran home. My head was pounding and my eyes were bleary, but I could see my poor brother standing there as the Nazi murderers counted "One, two, three, four. . . ."

CHAPTER 6

Guralis and Radishes

Our family grieved deeply for Bunio. We sat shiva for seven days on low stools and on the floor. Zachary led us in the Kaddish, and friends came to see us. They brought us cooked food, as much as they could spare. We were grateful for the food but mostly for their compassion. My heart was aching for my brothers, but my poor mother, who had now lost two sons and her husband, looked ghastly. I tried to stay near her all the time, hoping somehow to ease her pain.

For the rest of the winter and throughout the spring the Germans found ways to torture us further. They began by confiscating all radios and all fur coats. They continually demanded money and jewelry from the Judenrat, which it had to collect from the Jewish population. They also demanded food, which was very scarce. I heard the adults complain bitterly about the German demands. The Jewish community was being stripped of all it owned and needed to survive.

The German demands were doubly catastrophic because the summer of 1942 began with a terrible famine. The farmers had to deliver food to the German army: Most of the harvest of 1941 was confiscated by the Germans as soon as they occupied our part of Poland.

My own small and unhappy world was also affected. I still continued to trade at the market. The money I asked for each bar of

33

soap was usually the amount I had paid for it plus some bread—a meager but very important profit. But now the farmers were reluctant to part with even the smallest piece of bread. I had to literally beg them for it. I was discouraged, but I still continued to come to the market because even though I was only sometimes able to get some bread for my family, this was enough to make me very proud.

One day while in the market I sat down near a wagon and rested. Sounds of a conversation drifted toward me and, as I listened, it occurred to me that I had heard those sounds before. They did not sound like the Polish we spoke in Buczacz, or even like Ukrainian. They sounded more like a combination of both languages. And then it struck me. It was mountain talk, which I remembered from my childhood. How was that possible? Rosulna, the place of my birth, was so far away, and so was Solotvina, where Grandma and Grandpa Kurtz lived. Then I remembered having seen big barrels tied to the sides of the wagons and the unfamiliar clothing of the people riding on the wagons.

It was all falling into place now. Had I not been so absorbed in my own misery, I would have noticed all this, I thought. As I got up, I saw a woman sitting alone on the seat of the wagon and went up to her.

Without thinking, I spoke to her in the Huculi Ukrainian dialect. She answered me in the Gurali Polish language. As we talked, she told me about the hunger the people were suffering in the mountains due to lack of bread, and how they had come all the way to the Podole, where they heard the farmers still had some grain they might be willing to trade for lamb furs and blueberries. She was a friendly woman and kept on talking.

As she talked, she occasionally used Ukrainian words, which I thought rather odd. The Guralis lived all the way in the western range of the Carpathian Mountains, whereas the Huculi lived on the eastern side; our side included Rosulna and Solotvina. And then I remembered my mother telling me how Grandpa Kurtz had brought in Guralis and settled them around Solotvina to work in his forests and in the lumberyards.

Could it be possible that this woman came from that region? No harm in asking, I thought.

"Could you please tell me if you might perhaps come from Rosulna or Solotvina?" I asked.

"How do you know these villages?" she asked, eyeing me curiously.

"I was born in Rosulna," I said, and then asked her again. "Do you come from Rosulna by any chance?"

"No," she said. "I come from Solotvina."

"Then you must know my grandparents; their name is Kurtz, and they own the forests and the lumberyards in Solotvina."

"Blessed Virgin," the woman said, crossing herself and then called loudly.

"Stephan, Stephan, come here quickly! Hurry, Stephan!"

A young man wearing the same colorful mountain clothing as the woman came running to us. "Here, come closer, Stephan," and, pulling him to her, she whispered something in his ear.

As he listened to the woman the man, too, crossed himself and looked strangely at me. Something was going on. For a moment I thought it would be safer if I just ran away, but I stood rooted in place.

"So you are from the Kurtz family," the man was saying. "Come closer. Blessed God, I didn't know there were any of you left alive."

I gasped. "What do you mean by that?"

He nodded unhappily. "Well," he said. "They are all dead; it was the Hoculis, you know."

"What happened?"

He appeared agitated. "You know those Ukrainian bastards," he said hotly. "It wasn't our people; we loved your grandfather."

"I often did the laundry for the Kurtzes," his wife added.

"What happened to my grandfather?"

Tears rose to the man's eyes.

"He was buried alive," he cried, "forced to dig his own grave while those bastards stood around and laughed, and then—" He shook his head. "I am sorry, I really am."

I nodded silently. "What of the rest of the family?"

The way he looked at me I knew the answer.

"And what of you and your family? How do you survive?" he asked me.

I didn't know why, but I told them what happened to my family and, strangely, I didn't cry. The woman did, however, because I saw her wiping her tears with a corner of her shawl.

"This awful war," she said. "I don't understand it."

Then her eyes suddenly widened and, touching my shoulders, she said, "Why don't you come back home with us," and, looking at her husband, she asked, "Could she come, do you think she could?"

"Why, yes," the man said, his face brightening. "You could come as our adopted daughter. Yes, times are hard, but then, how much harder they must be here. And who would know?"

"Your neighbors would," I said.

"Then we would tell them that you were an orphan and we adopted you from an orphanage run by the church. No one would suspect. After all, you hardly look like a Jew."

His words had a twofold effect on me. *Look like a Jew, look like a Jew* spun through my mind. *You hardly look like a Jew.* Had my father and Bunio looked like Jews, with their blond hair and blue eyes? Would the Germans have known they were Jews if they hadn't been betrayed by those who knew them, our own neighbors?

"Well, what do you say?" The man's voice brought me out of my thoughts.

"I don't know. I will have to think about it," I replied. "How long will you be here?"

"We are leaving at six o'clock in the morning," he said.

The woman reached out once more and touched my shoulder.

"Oh, do come. We will treat you as our own child. It's the very least we can do for the Kurtzes."

"I will give it much thought," I told them. "But now, can you spare me some food for my family?"

They gave me a basket filled with blueberries and a small slice of bread. "Bless you, child," said the woman as she made the sign of the cross over me. I thanked them and made my way through the marketplace, back to the streets of our ghetto, and then home.

The offer to go to Solotvina with the Gurali kept me troubled for the rest of the day. Even though I wasn't sure I could trust the Gurali not to betray me when I got to Solotvina—or even not to throw me out of the wagon on the way—that was secondary. What really troubled me was the fact that I was even considering the offer. I wanted to leave the ghetto and all the terror in it. I wanted to eat apples and cherries and swim in a river again. I wanted to go back to a place where I had been happy once. I wanted to run from this life, to run far away. . . .

The day wore on, and my mother and brothers returned. Mother noticed my silence and knew that something was troubling me, but she didn't say anything. Several times I thought of talking to her about the Gurali in the marketplace, but I stopped myself. I had already decided never to tell what I had learned about her father and the rest of our family. I had told her of enough tragedies already. I thought about my opportunity to leave the next day, and I was sure that she would urge me to go.

I barely slept at all that night. When I did, I dreamed of my grandfather—when we children stood at the riverbank watching Grandfather and his crew as they drifted downstream on their rafts of freshly cut logs. There they'd be, stripped to the waist, sunburned, gracefully wielding the long, hooked poles used to break apart log-jams. We could always pick out Grandfather by his long reddish beard, and if we could catch his attention, he would wave his hooked pole over his head to salute us. It had been some years now since I had seen him. It is funny how you take people for granted when you know they are alive, but when you learn they are gone you grieve for them and you miss them until your heart is ready to break, knowing that you will never see them again.

I rose early the next morning while it was still dark and picked up my wooden-soled shoes. I intended to put them on outside so their heavy clunk, clunk on the floor wouldn't awaken anyone. Then I dropped them again. I wouldn't be needing them.

I was very careful as I walked to the marketplace. I would be in big trouble if I were caught, since I wasn't wearing my armband. As a matter of fact, I didn't even have it with me.

Finally the marketplace lay ahead of me. The sun was coming out, and the people were moving around the wagons.

Then I could make out the wagon I had been looking for. The woman and man were sitting in their seats. The man was holding the reins in his hands. I was now close enough to see them clearly. They were talking and looking around. My heart was beating strongly. I wanted to go to them and say something; I realized that I didn't even know their names.

As I stood there, I saw the wagons begin to leave. Still my Gurali didn't move. Then suddenly I heard the slap of a whip and a loud call for the horses to move on. Still hidden from sight, I watched as the wagon with my Gurali drove away, leaving a flurry of dust behind it. I watched them until they completely disappeared.

In spite of everything, life went on. We could do without many things, but one commodity that was essential and becoming increasingly scarce was firewood. We needed wood for cooking and to store for the winter months. One day I noticed children trying to sell cut-up branches to use as burning wood. When I tried to find out where they had gotten the branches, they wouldn't tell me. I had to bribe one boy with a piece of bread before he gave in. A group of boys would go into the forest just before daylight and look for branches left over from cut-down trees. Adults were stealing trees, and the boys took the branches.

I thought it was a splendid idea and, after a lot of pleading, the boys let me join them. We left at about two o'clock in the morning. We had to sneak over the bridge, go around the foot of the Fador, where it sloped to the river, and swim through the water. By the time we entered the forest I was shivering from cold, but I kept following the boys. They knew where to look for the branches. We tied them in firm bundles with thin twigs. Then we reversed our route and got home just in time to see the sunrise.

For the next two weeks I was busy carrying branches out of the woods into our home. Then one morning, as we were coming out of the woods, we were attacked by older Gentile boys. We had to leave our bundles behind and barely made it into the river and to safety. We waited a few days and then went back into the forest. The Gentile boys were hidden behind trees waiting for us. When we were just about to float over our bundles, the boys attacked us again and some of us were hit on the head with wooden bats. We managed to get into the river and swim over to the other side. But there we had a surprise. Another group of boys was waiting for us. We had no choice but to return to the river and swim until we could find a way to get out.

While swimming I noticed a large tree and decided to swim to it. The tree turned out to be hollow on the side facing the river and was a perfect hiding place. I swam back to the middle of the river and pulled a boy back to the tree with me. He was very frightened and had difficulty swimming. He was one of the boys who had been hit over the head. We stayed in the tree for a long time, and then I checked to see if anyone was around. But no one was, so we returned to the forest to hide. When it was completely dark, we sneaked into the ghetto. Two of our boys had drowned in the river.

During all this time my mother was the major source of our family's income. Each day she went out to the road near the river to trade with passing farmers and their wives. Sometimes she sold pieces of our remaining linens and other times goods belonging to our friends for which she got a commission. When mother became so ill with dysentery that she could not leave our house, I suggested that I go in her place.

"Please stay hidden in the ravine until you see a single woman on the road, and then approach her. There may be policemen coming that way. Please be careful," Mama said as she handed me a bundle containing two small kitchen towels.

"I will, Mama. I will be very careful." And I kissed her good-bye.

There were very few people passing the road that day, and I was about to go home, when I spotted an old lady with a basket. She was walking very slowly and looked tired.

I stopped her and, looking into her basket, saw bundles of small red radishes. They looked so lovely all tied up neatly with their roots cut off, leaving white little stubs in the middle of the red heads. We talked for a while, and she agreed to take my two towels in exchange for the radishes. I promised her that if I sold the radishes, I would meet her at the same place the next day and buy another basket from her.

I transferred the radishes from the basket into my apron, and, holding the two corners firmly, I returned to our neighborhood to sell the radishes. The first person I saw was a boy about six years old.

"Hello!" I said to the boy. "Come here and I will show you something."

Taking his hand, I let him touch a radish. "Please go into your house and tell your mother that she can buy radishes from me which will taste delicious with a piece of bread." The boy did as I asked and came back quickly.

"Mama said we don't have any bread to go with the radishes, and that they were probably hollow inside anyway."

My feelings were a little hurt, but I took his hand and let him touch a radish again. He put his two little fingers around the red head of the radish and suddenly pulled. This caught me by surprise, and I almost lost all the radishes from my apron. In the meantime, other children heard me scolding the little boy and came to see what was happening. There I stood, surrounded by little children trying to see what I had in my apron. I looked at their hungry faces, and, moved by the sight, I reached a decision.

"All right, all of you, sit down on the sidewalk," I called with a voice full of laughter. "I am going to tell you a story about Little Red Riding Hood. Now, listen carefully!" They were all sitting now, very close to one another. There were about ten of them.

"Here, have some radishes," I said, and, giving each a bunch, I told them not to eat until I started the story.

"There was a little girl who was sent by her mother to bring food to her sick grandmother. She carried a basket." Now I turned to the kids. "Start eating the radishes.

"The basket was filled with fresh white rolls, boiled chicken, strawberries, candies, and, of course, radishes."

At that point a cry went up. "Oh, no! Not radishes." The children were making faces as they munched on the sharp radishes but continued eating them.

I finished the story and was about to leave, when the little boy I saw first stopped me. "Will you tell us another story tomorrow?" he asked shyly. "You know, the radishes were really very tasty. See, I kept a few for my little sister!" He showed me his little fist with the radishes held securely. Suddenly I had such a feeling of love for this little boy. This poor and hungry little ghetto boy. I wanted to take him in my arms and never let him go.

I was worried about the loss of the towels, which I should have exchanged for much-needed food. But when I told my mother what had happened, she took me in her arms and told me not to worry, and that she wasn't really surprised.

CHAPTER 7

The First "Action"

Suddenly the summer was over. The new harvest eased some of the hunger, but only for those who had money or goods to trade. Most of us had lost everything, and we were facing a cold and hungry winter. I had only one compensation; my brother Zachary stayed home most of the time. With Zachary around, I relaxed a little and began sleeping more peacefully. It was, therefore, with some difficulty that I awoke early one morning to my mother calling my name and shaking my shoulder.

"Alicia, get dressed quickly, hurry up, take your warm sweater; we must go!"

There was such urgency in her voice that I didn't even ask where we were going. Within minutes the ten of us who lived in our house were at the stone wall in the backyard. The stone wall was against the hill leading to the Bashte meadow, and was not visible from the outside. It was still dark. Our landlord helped his wife, daughters, and their husbands into an opening in the wall, then my mother went in, followed by Herzl. When I climbed in, there was so little space left that I just fell onto the people. Zachary came in last. He picked up three large stones from the outside and very carefully pulled them over the entrance. Then he lifted up something that looked like a wooden box and fit it in to support the stones. The box had holes in several places to let in air. I found out later that this was intended to act as a buffer between the hollowness of the cave and the stones of the wall.

It was completely dark inside. No one spoke. I didn't realize that I

41

was holding my breath until I felt pain in my chest. Then I breathed out slowly, making a sound like a deep sigh. Fear was spreading through me, gripping me in a tight vise. My heart seemed to be beating loudly. I was fully awake now, and I realized that we were in a hiding place, waiting for something to happen. My eyes were on the box that Zachary was holding in place. A faint light was beginning to show through his spread fingers.

Suddenly I heard a shattering noise coming from inside the house. It sounded as though someone were trying to demolish the house, ripping it apart from all directions. Then a shout in German:

"'Raus, verdammte Juden! Out, damned Jews! Out of your hiding place! I know you are there. Out!'"

The voice was coming closer to us; it was coming from the backyard now.

"Look at the cellar inside the wall. They must be somewhere here; those damned Jews."

"Here, let's see," a voice said in Ukrainian. He was knocking on the stone wall near us. My heart stopped. And then someone called out again in German.

"Come, let's go. We will get them next time."

More noises of slamming doors. Then complete quiet. I felt warm moisture along my thigh and realized with great shame that I had wet myself.

The quiet was again shattered by gunshots and screams. Something terrible was going on outside. No one said a word, but Zachary moved over close to me and, taking my hands in both of his, held them tightly. How did this beautiful boy always know when I needed him? It was comforting to be linked to him, and I felt the warmth of life flow into me. My body, which started trembling after the Germans left, was relaxing a little. We sat there in the hiding place all day and half the night, without moving. During the day I heard someone entering the house, but no one came close to the wall again. In the middle of the night Zachary removed the stones, put them carefully back in place, and left us. He returned sometime later and told us that the SS policemen had left our town and that we could come out of the hiding place. From all the terrible noise, I had expected to find the house in shambles, but it wasn't. Although I could see some things missing from their places, I realized that the attack on the house and the terrible noises were to frighten us. If there were small children present, they would have started crying and revealed our hiding place. What clever murderers the Germans and the Ukrainians were!

About two thousand Jewish men, women, children were murdered in this first action in October 1942. They were taken out of hiding places or caught while trying to escape from the city. They were shot and buried in a mass grave on the Fador. Some were shot on the Bashte while trying to escape and were later buried in the Jewish cemetery by members of the Judenrat. A wave of sorrow enveloped us all.

For several days I stayed close to home. I was afraid the German troops, known as "SS" or "Gestapo," would return. Then I went to see Reb Srool. I needed to understand why all this was happening to us. I hoped he would be able to enlighten me.

Reb Srool was a very old man with a long white beard and very kind brown eyes. He lived alone in a basement room on Podhajecka Street. He had always been part of my life, and we still looked out for him. Before the war, when the weather was nice, he would have meals with us. He always sat near Papa in the place of honor. When Reb Srool spoke with his precise Hebrew pronunciation and musical voice, everyone listened with respect. I thought him the only person to turn to for my special need.

As I walked down the narrow steps to his room, my tongue moved to the gap where my tooth was missing. The tooth had been knocked out by a German policeman who had kicked me in the face a few months before when I had tried to help Reb Srool. I didn't really blame him for the loss of my tooth, but I could never understand what he had been doing at the water fountain at the beautiful monument called the Ratush in the middle of the city.

But there he had been, crying pitifully while two German policemen took turns pushing his head under the running water. I stood there for a moment watching, hardly believing my eyes. Then, trying to get my pail under the running water, I stepped in front of Reb Srool's head. The policemen looked startled for a moment and then, seeing my armband with the Star of David, one pushed me to the ground and kicked me in the face with his heavy boot. I screamed out with pain, and when I opened my mouth to spit out the blood, I saw my tooth. I was in such pain I didn't even notice when our torturers left. They had their fun, I thought bitterly.

Now the door to Reb Srool's room was slightly open. This was his way of telling visitors that they were welcome. As I walked in, I saw him sitting at his table, swaying back and forth, his arms holding a book close to his eyes. When he noticed me, he put down his book, looked up at me, and smiled.

"*Baruch haba* [Blessed be the visitor]," Reb Srool greeted me in Hebrew, and I answered with the traditional "shalom."

"Please be seated. I was just about to have a cup of tea. Will you join me?" I thanked him and sat down.

He brought out two cups and put them carefully on the table. Then he handed me a cup while shrugging his shoulder slightly. When I looked in my cup I realized that the shrug was Reb Srool's apology for serving me clear water.

We sat silently sipping the hot water. Once in a while I caught Reb Srool looking at my face, but he didn't say anything. He waited for me to tell him why I had come. When I finally spoke, I couldn't look at him.

"Reb Srool, could you please say Kaddish for my father, my brother Moshe, and,"—I nearly choked on my tears—"and Bunio."

Reb Srool looked at me with such sadness that for a moment I felt sorry that I had come to him.

"You are a good child; God will bless you," he said. "I will say the Kaddish memorial prayer for your family."

His mention of God reminded me that I had wanted to ask Reb Srool about God.

Coming from a traditional home with an atmosphere of love for God and Judaism, I was very bewildered and hurt by what was happening to us. With each additional disaster, I was beginning to wonder where God was and why he was letting such things happen. Perhaps he was dead, too, I thought, like all our thousands of Jewish people.

I had always pictured God as a person. I was too young to have a different conception of Him. Yet as I listened to Reb Srool speak of Him as a living God, I began to think that maybe God was alive but was so shocked at what people were doing to one another that He just left the world. Perhaps He was filled with shame over what He had created. Reb Srool continued. "We can't deny our God. Whatever happens, we must accept it as His will. We die for *kiddush hashem* [sanctification of His name], and we will earn our reward *b'olam haba* [in the next world]."

I thought I understood what Reb Srool was trying to tell me, but I couldn't agree with him. How could what was happening be His will? I was totally confused.

CHAPTER 8

My Brother Zachary

We began building a new hiding place in our house. We called these places "bunkers." Winter was coming, and it would not be safe to use the hiding place in the backyard wall again. The heavy rains might wash away the soil we put between the removable stones, and anyone passing the wall would be able to detect the irregularity between the stones. Also, we needed a bigger place. Our landlord's oldest daughter, Sarah, was expecting a baby soon. I don't know why, but I was very happy to hear this news.

We worked many nights building our new bunker. It ran under the hall, which had two rooms on each side. The entrance to the bunker was from the kitchen, which was occupied by the expectant mother and her husband. The opening to the bunker was under the big brick oven in which there were two small doors that normally opened to the firewood bin. We removed the wooden floor of the bin and dug a tunnel about ten feet under the hall in order to avoid the sound of hollowness. A wooden box filled with earth could be moved to cover the entrance in the floor of the firewood bin, completely sealing the bunker when in place.

Digging was very difficult. The landlord, his two sons-in-law, and Zachary worked for many nights. The rest of us carried the soil over the Bashte and spread it all over the meadows as far as the river. Herzl slept through all of this work. Children could talk and play, but I was not considered a child anymore, so I was included in the work. The work was finished before the first snow came; luckily, too, because it would have been very dangerous to spread fresh dirt over the snow.

In the middle of all the death and suffering a new life arrived. A baby son was born to Sarah.

"Alicia! Come look at the baby," called Herzl excitedly from the open door of the kitchen, where the baby lay in its cradle. "He is such a small fellow, but oh, can he cry!"

"I know he can cry. I can hear him through the wall, especially at night," I said. "I will see him later. Please, Herzl, I am tired now." But the truth was, I was not ready to show joy so soon after Bunio's death.

Even though I had not seen the baby since he was born, I felt that we had something in common. We both had cried a lot. He because he was hungry, and I because my heart and soul were hurting inside me. I was grieving for my brother, my family, and for my two best friends who had been killed in the first action. So the baby and I cried ourselves to sleep each night.

I finally went to visit the baby, Shmuel, after Herzl's endless pleas.

"Come in, children, and meet your new neighbor," his mother called to us cheerfully. "Shmuel loves company. He is about to wake up for his feeding. You may stay and watch him nurse."

We thanked her and seated ourselves to wait for the baby to awaken. He did as his mother predicted, and it was while he was nursing that I fell in love with baby Shmuel. He was very beautiful. He had brown hair and a soft pink skin, and later, when he opened his eyes, I could see they were light brown. He was wrapped in a white down-filled blanket with a blue ribbon tied around it. He looked like a little angel lying there in his cradle. This was the first time I had even seen such a young baby; a real wonder, I thought. I became his slave. Every opportunity I had I would peek in on him. I never hesitated, even in freezing weather, to go down to the well and fetch water for Shmuel's bath. Whenever I could find a piece of wood I brought it to Sarah to help heat Shmuel's room. While his mother napped I rocked Shmuel's cradle. I even had a fantasy that my brother Bunio was reborn in Shmuel.

I was not the only one who fell in love with Shmuel; all of us in the house did. Baby Shmuel meant life to us.

The baby and I shared the same wall. I was getting used to his cries. When I heard him cry I would wake up for a minute and listen. When he started to nurse I would fall asleep again.

One night I heard him crying; I heard someone screaming; and then my mother was shaking me.

"Alicia, hurry, get dressed, hurry!" Mama was urging me.

I have heard this before, I thought as I came fully awake. Something was happening again. I groped for my clothing in the darkness and joined the people in the kitchen, who were already crawling into our bunker.

More people came in. After we were all inside the bunker, Zachary pulled himself up into the bin. He moved the box into place, being careful not to dislodge the pieces of wood on the top of the box, and closed the opening to the bunker. He picked up a candle, looked around, blew it out, and then sat down near me. It was when total darkness came upon us that I suddenly realized that I hadn't seen or heard the baby.

"Zachary, where is the baby?" I asked in a whisper. He didn't answer me. "Please tell me, what did they do with Shmuel?" I asked again frantically. "Where is he!" I was shouting now.

"Alicia, be quiet," Zachary said sternly in Hebrew. "The baby is in the kitchen hidden behind the bed. His father took care of him. He fed him strong camomile tea. He will sleep now for a long time. He couldn't come into the bunker with us. He might wake up and cry and give away our hiding place. It was his father's decision. Don't worry, Shmuel will be safe," he added in a not very convincing voice.

But I did worry and I felt a cold fear spreading all over me. My stomach was hurting me and I felt miserable.

Suddenly everything around us shook. It came from upstairs, and then there was the impact of footsteps over our heads and voices in German and Ukrainian. "Out, you damn Jews! Get out!"

My heart was pounding; I was afraid to breathe. Then I heard a shot that echoed into the depths of my soul. There was more slamming of doors and then quiet.

I don't know how long we sat there in terrified suspense until Zachary suddenly said, "They seem to have gone, but we must be very quiet. They may be listening for sounds from hiding places. We must be absolutely quiet."

A little while later Zachary turned to me. "Alicia, if you need to empty your bladder, you can do it now." He handed me a chamber pot. It was too late. I had already wet myself.

The rest of the day passed in total silence, waiting for the night and hoping that we would be able to get out. But Zachary told us that those on watch had seen a large number of SS men and that we would have to be careful; we must wait.

But how can we wait, I thought, the baby needs to be fed. The mother was here. I had heard her whispering a while ago, but now she was quiet. Suddenly I had an idea and I turned to Zachary.

"Zachary," I whispered, "I will go out and feed Shmuel. I know where his mother keeps the bottles of tea. I will feed him and then I will go up to the attic and stay in the hiding place you showed me the other day. Remember, the one where you keep your old violin. I could look outside and see if any of our Jewish neighbors are outside. If they are, I will come down and knock three times on the door of the wood bin. You know I am slender enough to squeeze into the hiding place. I will be very careful; I will be very careful," I assured him again. "This is the only way. Please, Zachary, talk to Mama," I begged him, "and tell her that I will be safe in the attic."

It took some time for Zachary to convince Mama to let me go, and finally she did. Zachary held me tightly for a moment, and then helped me out of the bunker. It was completely dark in the kitchen. I was terribly afraid, and for a moment I regretted leaving the safety of the bunker. Carefully I felt my way to the bed. I was puzzled by the bed being out of its place. Between the wall and the bed was the baby's crib. He seemed to be sleeping quietly. I bent down to pick him up. My hands felt his head and I screamed and screamed, and then seemed to spin into darkness.

When I woke I didn't know where I was. It was lighter in the kitchen. Then I remembered what had happened, that I had fainted and why. I had hit my back as I fell, and it was paining me now. I tried to remember what I had come to do. But Shmuel was dead. The shot we had heard when the murderers entered our house had killed the poor baby; yet, I remembered, I also had to find out what was going on outside.

I climbed up to the attic. I don't remember how I got into the hiding place, but I did, nearly crushing Zachary's violin. I picked it up and held it close to my heart, deriving comfort from something familiar. This was his old violin. He had sold the new one some time ago to buy us food. Daylight was coming through the opening in the wall where I hid. I leaned over to see what was going on outside.

I saw about a dozen SS men and Ukrainians. They were approaching a house nearby, and then they surrounded it. In seconds I heard the terrible sound of broken doors and loud shouting. "Out, damned Jews!" I heard children crying and then I saw them. They looked dazed from the sudden daylight, and they were staggering as they walked. Men, women, and children, half naked. They were being pushed by rifles and being hit over their heads and backs. As I looked, I suddenly heard a terrifying scream followed by a shot and saw a girl falling out of an attic window. She fell sprawled on the snow like a shot-down bird. Her legs were uncovered and the blood running from her shattered head was spreading into the white snow.

All through the day I heard screams and shooting. I heard children cry and dogs bark. I didn't look outside again. I didn't know when night came. Sometime later I heard a voice calling. I thought it was calling my name. The voice penetrated my mind, and then I heard it distinctly. I thought it was Papa calling me; I tried to call out that I was here, Papa, but I couldn't.

"Alicia," someone was saying in Hebrew, "don't be afraid. It is I, Zachary. I have come to take you down."

I tried to say something but I couldn't. I removed two boards and literally fell out of the hiding place. I was so happy to see Zachary that I started crying. He helped me crawl back into the bunker. There, my mother pulled me into her lap and held me tightly. I could feel her body tremble. Poor Mama, how she must have worried about me. She had probably heard my screams when I discovered the baby, or did she? There was so much I wanted to tell my mother, but I was unable to utter a word. I had lost my voice.

Zachary was putting something between my lips. "Drink it down, Alicia; it will help you stop trembling."

I did as he asked. It was burning my throat but I swallowed it. I felt a warmth spreading all over me. My head became heavy. I felt so tired.

I must have fallen asleep, because now I was waking up. I could hear people whispering around me. Someone stepped on my foot. The people were getting out of the bunker. I will wait a little longer, I thought. I felt warm under the blanket Zachary must have put over me.

Suddenly someone screamed. My first thought was that the Germans returned again and that they had finally found our bunker. They will have to shoot me right here, because I am not getting out, I decided. The screaming stopped as suddenly as it had started, and I heard someone crying. They must have found the baby. Poor mother; poor baby; why did they have to kill him? I felt a fierce anger and an emotion that I couldn't identify taking hold of me. It was born there in the depths of the earth. It was like a fire inside me.

Thousands of Jewish people were murdered in that action. The discovery of many bunkers was due to a young Ukrainian dogcatcher who used his dogs to find the hiding places. He was later killed by an unknown person. The people were murdered in front of mass graves on the Fador and over the Bashte near the Jewish cemetery. Some were buried where they were killed, like the ones near the water well at the end of Podhajecka Street: Their blood seeped into the well, and the water was discolored for days. On the streets the snow was colored a reddish-brown in places where Jewish blood had spilled. Toys were scattered over the streets of the ghetto, lost by children or knocked out of their hands when they were taken to their death by their murderers. The ghetto was half empty. At night the houses on the streets appeared ghastly, and the people left alive had a ghostlike look about them.

One late afternoon when I returned home I found two little girls, about five or six years old, sitting on my bed. They looked dirty and very scared. They were huddled together as if they were trying to disappear into each other. Since I couldn't speak to them because my voice hadn't yet fully returned, I just sat down near them and smiled. They didn't smile back. They just looked at me with frightened eyes.

My mother came home shortly after and explained the children's situation to me. They had been separated from their parents during the action. They were sisters. My mother had found them in an empty house. She had heard them crying and brought them home. They were going to stay with us until we could find out if they had any family and, if not, my mother would find them another home. Mama asked if in the meantime I would mind if they slept in my bed and I shared hers.

As I lay snuggled in near my mother, I heard sobs coming from my bed. Poor children. I got out of Mama's bed and, lifting the covers off the children, squeezed in with them. I put my arms over their trembling bodies, pulled the blanket tightly around us, and tried to fall asleep.

My mother was very kind to them, and I was very glad to have them with us. So far, they just stayed in our room. We had to let the landlord know about them in case they had to hide with us. How would he react? How were we going to feed them? Herzl promised to make a greater effort at the market, and I decided to go back to selling soap with Herzl as my spokesman until I regained my voice. I had two pieces left over from before the action, and I had to sell them before they dried out. We had to be very careful. Two children trying to sell would arouse some attention. So I stayed some distance from Herzl, and when he had a customer, he would call me over. It was working out just fine.

One afternoon as I was leaning against a sleigh, waiting for Herzl to call me, I heard loud voices and laughter mixed with the crying voice of a child. It was coming from the direction in which Herzl had gone. Something was pulling me to go and see what was happening. When I pushed through the people I saw my brother kneeling on the snow trying to pick up his spilled flints. A big farmer was kicking him in his behind. Each time my brother tried to get up he was kicked by the farmer again, who was encouraged by shouts of laughter from the onlookers. I felt a wave of hatred envelop me as I threw myself at the farmer, beating him with my fists and screaming curses at him.

"Alicia, your voice, your voice!" Herzl, who was on his feet, screamed at me. I was so stunned, I stopped hitting the farmer. I turned to Herzl, grabbed his hand in mine, and we shot off like two arrows.

As we ran, our wooden-soled shoes slapping the frozen snow, we could still hear the distant laughter of the cruel farmer. We were stopped several times by people who wanted to know why we were running. We just smiled at them and didn't explain why. I was afraid to talk.

One afternoon Zachary suddenly appeared in our room and, without saying a word, collapsed on his bed. He lay there moaning and shivering violently. I acted immediately. I pulled off his coat and took off his hat. To my great surprise he was wearing one of those hateful

Ukrainian blue hats, which I threw on the floor and disgustedly kicked into the corner. His hair was matted with blood, and he moaned deeply when I touched his head. His shirt was covered with blood. I rolled up the sleeve that looked the most bloody. It looked as though something had pierced his arm.

Now, Alicia, I said to myself, don't panic. Remember what Uncle told you. When someone is bleeding, the first thing you must do is stop it by using pressure on the wound. I felt a calm settling over me. My hands worked steadily as I tore up a sheet and bandaged Zachary's arm. I did the same with his head. I covered him with blankets and told him I was going to get Mama.

Outside, I instinctively looked to see if someone might have followed Zachary. I hesitated for a moment, thinking that perhaps I should hide him in the bunker but decided not to as it would not be wise to move him. I ran toward Mrs. Kovalsky's house, where my mother now worked, slipping as I went.

If I only had a pair of leather boots in place of the wooden-soled shoes I was wearing, I thought as I picked myself up for the third time. The earth was frozen underneath the soft thin blanket of snow, and I couldn't see where I was going.

I was out of breath by the time I reached Mrs. Kovalsky's home and knocked on her front door. She opened the door so suddenly that I nearly fell into her arms.

"Alicia, you shouldn't have come here; you know you are not allowed in this neighborhood. What do you want?" she asked.

"Please tell my mother—she is working here, isn't she?—that she must return home immediately. It's urgent!"

"What has happened?" She looked frightened now. "Are the Germans . . . ?"

"No, no, they are not. . . . Those murdering cowards come only at night."

Then I realized what I was saying. Mr. Kovalsky was some kind of official in the German police.

"Please, Mrs. Kovalsky, I must see Mama," I said with a pleading voice.

"Wait outside, near the wall," she commanded. "I will tell her you are here."

I was shivering from cold and anxiety. The perspiration from my run was now chilling me thoroughly. Most of all, I was worried about Zachary. As I was waiting impatiently for my mother to come out of

Mrs. Kovalsky's, I thought how ironic it was that my mother was busy treating sick children of our former neighbors, now our enemies, when her son might be bleeding to death. My mother applied *Banke* to their backs and chests. The *Banke* were delicate, bell-like glasses that were warmed and applied to the skin of the patient. The cups left deep red circles when removed but helped reduce the pain caused by influenza. I had had it done to me several times. My mother had a very gentle hand and was often called in to give this treatment.

It seemed like ages until finally the door opened and Mama appeared, looking white and frightened.

"What happened, Alicia?" she asked in a trembling voice.

"Zachary has been hurt. I took care of him, but let's hurry. Let me take your bag; I will be careful. Please go first, Mama, I will follow you."

It took two weeks of tender care by Mama and the rest of the family to get Zachary well enough to get out of bed. Finally one day after supper he told us what had happened.

It had begun when my mother found the oldest sister of the two little girls who now lived with us. During the second action the sister had been away from home in a nearby village, tutoring a farmer's son for his gymnasium [high school] exams. When she had returned home, she found all her family gone, but she learned from the neighbors that her sisters had survived and were living with us. This was how we met Lena. Lena was a lovely sixteen-year-old, and it was not at all surprising that she had captured our hearts, especially that of my brother Zachary. As young as I was, I could not have missed the looks that passed between them, and I knew that Zachary and Lena were in love. Since I loved my brother dearly, I had been willing to love Lena as well. It was good to see my brother joke and smile again. We had been ready to think of Lena and her sisters as family, when I came home one day to find them gone. I was upset, and when I asked Zachary where they were, all he said was that they were safe.

Now Zachary told us that Lena had returned to the farmer whose son she tutored and had taken her sisters with her. She had been assured by the farmer that he would build a hiding place for them, and Lena would continue to help their son during the evening hours while hiding during the day.

Zachary had taken them to the farmer at night and was relieved to see that the house was some distance from the other farmhouses, and that it was near a small forest. He had been hoping, he told us, now almost crying, to eventually find a safer place for the girls, and for us, as soon as spring came. But at that time they had seemed better off outside the city.

Lena and her sisters had stayed with the farmer about a month. Then the farmer brought them into the city to the German police, who took them to the Fador and shot them. One of Zachary's friends had seen them brought in and told Zachary what had happened. My brother was overcome with grief and went to kill the farmer. He waited for him in the barn, and when the farmer came to feed the horses, Zachary attacked him. Zachary was barely a match for the strong farmer, and the farmer pierced Zachary's arm with a pitchfork. But eventually Zachary managed to knock the farmer unconscious.

"I was about to drive the same pitchfork into his heart, but I couldn't." Then, looking at Mama, he said again, "I just couldn't kill him."

My poor brother, I thought as I listened to this tragic story; he must have loved Lena very much. And now Zachary was telling us that more farmers were bringing their hidden Jews to the police after taking away their money and clothing. Some farmers did not even bother to bring the Jews into the city; they were taking them out into the fields and forests and killing and burying them right there. Zachary told us that he and his friends would have to do something to stop these murders and to punish the farmers who committed such crimes.

After Zachary got well we saw very little of him. My mother, Herzl, and I worried about him; but we understood his need to fight murderers in his own way. To sit and wait, as most of us did, was unbearable for my brother. Somehow I believed that Zachary and his friends would find a way to save at least some of us.

One day, in the late afternoon, as I walked up to a group gathered on the street corner, I clearly heard someone say, "Shh, here comes his sister."

"What do you mean, here comes his sister?" I demanded to know. "Please tell me."

I searched each face for an answer while my heart started beating wildly. Some turned away, and others stared, saying nothing. I knew something was wrong; I didn't want to know what it was, but I had to know.

"Nathan!" I turned to one of the boys. "Where is my brother Zachary?"

His eyes darted nervously to the faces of the others.

"You are his best friend; you should know. Please tell me!"

Reluctantly Nathan looked into my eyes. "Alicia," he said slowly, forcing the words out, "Zachary has been hanged."

I staggered back as though from a blow. My knees felt weak, and I thought I would faint; but I didn't. I felt the burning sensation of hatred that I now knew so well.

"Where is he?" I asked. Nathan only looked away.

"Where is he?" I was screaming now.

The boy who had spoken before stepped forward. "I will take you to him," he said. "He is at the police station, the one with the prison."

Just before crossing the bridge leading to the police station, the boy, whose name was David, put on a blue Ukrainian hat, pulled off my armband, and taking my hand, dragged me to the station.

In front of the building, hanging from a tree, was the lifeless body of my brother. His clothes were torn, and all over the body there were marks of torture.

I freed myself of David and ran to my brother. I just managed to touch his legs, when I felt a terrible pain in my back. I fell down.

I pulled myself up to a sitting position and saw a Ukrainian policeman pointing a rifle at me, ready to shoot. I didn't really care if he shot me right there. I would have welcomed it. I wasn't at all afraid. I must have gone crazy, because I was screaming at him and cursing him for what he had done to my brother.

"Be gone or I will shoot you," he screamed back at me.

"Shoot, shoot, I don't care!" I screamed back.

He kicked me with his boots and then left me alone. I don't know how long I sat there sobbing.

When the policeman left, David appeared and urged me to leave.

"David, we must . . ." I choked on the words.

"It is impossible," he said. "In a few days, perhaps. The Germans will never let us take him down until the whole town has seen him. You know how cruel they are."

"We must do it," I said, wiping my eyes dry. "I can't leave him there. What if my mother and Herzl hear about him."

For a moment we stared at each other, this young stranger and I. Finally he conceded. "All right," he said quietly. "But we will need help."

"Can you get someone?"

"I am sure I can," he said. "Your brother helped so many others; I am sure someone will help us now."

I waited at David's home. He returned shortly with Nathan and two other boys. In the darkness, after the curfew had begun, we crept back to the police station.

To be caught in the streets after curfew was a crime punishable by death, and I knew the risk these young people were running by helping me. It touched me deeply to realize how much they loved my brother. In my anguish I didn't even think that the policeman might stop us.

There was no one there.

All the way to the Jewish cemetery I held my brother's hand and cried and cried. When we put him into the freshly dug grave, all I wanted was to be buried with him.

CHAPTER 9

Bella

As if it were not bad enough that the Gestapo and their helpers were trying to wipe us out, another enemy from which we could not hide appeared in the ghetto—typhus. Especially in the winter, the conditions under which we lived were very unsanitary. There was never enough soap or hot water, toilets were primitive, and there were lice. Typhus furiously attacked our weakened bodies and, within weeks, hundreds died.

My mother and Herzl were the first in our house to become ill. The anguish my mother suffered after Zachary was killed and the lack of food made her a ready victim. Herzl had a bad cold, which further weakened him. My greatest worry was that my mother didn't seem to care whether she lived or died. I had two very sick people to take care of, and I don't know what would have happened if Sarah, Shmuel's mother, hadn't helped us.

She walked into our room one evening.

"Good evening, Alicia. I have come to help. My husband is away building an aluminum roof for a farmer, so I can stay with you."

She took my hand gently. "You know, Alicia, I have never forgotten how you tried to save my baby."

With Sarah's help we were able to work around the clock, sponging the hot bodies of my mother and brother and forcing hot tea between their parched lips. We kept them covered when they tossed off their blankets and took turns resting. I was not even aware when the day ended and the night began. Sarah disappeared occasionally into the kitchen and came back with tea or soup. Thus passed two nightmarish weeks of worry and devoted nursing.

As suddenly as the fever came, it disappeared. The crisis was over. Mama and Herzl opened their eyes almost at the same hour. Mama smiled when she saw us and went back to sleep. Herzl drank some tea, and then he, too, went to sleep.

Shortly after, I became ill with typhus. I had terrible nightmares. I dreamed that I was trying to escape bullets the Germans were shooting at me, but I couldn't run. I vaguely remember people saying things to me; I felt very hot; and then one day about two weeks later I awoke. I saw Mama and Herzl, and suddenly I felt peaceful and content.

I remember dozing off and waking, to find my mother near me, saying loving words to me and encouraging me to drink. I was too weak to lift my head, but there was Mother's arm holding me gently and tilting the cup to my mouth.

Mama came by often and stroked my head. I didn't know what it was, but her hand, which usually felt soft as it glided over my hair, now felt strange. I lifted my hand to my hair and was shocked. My hair was short and bristly. All my curls were gone. Suddenly I understood. My mother must have cut off my hair to stop it from falling out during my illness. I remembered that my mother had told me about this. I had not known about it in time to cut her hair when she was ill, and as a result her beautiful hair was now very thin. But Mama wasn't taking any chances with me; she just cut my hair off. I was going to look terrible and would have to wear a kerchief on my head like others who had survived the typhus epidemic.

Soon I was feeling much better, although still weak. We needed food desperately. I decided to try to get more soap from Mr. Gruber, who had been supplying it to me. I took the road to his house, hoping he would let me have a piece of soap on credit. I could go to the market and try to sell it.

It was a short walk, and soon I saw the house. It looked so majestic in the sun. I quickened my steps and was about to knock on the door, when I noticed something unusual. Chickens were walking around the yard. Chickens? I hadn't seen chickens for such a long time that I stood hypnotized. What's more, they were picking corn seeds from the ground where the snow had melted.

I was just about to knock on the door, when it opened and a woman I had never seen before said in an angry voice, "What do you want here? Be gone or I will set the dogs on you!"

"I mean you no harm. I am looking for Mr. Gruber," I said.

"They took him and his family away. I live here now."

I got out of her way just in time. She was about to hit me. A crazy woman, I thought as I walked backward still looking at her. I wondered if she hadn't deliberately sent the Germans to kill the Grubers so that she could live in their house. She sure acted guilty.

I dismissed her from my mind, but I couldn't dismiss the Gruber family. They had had four children.

I felt a burning sensation inside me again, a feeling of hatred for the Germans, the Ukrainians, and for our former neighbors who had helped kill us in order to get our homes. I hoped God would punish them for their evil deeds.

Thinking again of God, I thought of Reb Srool. I hadn't seen him for some time, and I also needed to ask him to add Zachary's name to the mourners' prayers he was already saying for my family.

The door of his room was closed, and at first I thought he might not welcome a visitor. But it was winter, and I concluded that his door must be closed to keep out the cold. I knocked several times. When I didn't get an answer I turned the doorknob and entered the room. For a moment I just stood staring. The room was in shambles. The books normally stacked neatly on shelves were thrown around, the bed linen lay crumpled on the floor, and I saw his tefillin (phylacteries) near the sink with their straps spread about like winding snakes. My head started pounding with fear, and I ran out of the room. I saw a woman standing on the steps outside the house.

"Have you seen Reb Srool? He is the old man who lives downstairs, the one with the long white beard."

She said something to me in a language I couldn't understand. She kept repeating the word *nem*. Suddenly I was screaming at her.

"What happened to Reb Srool? What happened to Reb Srool?"

Something snapped inside me because I was screaming loudly and crying at the same time.

A man suddenly appeared, grasped my arm, and was pulling me away, saying, "Stop, you crazy girl! Stop screaming! Do you want to scare the people here? Don't they have enough trouble already? If you don't shut up, I will hit you!"

"I am not a crazy girl, and you should apologize to me for calling me such a name." Then I added, "I had a bad day today."

"I know you are not crazy," he answered. "I will take you to meet someone who they say is crazy but just had a bad time, like you."

And that was how I came to meet Crazy Bella, who wasn't crazy at all.

"Bella, my dear, let me introduce you to a ghetto rat," the man said. "I caught her when she came out of a basement and began screaming at a poor Hungarian woman, whom she scared half to death.

"She is really a good girl, though," he added with a smile.

"What is your name?"

"Alicia Jurman, and my mother is a Kurtz from the Carpathian Mountains," I answered with dignity as I looked up at the lady.

Before me stood a woman who looked like a princess in biblical stories I had read.

Bella was about six feet tall with two long red braids hanging down on her chest. She had green eyes and lots of freckles. She wore an embroidered peasant blouse and a wide peasant skirt. On her feet she wore high-heeled red boots. She looked like a flaming torch. In her arms she was holding a little girl about two years old who had the same coloring but short, curly red hair. Sitting at the kitchen table was a young girl about my age, with the same red hair falling in gentle curls to her shoulders, apparently Bella's sister. The third child, a boy of about six, had brown hair and brown eyes.

I looked closely at the man who had brought me there. He was very handsome, as tall as Bella, with blond hair and brown eyes. Bella called him Beniek.

I had never seen these people before. Apparently they had come to live in the ghetto after the second action. There was something about them I couldn't understand at the time, but I felt drawn to them. I wished that they would let me stay with them for a while. I didn't know what impression I made on them. Before them was a skinny twelve-year-old girl with a kerchief on her head and a tear-stained face, with a trace of a smile on her lips but not in her eyes.

"Why don't you sit down near my sister Rachel and have some soup? Would you like that, Alicia?"

What a gracious lady, I thought as I curtsied and sat down. The boy made space for me at the table. He was Bella's son, and his name was Danny. He was six years old, and I liked him. I also liked Rachel and Bella very much. I was hoping that they would like me too.

Our life in the ghetto, the constant hunger, the gradual loss of family members, the horror of being hunted by the Gestapo and killed, left very little hope of survival in the hearts of the Jewish children. I wasn't different from the others. What kept me going was my love for my mother and brother and the wish to see our murderers punished for their crimes. There was a balance between love and hate in my heart. Meeting Bella and her family tipped the scale a little in favor of love.

Every day I stopped by to say hello to my new friends, and when I found out that Rachel was very ill with tuberculosis, I spent hours with her, just talking and reading aloud to her from the many books she had found when they moved into their home.

One of the books interested me because it dealt with the changes that were taking place in my body. The book was written in Polish and was called *Zagadnienie Seksualne*, "Sexual Problems." Rachel, who was two years older than I, was glad to enlighten me when I couldn't understand some of the words. As we became close friends we talked about our families. Rachel told me about hers and how they had come to Buczacz.

They had lived in a small village nearby. Her father was a furrier who made fur coats out of lambskins for farmers in the neighboring villages. He made a good living and was able to send Bella to school in Buczacz. Bella was a free spirit. She rode horses with the village boys and swam in the river. Here Rachel stopped her story and smiled.

"This worried Father, and do you know what he did?" Rachel said, lowering her voice.

"No, what did he do?" I asked somewhat worriedly.

"He married Bella off to a very religious yeshiva boy in order to tame her."

"And what happened next?" I asked.

"Well, she had children. Danny is six now and Hanale two. Danny is a quiet boy, just like his father, but Hanale is a little red-haired flame," she said with pride.

The Russians took Bella's husband into the army in 1941 and they hadn't heard from him since. I could sense that Rachel was getting tired, so I suggested that she finish the story another time. I could not have been very convincing, because Rachel continued. I really did want to hear the rest of the story.

"My father and mother disappeared shortly after the Germans came. I was visiting Bella, who lived at the other end of the village. No one could tell us what had happened to them. But we found out that the Ukrainian police had taken them away, and we assume they were killed.

"Can you imagine such a thing?" Rachel was crying now.

"Someone told me it was the son of one of the farmers who brought the police to our house. His father owed my father for a fur."

Here I really had to stop Rachel. A week passed before I heard how they had left Bella's home and moved into a hiding place in the forest.

For a while they managed well. Bella would go out and get food from some of the farmers who owed her father for fur coats. Bella, as always, carried a whip in her boot, so she felt relatively safe.

Then one night Bella was followed by farmers to her hiding place. They waited long enough for Bella, her children, and Rachel to fall asleep, and then attacked them. The farmers bound them with ropes, put them on a wagon, put rags in their mouths, and then covered them with straw. The other farmers went home while one of the farmers drove the wagon. Sometime later the wagon stopped and the farmer pulled Bella down by her hair. Rachel couldn't see what happened next, but suddenly her sister was screaming, and she heard the whip whistling and the farmer yelling and cursing. Bella eventually untied the others and, whipping the horses with all her might, drove into Buczacz.

Sometime later Rachel heard Bella tell Beniek what had happened. The farmer decided to rape Bella before bringing her and the children to the police in Buczacz. Bella managed to free her hands and nearly whipped the farmer to death. She then took off his boots and his clothing and left him naked on the road. Before leaving she made sure he understood that if he told anyone what had happened she would come back and burn his home and the homes of the other farmers who had been with him.

I could see that Rachel was glad to have finished telling this horror story, but I wanted to know one more thing.

"What happened to the wagon and horses?" I asked Rachel.

"Oh, Bella sold them in the market. How do you think we can buy food now?"

"But aren't you afraid that the farmer will find you and kill you?" She frowned.

"Well, yes, that is why we stay in this house and try to keep watch from the balcony."

I was really in awe of Bella's bravery and wondered why she was staying in the ghetto. Surely she could hide somewhere else. Then I realized that Rachel was too ill. She couldn't live in a hole in the ground anymore. My heart went out to them. Trapped, I thought. We were all trapped, one way or another.

CHAPTER 10

In Chortkov Prison

"I said Alicia can't see you now," came Herzl's angry voice from outside. "She's busy. Come back another time."

"I'll wait, if you don't mind."

"You have to wait outside," Herzl said.

"I will wait inside," the visitor said firmly.

If this visitor insisted on entering our room, I thought, Herzl would have to prevent him by force, and there might be a fight. He had orders not to let anyone into our room while I was under the bed digging a new bunker. I pulled myself out of the hole and crawled out from under the bed.

Not taking time to brush the soil from my clothing, I went to the door.

"What's so urgent that you have to make my brother angry?" I asked the intruder. He was facing me now, and as we stood looking at each other, I recognized him. He had grown a lot since I last saw him four years before. He was very slender and his clothes were about two sizes too small, but his eyes were the same deep blue, with a special twinkle in them that gave the impression of a lingering smile.

"Milek? Milek?"

"Yes, it is I in person. How are you, Alicia?" he asked softly. Then, changing his tone, he said, "My, you look like . . . like"—he paused—"a chimney sweep," and began to laugh.

"Oh, no, Milek, you are wrong, very wrong. I look more like a gravedigger," and I also burst out laughing. It was just like old times in Stanislavov. Milek would say something funny and I would become hysterical. My dear friend from Stanislavov had come, and there I stood all covered with dirt and not even able to offer him a chair to sit on. We had traded all our chairs for food.

Milek had escaped from Stanislavov with his friend, Bolek, just before the ghetto was made Judenrein, or free of Jews. I never asked him about his family, or about my uncle. From the way Milek and Bolek looked, I could see that they had suffered a lot. They were now living with Bolek's aunt, who had lost all of her family and was glad to have them in her house.

In a very short time Milek became a member of our family as well as that of Rachel's. Rachel and I tried our best to interest Milek in our books, or just in storytelling; but although he would listen for a while, we could see that he was only being polite to us, and his thoughts were far away. The only times he showed genuine interest were when Beniek was visiting Bella. Beniek usually had some kind of news— sometimes good but mostly bad—which he told us in such a way that we could handle it and not get too upset. Beniek was an optimist in a pessimistic world.

Beniek and his friends were well known in the ghetto. There were ten of them living across from Bella's house. They had escaped from Horodenko ghetto, which was quite a distance from Buczacz. Rumor had it that they had fought the Germans and the Ukrainian police in their area and were planning to do the same in Buczacz. Perhaps, I thought, they will be able to do what my poor brother Zachary couldn't. Fight back. We all knew that our chances for survival were very small and that the Germans planned to destroy all of us.

Milek wasn't the only one to enter our lives as a dear friend. One day I came home from visiting Rachel and found a woman and two boys in our room. My mother introduced them as Mrs. Eckerberg from Bielsko and her sons, Samuel and Joshua. Samuel was about fifteen years old and Joshua looked about my age. Mrs. Eckerberg was a very beautiful lady. I remembered that Mr. Eckerberg and Papa had been business partners in Bielsko. For a moment I wondered where Mr. Eckerberg was, but I didn't ask. If he were alive, he would have been with his family. Poor people. They must have had a very difficult time getting to Buczacz. Bielsko was occupied by the Germans in 1939, and it was now 1942. Three years of hell, I thought as I looked at them.

Mama and Mrs. Eckerberg became good friends. The Eckerbergs lived in a room one street below ours. Mama told me that the house had a bunker, a necessary part of every ghetto home. Mrs. Eckerberg had brought very little money with her and practically no clothing. We shared what little we had with them. The boys were given some of my brother's clothing. When I saw them wearing the familiar garments, I found it hard to go near them. Mama must have cared very deeply for these boys to give them her dead children's clothing. She hadn't even touched it when we were starving during the famine.

The new people who had entered our lives put additional pressure on me to look for new sources of food. One day, as I was standing on Rachel's balcony looking down on Chechego Maya Street, one of Buczacz's main streets, I had an idea. I saw the farmers bringing their quotas of sugar beets to the Germans. I stood watching as sleighs, heavily loaded with sugar beets, moved slowly along the street. They were coming from the Charny Most (the Black Bridge), which was the western entrance to our city. I knew the place well. The sleighs coming that way had to pass a hill in order to get onto the bridge. That's it, I told myself. That could be the place where I could get some beets.

"I will see you later," I said to Rachel. "I have to go and talk with Herzl."

"Wait a minute, Alicia; here, take this." She handed me a piece of white pork fat. "Eat it here. It will take only a moment. I don't want anybody to see you eat it. It will help your cough, although you don't seem to be coughing much lately.

"You are feeling better, I hope?" she asked, looking anxiously at me. I had developed a mild case of tuberculosis and my lungs were weak.

"Thank you, dear Rachel, I'm much better. The fat is really helping me. My cough is almost all gone and the pain in my chest too. This is it, the last piece of fat I will need. Thank you again. I really must go home now."

I found Herzl at home and immediately told him what I was planning to do. He thought it was a good idea and said he would get two of his good friends to come along with us.

Early the next morning the four of us were hiding in the bushes near the Black Bridge. I was going to perform an experiment. I cautioned the boys to stay in hiding no matter what happened. We did not wear our armbands, and it would be very dangerous for us if we were to be discovered by the police, or by anybody, for that matter. It was a cold morning, so I was shivering as we huddled together. I was also afraid of what I was going to do. My stomach was churning from hunger and fear.

Suddenly I heard the sound of an approaching sleigh. It was coming slowly up the hill. There were two people sitting on the driver's seat. They had bundles inside the wagon, but not beets.

Some time passed before I heard the sound of the next sleigh. The farmer was urging his horses to pull, so I assumed that the sleigh must be carrying a heavy load. Then I saw that the sleigh was loaded with sugar beets. I waited until it passed us and then, stooping over, I ran after the sleigh. As quietly as I could, I pulled myself up into the back of the sleigh and kneeled down on the short boards. Holding the side of the wagon with one hand, I used my other to reach down inside. I grasped the leaves of a beet and pulled it out gently. I put the beet in my apron and then pulled out three more beets.

I waited for the right moment to get off. When the farmer called out to the horses to move on, I jumped. I landed on my behind and the beets spilled out of my apron and scattered around me. I looked around to make sure that no one had seen me, quickly picked up the beets, and ran to where the boys were hiding.

My heart was beating wildly, but I had four large beets. One for each of us. I should have been glad about the success of my experiment, but I wasn't. As a matter of fact, I felt sudden anger and humiliation. I was angry with myself, with the farmer, and with the whole world. I was also very ashamed. I had violated the commandment that tells us not to steal.

Herzl sensed my change of mood and, putting his arm around my shoulder, said, "I know how you feel, Alicia. This is the first time in your life that you have stolen. 'Thou shalt not steal' is a commandment we were taught to respect, but what about the commandment which says clearly 'Thou shalt not kill'? What about that one?" he said forcefully as tears gathered in his eyes.

I looked at my ten-year-old brother with gratitude. He understood what I was feeling deep inside me. At that moment I loved him with all my heart. I made up my mind not to subject him and his friends to the humiliation I had just experienced. I would have to find another way to get food for us.

*   *   *

One day I was sewing up a torn sleeve on Milek's coat. The coat looked too large for him, and I wondered where he had gotten it.

"Milek, I hope you will forgive me for asking, but where did you get this coat? It is really a nice coat," I added hurriedly. "I was just wondering."

"Oh, that!" He laughed. "Bolek and I found a whole trunk filled with clothing in the attic of our house. Bolek took a jacket, and I took this coat. The rest were ladies' things, and we left them in the trunk."

Ladies' things. Maybe some of them would fit Mrs. Eckerberg, or even Mama, I thought.

"Do you think I could have a look at those ladies' things?" I asked Milek.

"We can go as soon as you have finished sewing up my coat."

The ladies' things turned out to be real treasures. Mama said they were fashions of the 1920s. She washed some of the dresses, repaired them, and gave them to Mrs. Eckerberg to wear. A few of the dresses were ripped apart, and we traded the fabric for potatoes. A lovely taffeta skirt was exchanged for eight potatoes. My mother made me a green pinafore trimmed with white silk, which covered my shabby dress. "Green for hope," my mother said as she tied the ribbons in the back.

This find gave me the idea that all Herzl's friends should look in their attics for old clothing. Soon I was busy washing old clothes and hanging them out to dry in the attic. Since all my washing was done without soap, some things could not be saved, but those that came out relatively clean were traded for food. Among the old things, I found a nice shirt for Milek. I washed and mended it. Actually this shirt was to be in exchange for a favor I was going to ask him. I wanted him to help Bella build a bunker.

I found Milek at Rachel's house. He was spending a lot of time there. Rachel and Milek were the same age, and I was a little jealous of the attention he was giving her. But both Rachel and Milek were my best friends, and I felt ashamed to feel anything but love for them.

I waited until Milek finished his soup and then asked him to go for a walk with me. I said I needed advice. I gave him the shirt and told him I wished him to wear it in good health.

I could feel that Milek was annoyed with me.

"Well, what is it you have to tell me that couldn't wait a little longer?" Then more gently, "What is it, Alicia?"

"It is about Rachel and her family," I said. "I am very worried about them. Winter is coming and they don't have a bunker. Rachel will not be able to run over the Bashte and hide when the Germans come again to kill us. What will happen to them, please tell me?" I asked in a pleading voice. Tears had gathered in my eyes and started running down my face.

Milek stopped and looked at me. He took out a handkerchief and wiped my face, which made me cry even more.

"You are right to be concerned, Alicia. Rachel is too ill to run now and stay outside for long periods of time, especially in this weather. I heard Bella talk about this with Beniek.

"They are all worried, and so am I," Milek continued. "They decided to build an extra wall somewhere in the house. I don't know where, but if they need my help, they know they can count on me. I love them too, you know. I really love them," he repeated again.

I was so relieved to hear this news that without thinking I kissed Milek on his cheek. For a moment we just stood looking at each other. Then I blushed and wished that the earth would swallow me.

One morning as I looked out the window I saw the ground covered with freshly fallen snow. I loved the snow, and I remembered how much fun we used to have, my brothers and I, skiing and sliding down the hills on our sleigh. And now . . . I pushed the sad thoughts away. I was going to visit Rachel this morning and bring her a snowball. In the meantime I went back to bed to snuggle into the warmth of my blanket.

I must have dozed off, when I thought I heard someone calling my name and tapping on the window. I came fully awake and immediately felt the familiar sensation of fear. I jumped out of bed and looked out through the window. Rachel was standing outside. Now I was really frightened. What could have brought Rachel here? She rarely came to my home, and never so early in the morning. I didn't even put on my coat but quickly opened the front door and pulled Rachel into our room.

She was out of breath and coughing; I was trembling from cold and fright. Then Rachel smiled at me.

"Alicia, forgive me; I can see I frightened you, but I had to come and tell. I couldn't wait for you to come to us. I have some wonderful news for you. You'll never believe it, but it is true. America is at war with the Germans and with Japan, and the Russians are getting help from America, and they, too, are able to fight the Germans. We are going to be saved!"

"Mama, did you hear the news Rachel brought us? Do you think that the Americans or the Russians might get here in time to . . . ?"

A shadow crossed over Mother's face. It disappeared as quickly as it had come, but it lasted long enough to bring us back to reality. We will have to try to live through each day as it comes, I thought. There was some hope now, but not enough to quiet my constant fear.

I turned to my mother and said, "Mama, I will go home with Rachel now. Bella is going to be very angry with her. Maybe we can get back without Bella noticing. I will also go and see Beniek and find out a little more about the news. There is hope now, dearest Mama." And so saying I bent down and kissed her. I threw my pillow at Herzl as I was leaving the room and heard him laugh.

Hope! What a wonderful word for a child in the ghetto. A spark of light in the darkness. How I wished it would grow! But I knew that for us, rescue might come too late.

All of my nightmares became reality one late afternoon in December 1942, about four o'clock. I had just returned from pumping water for our tiny household. I had set the water buckets down in their usual place in the hall and pushed the front door shut, when suddenly there was a heavy knock. I still had my gloves on, and my heavy shawl was wrapped high around my head, covering my nose and mouth against the bitter outside cold.

I opened the door and saw a Ukrainian policeman. He held a pencil and a small notebook, and seemed to be checking things off some sort of list. "Frieda Jurman?" he asked.

I swallowed hard, and a wave of sickness swept over me. "Yes," I said.

He made a check in his little book. "Come with me."

And so I went. I said nothing, fearing he would realize that my voice was too high and childlike to belong to a woman. It may seem strange that he thought me an adult, but I was tall for a twelve-year-old, about five feet six inches, and the coat and shawl disguised my body well. The thing I most feared had happened. They had come for my mother. I wanted to get away from our house as soon as possible, so I walked quickly in the direction the policeman indicated.

He brought me directly to the police station, where I was put into a cell with many others. It was a bare cell. The people were sitting on the stone floor all huddled together. I found a corner and sat down, pulling my legs up and encircling them with my arms. I put my head down and closed my eyes. I made up my mind that I wasn't going to cry or think about what was going to happen to all of us. Instead, I was trying to listen to what the women near me were saying. They were talking about a street action they were caught in. This was odd, because the policeman had come into our house to ask for my mother by name. Street actions were something new. We were now being picked up at random in the streets. What new horrors would that bring to the ghetto, I wondered.

Dawn was just breaking, when a prison guard came and unlocked the door to our cell. "Everybody line up and go upstairs into the waiting room," he called out. The people who had remained awake were heavy with fatigue. I, like some others, had taken the opportunity to get some sleep; I knew I would need to be alert later.

As the line moved, I could see that the people were stooping and writing their names on a yellow ledger in front of a policeman seated behind a table. I blinked hard when I realized that I knew the policeman. I felt ill inside.

This man, who was helping murder my people, was the father of my childhood friend, Olga. As I came nearer, I watched him silently. He did not look much at the people who approached him, but kept his eyes on the ledger.

When it was my turn I stepped up, took the pencil, and wrote "Alicia Jurman" on the yellow paper. I did not sign my mother's name, as I feared Olga's father would recognize me, realize what had happened, and send for my mother. His eyes widened as he recognized the name. "Alicia"—he looked at me—"what are you doing here?"

I straightened my shoulders. "I was taken here like the others," I said. He seemed baffled; clearly there had been a mistake. All of the others were adults; they had not meant to include children in this action.

Olga's father looked around to see if any of the other policemen had noticed his outburst, then motioned for me to come closer.

"Look," he said, "the Germans will be here soon to take you away. When they get here, I want you to get down on your knees and beg for your life."

He searched my face for a nod or some other sign of acknowledgment, but I only stared back. His words "beg for your life" were still ringing in my ears. He looked uncomfortable under my gaze. "All right," he said. "Move on."

I took my place with the others. I still couldn't believe that Olga's father could be part of this. I still remembered when he had told his daughter how fortunate she was to have me help her with her homework and how glad he was that we were friends. Friends, I thought bitterly, and hatred began to settle into my heart. Will he accompany the Germans and help them shoot us? Will his bullet find its target in my heart or head?

It wasn't long before the Germans came. I could see by their uniforms that they were not the usual SS men, known to us as Hitler's most brutal killers, or even the Wehrmacht (army). They were the local German police.

As one of them explained that we were to be loaded into sleighs for a journey to another city, I watched Olga's father. Our eyes met. I could almost hear his thoughts. *Say it! Do it now!* I looked back at the German. He was winding down his talk; time was running out. Olga's father looked at the German, then at me again. Beg for your life, his eyes commanded me.

But I would not. Never! Never! I was frightened but angry at him, at the Germans, at the whole world. I wanted desperately to live, but I didn't think for a moment that going down on my knees before a heartless German murderer would save my life. If they released me, would they look for my mother again? Call it what you will, anger, dignity, courage, or just hatred, I couldn't beg, and the moment passed.

Finally the German finished. The doors opened, and the people were being pushed outside. Suddenly Olga's father stood up and came over to me. Swiftly he swung his open hand at me. The blow caught me on the cheek, throwing my head to one side. Then his hand swung back, connecting against my other cheek. The force of his slap threw me off my feet, onto the crowd of the people. Hands reached out to catch me, and I was quickly steadied.

Olga's father stood in the middle of the room, his body stiff, his eyes glaring at me. Then something seemed to break inside him. He turned and went back to the table, where he sat down. He folded his hands in front of him and studied them. He did not look up again as we left the room.

A blast of bitter cold air hit us as we stepped into the street. It must have been four or five in the morning, and the sky had taken on the eerie hue it often had when it had shaken off the night but not yet accepted the day.

At least now I knew we weren't going to be shot immediately, a fate we in Buczacz had come to expect for anyone caught in an action.

Had that been the case, they would have taken us to the Fador, or the Bashte. But we had turned in the opposite direction and were now a long way from those places.

Soon we drove past the ghetto. I craned my neck, straining to see our little house just beyond the hill. But I couldn't see it. I thought of my mother. Would she be asleep, or would she be pacing the floor, sick with panic and grief at having lost her fourth child in so short a time? If only she had known how much I loved her. Would it have comforted her or pained her even more, since she was helpless to save me? Tears that I had held back for a long time were finally streaming down my face.

Then we were crossing the Black Bridge at the edge of the city. And suddenly we were in the country, traveling into the misty morning.

Two Ukrainian policemen were assigned to each sleigh. One faced the horses and one faced us, holding a machine gun in his lap. Maybe if I waited until this man's back was turned, I could leap into the snow and run for cover. It wouldn't be so hard. I could roll into the ditch on the side of the road.

But what might happen then? Bunio had been killed because one of the other slave laborers had escaped. They might line up nine people from the sleigh and shoot them on the spot. They might even kill all sixty. Or they might simply find some unfortunate person to take my place. No, I just couldn't take that chance.

Our journey wore on and on. Six o'clock came, then seven, then eight. I could almost tell the time by the rising sun.

In the next village we passed children bearing knapsacks on their way to school. Their faces were partially hidden under shawls and hats, but I could catch glimpses of noses and cheeks red with the cold. As they stopped to let us pass, they looked from the policemen to us with puzzled eyes, not understanding but sensing—the way children often do—that something was wrong with the huddled people on the sleighs.

The sun rose higher; it was midday. I could see the outline of a city in the distance. It was a big city, much bigger than Buczacz. I had a terrible feeling as we headed toward it.

There was something familiar about that place. I had the feeling that I had been there before; a memory was fighting to break through to my consciousness. Did I really recognize that sign? Or did I just think so? I had seen the building before, hadn't I? But had I really? The streets were crowded, and sleighs had to pull to one side to let us pass. People in the streets were shouting things at us, cupping their hands around their mouths, or shaking their fists. "Cursed Jews! Christ killers!" Some spat in our direction.

It was around noon. We had been traveling about eight hours, when the sleighs arrived at a huge compound. They stopped while massive gates were pulled open and then continued through. As we pulled up before a large stone building, I saw that we were in a prison yard.

"It is the Chortkov prison," I heard one man tell another. "They have brought us to Chortkov."

We were quiet. Everyone knew that this was the city where the Gestapo was headquartered, and the central base for murdering actions in ghettos, including Buczacz. Chortkov had distinct memories for me. It was in this city that I was blessed by the Chortkov rabbi, and it also was in this very prison that my brother Moshe died during the Russian occupation.

"Get out of the sleighs!" The order broke through my reminiscences and jerked me back to the present. Suddenly there were SS men everywhere, barking orders and insults. People were getting off the sleighs. Those who weren't fast enough were pulled or pushed to the ground. Rifle stocks and long sticks seemed to fly through the air as the Nazis beat and jabbed us. Arms were lifted to shield faces and bodies from blows. All around me were cries of pain. More SS men appeared. They were wearing ski boots and carrying ski poles; I had the impression that they had stumbled onto our reception and decided to join their friends.

The woman in front of me caught a blow on the back of her neck and dropped to her knees. An SS man was moving closer for a second strike.

"Get up," I urged her. I thought that if I could just get her to her feet, maybe he wouldn't be so angry with her. I bent over and wrapped my arms around her waist, struggling to pull her up.

Crack! A sharp blow caught me right across the back, nearly knocking the breath from my lungs as it drove me to my hands and knees. I gasped from surprise and pain. Looking up, I saw the SS man swinging his bamboo ski pole directly above me. The pole made a whistling sound as he whipped it through the air to beat me again and again.

I felt a click in my back, then knifelike pains that made it difficult for me to inhale. I knew he had cracked some of my ribs. I squirmed to get away but could barely crawl, the pain was too great. Again and again he stuck me. Then I heard another click, different from the first, and the sound of wood splitting. The prong of the ski pole fell into the snow beside me. He had beaten me so hard, he had broken the pole. This enraged the SS man even more. "Damned Jew!" he screamed, kicking me with his heavy boots. I tried to shield my body, but he kicked at my arms and hands too. Then, as quickly as it had started, the abuse seemed to end. Orders were shouted for us to enter the building.

A woman helped me to my feet. "Come, Alicia, we have to go inside now." I stared dumbly at her. She knew me. She knew my name. Mrs. Eckerberg had been caught in this madness with me. I didn't remember seeing her at the police station in Buczacz. Her presence was calming but disorienting too. It was almost as though she had appeared out of thin air.

Mrs. Eckerberg tried to smile reassuringly, but I could see that she, too, was in a great deal of pain. Blood ran down her cheek from a cut in her forehead. I felt my tired body relax against hers as we plodded slowly and painfully through the snow and into the building.

The prison was made entirely of stone. The solid walls had kept out the warmth of the morning, and the chill went through my coat and shawl. Now we were ordered to remove our overcoats and put them on a huge pile, and then to stand in a circle. It was terribly difficult to get out of my coat; my bruised and stinging fingers fumbled painfully at the buttons. It was lucky that I had been wearing this coat at the time I was beaten; otherwise my back might have been broken.

Without my coat the cold felt even more bitter. In moments I was shivering, which shook my cracked ribs, sending bursts of sharp pain through my back and chest.

Next we were ordered to remove all of our jewelry. No one resisted; but those who were slow in unfastening snaps or pulling off rings were beaten. I saw some necklaces ripped from around necks, and knuckles made bloody by pulling off tight rings.

Quickly I began to remove my only jewelry, a pair of pierced earrings I had worn since I was six years old. I was able to take one earring off easily, but the other one had always been a problem. The closer the Germans came, the more frantically I worked with the difficult earring, pulling and twisting.

Finally two Nazis stood before me, one holding a sack containing all the jewelry, the other ready to help remove the pieces. Quickly I handed over the first earring. "I will have the other for you right away," I said in broken German, twisting at the gold ring.

The man did not hesitate for a moment but reached over, slapped my hand away, and grasped the tight gold ring. He jerked his hand sharply downward, and pulled the earring out, tearing the earlobe. I felt dizzy as the blood flowed freely down my neck from the burning wound.

Suddenly my legs gave away, and I collapsed to the floor. Unfortunately I did not faint, but remained conscious as two guards hurried over to kick me back to my feet. It was as though I were in the middle of a bad dream. I saw Mrs. Eckerberg reaching over to help me, but she was pushed back. I could hear the Germans shouting at me and could see the toes of their boots coming toward me, but their blows felt muffled.

I saw their mouths twisting grotesquely and their teeth bared, but I could not understand them. I could hear only a loud rushing in my ears, like a waterfall. Everything looked white and misty and seemed to be in slow motion. Finally I could not look anymore, but slumped my head forward against my chest, my eyes gazing unfocused at the stone floor.

I don't know how long I remained there unconscious. Sometime later I felt myself put onto a sack and pulled along the floor. I was pulled roughly down the stone steps, each one jarring my ribs with increasing pain. The pain actually seemed to reawaken my senses, because by the time I reached the cell door I felt more coherent, more conscious of my surroundings. I was pushed to a corner while the other people were herded past, and then I was dragged in through the barred door. I heard the door clang shut behind me.

I awakened early the next morning to the sound of clanking metal and bootsteps. Several Germans had entered the cell and were ordering people to their feet, jabbing at them with the muzzles of their guns. I huddled in the corner, hoping I wouldn't be noticed. My body was stiff with cold and it hurt a lot to breathe.

About eight women were pushed outside the cell, and the rest of us were left alone. I tried to pull myself into a sitting position which took me quite a while to do. I had to move very slowly so as not to jar my ribs. The cell was freezing. I could feel the blood from my torn ear caked on my neck and face. When I scratched lightly I was able to flake much of it away. The ear itself was very tender and felt swollen.

I looked for Mrs. Eckerberg. And when I found her, I saw that she was very ill. Her head was all matted with blood from the wound on her head. When I called her name she opened her eyes, and to my great relief, she recognized me.

"Alicia, will you take care of my sons? You will do it for me? Please," she whispered. I couldn't sit for too long, so I lay down and pulled her head onto my hip.

I could hear sounds coming from the courtyard. There was a small window in our cell but it was too high, so we couldn't look outside. The sounds I heard were terrifying. There were the cries of people and shouts in German; but even more chilling, I could also hear snarling dogs. Soon the air was filled with the blended sound of barking dogs and the shrieks of human beings.

I pulled my sack over Mrs. Eckerberg and lay listening to the horrible sounds. How I would have loved to put my hands over my ears and muffle out the screams and growls, but I couldn't touch my torn ear. Many in the cell did cover their ears; others huddled together, weeping. Still others like myself lay still. No one could sleep.

Some time passed and it became quiet outside. Three women were returned to the cell. Each was dragged in and thrown on the floor; not one had had the strength to walk by herself. Cellmates moved forward to help, but the poor unfortunates cried out at the touch of a hand on their ravaged bodies. Their arms and legs were torn by dog bites. We didn't have to ask about the others; we knew they had died. Two of these survivors also died during the day.

Throughout the day, every few hours more people were taken out to the courtyard. Many were torn by the dogs, others were beaten severely. Some were brought back to the cell; many were not. There was very little talking; people were immobilized by fear and suffering. Many stared straight ahead; some, like myself, tried to sleep off and on. The reasons I sought sleep were many; sleep erased the pain, the fear, the cold, and the hunger. I had not eaten nor had I had a drop of water in two days, but I sought sleep, especially because I didn't want to see the faces of the Nazis when they eventually pulled me out of the cell.

On the third day of my imprisonment a German guard brought in a bucket of water and a ladle. "Drink all you want," he told us. "When you want more, call out." The water was cold, with pieces of ice floating in it; we drank it all, and the bucket was refilled several times. But no food came that day or any other. We were slowly being starved to death.

Night came again, but the raids on the cells did not stop. Again and again we heard the screams in the courtyard; and never did as many return as had left. People began to die in the cell, either from the beatings or the dogs or exposure to the cold.

Poor Mrs. Eckerberg died one night just as I was trying to pour some water between her lips. She opened her eyes for a moment, looked at me, and died. I thought she went to sleep, but the woman next to me recognized death. Now she will not have to suffer anymore, I thought as I covered her face with my sack.

The Germans came in the next morning and went about the cell, kicking at us to see if we were still alive. Those who did not move were kicked again, more severely. And if they still didn't move, they were carried away for dead. I felt as though I ought to mourn poor Mrs. Eckerberg, who had brought me a bit of comfort days before, but actually I felt very little. I was beginning to die myself. I realized that a person could actually become one of the living dead; could go on living but feel nothing, not pain, not fear, not sorrow. I was very near to this state.

I was still able to think, and my thoughts went back to the time I was thrown out of the train. I was with the doctor, and heard him say again that he didn't want to be part of the human race anymore. Now I clearly understood what the doctor had meant. But then I heard him say to me, "You must live, Alicia. You must live."

My mind raced. I thought about my mother and brother. I thought of their anguish over losing their family one by one. I also remembered how I had promised myself to protect my mother with my life. I felt the familiar sensation of hate burning within me.

Damned Nazis, I thought to myself. *I'll show you. I won't die. You will not be able to kill me. I will live to see you pay for your crimes and to have your name erased from this world.*

When I awakened, I was no longer in the prison. I was in bed in a darkened room, and I could see light coming in through the doorway. I didn't recognize the room at all. Was I dreaming? Or could I actually be dead, and at some stopping station on my way to heaven?

I felt terrible: hot, clammy, then cold and very ill. My joints ached and my head hurt. I felt tightness around my back and chest. I tried to get out of the bed, but I was so weak that I could barely even roll over.

Soon after, a woman entered my room.

"Oh, you are awake!" she said. "That is wonderful. Oh, Jules"—she called to someone in the outer room—"the girl is awake."

A man entered. He smiled at me. "So, dear one," he said, "how are you feeling today?" He felt my forehead. "Hmm, still warm, but I believe you will recover now."

"Where am I?" I asked.

"In our home, in the Chortkov ghetto," the man answered. He was a gentle man, and I felt very safe with him and the woman.

"I am Jules Gold, and this is my wife, Sala. You have been with us for two weeks."

Two weeks! It didn't seem possible. I had been unconscious for fourteen days.

"Do you feel like having a little tea, or soup?" the woman asked.

Until she mentioned food I had not thought of it, but suddenly I realized I was ravenously hungry.

"Yes, please," I replied.

While Mrs. Gold prepared my soup, Mr. Gold propped some pillows behind my back and began to tell me the story of the last two weeks. I was in their home, Mr. Gold told me, because he had discovered me in a pile of dead bodies awaiting burial at the prison cemetery.

The earth had frozen badly, so the Germans called in additional help to dig graves. Ghetto Jews were forced to bury the corpses of their own people who had died in prison. Mr. Gold, as a member of the Judenrat, accompanied the men from the ghetto to the cemetery so that in case the Germans decided to shoot them, he could at least try to plead for their lives.

Apparently, after I had become unconscious in the prison cell, I had been assumed dead, either by my cellmates or by the German guards. At any rate, my body had been thrown onto a pile of bodies, in the middle of the room, which was then carried outside and left in the snow for burial. Mr. Gold told me that when he picked me up, he thought he heard a moan, and then he realized that my body was warm. The Jewish burial party pretended to bury me and actually put me in the grave. But when the German guards left, they pulled me out, wrapped me in a coat, hid me under the straw of their sleigh, and brought me into the ghetto to Mr. Gold's home. Since then, he and Mrs. Gold had cared for me as though I were their own child, not knowing if I would live or die. For two weeks I had tossed and turned in the bed, moaning, talking in my sleep, sometimes calling for my mother, sometimes for my father. They had been very concerned that an action might take place while I was sick. It was a true miracle that I was still alive, and they were determined that I stay that way. Two angels from heaven, I thought.

Mrs. Gold brought in a cup of tea and a bowl of broth.

"Now, don't eat this too quickly," she cautioned. "You may get pains in your stomach."

I tried to do as she asked me, but in the end I gulped the soup down. It was thin and watery, but to me it tasted wonderful. When I finished, Mrs. Gold tucked the blanket tightly around me.

"Too much excitement at one time is not good for you," she said. "We will talk more later; but for now, try to get some more sleep."

I was still so weak that it wasn't at all difficult to drift back to sleep. But this time I was aware of the Golds coming into my room to check on me. I could tell the difference between day and night. I could hear voices as the couple talked in the next room. After two weeks of nonexistence I was overjoyed to be able to make use of my senses once more.

Every day I ate soup and bread for breakfast, lunch, and dinner. I was so hungry, I could have eaten around the clock. But I knew the Golds must have the same difficulties in getting food as every other Jewish family in Poland, and I knew they were giving me food they could have eaten themselves. I was deeply grateful for their sacrifice and felt very guilty about it.

As I grew stronger, we talked more and more. They wanted to know where I had come from, and how my family had been able to survive. I told them about the deaths of my three brothers; how my father had just disappeared and we believed he, too, was dead; how Mama, Herzl, and I peddled goods in the marketplace for bread and potatoes. I also told them about Rachel and her family, about Milek and Beniek.

"Alicia," asked Mr. Gold, "can you remember when you first became ill in the prison?"

"I don't really know exactly when, but it must have been on the third or fourth day."

"Did others become ill at that time?"

I told him I didn't know, but that many people had died during the time I was in the cell. I told him about Mrs. Eckerberg.

"Alicia," Mr. Gold continued to question me, "did you have typhoid before you came to Chortkov prison?"

"I was ill with typhus last winter, or rather early spring. Had I been ill with the same disease again?" I asked him.

"Not exactly; you had typhoid, which is a little different. But you are well now," he added quickly.

I was curious about his interest in the illness, so I asked some questions myself. Mr. Gold told me that we were apparently given water to drink that had been contaminated with disease. So that was it. The Germans had given us all the water we wanted to drink, which was not in character for them.

"Did all the people who came from Buczacz die in prison?" I asked Mr. Gold.

"No, some were released and sent back to Buczacz."

I understood it all now; the Nazis were trying to kill us by disease too.

I stayed about a month in Chortkov at the Golds' home. My health improved, but slowly. After three weeks I was finally able to get out of bed, but I was so weak I could barely stand. My ear had begun to heal, and my back didn't hurt so much, although it was still very tender. I continued to wear bandages to keep my ribs in place and knew that I would have to wear them for some time.

The first day I was able to stay out of bed for a while, Mrs. Gold gave me a pair of boy's pants and a shirt to wear. It surprised me that they had children's clothing. As I took them from her she must have seen the question in my eyes.

"They were our son's. He was killed before you came to stay with us."

I went over and hugged her. "I am very sorry," I said.

"Thank you, my dear," she said, patting my hand. "I am sure he would have liked you very much. Sometimes I feel as . . . as though our son returned. . . ." She could not complete her sentence because she started to cry. She didn't have to finish. I knew what she meant. How she must have loved me to give me her son's clothing. I remembered how Mama gave her son's clothing to the Eckerberg boys. I thought, how heavy with sorrow are the hearts of Jewish mothers.

One evening about six weeks after they found me, Mr. Gold returned home and announced that he had found a way to get me back to Buczacz. "In two days you will be with your mother and brother," Mr. Gold said as he put his arm around me.

"We will put you under the straw in a sleigh, where you will be nice and warm and no one will even know you are there. Is that all right with you?"

I nodded. Then something clicked in my mind. A sleigh driven by whom? I hesitated whether to ask. I was afraid to hurt Mr. Gold's feelings. But I had to ask.

"Mr. Gold, please forgive me for asking; I am really very grateful for what you have done for me, but who is going to drive this sleigh into Buczacz? I hope it is not some farmer. I have such bad memories . . ."

"You can trust me. You will be in very safe hands." He smiled. "Good, then. Mama," he addressed his wife, "Alicia will be leaving in two days. Let's see if we can find something warm for her to wear."

I burst into tears. Mr. Gold put his arms around me and held me tightly. "Shush, darling, no more tears," he said. "Now is the time for us all to be brave."

Two days later Mrs. Gold awoke very early, about half past four in the morning. Mr. Gold was already awake. Because of the need for secrecy, they lit only one candle. Mrs. Gold gave me a piece of bread and some tea. She also gave me a small package, which I put in my coat pocket. "Chew slowly, my dear," she said. "This will be your last food until you get home."

Suddenly there was a knock on the door. "Ah," said Mr. Gold, "that should be our friend." He told me to wait in the other room and then opened the door. I heard some voices in a different language. For a moment I thought it might be Hebrew, but I couldn't be sure. I felt excitement mounting in me together with a certain amount of apprehension. Mrs. Gold called for me to come out. There was a man in the kitchen who seemed to fill up all the space there. He was big and burly.

"So," he said, looking at me, "this is to be my traveling companion, eh? We will do our talking now, little friend. Once we are on the road, we take no chances."

The man's name was Ivan. He and Mr. Gold explained that they were going to smuggle me out of the ghetto. I would have to be in a potato sack under the straw; and whatever I heard, I was not to make a sound. Once we were out of the city it would be a little easier. But now they had to put a kerchief over my mouth and nose, which I could remove when we left the city. Ivan would stop before the Black Bridge in Buczacz and let me off there. "Now," he said, "it is time to say good-bye. We must leave without delay."

I turned to the Golds. Mrs. Gold's eyes were brimming with tears as she hugged me tightly. "We will miss you, Alicia," she said. "Try not to forget us."

"I won't, Mrs. Gold," I said. "I won't ever forget you."

When I went to hug Mr. Gold, I could feel that he was warm. I touched his forehead and it was hot.

"I hope you are not getting sick, Mr. Gold," I asked with concern in my voice.

"It's all right, Alicia, don't worry. I have had typhus already, so if I get ill, I will get well again."

"I am sorry if you got sick because of me."

"No, no, child. Not because of you. There is a terrible epidemic in the ghetto. Don't worry, I will be all right. Good luck, Alicia. Take care, dear child."

"God bless you, Mr. Gold," I said, giving him a last kiss on his cheek, and then I quickly followed Ivan to the sleigh.

I stepped into a sack, which Ivan tied. He lifted me in his arms and pushed me under a kind of wooden platform on the bottom of the sleigh; then he put straw on top of me. The sleigh moved for a while and then it stopped. I heard voices, and things were put on top of my platform. Then we moved again. And then someone was asking something. I heard loud laughter and the words "the usual," and the sleigh moved on. Perhaps a half hour passed before we stopped again. People were talking and unloading the things that had been put on the sleigh earlier. Now I heard distinct voices saying, "We will not be able to bury them today. The earth is too frozen."

The sleigh jerked and moved on. I began to perspire when I realized that I had been under dead people and had been brought back to a cemetery again. Now I understood why they put a kerchief around my mouth and nose; to prevent me from making a noise. I was supposed to be dead too.

"You can remove your kerchief now," came Ivan's loud voice. "We are out of the city. Best go to sleep; it is a long way home for you!"

I stayed awake for the first hour or so of the trip, thinking about the Golds and about the prison and wondering what would await me back in Buczacz. I was filled with both joy and worry. Then I drifted off to sleep and slept through much of the remaining journey. When the sleigh stopped I found myself lifted out from under the wooden platform. Ivan removed the sack and I stepped out. "Thank you very much for bringing me home," I said as I looked at Ivan. There was something about his eyes that caught my heart. They were so sad. I was stunned. They simply did not suit this big man. Who was he anyway, I wondered.

"All right, I am off," said Ivan, and he jumped up on the seat. I watched him turn around to go back to Chortkov.

It had started snowing, the new flakes falling gently down on the older, hardened snow. I put out my hand and caught some. They looked so beautiful that I licked them with my tongue. My joints ached; I shivered as I made my way over the bridge, down the street, and into the ghetto. But it wasn't only the January weather that made me shiver—on many of the doorways I saw signs in Polish and German saying "typhoid." So, I thought bitterly, I was not the first to make it home. The typhoid was already here.

My anticipation mounted as I came closer and closer to our house. My heart sank when I saw the sign on our door. I paused for a minute to catch my breath and compose myself, then pushed the door open. It was deathly still inside our room. I looked around and saw Mama and Herzl lying in their beds. I approached slowly, fearfully, not knowing if I would find them dead or alive. Reaching the bed, I gently touched Mama's shoulder. Her head turned toward me and her eyes opened. She was very ill.

Then she smiled weakly. "Alicia," she whispered, "you have come home to us."

"Yes, Mama," I replied in a choking voice. "I have come home."

CHAPTER 11

Milek

As I stood at the window watching the falling snow, I saw Milek walking toward our house. I felt a surge of happiness at seeing him again, and suddenly I realized how good it was to be alive and home.

Later, I sat in stunned silence as Milek told me what had taken place in Buczacz while I was away. Each word was a blow.

"Alicia, your sudden disappearance was discovered in the evening. It was too late to get information from the Judenrat, so your mother, Herzl, and I went from door to door asking if anyone knew what could have happened to you. After all, there had been no general action. The Gestapo did not come from Chortkov, and there had been no shooting or disturbance.

"The next morning we went to the Judenrat. They told us that about sixty Jewish people had been picked up in the streets and were taken to Chortkov, and that the Judenrat had been told that the captives might be returned to Buczacz, but no one believed that. Then about two weeks later twenty people returned and told of their experience. They told your mother that all the rest were probably dead, that there would be no more returnees. You can imagine," Milek said, "the anguish felt by your mother and Herzl; by all of us!

"Then"—Milek's voice broke—"Rachel fell ill and died of a lung hemorrhage."

We sat for a while, silently watching the fire that could be seen through the opening around the door of our little iron stove. After a while Milek continued. "Typhoid hit the ghetto about two weeks ago.

Bolek and Joshua died in the early stages of the disease. And then one day Bella and her children as well as Beniek and his friends disappeared."

Poor boy, I thought as I listened to Milek. The world around him had collapsed. Suddenly I realized that it was also my world, and I felt overwhelming sorrow. The joy over my miraculous escape from Chortkov and my return home was completely erased by these new tragedies.

Herzl and Mama were moaning. They needed my attention now. Somehow I would have to find the strength to help them through this terrible illness. They had to live! It was only because of Milek's kind and loving care that I had found them alive when I returned to Buczacz. He had taken care of them from the moment they collapsed with high fever two days before. I thought of Milek's interest in medicine, his devotion to people and instinctive knowledge of what to do in an emergency. It would help him become an excellent doctor . . . someday?

Milek sponged Herzl while I did the same for my mother. We changed the wet sheets and forced warm water between their parched lips. Their bodies were very hot.

This time I remembered to cut my mother's hair. I cut it as short as I could. Then I went to Herzl's bed and cut his hair as well.

After we finished taking care of Mother and Herzl, Milek showed me some flour and potatoes that he had brought from Bella's house. He had gone to visit them and discovered they were gone. He used the key Bella had given him, went into the house, and found a note addressed to him telling what to do with the food and firewood she had left. Dear Bella, always thinking of us.

"I have to go now because it is getting late, but I will be back in the morning," Milek said. "I wish I could stay, but you know how it is. In case of an action, you have to be near your bunker, and Bolek's aunt is sick and needs help. Besides, Samuel will worry about me. He is living with us now." I nodded my head.

"It is good to see you again, Alicia. Try to get some rest." Milek opened the door and let himself out of our room.

True to his promise, he was back the following morning; we sponged my mother and Herzl and spoon-fed them throughout the entire day. I had enough time to see Sarah. She was very happy that I had returned. She, too, was recovering from typhoid and had barely enough strength to cook some soup, which she shared with us.

Slowly my mother and brother were getting out of danger, but they were still very ill. They dozed on and off most of the day and night, but now there was hope that they would live.

Then a most frightening thing happened. Sarah woke me up at the crack of dawn to tell me that the Gestapo had arrived from Chortkov and that there was going to be an action. She took my arm and pleaded with me.

"Please Alicia, your family is still very sick and might call out. Please don't fight with my father about taking your mother and brother inside the bunker. It will only delay us in getting down, and waste the precious time you need to hide your family elsewhere. You've told me that you built another, smaller bunker. Could you use it this one time?"

She was about to cry, so I assured her that all would be well, and that she should hurry up and hide in the main bunker. Then I went into action. I went to her bed and awakened my mother.

"Mama," I said, "the Gestapo is in Buczacz. There is going to be an action. We must hide."

"How?"

"I have a plan, but you must help me. You and Herzl will get into the hole I made under the bed. I will lie near the opening. I will have the boards near me and, in case I am discovered, I will push the boards into place. You must promise me that you will not cry out, and not let Herzl cry out if you hear me being taken. Please, dear Mama, promise me! But," I added hastily, "I hope that they will not discover us."

I moved the bed away from the wall to make enough space to get to the hole. I spread blankets inside, then I eased my mother slowly inside the hole. I put a pillow under her head and covered her with a blanket. Next I went to Herzl.

"Come on!" I shook him. "The Gestapo is coming, don't you understand?"

He was so weak, that little boy. I half carried, half dragged him out of the bed, and eased him into the hole and into my mother's arms. He put his head on her shoulder and she wrapped her arms around him. I placed a blanket around them, then wiped my tears. I would have liked to be held and comforted by my mother, too, but that was impossible.

Once they were inside, I went through all the rooms and turned over the chairs, pulled down the bedding, opened all the doors, and scattered bits of clothing around. I wanted it to look as though our murderers had come already and as though the people who lived there had left in a state of panic. I left the doors open because I remembered how much noise the Gestapo and the Ukrainians made when they broke into the house in earlier actions. I was very afraid that my mother or Herzl might hear the noise and cry out.

The last thing I did was go down the hall and get the pail that the families used as a toilet during the night. I spilled it all over the floor of the hall, then threw the pail outside. I almost laughed out loud when I realized that this time the Gestapo would be right in calling us stinking Jews. I hoped they would slip and break their necks. After having been captured by them twice, I had developed such a hatred for the Germans that I could hardly control it.

After I had done everything I could think of to secure our safety, I crawled under the bed near the hole and put the boards in front of me. In case someone should poke around under the bed, he would hit what I hoped he would think to be the wall. I found Mama's hand and, squeezing it gently, signaled to her that now we must be very quiet.

I lay waiting and listening for any sounds. Then I heard them coming closer and closer. "Damned Jews out! Come out!" I heard them cursing because of the human waste, and then they were in our room. I held my breath, terrified that at any moment my mother or brother might moan or call out, or that we would be discovered.

After what seemed like an eternity, our door slammed shut. There were loud noises from other rooms, then no more sounds in the house. Still, I was afraid to breathe freely. Our murderers often would keep quiet and listen. Perhaps a child or a sick person would betray his bunker by making a sound.

All day I heard shooting from the Fador and the Bashte. We remained hidden in the house, I and my family under the bed, the other families bunched together in the bunker in the kitchen.

Finally I had no choice but to get out from under the bed. My mother and Herzl were moaning and I was afraid they would not be able to endure staying in the hole much longer. I looked out through the window and saw people moving around. I recognized some of them. The Gestapo had left. The action was over. Probably many of the ghetto people had been murdered. As I thought about it, I became so angry that I felt a fire inside me. I had to do something before I lost my sanity. I turned to Mama and Herzl and put them into their beds. They were feeling very ill and their fever had returned. I gave them a lot of water to drink and they went to sleep. Then I took the soiled blankets out of the hole. Looking into it, I shivered. It looked like a grave.

Next, I locked the front and back doors of the house. I bent over the doors leading to the kitchen bunker and called out softly.

"Sarah, this is Alicia. It's safe to come out."

I heard the sound of a box being pushed up and branches moved aside.

"Are you sure it is safe to come out?" Sarah was asking in a whisper.

"It is safe now. I saw people walking on the street. I put Mama and Herzl back into their beds. Trust me, Sarah!"

One by one the people crawled through the stove opening. They looked frightened and a little disoriented. They blinked, shielding their eyes from the daylight, and rubbed their joints to relieve the cramps resulting from sitting in fixed positions for such a long time.

"Were they in your room?" the landlord asked.

"Yes, they came into our room."

"Your mother and brother . . ."

"They're safe, but still ill."

Our landlord sniffed and made a face as he recognized the awful odor now permeating the entire house. Then he smiled and patted me on my back.

"What a clever girl," he said. "Now, why don't you clean that up?" And I did.

No one knew how many people were killed in this February action, but Milek told me that the ghetto was now half empty. Soon new people would be coming in, I thought, and the Germans would continue their murdering cycle. In the meantime, my immediate worry was how to get food for my family. The food that Bella had left us was gone. Then I remembered the package Mrs. Gold had given me in Chortkov. It was still in my jacket pocket. I opened it and stood stunned. I held in my hand what looked like quite a lot of money. There was a note attached.

> Dearest Alicia,
> This is my son's money, which he normally carried with him in his jacket so that he could try to buy his life if he was caught. When he was finally caught, he was not wearing his jacket.

Tears blinded me, and I couldn't read the rest of the letter, but I promised myself that if, by some miracle, we lived through this hell and were free again, I would be like a daughter to the Golds. I would love them and care for them with all my heart. I wished I could write and thank them, but I didn't have their address and, anyway, I didn't expect that anyone could receive mail in the ghetto.

I now had four hundred zlotys that I could use to buy food. I gave Milek fifty zlotys for his household, and I used the rest very frugally. Thanks to the generosity of the Golds we did not starve to death that winter.

When my mother was well I gave her the money I had left. She kept us eating soup and bread that quickly restored our strength. Occasionally she bought some sunflower oil, which she put in the soup. We also shared our food with several children who were orphaned during the actions. My mother was a real angel.

One day I told Mama what had happened in Chortkov. While she listened, silent tears rolled down her cheeks, and she did not even try to wipe them away. It frightened me to see my mother cry, but I knew that crying was the only way she could find some relief from the anguish she felt in her heart. She knew how Mrs. Gold felt, since she had lost three sons herself. One day I saw her holding the jacket the Golds had given me. I saw such pain in her eyes that I quickly moved away, not wanting my mother to know that I had seen her.

I was deeply troubled. The ghetto remained half empty. There was no sign that new people were coming in, as usually happened after an action. It was possible that everyone in the surrounding small cities and villages was already dead, or had left a long time before. I developed a persistent nagging fear, a premonition that would not leave me.

Spring came early in 1943 and was welcomed by all of us in the ghetto. It seemed as though it brought new hope for life. When everything began to bloom, we could not help but respond. Our eyes took in beauty eagerly, even though our spirits were despondent.

I walked around the ghetto, attaching myself to groups of people and listening to their conversations. I heard rumors of the war, that the Germans were stopped somewhere in Russia and that there was fierce fighting. Everybody predicted that like Napoleon, Hitler would also be defeated. There was talk about second fronts, and it always came down to one question. How could we survive to see what would really happen?

There was one rumor that disturbed me very much. A young girl, perhaps eighteen years old, was talking about forty Jewish girls that the Germans had asked the Judenrat to supply for a work camp in Chortkov. As soon as she mentioned Chortkov, my heart started beating violently. I didn't believe there was a work camp in Chortkov. I believed that they would be taken to prison to be torn by dogs, or would die by other cruel means.

I turned to the girl and said, "Please, whatever you do, don't go to Chortkov. I was there in prison and it was terrible. They don't have a work camp in Chortkov, they have a ghetto like ours. Please go and hide somewhere, but don't go to Chortkov!"

"Go and hide! Go and hide!" the girl said angrily. "Do you have a safe place I could go and hide? And if I found the place, how would I get food? From the Poles or the Ukrainians perhaps? We are all doomed, that is what we are." Pointing a finger at me, she said, "Look at you! You look like a walking skeleton. How long do you think you will live, even if the Gestapo doesn't kill you first? Tell me, you, with your smart advice!"

I thought for a minute that she was going to hit me, but she was just angry, unhappy, and lost. So very lost.

"I don't know how long I will live, but I will try to live long enough to see the Germans rot in hell. I will see them defeated, you'll see!" I said with such determination that the girl burst out laughing. It occurred to me, while we stood facing each other, that one of us was mad, but in all honesty I couldn't say which one.

During the second week of April my nagging fear materialized in the form of a new tragedy. The fourth action took place in our city, and again the Gestapo murdered many of us. Then the final decree came. Buczacz was to become "Judenrein." Those who survived the action would have to move to the Kopechince ghetto. We were notified by the Judenrat that wagons would be available for our transportation to Kopechince. We had to leave Buczacz within one week.

So it had finally come, I thought. Now we will arrive in another ghetto after the Gestapo had killed as many of its inhabitants as they could find. And the cycle of terror and murder will start all over again for us.

My mother acted immediately.

"If we have to go to Kopechince, then we might as well be among the first," she said. "The earlier we leave, the better chance we will have to find a place to live."

She went down to the Judenrat to find out when the first wagons were leaving and arranged for our departure. The day before we left I had two things to do. I took my sketchbook, with some of my sketches and watercolors, removed my armband, and went to my friend Slavka's

home. When I knocked, her younger brother, Bohdan, opened the
door. He was startled to see me.

"Bohdan," I said, "please give this book to Slavka. We have to
leave Buczacz. We are being sent to Kopechince. You probably know
about it from your cousin, the policeman." He nodded his head.

"Please tell Slavka that I still consider her a friend, and that I don't
hold her responsible." Then I saw Slavka. She came out of the living
room, looking so lovely in her school uniform. She had grown since I
last saw her. I pushed the sketchbook into Bohdan's hand, turned, and
ran down the steps. I heard Slavka calling my name.

"Alicia, wait! Wait just a minute!" she was calling.

But I couldn't wait. I didn't want her to see me cry. Now Slavka
had the sketchbook she had always admired. It was the last thing of
value I had. It was my way of telling her that she was still my friend.

The second thing I had to do was say good-bye to two people I
loved and missed very much. My brother Zachary and my friend
Rachel. I picked up two stones and put them on their graves. I said a
silent prayer and cried and cried.

When I got home, Milek was there talking with Herzl. Since
Danny had left, Herzl had become very attached to Milek, and they
were becoming good friends. Herzl's two best friends had been killed,
and he missed them very much. Milek helped fill the void they had
left. I was very grateful to him.

"I was worried about you, Alicia," Milek was saying. "Where have
you been?"

"Oh, nowhere, just out," I said. But Milek knew that I had been at
the cemetery. My swollen eyes betrayed me.

Then he asked me to go outside with him for a moment. I followed
him and we sat down near the house on the hill leading to the Bashte.

"Alicia, I want you to have this." Milek took my hand and put a
small gold ring into my palm. "Take good care of it," he said, closing
my fingers over the ring.

I was very touched by his gift and couldn't think of anything to say.

"Samuel and I will be going to Kopechince, too, but a few days
from now. We will meet you there." He lifted my chin and looked
deeply into my eyes. Then he was gone.

Some time passed and then I got up and went to the stone wall in
our backyard. I removed the loose stone near our old bunker and,
wrapping the ring in my handkerchief, I put it inside and replaced the

stone. If I lived, I would come back someday and get it out. I was sure of one thing. I would not let the Germans take it away from me, as they had my earrings.

There was a world of difference between this journey to Kopechince and my last journey—to Chortkov. Now it was a beautiful spring day, and I was with my mother and brother. When I was taken to Chortkov, I was alone and it was winter.

We stopped a couple of times to feed and water the horses and stretch our legs. We reached Kopechince in the late afternoon. The wagons drove straight to the street where the offices of the Judenrat were located and, within an hour, we were assigned places to live. Our house was large with a nice backyard. It had six rooms. It would eventually hold six families, with two or three people in each family, but at this time it was not completely filled and we were able to make a choice from the remaining rooms. My mother selected the kitchen as our room; she explained that with the stove there, it would be one of the warmer rooms in the house. At least this is what she wanted us to believe, but I really thought that Mama couldn't make herself move into a bedroom knowing that its previous occupants had been taken in an action and killed. She couldn't bear to see the children's toys or personal items left in those rooms. I understood how she felt and was very glad that we chose the kitchen. People would have to come in to cook periodically, but that wouldn't disturb us much.

There were two families already living in the house when we arrived and then three more joined us. They were all very nice people. Then I discovered that two of the families had babies. I shuddered to think what would happen if there was an action. I had never forgotten little Shmuel, Sarah's son, and how the Germans had shot him.

Herzl and I were soon busy exploring the neighborhood. It was an open ghetto like Buczacz, as it didn't have a wall or barbed wire around it. To go anywhere else was punishable by death; that was wall enough.

We found out where the marketplace was, and how we could buy food or trade for things we found in the house. We had to take off our armbands because here, too, Jews weren't permitted to go to the marketplace. It was very dangerous, but we did not have much choice unless we wanted to starve to death. It was out of the question to let Mama go to the market. There was so much sadness in her eyes that anyone would see she was a Jewess. It was up to Herzl and myself to get food for us.

During the second week in the new house I was in the kitchen baking a grain patty on our stove, when I heard a couple of familiar voices. I couldn't leave the patty to burn, so I stayed and watched it carefully. Suddenly there were people in the kitchen. I nearly burned my hand trying to rescue the patty and hug Milek and Samuel at the same time. Milek, Samuel, and Bolek's aunt had been given a room in a house next to ours, and we shared the same backyard.

We lived in Kopechince as we had in Buczacz—from hand to mouth. The most important thing to us was to live through each day. We would worry about the next day when it came. Everyone in our house got on well. If one person obtained some food and knew that another person had none, he would share it. The main items in our diet were little grain patties that we would bake on top of the stove. We would grind the grain between two stones into flour, then mix it with water and—when we had it—salt. These patties had very little taste, but they filled our stomachs. When we could get potatoes, we would cook soup, but the biggest luxury was to actually eat the potatoes. We would slice them into very thin slices and bake them on the flat top of the stove; they were delicious.

Once we were settled, it was time to find out if there was a bunker in the house or, if there wasn't, to build one. To be without a bunker was unthinkable to me, and I asked my mother to find out from the families who were living there. There was a bunker, but it was very small. It would have to be enlarged. The men in the house were working on it already, and Herzl and I were soon drafted to help dispose of the earth in the meadows near the lake. This lessened some of my worries, but the rest remained deep inside me, especially whenever I caught a glimpse of the babies in our house.

The action began early in the morning, about three weeks after we arrived in Kopechince. Since the Gestapo was stationed in the city, we had no advance warning. We could only know an action was taking place when the SS men were already in the ghetto rounding up people and shooting them. When the news reached our house, there was complete panic. Then one man took command. He had us all gather in the hall and declared that since the enlargement of the bunker was not completed, only a certain number of people could go inside, only the younger children. The older children would have to run and hide in the meadows near the lake, or find a place in the attic. Babies couldn't come into the bunker at all. They would have to be hidden in the rooms. The man's declaration sounded cruel, but if we hadn't moved immediately, we would have all been caught outside the bunker.

I made sure my mother and Herzl were inside the bunker. I had enough time to kiss them. I closed the top of the bunker and put a lot of junk on top of it. Two boys and myself remained outside the bunker. The boys went out of the house and I decided to hide in the attic. I was partway up the ladder, when I heard the babies cry. I stood there frozen for a second, then climbed down and went into the babies' room. I found the half-empty bottles of camomile tea that the mothers had been feeding them. One baby finished his bottle and had fallen asleep, and I was almost finished feeding the other, when suddenly there was a shattering noise. The house filled up with SS men and Ukrainian police. The babies woke up and started to cry. Two Germans entered the room where I stood. One of them went to where the babies lay in their cribs, looked down at them, pulled out his pistol, and shot both babies through their mouths. I must have cried out in protest, because he turned to me and struck me in the face with the pistol.

"Out, you damned Jews, out of the house!" I heard the now familiar calls of the SS men, mingled with curses in Ukrainian, more noise of turned furniture and more screaming.

A rifle butt hit me in the back and a Ukrainian policeman commanded me to move out. At least, I thought, I was the only one being taken from the house.

How can one describe the death march of what seemed to be a sea of men, women, and children? We were defenseless, demoralized people being pushed, hit, and even killed by the Germans and Ukrainians, who were driving us to some unknown destination. As I stumbled along on that street I began to experience that familiar feeling of hate. It acted in a strange way. It actually cleared my brain. I felt like a spectator who wasn't personally involved, and I was clearly aware of what was going on around me. People along the sides of the streets were cursing us, and some were throwing stones at us as we were driven along.

Finally, after some time, we were pushed into the courtyard of a prison where more Jews had already been collected. I recognized a girl from Buczacz. She told me that people had been taken off the wagons as they came into the city from Buczacz. The Germans were waiting for them. Many were killed on the spot, and some were brought here. She also told me that they had had another such action in Buczacz in May and that very few Jews remained.

Now the Kopechince ghetto was being liquidated. The action was probably going to go on until everyone was killed. I was afraid to think what would happen to Mama, Herzl, Milek, and Samuel. I had to stop thinking about them or I would lose my mind.

We stayed in the courtyard all night. The following morning the Germans took out groups of people and marched them in the direction of the forest. My turn came around noon. As we walked, many of us began to stagger and stumble. The older people and children were suffering the most. Some of the older men could go no farther and were shot as they lay on the ground, gasping for breath. The longer we walked, the more bodies we saw along the side of the road. People tried to help one another, and I did my share, but I also remembered my broken ribs from Chortkov, and I helped as quietly as possible so as not to call attention to myself. If I stood any chance at all of escaping, I would have to be in the best possible condition.

We stopped at a large meadow near the forest. A large trench had been dug. There were many Jews at the trench already, some undressed and some still undressing. Then the shooting started. We were pushed from the back by the barrels of machine guns and, as we approached the trench, we were confronted by more machine guns. Some people in front fell into the trench dead, and some still alive. Then there was more pushing from the back and, as I was nearing the pit, I thought I heard my name being called. No, I was imagining it! Then I heard it again. "Alicia—Alicia Jurman!"

All of a sudden we heard machine-gun fire near us—not directed at us—coming from the side where the Germans were standing. I turned my head to see what was happening and saw Milek holding a machine gun in his hands and shooting at the Germans.

"Alicia, run! Get out of here! Run!" Milek was calling as he kept shooting at the Germans.

I stood a moment, paralyzed at this unbelievable scene, and then without waiting a moment longer I started pushing my way through the people and ran into the forest. Other people followed me, running and screaming as they came. Then the firing stopped, but I kept on running and running. I stopped for a few seconds to catch my breath and listen. I could hear machine guns firing again. I ran on. I ran for an hour, perhaps longer. Finally I could not take another step and collapsed on the ground. I remember thinking about Milek; then the reaction to the horrors of the last two days set in, and I began shaking and crying uncontrollably.

CHAPTER 12

Reunion

I awoke the next morning to the soft buzzing of bees. I yawned and stretched, and looked around me. The sounds of life were everywhere; birds singing, leaves rustling. Above me the trees rose high to form a sort of ceiling with only patches of the sky peeking through. The forest was safe and self-contained, needing nothing from the outside world but to be left alone. If I could just find a way to get food, I thought to myself, I could stay here forever. The forest would protect and hide me. But could it feed me? I didn't think so. I got up and brushed the crumbled bits of dried leaves and pine needles from my hair and clothing. I felt sore and stiff from sleeping on the ground. I wasn't planning to stay in the forest, but it was comforting to know it was there for me.

That was something to consider for the future. But my immediate plans were to go home, back to Buczacz. Oh, yes; even though the city was now Judenrein, that's where I would go. Only a month earlier my mother had hugged Herzl and me very close and together we vowed that if we were ever separated, we would each find our way back to Buczacz, where we would reunite. I thought of my mother climbing out of the bunker and not finding me in the house. Perhaps she had heard everything through the floorboards; or did the earth muffle the sounds as the Gestapo shouted at me to get moving? Surely she must have heard the shots—what a horrible shock for those poor mothers to come out of hiding and find the bodies of their babies, those unfortunate little lives I had tried to save.

There was something no one in my family knew, something I had never told anyone. I had decided that if there were going to be any more deaths in our family, I wanted to be the one to die. It wasn't bravery that kept me volunteering to close and disguise the hiding place time after time; it was cowardice. I couldn't see any more of my family die.

But now the problem was—where was Buczacz, anyway? I couldn't very well stop someone on the road and say, "Excuse me, but is this the way to Buczacz?" When one is a fugitive, one doesn't even think in terms of road travel. I would have to make my way back through the forest and fields. One thing I did know: Buczacz was terribly far away.

My immediate need was food. Only after that would I worry about what direction Buczacz lay in. I headed into the forest, and after a while could see I was coming to a clearing. It was a wheat field, not quite ready for harvest, and there was no one there.

About a mile farther on there was another field, and this time I could see workers, stooped over rows and rows of small plants.

I studied the field carefully. This field seemed far removed from city life; they had probably not seen a Jew here in quite a long time. And, of course, not every dark-haired, dark-eyed person was Jewish; there were also a lot of Ukrainians and Poles who fit that description. I remembered what the Gurali people had told me that day in the marketplace; that I could easily pass for a mountain girl and that if I went back with them, no one would ever suspect I was Jewish. I got up my courage and walked down to the field.

The first person I encountered was a girl not much older than I. "Who is the owner of this field?" I asked. She straightened and looked at me coolly before motioning.

"Over there," she said. "The one with the vest." I looked in that direction and spotted the man, far away on the other side of the field. "Thanks," I said. She did not respond, but went back to her weeding.

I approached the man, a red-faced Pole who looked to be in his early fifties. "Can you use an extra hand?" I asked. "I'm very good at weeding, and I ask only for a slice of bread and a cup of sour milk at mealtime." The man studied me silently, then nodded his head toward the girl I had just spoken with.

"She'll show you," was all he said.

I went back to the girl stooped over the small plants with her back to me. "He said you'd show me," I said, hoping that would be all the explanation necessary.

"What?" she asked curtly. "Show you how to weed?"

"Oh, no, no," I said. "I know how to weed. But where do I start?" She snorted. "Wherever you see weeds."

This girl was making me very nervous, but I knew I must not show it. I had to be just as normal as everyone else. My life depended on that. So I squatted down and began to weed between the young potato plants.

Mealtime finally arrived. The workers all left their places in the field and gathered together near a wagon where lunch was being prepared by an older woman. I brushed the soil from my hands as best I could. Someone handed me a tin cup, and someone else poured me some sour milk from an earthenware jug. I also received a slice of bread, not as large as I had hoped; but I did not dare to ask for more.

Everyone sat down in a sort of half-circle. I knew that this time when all the workers were brought together would be risky for me, but of course I had to stay and take my chances; I couldn't appear to be different from these people in any way, lest they suspect me.

"Where are you from?" someone asked.

I thought quickly. "Kolomeya," I answered, pulling the name of one of the villages near Rosulna from the air and hoping no one would recognize it and ask why I was so far from home. Luckily my answer was not questioned too much, except for one man, who wanted to know in what direction was Kolomeya.

"Up north," I explained; but that didn't satisfy him.

"What are you doing down this way?" I chewed my bread slowly, my mind racing for a logical explanation.

"I'm an orphan," I finally answered. "There was nothing left for me up there, so I decided to come down to the cities to work as a maid. I have an aunt in Kopechince. Is that far from here?" I asked my question, turning to the girl who had been studying me closely, but she quickly looked away. But the others, hearing the name Kopechince, laughed lightly. "Why, that's kilometers from here," one man said, "over a day's walk at the very least."

"So long still," I said. "But of course I don't have to go down that way. This seems like a nice area; is there work here?"

"Oh, yes, there's work. And we've had no trouble from the Banderovcy, these godforsaken Uk—" He cut himself short, and I realized that he suspected I might myself be a Ukrainian; but that was good, I decided. Let them think that.

For something was happening now in this part of Poland that the Poles had never anticipated. Now that most of the country was Judenrein, the Ukrainians were turning their guns and knives on the Poles, mostly in the outlying villages to the east and north. So, I thought, when you heap suffering upon others, some of it can't help but fall back on you. It gave me a perverse pleasure for the moment to think I posed a threat to those people; that they would feel they had to watch their words around me.

After another two hours or so the workday was over, and people began packing up to go home. I went up to the farmer and thanked him for giving me work, and asked him if I might come back again the next day. Of course, by then I would actually be long gone from that area, but I wanted to leave the impression that I was very comfortable in my surroundings and might even be there to stay. After receiving his assurance that I would be welcomed back, I turned and headed in the direction of the forest.

In doing so I had to pass the peasant girl, who was fumbling with something in her bundle. As I passed her I had a sudden urge to communicate to her that I was, after all, a human being; that her day of treating me otherwise had not diminished that. "Well," I said, "nice working with you. Good-bye for now."

"Wait," she said. I stopped; what now? But then she pulled two thick slices of bread from her bundle and gave them to me. "Here," she said. I took the bread dumbly, trying to think of something to say. I stammered out my thanks, but she only half nodded and turned away. I walked briskly back to the forest, not daring to run, as I would have liked.

I walked for several more kilometers before stopping for the night. The bread was so tempting, but I didn't dare touch it. I would need it for the next day, and perhaps even the day after. I still didn't know where Buczacz was, but now that I knew roughly where Kopechince was, I was able to work out the rest. I had also figured out an easy way to get my bearings. If I could only find out how to get to the river Stripa, then I could follow it back home.

The following day I found work in a field again. This time I was given a couple of small cooked potatoes along with my cup of sour milk. While the workers were together eating, I asked in what direction the river Stripa lay, and someone pointed to the northwest. At last I was on the right track.

After about two weeks of working and walking, working and walking, one day I finally recognized my surroundings. When I came within a kilometer of the city, my pace became faster, and soon I was hurrying along.

But in a little while I was forced to stop and take cover. Up ahead of me was the river Stripa. I could see children splashing by the shore, and where the water was deeper, swimmers were taking advantage of the water on an unusually hot day. I was close enough to be within hearing range, although the voices were muffled and all I could hear was the sound of laughter. Oh, how I longed to dive into the cool water! But, of course, that was impossible. I was a condemned outcast, and, if caught, I knew I would be shot.

At long last, after hours of waiting, the last person had disappeared, and it was almost completely dark outside. Quickly I crossed the narrow bridge over the Stripa and climbed the hill over the Bashte, skirting along the edge of the Jewish cemetery. There, spread before me, were the twinkling lights of Buczacz.

I knew that being out after curfew was no longer a risk. It would have meant death only a month before, but now that there were no more Jews, there would be no curfew. No, my only danger lay in being recognized by my former neighbors and taken to the police station to be killed.

Carefully I walked down the hill to our house inside the ghetto. Most of the houses were dark; only a few lights shone in windows, not Jewish lights in Judenrein Buczacz. I looked at those empty husks, where only a short while ago there had been life, so much life! Suddenly my throat ached fiercely, and my eyes burned but would not tear. My mother would not be here; somehow I knew she would not.

Careful not to make any noise, I walked around the house to the back, to the wall where we had buried the things precious to us before we left for Kopechince. My mother had hidden a small box behind that chink of stone there; I didn't ask what was in it. I had buried something of my own behind a chink farther down the wall: the ring Milek had given me.

It was a sort of wedding ring, actually. I never asked how he'd gotten it, and he never volunteered the information. Of course, Milek had no idea I was madly in love with him. Perhaps Milek thought of me as his childhood friend; perhaps not. But he had given me that ring and I cherished it, so much so that I had been determined to hide it safely.

But now, after the open grave, I decided I wanted that ring. I wanted Milek to be always with me, if only in spirit. He was the reason I still lived, and I wanted his ring.

The problem now was how to find it in the dark. I felt carefully along the stones, looking for any that seemed loose. I pulled out a stone and felt quickly behind it. Nothing. Again with another stone. Nothing. And then finally my fingers felt the handkerchief I had wrapped the ring in. Quickly I pulled out the small gold band and slipped it onto my ring finger. It was too big; I put it on my middle finger, where it fit better. Then I replaced the stone. I thought for a moment to check for my mother's box, but I knew I would have to go through the same amount of work to find it; and besides, if Mama was alive, she might need whatever was there.

Crouched in the darkness, I could see the light next door in Mr. Orlovski's cobbler shop. He had often worked into the night, I remembered. I watched the light in the window for a long time, wanting to approach it, but afraid—afraid the Orlovskis hadn't heard from my mother, and afraid that they might not be friendly, particularly since their son was a policeman.

Finally I got up the courage and walked up cautiously to the door. "Mr. Orlovski," I called, tapping lightly. "Mr. Orlovski." After a moment I could hear the wooden floor inside creaking with approaching footsteps, and I shrank back into the darkness. The door opened, and Leon Orlovski looked out. "Mr. Orlovski," I stepped into the light. "It's me, your neighbor Alicia."

Mr. Orlovski looked at me in wild fright, as though I were a ghost, glanced from side to side, apparently to make sure no one had seen me, and then motioned me inside. I rushed through the door, which he slammed behind me. Once inside, he stared at me nervously, seemingly speechless. Then, "Wait here," he said. "Don't make a sound." And with that he went through another door into the main house.

A moment later he reappeared with Mrs. Orlovski.

"Have you seen my mother?" I asked. They seemed surprised.

"Why, no, Alicia," Mrs. Orlovski said. "Why should your mother be here?"

"My brother?"

"Of course not." A note of defense had entered her voice. "There are no Jews in Buczacz now. The city is Judenrein!"

I wanted to say "You needn't point that out to me; I'm well aware of it," but I did not. For all I knew, I could be out the back door and they out the front, running to the police station to tell them that Jews had returned to Buczacz. You never knew if a neighbor was about to turn on you; in those times plenty had.

"Yes, I know," I replied, looking at them both with a steeliness that made Mr. Orlovski avoid my eyes. Mrs. Orlovski hesitated a moment, then said, "Wait here." She hurried through the door, leaving Mr. Orlovski and me face-to-face in an uncomfortable silence. "Well," he said finally, "how were things in Kopechince?"

"Mr. Orlovski," I said, "I was picked up in an action in Kopechince two weeks ago. Thousands of Jewish people were marched to their deaths. I escaped from an open grave to come here. I don't know if my mother and brother are dead or alive."

Shock flooded his face. "I don't know what to say, Alicia."

"And before that, when the wagons were taking the people from here to Kopechince, the last wagons were stopped and all the people murdered. Most of those who were living here are dead now." I could sense the effect of my words, his brain trying to absorb this shocking new information. Did he believe me? I didn't know. Perhaps he was glad that no one remained to reveal the participation of his son, a policeman, in our total destruction.

Just then Mrs. Orlovski returned with a small bundle. "Here, Alicia," she said, thrusting it into my hands. "This is for you."

Outside I ate a little of the bread and then started to look for shelter for the night. I had to stay close to Buczacz and continue to wait for my mother and brother. I waited for three days near the river Stripa, and then I moved on. I passed the outskirts of several villages, hoping that I would find a place to hide. I rejected village after village for one reason or another—the homes were too close together, or they just gave me an uneasy feeling; perhaps I would be betrayed to the Germans! After a few days I was beginning to wonder if, under the circumstances, I wasn't too fearful. But then I found a place I knew immediately would be perfect for hiding.

In Poland, as in many European countries, the fields are actually far away from the farmer's homes. Sometimes a man's field may be ten kilometers from the village where he lives. So the farmers build little shacks on their fields to store tools and straw to be used during the summer, and to give a bit of shade to workers who come to harvest the crops. Sometimes you could see several such shacks dotting large expanses of land, one shack on each piece of property.

I came to one such shack that didn't look as though it had been used much since the previous summer. There was some stale straw left and some hand tools, most important among them a small shovel. It occurred to me that I could dig my own bunker right there; no one should be coming around to check on the place for at least another month. There were a couple of poles in one corner which I could lay across the hole and cover with straw. For the time being, it looked safe.

The earth was cold and hard, but as I dug deeper it became softer and easier to work. After several hours with the shovel I had managed to dig a hole three feet deep and almost six feet long. With the poles laid over it and the straw piled high, no one could tell there was a hidden bunker there. I was very pleased. I thought, if only I could find my mother and brother and bring them there. I fell asleep with an ache in my heart.

I made the food the Orlovskis had given me last a full eight days by eating only when I couldn't stand the hunger another minute, and then only a small amount of bread, enough to mute the pangs. On some days I might take only four or five bites for the entire day; I never had the feeling of not being hungry; but I had learned over the past year that one could distinguish between degrees of hunger and could learn to live with it.

One night I had not been able to sleep particularly well and the next morning I slept later than usual. I had had a night full of fitful dreams, and so when I awoke to hear children's voices nearby I thought that I must still be dreaming. Then, without warning, my little straw bunker came crashing in on me. I shrieked in terror and frantically clawed my way up through the straw. I heard other shrieks and could just see the leg of someone hurrying from the shack as my head rose above ground level. I jumped to my feet and hurried to the door; there, on the open field running as fast as they could, were three children. One of them looked like a girl I had gone to school with.

The thought of those children running to someone and telling what had happened jerked me into action. "Wait, wait!" I called, running after them. "Lala, stop! It's me, Alicia Jurman! Lala, I knew you in school! Stop!"

I called out the name, not really being sure that the girl was my former schoolmate, but when she stopped running and turned around, I knew it was.

"Alicia," she said, gasping for breath as I caught up with her, "what in God's name are you doing here?"

She quickly crossed herself, a common gesture among the superstitious Poles.

"I'm hiding," I said. "You know what happened to us. I am trying to find a way to survive. But, Lala, what are you doing here?"

"I am visiting relatives," she said. "These are my cousins, Josek and Sosia; this land belongs to them." Sosia said hello, but the boy eyed me silently, with a kind of speculative look in his eyes, unfriendly and maybe even cruel.

"What's on your finger?" he asked, pointing to my hand. I quickly hid it behind my back. "It's only a ring that I have had since I was little."

"Let me see it." Warily I held out my hand. "No," he ordered, "take it off."

I pulled back my hand. "No!" I cried. "I love this ring. It's the only thing I have left. Please, Lala." I turned to her, pleading.

"Josek . . ." she began.

"Come on, Lala, I only want to see it," he said, and, turning back to me, added, "The owner of this shack doesn't know you're here, does he?" We looked at each other with hatred. I thought of fighting him, but he was so much stronger. I knew I had no choice but to give him the ring.

He turned it over and over in his hand. "This looks like gold. Is it?" I shrugged, although I was sure it was. "I could get a little money for this," he said.

"Give it back to her, Josek," Lala said. "Didn't you hear her say it's all she had left in the world?"

"Oh, no, Lala," the boy said in mock innocence. "I think she wants me to have it. Don't you? What is your name?"

I watched with fury in my heart as he slipped my ring onto his finger, a mean smile slowly crossing his face. I looked once more at Lala, silently pleading with her to stop this, to make her cousin give back my ring, but she avoided my eyes. I had not met one Pole yet who would stand up for a Jew, I thought bitterly. Why should Lala? "Goodbye, Alicia," she said sadly, her eyes nervously darting across my face but never making contact with mine. "We won't tell anyone where you are, I promise." I said nothing; I knew she was helpless to enforce such a promise.

The three of them turned and headed away across the field. I wiped away the tears and went back to the shack for my bundle. Then I, too, headed across the field, in the opposite direction. But my tears would not stop coming; slowly they oozed from my eyes as though from a bottomless well. After a while I no longer tried to wipe them away.

I walked for the rest of that day. The river and forest were far away now; all around me were fields broken up by rows of bushes. About a kilometer away from the shack where the children had found me was a ravine that I felt would make an excellent hiding place. It was separated from the fields on either side by tall hedges. Once you were in the ravine, no one could see you from either field, and if someone entered, you only had to hide in the bushes. It was perfect.

That night I slept fitfully. I dreamed that the ghost of my mother came and hovered over me for the longest time. Her face was deathly white with dark circles under her eyes, and her beautiful raven hair had been chopped short. Seeing my mother this way was frightening as well as heartbreaking. Was this a sign that she really was dead and had come to tell me so? And yet I felt strangely comforted by her presence and prayed she wouldn't leave. She said something to me, but there was no sound, only her moving lips. I listened hard, trying to hear what she was saying but couldn't. Over and over again she seemed to be repeating the same thing. Eventually I began to hear her voice, first very soft like a murmur, then a little louder.

"Alicia," she was saying. "It's Mama. It's Mama. Alicia, it's Mama. Wake up. Wake up, sweetheart; it's Mama; it's Mama."

At that point I opened my eyes and screamed. The ghost of my mother hadn't left; it was still there, bending over me. I squirmed away. Half awake, half asleep, I struggled clumsily to my feet and started to run.

"Alicia!" my mother called out after me. "Darling, don't run away, it's Mama. Alicia, please!" I stopped and turned; my mother was rising to her feet, holding her arms out to me. At first I stood, frozen; fearing that if I reached back to her only to have her fade into mist, I'd go mad. But the urge was too strong, and I found myself running, running into my mother's arms. She was real! She was alive! I sobbed like a baby and she cried, too, holding me close. We cried together for a long time and then we sat for quite a while longer, not talking, my head on her shoulder and her beautiful fingers stroking my cheek.

My mother's description of what happened at the end of the action was much as I had pictured it. After three days the people came crawling up from the hole under the house, its air stale and foul with the odor of body waste, to find the house empty but for the corpses of the babies. Herzl was sent right away to find out what had happened to me, and he brought back the news of the death march. So, she concluded, she had probably lost her fourth child. But she wouldn't know for certain unless she went to Buczacz; she began to prepare for her departure immediately.

In a few days she had gathered enough food to feed herself and Herzl for a week. She bundled it up with her shawl but took nothing more. Herzl planned to take along a blanket.

But when the day came to leave Kopechince, my brother could not be found. Mama waited all day, and the next, and the next; but Herzl did not return. My mother was torn—should she stay and wait? Should she leave without him? Should she risk being separated forever from her last child? Should she search for the child she couldn't know was still alive?

Rumors were going around that a new action was imminent—a final action to make Kopechince Judenrein. In the past such rumors had always proven true. She dared stay no longer. Herzl knew that we had agreed to meet in Buczacz when and if we could, and my mother tearfully left.

She had been able to progress much faster than me, since I, having no food, had to stop every day and work for my meals. Mother couldn't have stopped; couldn't even risk being seen. She was gaunt and white from malnutrition; the bites from her head lice had erupted into open sores, and before she left Kopechince, Mrs. Kaplan at our house had helped her cut her hair short again. One look at a woman in such misery and any Pole in the country would have known she was a Jewess.

So Mama hurried on, stopping only to eat and sleep for a few hours at a time. Of course she had to stay out of sight during the day, and like me had followed the river as much as she could. She arrived at the Orlovskis two days behind me, and learned, much to her relief and joy, that I was alive. Of course I had not told the Orlovskis in what direction I would be heading, for fear their policeman son might get wind of it, and so my mother, knowing I was only two days ahead of her, had to make a quick decision—which area around the city should she search? By sheer luck she decided to head in my direction. For nearly a week she roamed the fields at night, calling my name, praying I would answer. During the day she crawled through the wheat as close as possible to the people working in the fields, hoping to spot me among them.

Then a day earlier, while hidden in a ravine, she overheard children argue as they passed close to her hiding place.

"Why did you take the ring? You heard her say it was all she had left in the world."

"What's the matter with you? She's lucky we don't turn her in."

"Josek, I went to school with Alicia. I've known her for years. You just took her last possession. Doesn't that even bother you?"

"I don't want to hear any more about it."

My mother said that when she heard my name mentioned she knew I must be nearby. She hurried in the direction from which the children were coming, hoping to catch up with me. She found the hut, and the bunker partially covered in straw. Her heart sang. She searched the field, and the one next to it, and the one beyond that. Nothing. Frustrated, tired, and weak, she wouldn't consider stopping even briefly. The fear of losing me after coming so close was driving her on. She searched through the night, calling and calling. Exhausted, she finally arrived at the ravine as morning was just beginning.

I can't describe my joy at being with my mother again. I told her all about Milek and how he had saved my life, about working in the fields, and the ring. We didn't discuss Herzl's fate beyond what she had already told me; it would have been too painful. We would continue to search for him, because we couldn't give up hope completely.

Now that my mother had found me, all her remaining energy seemed to fade away. I had her lie down and rest her head in my lap so I could wrap my arms around her thin body. I had lost my ring but found my mother. As she drifted off to sleep in my arms I made a silent promise that from then on I would guard her with my life.

CHAPTER 13

In the Fields

The next day my mother and I decided to remain where we were. Since we had a little bit of food left, we agreed that I would not rush to find work. Instead, we would study the countryside, the fields, and the farmers who worked them. There was a village close by—I would have to find out if it was Polish or Ukrainian. It was not a matter of languages; I spoke both languages fluently. But we feared the Ukrainians very much, whereas I hoped the Poles, who had become the new target of Ukrainian gangs, might have some understanding of our plight.

We were in the Podole, a part of the Ukraine that had been annexed by Poland after the First World War. This was the reason for the friction between the Ukrainians and the Poles. The Ukrainians wanted an independent Ukraine, without Poles. The Poles, on the other hand, had lived in this area for a long time and now felt that it was their home.

The war had given the Ukrainians the upper hand. The Germans promised them a free Ukraine, free from Poland and from the Soviet Union, in return for their collaboration, and they gladly gave it. Ukrainians cooperated zealously in the elimination of the Jewish population. As the war progressed, and the Jewish people were all but eliminated from the area, the Ukrainians turned their attention to the Poles. The Banderas, a national Ukrainian group, would sweep into Polish villages pretending to look for Jews, and more often than not would leave the villages in flames.

Most farmers, Polish and Ukrainians alike, lived in small villages. If one were to look down from the air, one could see a patchwork quilt made up of dozens and dozens of small fields separated from one another by hedges, roads, or ravines. Dotted among the fields would be small villages, each no more than twenty or thirty houses on both sides of a road. There would also be a church, a school, and occasionally a small store.

Very few farmers were lucky enough to have connecting fields, and most farmers did not have all of their land next to their villages. In most cases a farmer's fields would be scattered over many kilometers. A man might inherit a piece of land in one place, while his wife might have received, as a dowry, land near the village she came from.

Farm people generally lived on their own produce—even spun their own linen—and the highlights of the week or month would be the trips to the nearest city on market day to sell or trade goods.

Even in the largest of farm families there were rarely enough field hands. So the people of the region helped one another. In the late spring one would go to a neighbor's field to help weed potatoes. In August the neighbor would reciprocate by helping harvest one's wheat. There were also those who did not have enough land of their own to keep busy, who worked for produce such as wheat or potatoes. All of this cultivating and harvesting was done by hand and always in a great hurry because of the weather. The owner of the farm would feed the workers in his field during the day.

Even considering the murdering Banderovcy and other pro-Nazi Ukrainians and Poles, the villages still constituted almost the only refuge for the few surviving Jews such as my mother and me. Rarely was a German soldier to be seen in this region, unless directed to a specific place to find Jews who were betrayed by local residents. They would then come and take the Jews into the city to be killed, or would kill them in the nearest forest. Otherwise the Germans stayed in larger cities such as Buczacz, which was several hours away.

Spring was passing into summer, and the fields would soon need harvesting. All kinds of crops were growing: flax, wheat, barley, oats, potatoes, sugar beets, and corn. Some of the early corn in the fields, especially close to the village homes, had already been harvested. I could tell by the chopped stalks still in the fields, waiting to be plowed under. There were also hay fields, grazing land for cattle, and fields left to lie fallow for a season before replanting.

My mother and I decided on a plan that called for her to remain hidden in the ravine while I worked on building up a rapport with the local farmers. It wasn't enough just to work for them in the summer; I also had to earn their fondness and sympathy for the wintertime, when there would be no work and I would have to go begging. It was out of the question for my mother to try to work; she would be too easily recognized as a Jewess. The sadness and pain that had settled permanently in her eyes would betray her.

We agreed that she would hide in the wheat fields or in the ravine during the day, and I would bring food for her after my work was through. When I thought of my mother hiding day in and day out in the wheat—trembling at every sound, wondering if I would come back or if I had been found out and caught, and waiting, waiting all day with nothing to do, totally dependent on her child for survival—my heart ached for her. But that was how it had to be if we were to remain alive.

For myself, I was not too worried about being discovered. I had learned to approach people carefully and to live with constant fear. I felt a cold hand lodged inside me, twisting my insides whenever danger was present. I learned to control the fear to a certain extent by ignoring it. I had to go out early every morning, face the fields with the people working in them, and become part of the working force in order to get something to eat. I concentrated on becoming a good worker, however inexperienced, and I learned quickly. Field work is terribly hard on the back, but with my health weakened as it was from the beating, and typhoid, and tuberculosis, it was even more difficult for me. To lift a sack of potatoes was torture; yet I had to make the effort. I could not slack off in my work. This I knew.

My first job was weeding potato patches for a Polish family. I introduced myself as Helka, a good Polish name. I told them I had been forced to leave home by my stepmother, although I doubt that they really believed me. I was pointed to a line of potatoes, given a small hoe, and went to work alongside their two sons. We worked in complete silence until noon, at which time we broke for a meal. I was given a nice slice of bread and a cup of sour milk. I ate part of the bread and was able to conceal part in my blouse for my mother. At the end of the day, as they were readying to leave, the farmer's wife handed me an extra slice. "In case you get hungry later," she said, avoiding my eyes. I hurried back to the ravine to share the food with my mother.

Thank God it was summer and not winter. The nights cooled, but were still comfortable. Had we arrived here in November, or even

October, the crops would have been in; there would have been no need to hire an extra field hand like myself, and the farmers would certainly not have reacted well to a stranger begging at their door. I am convinced that we would have frozen to death, or if not that, starved. But here it was, nearly July. A beautiful, warm month. Blue skies, cottony clouds sweeping by overhead, a hot, happy sun. My mother began to sit out in the sun, safely hidden in the wheat field, to gain a little color and to help heal the sores on her scalp while I worked in the fields of local farmers.

A few weeks after we had arrived in the area I returned to the field of the family who had given me my first work. They had been kind to me, and I had gotten along well with the sons, one about ten and the other about thirteen. They seemed pleased to see me, and at day's end the older boy invited me to come and visit them at their home in the nearby Polish village of Wujciechovka. "We could give you some sour milk," he said. I looked quickly to his mother and could see her face clouding. The polite thing would have been for me to say, "No, thank you, I couldn't really; but thank you for your kind offer." But I couldn't afford to be too polite if I were to stay alive; I needed to take advantage of every friendly gesture that came my way.

So I said instead, "How very kind! I would love to come. When?" The parents exchanged quick glances.

"How about tonight, Papa?" asked the boy.

The man coughed a little and, clearing his throat, said, "That should be all right. But I think you should wait until nightfall. It is the eighth house from the corner as you come into the village from the road." He pointed with his finger to the road in front of us. "Look for the sheet-metal roof, and come to the back door."

I was about to inquire about a dog, but he read the question in my eyes and said not to worry about the dog. The boys seemed puzzled at his mention of the back door, and I knew immediately that the farmer suspected that I was not who I said I was. There was an element of danger surrounding me. He could sense it, for why else would he ask me to come in stealth? And yet he had not forbidden me to come; he even said he would keep the dog inside so that it wouldn't bark at my approach.

Fortunately there was a moon out that night; otherwise it would have been difficult to find the house my first time in Wujciechovka. I came in on the main road. There was a risk, I knew, in walking in the open; but on the other hand, why shouldn't a person who had nothing to fear walk on the road? I had to look like such a person, and besides, I didn't yet know the village well enough to take the back paths from the fields.

It seemed like a nice little village from what I could tell in the dark. There was a church and behind it some ways back what seemed to be a school. The houses all had very small front yards prettily planted with flowers. I learned that on almost every back lot there was a barn and vegetable garden.

I began counting from the first house I saw. I counted eight houses down on the right to the one with the sheet-metal roof. A galvanized metal roof was a sign of prosperity. Most homes had thatched roofs. I found the house and made my way around to the back door.

I had raised my hand to knock, when suddenly the door flew open, startling me. It was the farmer. "Blessed be Jesus Christ," he whispered. "Before we invite you in, would you follow me for a moment?"

Fear shot through me. Was this a trick? Where would he take me? Was he going to kill me? He must have read what was in my face, and his suspicions about me were probably confirmed. "Don't worry," he whispered. "I only thought it would be safer if we talked in the barn."

My fears not completely put to rest, I nevertheless nodded and followed him. He took me to the barn, and after we were inside lit a small lamp. I felt terribly afraid, suddenly unsure of this man who had been so kind during the day. Then he spoke. "Helka, my wife and I have discussed the matter, and we believe it best if you make this your last visit to our home. We hope you will understand. We have also told the boys it would be better not to mention you to anyone."

I swallowed hard. He knew I was a Jewish girl. I had not fooled him.

"Can I still come and work for you?" I asked. He thought for a moment.

"Yes," he said slowly. It was a lot to ask under the circumstances. Then with more conviction he said, "We can always use a good worker in the fields. But don't come every day. Let a little time pass in between."

"Thank you," I said, feeling my tears beginning to choke me. "I will be going then."

"First come and visit for a minute. The boys stayed up to see you." He was trying to be kind in his own way. "Besides, my wife has some food for you."

I followed him into the house gratefully. It had been years since I was last in a farmhouse. The room was fairly large. A big bed covered with a colorful blanket stood near the wall. On top of the blanket were scattered large pillows with hand-embroidered covers. The boys probably slept on a bench placed under the window, which was converted to a straw bed at night. An oven with cooking surfaces on top caught my eye: The aroma of freshly baked bread was coming from that direction.

I talked for a few minutes to the boys and left the house with a jug of sour milk under one arm and a full loaf of bread under the other. So my first contact with the people of this region had brought mixed results. They did suspect me of being a Jewish girl; they did recognize danger hovering over me; and yet they still helped me. That was very comforting. Our chances for survival were good if everyone else reacted the same way . . . but that was a lot to hope for.

I decided I liked this Polish village called Wujciechovka (which in English means "the village of uncles") and hoped my mother would agree to move closer to it. If only we could find a safe enough hiding place. I would have to look for one.

In the meantime I continued to work in the fields while my mother hid in a different field each day. She preferred wheat fields, which are wonderful hiding places if one takes care to part the tall and delicate stalks gently before passing through. If the stalks were crushed, they would leave a trail, and a farmer passing from time to time to inspect his fields would immediately see that someone had been sitting there. Who would be sitting in his fields during this busy season but a person who was trying to hide, and who would be trying to hide these days? The farmer might become angry enough to hunt down the hider and kill for even the slightest damage he had caused to his field.

But Mother handled the wheat stalks very gently, entering each field carefully in a zigzag fashion. Each morning we left the ravine together, and I left her at her hiding place for the day before going on alone to look for work.

With my hair braided and bandanna I looked like a typical peasant girl, Polish or Ukrainian. I tried to imitate the free, swaying walk of the village girls and was able to do so because my feet had become callused enough to step freely on the hard earth. Each day I tried a new field, which seemed like a safe thing to do. I had to be careful approaching the farmers to ask for work; what if I addressed one in Ukrainian and he turned out to be Polish? He would certainly turn me away, and then I would have lost the chance to work and get a piece of bread for my mother. On the other hand, if I spoke Polish to a Ukrainian, something even worse could happen—the man might come after me with his shovel. So the first moment that I approached the farmers was always crucial. On my way across the field I always tried to swing close to other workers and listen to their conversation to find out which language to use. If I had no choice and had to approach the farmer directly, I mumbled my greeting and waited to find out in what language he would answer.

By now I had prepared a number of stories. The evil-stepmother story had not seemed to do well, so I modified it. I said that our family was so poor that I, being the oldest child, had been sent out to fend for myself. Another good story, but only with Poles, was that my village had been burned down by the Banderovcy, and I was one of a handful of survivors.

As I have said, this was a big area, and every day before going to find work I would explore it a little more. One day to the south, another to the east, another to the west—the fields stretched on and on. One morning I headed northwest looking for work, near Wujciechovka, crossing ground that was slightly uphill. There was no one around, only wheat fields. Suddenly I spied a puff of smoke; there had to be a house somewhere around. I headed toward the smoke, crawling low through the wheat. I came to the edge of the wheat and peeked beyond it.

In front of me was a small clearing in which stood a little house. Actually it was more like one of those hay and tool shacks. It was similar to the one I had hidden in, only larger; a room had been added. I couldn't see any windows from where I stood; they were probably on the other side of the house. Next to the house was a small garden: I recognized onion and potato stalks pushing up through the soil. There was smoke trailing from the chimney but no other sign of life around the place. As I came closer, I could hear a familiar hum; it grew louder as I passed the side of the house and turned the corner. In front of the house, not twenty feet from the doorway, were five beehives, each with a little cloud of bees buzzing happily around. I had never seen man-made wooden beehives from close up before, but I was not frightened. I respected and appreciated bees, and hoped that if I did not disturb them, they would not sting me.

My attention had been so drawn to the beehives that I had let my guard down. Suddenly I jerked back to awareness and realized there was a body lying facedown on the ground between the house and the hives. I approached cautiously. There was a man on the ground. Was he dead? If he was dead, then why the smoke coming from the chimney? Was someone else in the house? I could not see anyone. I stepped carefully around the body and looked in the front door of the house. I called out, but there was no answer. I went back to the body. It was an old man dressed in an odd fashion. His shirt was of a military style, very aristocratic, yet the pants were typical peasant garb. He was barefooted. I reached out and touched the man's hand. It was warm and soft, not cold like death. Very gently I rolled him over onto his back. I put my ear to his chest. He was breathing.

"Hey, mister," I said in Polish, shaking him gently. "Wake up. Are you all right?"

The man opened his eyes, and was startled to find me leaning over him. He scowled darkly, his thick brows furrowing.

"Who are you? What are you doing here?"

"Does that matter?" I replied quickly. "It should only matter that I found you, and that you are not dead."

He struggled to reach a sitting position but waved me off as I tried to help him. He put one hand on his head and the other on the ground to brace himself, resting for a moment in that position. He looked in a strange way like a sort of nobleman, with his white mustache sweeping upward, clipped in the fashion of the late emperor of Austria, Franz Joseph. His eyes were pale blue, a sharp contrast to his sun-reddened scalp and face. The Polish he spoke was that of an educated man.

"Who are you, anyway?" he said. "And what are you doing here?"

"I am an orphan looking for work. I saw the smoke and thought there might be a house up here."

"Well, there is no work for you here." He looked at me with an expression that was rapidly becoming one of amusement.

"Where are you from, then? Certainly not from here."

I stiffened a little. "How do you know that?"

This man seemed to look right through me, and yet he appeared to offer no real threat, although I couldn't be sure.

He nodded toward the hives. "Aren't you afraid of the bees?"

"No," I replied. "Why, should I be?"

"Everyone else is. You are the first visitor I have had in"—he tried to remember—"a very long time."

"You seem friendly enough," I said. His face suddenly lit up with a most beautiful smile, and he laughed.

I felt I was winning him over.

"You are a very smart girl. What is your name, miss."

I curtsied and was about to say Alicia but changed my mind.

"Helka; I am called Helka," I said, trying to sound convincing.

"And you are how old?"

"Thirteen."

"I see. And you are not afraid of me?"

"What is so bad about you?"

He laughed again. "An old man with fits?"

"You have fits?" I was intrigued. "Is that why you were . . ."

"Yes, my dear, that's the reason. I have fits. They come on without warning. I can't predict them and I can't prevent them." He looked at me again, a long, searching look.

"Something tells me you are not a village girl."

"Why do you say that?"

"The villagers are all afraid of me."

"But why?"

"Ah, you see?" he said, shaking a finger at me cunningly. "If you were a village girl, you would know the answer. They say I am possessed by demons."

I looked at him blankly. Was this some aspect of the Catholic religion I had missed? I knew they believed in saints and the devil, but did they think that demons inhabited this old man?

The old man watched my bewilderment with an amused smile.

"So," he said. "Knowing what you now know, aren't you even going to cross yourself?"

"Perhaps I had better." I lifted my right hand and slowly made the sign of the cross, touching first my forehead with three fingers, then my heart, my left shoulder and the right. This was something I would have to remember to do, and do frequently, if I wanted to move among the village people. The old man had tripped me up. Now I understood; a village girl would have left the man lying in the dirt and hurried away as quickly as her legs could carry her. So he knew, at least, who I wasn't, and he was still smiling. I decided not to run, not yet.

I straightened my shoulders and said, "Did you ever consider that maybe people don't come to see you because you are not a very good host?"

At this the man laughed outright. If you can make someone laugh, I have always felt, you can win them over.

"Well," he said, "I do seem to have forgotten my manners. May I offer you a cup of tea?"

"That would be very nice. Thank you very much."

I followed the man into his house. The front door opened onto a small hall leading into a tiny kitchen. It was sparsely furnished, only a brick stove with an iron plate on top, a small table, and one chair. But it was amazingly clean. For an old man, he kept a very neat house. There was a door leading to a second room, where he kept his foodstuffs and the straw which he used for sleeping.

The old man put a pot of water on the stove.

"How about a slice of bread and some honey?" he offered.

"I would like that very much," I replied. I couldn't remember when I had last tasted honey. This man was so lucky to be able to have it all the time.

"So you own this land, then," I asked.

"Oh, no. This land is owned by the Sobiesky family."

I was sitting on his only chair and felt uncomfortable, but knowing how important it can be to be a good host, I just continued sitting while he stood. He continued to talk.

"Yes, they let me live here in exchange for the honey from the hives, and for not putting any curses on them." He winked mischievously. "I don't encourage them to think I'm possessed, but as long as they do already . . ." I smiled.

"And no one ever comes to visit you?" He shook his head.

I felt such compassion for this man, to be cast out this way because of ignorance and superstition.

"Do you ever leave your home?" I asked.

"Oh, yes, I take honey into the village now and then, and a few times during the year I beg a ride into our nearest city, Buczacz, for the market day."

"Buczacz?"

"Yes, it's down to the south of here and not too far. A nice place, really, if you like cities."

I felt a wave of pain shoot through me at the mention of Buczacz. My hand holding the cup started to tremble, so I put it down quickly.

"I hate to leave," I said. "But I really must be going. I have work to do."

He bowed slightly, another indication that he wasn't a peasant.

"And I must say I have greatly enjoyed your visit." Somehow I managed to swallow the lump in my throat. How long had it been since I heard such kind words. I felt like crying. *Stop it, Alicia! Stop it this minute,* I said to myself.

"May I come back again and look in on you?" I asked, hoping he did not detect the tremor in my voice.

"And have some more honey?" I stiffened somewhat at this suggestion. He thought I valued him only for his honey. I had to admit that at least partly he was right. I valued not only the honey, but his kindness to me and, most of all, the privacy his home could offer. A place to hide.

I thanked him for the tea, bade him farewell, and started out of the house. As I turned the corner leading toward the path to the right of the house, I was struck by a wonderful sight. Directly ahead down the sloping hill was the village of Wujciechovka, about a kilometer away. When I had visited the farmer at night I couldn't see very much of its beauty. But now I was so carried away with admiration of the village that I must have called out, because the old man was suddenly beside me.

"What a wonderful view of the village you have!"

For the rest of the day as I worked I could think of nothing but the old man and his house. At the end of the day it was difficult not to run straight to the field where my mother was hiding. But I had to start out in one direction until I could no longer see the field I worked in, then reverse my steps and dart across another field, through the ravine, across another field, and finally to my mother's side.

Mother did not share my excited enthusiasm for adopting the old man, even though this might assure us a place to stay in the winter.

"Are you sure it is safe?"

"Are you sure he is not a Jew-hater?"

"Did he say anything at all about Jews?"

"Did he say anything at all about wanting company?"

"Are you sure?"

Suddenly, in the face of my mother's fears, I came to doubt, as she did, the safety of the old man's house.

In the meantime I was worried about Mama. The sores on her scalp were not healing, even though we made compresses of babka leaves for them, and even though she spent hours under the sun. Her hair, which she last cut in Kopechince, was beginning to grow back in. This was bad because her scalp needed to be exposed to the sun's rays and we had no means of cutting it. The sour milk, pieces of bread, and an occasional boiled potato I brought her kept mother from starving but not from going hungry, and they certainly did not give her the nutrients she needed to help heal her sores. Both of us, we knew, were suffering from malnutrition. But to be both alive and healthy was too much to ask for; for the time being we would be thankful to be living.

One day I was weeding yet another potato field, when I overheard the owner's wife talking with someone.

"I don't know what I am going to do," this woman was saying, "With my husband, Jan, so ill, and the children too young to be of much help, I don't know how I can keep up with all the work. If only I could find someone to help me."

I felt sympathy for the poor woman, but at the same time my survival antenna was vibrating. I waited until the woman was standing alone and said, "Please forgive me for eavesdropping, but I heard about your poor husband. I would like to work for you and help you."

"Really?" Her eyes showed both relief and doubt. "But what can you do?"

"Oh, I can do everything," I said. "I am very experienced at farming. I can milk, tend horses, feed chickens, and help with children, and I only ask for my meals and a place to stay. Your barn would be fine for me. I also know a little about nursing; my mother taught me."

She hesitated at first, then gave me directions. Her farm was almost ten kilometers away. When the workday was over, I hurried to the ravine to tell my mother. All thoughts of the old man and the bees faded in the face of this new opportunity—to work safely away from prying eyes and to have my mother hiding close by at all times.

Mama, too, was excited about the possibilities, and after eating we decided to start out right away for our new place.

We reached the woman's house in not quite five hours despite my mother's weakened health. We were motivated, to be sure. The night was the only time we could walk freely on the main road. But we had much to do: We had to find the farm, and find a hiding place for my mother, all before dawn.

We had no trouble finding the house. Mama stayed some distance away while I went ahead to learn the farm's layout—and where the dogs were. Farmers almost always had dogs at their homes in the village. The house looked prosperous, with a sheet-metal roof, and some thirty meters behind it was a barn. I saw no dog, but that didn't mean there wasn't one there.

As my eyes became used to the dark I looked around the barn. It was a nice barn, of a good size. A ladder was leading to the hayloft. This would be a wonderful place for my mother. Two cows were lying on the straw at one end, and a horse was tied to a pole at the other end. There was no sign that anyone was disturbed by my presence. I was very careful not to stumble over the buckets and various tools scattered around. I climbed up the ladder to see the hayloft. It was nearly full of hay and straw. Somehow I would have to arrange a way to handle the straw and hay so that the owner's wife would never have a reason to go into the hayloft herself. Then my mother could hide there safely. For the time being, I decided not to tell the woman about my mother. It might confirm her suspicions about who I was. When I knew her a little better, I would tell her.

I settled my mother comfortably into the hay. For myself, I found straw downstairs in the barn, curled up, and dozed off. I was a very light sleeper, and if I knew in advance what time to get up, that was the time my eyes would open. I was also always quick to start at any sound. A footstep outside a door would bring me to full alert. I hadn't been asleep for very long, when a noise awoke me. I saw a light and realized that the farmer's wife had come in and was walking in my direction.

I called out. "Panie, Panie," I said. "It is I, Helka, from the field. Don't be afraid."

She was understandably startled. "My God! How did you get here so fast?"

"I knew you needed help urgently, and I know how busy it must be for you, especially in the morning.

"I will do a lot of work; you will see," I said in a pleading voice. I was so afraid she might have changed her mind and would send me away. With Mother in the hayloft, I would have had to wait until nightfall to get her away. Luckily she could hear our conversation. My thoughts were racing. Finally the woman spoke again.

"Well, now that you are here, let's begin with the milking."

Wiping her hands on her apron, she took two pails from the floor and handed one to me. I swallowed hard. I had never milked a cow before. I had been hoping to get a little experience before I had to milk in front of anyone.

She introduced the cows. "This is Sosia, our blondy," she said, patting the back of the cow nearest her. "And that is Rosa. Her red and white color suits her. She is quite something, that cow," she said, smiling. "Well, shall we begin?"

We washed our hands in a wooden keg filled with well water and wiped them on her apron.

I copied the woman's every move, getting the stool and setting the pail in place. I watched her for a minute as she milked Sosia, while talking softly to the cow.

As I set up my stool, Rosa turned and looked at me warily, all the time chewing her cud. "There, Rosa," I said softly. "There's a nice cow. We are going to be quite good friends, you and me." I reached down and felt along the udder for the teats. I was good at handling horses but not cows. I had watched others milk, but had never touched a cow's udder myself. Rosa was quick to realize it, too, and she shifted her weight from side to side.

I pulled the stool closer, placed the pail between my knees, where I expected the milk would land, gently put my hands on Rosa's front teats, and began to pull. I could hear the soft zsh, zsh as Sosia's milk hit the bucket, but from Rosa came nothing. "Come on now, Rosa," I coaxed. "Please?"

Somehow, miraculously, I felt milk begin to stream in spurts into the pail. I relaxed. This wasn't too hard after all. As soon as the milk flow slackened from the front teats, I moved my hands to the back teats.

Swat! Suddenly I felt myself flying backward, my face wet and stinging. That devil cow, darling Rosa, had slapped me with her tail, which was muddy and matted with burrs. As I went over, I could see the pail flying right toward me, milk splashing everywhere. Rosa, not content to brush me off like a fly, kicked me as well. There I sat, my face hurting badly, as was my thigh where Rosa had kicked me. The milk had all soaked into the straw with only a slight foam remaining. And there was Rosa, turning her head casually to see where I had landed. I began to laugh hysterically, pressing my hand to my painful cheek and casting a furtive look in the direction of the woman. To my great relief, I realized that she was laughing too. Tears were actually streaming down her cheeks, she was laughing so hard.

"That Rosa," she exclaimed. "What a scamp!"

"I am sorry about the milk," I managed to blurt out between bursts of laughter.

"Don't worry," she said, turning back to her milking. I thought for a moment that maybe Sosia would kick her, too, but the woman finished her milking and put the pail safely aside.

I replaced the stool, gripped the pail between my knees, wiped my hands on my skirt, and with sure strokes started milking the back teats again while keeping an eye on Rosa's treacherous tail.

Following this dramatic beginning, I settled nicely into a daily routine. My days were very busy. I got up before sunrise to take Rosa and Sosia out to pasture and brought them back around six A.M. for milking. I cleaned the barn, fed the chickens, worked in the vegetable garden, did the laundry, and helped spoon-feed the sick husband when Maria, his wife, was away working in the fields. At about four P.M. I took the cows back to pasture and then milked them again. I was becoming very proficient in this task and occasionally treated myself to a long gulp of fresh, foamy milk. The work I would have liked to have done most was to take care of the horse, but it was on loan to a neighbor in return for the heavy plowing he did for the farm. Each evening after supper, which was fairly early, I had enough time to sit with the older girl, Ania, and go over the lessons that she had learned the previous year in her first grade. She was eight years old, a friendly girl who was in delicate health. Her nose was constantly running and she coughed a lot. She was very good with the younger children, and very kind to her sick father. We took turns caring for him and sometimes I pretended he was my father too. It was a pleasure to write and read with her and to touch a schoolbook again. The first time I did it I had to use all my willpower to stop tears from running down my face. I tried not to remember my own school. Maria encouraged our lessons and tried to keep the younger three children quiet. Just the same, I had to be careful when helping with the lessons; I couldn't be too smart. I was supposed to be only an orphan who, at best, had completed only three classes at a village school.

For all this work I had my meals with the family, ample portions of bread, sour milk, potatoes, cooked corn meal cereal, cabbage, carrots, and on Sunday, a piece of chicken. My stomach was so shrunken that the food I received was enough for both my mother and myself. Each night I would bring Mother bread and other food that I would hide on my person or put aside when cleaning up after meals.

I continued to sleep in the loft, although Maria would have let me sleep in the house if I had asked her. Naturally I wanted to be with my mother and, secondly, it was safer to be out of the house in case someone came calling at night.

The hardest part of farm life, with the exception of working in the fields, was getting up before sun-up, about four in the morning, to take the cows to pasture. It wasn't enough to take and leave them there; I had to stay and watch them.

Rosa, I soon learned, was a notorious wanderer. Turn your back on her for a moment, and she was off in the next field trampling down plants with reckless abandon. I had to follow her and Sosia with a switch to keep them from straying out of their pasture.

One morning I was so sleepy I could hardly wake up. Even in the summer the mornings were cool, and I was shivering a little as I led Rosa and Sosia out. The walk to the pasture warmed me up a little, but my feet were wet and cold from the early morning dew, so my chill persisted. I was getting very sleepy again, so much so that I didn't see how I would be able to keep my eyes open. Then a solution occurred to me. I tied the long rope that was around Rosa's neck to Sosia's neck, so that they could graze side by side with enough space to move around. Then I made a loop on the end of Sosia's rope, put my right foot through it, and tightened it around my ankle, making myself a sort of human anchor. I settled down in the grass and planned to sleep for the next hour or so. I should have known better.

Rosa suddenly and rapidly began to move off. Sosia was tied to her and therefore had no choice but to follow along, and I was dragged behind by the rope that was tied firmly to my ankle.

"Rosa," I cried. "Halt! Slow down! Sosia! Stop!"

But they didn't stop; instead, Rosa made a beeline for the gate.

Openings to fields of corn or garden vegetables would often be blocked by horizontal poles that could be slipped in and out of openings on gateposts. I could see Rosa heading right for the gate leading to the next field, the corn field. Here the poles hadn't been placed properly, someone had only crisscrossed them. Over Rosa went; over went Sosia after her, without a single hoof making contact with the wood. Then came Alicia [Helka], boom, right onto the poles. Ahead of us, directly in Rosa's path, lay the corn field, the harvesting over, only jagged stalks remaining.

I breathed a hurried prayer that Rosa would stop before she came to the stalks, but no. She trotted happily into the field. I was pulled over every stalk, every stone, every barrier Rosa could spot. Finally I was able to undo the rope and free myself. Rosa, then not more than ten feet away, looked at me, let out a bellowing, "Moo, moo, moo," and calmly resumed her grazing.

I was a mess, covered all over with dirt, smarting from bruises, and bleeding from scratches. I rose to my feet painfully and went over to

Rosa and Sosia, who were standing still. "Rosa!" I yelled, fury raging inside me. I looked around for some kind of stick, as mine was back in the pasture. When I finally found a stick big enough to do some damage, I hurried back to the cows, who had not moved a bit, and herded them back into the pasture.

When I returned to the barn I washed up a little, milked the cows, set the milk on the family table, took a piece of bread, and went to see my mother. I woke her up to complain about my mistreatment. My poor mother, seeing me covered with dirt and my clothes torn, became very frightened. I immediately went into my story. She listened, nodding her head sympathetically. I was so carried away with my story, it took me a while to realize that my mother was making strange noises. I stopped and looked at her with amazement. Apparently, as valiantly as she had tried, she could not stifle what had started as a giggle and built into hysterical laughter. She pulled me close to her and hugged me tight; but that did not fool me; it was only to prevent her from seeing my funny, dirty appearance. Every time she regained her composure and tried to look at me again, the laughter would come bursting out, and she would hold me a little tighter. Although I pretended to be indignant, secretly I was glad to see my mother laughing this way; it was her first laugh in a long time.

Almost two weeks had passed since I came to the farm. I worked from the very early morning until night or, rather, until I fell off my feet. I was tired, but I made every effort to give my best, especially since I had told Maria about my mother and that we were Jewish. Maria started giving me a little more food for my mother and otherwise completely ignored her existence. In return I tried to protect the family. I knew instinctively that I should disappear whenever someone came calling at the farm. I always remembered that I was not an ordinary farm worker; I was a Jewish girl in hiding, and there was a very big difference. Apparently, though, someone had spotted me. Maria came into the barn one evening after the children were asleep and called me to come down.

It was awkward for her, I could see, but she nevertheless came right to the point.

"I have to let you go, Helka," she said, trying not to look at me. "I am so very sorry."

"But why?" It was a silly thing to ask, since I already knew the answer.

"A friend of ours saw you on the pasture field and mentioned you to me. I discussed it with my husband, and . . . Helka, we have worked so hard for what we have."

"I understand," I said. "I thank you for giving me this work. I like you very much, and I had hoped to stay here . . ." My first thought was to say "through the war," but I stopped myself and instead said "for quite a while."

"Well," she said, "at any rate, my husband should be back on his feet soon, and then we won't need any help, anyway." She knew, poor woman, that her husband would never get on his feet again. He was very ill.

"Could I still help you on the fields near Wujciechovka?"

"I don't know," she said. "We will have to see. But," she added hastily, "you can sleep here tonight and leave in the morning."

She walked out of the barn quickly. I stood rooted in place, feeling anger beginning to overcome reason. Hold it, Alicia, calm down. Think . . . think, I said to myself.

I tried to put myself in Maria's place. She was right to let me go. If her "good neighbor" would tell another "good neighbor" that Maria had an orphan girl helping her, and they put their heads together, they would know it could only be a Jewish girl. If someone betrayed me to the Ukrainian police or the Germans, Maria's family would be in danger; so I had to go. But my heart was aching with disappointment. I felt rejected and very lonely. I climbed up the loft. My mother met me as I was just stepping off the last step and pulled me into her arms. She had heard our conversation and understood how I felt. I knew my mother was disappointed too. She had been doing so much better: I had borrowed a pair of scissors from the house and trimmed her hair; with that and sufficient food, her sores were beginning to heal. In the effort to reduce my pain, Mama assured me that she would rather be outside anyway, to enjoy the sun and be able to see what was going on around us.

We decided to leave that night. It was safer to walk in the dark. As I was leaving, I turned to say good-bye to Sosia and gave Rosa an extra pat on the back. By now we were very good friends and, having discovered each other's stubborn natures, we had developed a mutual respect. Rosa emitted a long "moo" and turned her head to look at me. I wondered if she knew that we were never going to see each other again. At this moment I was sure that animals had more feelings than human beings. On our way to the field, we detoured past the chicken coops, and I relieved the chickens of two eggs.

My mother handed me the few things I now owned, thanks to Maria, and we left the farm. Returning to our old ravine took us much longer than had our trip to Maria's house. We arrived in the early morning as the sky was beginning to lighten. The test stick we had set up in the ravine had not been disturbed, and we were grateful for that.

Of course, my thoughts turned immediately to the old man with the bees, and the next day I decided to pay him a visit. I approached his house through the wheat field and looked carefully around before emerging from cover. The old man was hoeing in the garden on the other side of the house; I came upon him from behind.

I called out the customary greeting, praising the Lord, and added my name.

The poor man dropped the hoe and whirled around, clutching at his heart. He seemed so agitated I thought he might go into a fit.

"Jesus Christ," he cried, crossing himself. "Do you always sneak up on people that way? You could have killed me."

"I'm sorry. Are you all right? Maybe we should go into the house."

"No!" He seemed surprisingly adamant. "No, I have to finish my work."

"Then maybe we could just visit while you do your work."

"Oh, no. No. Much too distracting. Oh, no. That wouldn't do at all. I think you should go then."

Now I was really puzzled and even a little bit hurt. Had I done something wrong? Was he angry because I had surprised him? I really couldn't understand his strange behavior.

"I hope I haven't offended you," I said. "I enjoyed our last visit so much, I wanted to see you again, to see how you were getting on."

"You haven't offended me," he said abruptly, now turning his back to me as he worked. "But I do think it would be better if you left now."

When I got back to the ravine I told my mother about the old man's strange behavior. "What do you think could be the matter?" I asked.

My mother looked thoughtful. "Perhaps it occurred to him that you were Jewish."

"But if that were so, why was he so friendly to me the first time? No. I think it's something else."

"Maybe someone spotted you at his house that other time. Maybe someone warned him about you."

"No one ever comes to see him; that's what he told me. And I am sure no one was around that day."

"Maybe there was someone in the house. Maybe he was trying to protect you."

"Mama," I said, "I want to go and visit the old man tonight, to see what is wrong with him. Would you like to come along?" Poor mother, I shouldn't have asked her to accompany me, but I was always so upset when I had to leave her alone. She must have read my thoughts.

"Dear daughter, if you want me, I will come with you." Having said it, she smiled a sad little smile, which gave us both courage.

As we came out of the field at the rear of the old man's house, we could see a light coming through the window. I remembered from my previous visit that only one room had a window and that was the room he occupied as living quarters. Silently I moved to the side of the house and looked into the window. I saw the old man sitting on a chair near the table. A shirt was spread on top of the table and his hands, or rather his fingers, were moving over the seams of the shirt. For a moment I thought he was sewing. As I watched him, his expression suddenly changed from one of concentration to a look of sheer joy as his fingers tightened on something in the seam. I nearly burst out laughing when I realized that he was delousing his shirt. Poor man, he, too, was afflicted by the little bloodsuckers.

I motioned to my mother to stay hidden near the field, went to the front of the house, and knocked on the door. The door opened a crack, and I saw the old man's frightened face. He was holding a lamp in his slightly trembling hand.

"What is the matter?" he asked. "What happened?"

"Nothing happened," I said quietly. "I was just concerned about you, so I came back to see how you are. May I come in and rest a little? I am very tired."

He sighed deeply, then said, "All right, you want to come in, so come in."

The old man was standing in the middle of the floor, still holding the kerosene lamp which lit up the whole room. Suddenly I knew why he had behaved the way he did. He had visitors. They were sitting on the floor in the corner all huddled together. There were three of them. They looked to me like a mother and two daughters. I didn't have to ask who they were. I knew. I felt very bad about coming at night. I must have given them a terrible fright. How could I have known that there was anyone sitting on the floor? I saw only the old man through the window.

I stood there looking at them openmouthed and they in turn stared at me with frightened eyes. No one said a word. The girls on the floor were leaning against their mother. One was about ten and the other about my age, thirteen. I noticed the older girl. She was very beautiful and, as we looked at each other, there was an instant rapport between us. The old man didn't move from his place. I took the lamp out of his slightly trembling hand and put it down on the table. My first impulse was to put my arms around this saintly man and kiss him. Because what else but real kindness would motivate this man to take us into his home? We didn't have money to offer him. I didn't kiss him. I just took his hand in mine and shook it. I was choked with emotion and filled with gratitude.

I asked, "May I come and stay here, too, and may I bring my mother with me? Please, may I?" I looked at him with pleading eyes. He looked at me and just nodded his head.

I ran out to get my mother and brought her to the house.

"My daughter told me of your generous offer to take us into your home. We will be forever grateful to you. We will never forget you," my mother said.

He just smiled and pointed to the family on the floor. We were introduced, but all I caught was the older girl's name, Basia. I was glad to have someone my own age to talk with, and I was sure that my mother was equally glad to have Basia's mother. But tonight there wasn't much conversation. We got some fresh straw from the other room and spread it in the corner near the window, where we settled down for the night. The old man went to sleep near the stove on a straw pallet. The kerosene lamp was turned out, and all we had was moonlight coming through the window. Before I fell asleep I looked at the old man. I could see his face clearly. I wondered what this man's kindness would mean for us and what price he might have to pay for his good deed.

CHAPTER 14

Wujciu

I started calling the old man Wujciu right away. Wujciu is Polish for "uncle." It is an affectionate title applied to older men, and I wanted to endear myself to Wujciu. We were, after all, not only imposing on his good will and intruding on his privacy, but we were risking his life as well. By allowing us to stay in his house, Wujciu had linked his fate with ours.

However, Wujciu did not fare too badly with a sudden flock of women around him. We cooked his meals, did his laundry, and, at night, took turns delousing his clothing for him. Delousing was a regular part of our daily lives. No amount of washing would keep the lice from our bodies and our clothes. We thought it had something to do with our living conditions and with our food, or rather the lack of food. Wujciu's vegetable garden and his small income from selling honey were barely enough to feed himself, never mind all of us. We had to provide our own food in order to survive.

My mother and I developed a new routine. I thought it best not to work in the immediate area anymore. I didn't want to risk being seen coming to or from the direction of the beekeeper's house. I began to leave the house before dawn, and walked three or four kilometers away to find work. My mother also left the house in the morning and hid in fields or ravines. It would probably have been better for her to remain at Wujciu's and talk with Basia's mother, but my mother needed the sun. She would tell me where she planned to hide that day, and on the way home from work I would sometimes meet her, and we would walk back to Wujciu's together; but most of the time we just met back at the house. While it was summer and still comfortable outdoors, I preferred to stay away from Wujciu's as long as possible. I would sleep out in the ravine, where Mama could join me and we had a chance to talk. Although Basia and her family stayed in the house most of the time, they, too, disappeared occasionally to get food. I never asked Basia where and how they did this; it was strictly her business.

I continued to work in the fields for my slice of bread and cup of sour milk, plus an additional piece of bread if any was left over from lunch. I had learned a neat trick to discover whether the farmers were Poles or Ukrainians. I have said before that the people of that area were highly religious. The Poles were Roman Catholics and the Ukrainians, Greek Orthodox. The standard greeting in both languages was "Praised be Jesus Christ" and the response would be "Forever and ever, Amen." Polish and Ukrainian are very similar languages. I decided to mumble the greetings. The listener really could not tell which language I was using. I would listen carefully for the reply and then use whichever language I heard. This worked wonderfully well and gave me a chance to select either my Polish name, "Helka," or the Ukrainian name, "Slavka," which I had borrowed from my friend.

I also tried, whenever possible, to work the fields where there were only women, children, and older men; I avoided fields where young men worked. If the field belonged to a Ukrainian farmer, such young men might belong to the police or to the Bandera national organization. They could be on leave to help their family with farm work and would be more likely to notice me and turn me in.

On this particular morning, however, I could find work only in a Ukrainian field where there were young men present. Looking back on it, I think it must have been fate that placed me there in that particular spot at that exact time, because as I weeded I overheard part of a conversation between two other workers weeding nearby.

"Are you certain they were Jews?" asked one fellow.

"Of course! Who else could they be?"

"Gypsies, maybe?"

"Jews."

"Did you give them anything?"

"What do you take me for?"

"Jews in this area. I can't get over it. How long has it been?"

"Not long enough." The two men laughed. Then:

"What is being done about taking them to Buczacz?"

"Don't worry about that; Stephen is already seeing to it."

"How so?"

"He followed them after they left the village. Tonight he and the boys will bring them to the police station in Buczacz."

"He knows where they are, then?"

"In the wheat field. You know, the one near the flour mill."

"It's funny, you know? I thought all the Jews were dead."

"Oh, they are; these are just the last few. Don't worry, we'll get them too."

Laughter.

It was only a brief conversation, but it was all I needed to hear. My first fear, of course, had been that they had discovered my mother, who was hiding in a wheat field. But not a field near the flour mill, thank God. And the man had said there was more than one. Who could it be? Basia, her mother, and sister? God forbid; I felt a cold fear grip my insides. I began to tremble, and had to sit down for a moment to control my wobbly knees. But I knew I must not attract attention; in fact, I must find a way to disappear from the field altogether.

I continued to weed around the same spot, not moving forward row by row as the others were doing. After a while everyone else was ahead of me; no one behind. I crept backward a few inches at a time, still facing forward in case anyone looked back. When the others were far enough away I bolted from the field, running for the nearest row of bushes. I gasped for breath and peeked through the leaves; no one had followed me. Good. Now it was onward to the field near the flour mill.

That field was actually quite a distance from Wujciu's. People went to the mill regularly. Basia and her sister and mother were not likely to hide there if they had decided to spend the day in the fields. Besides, they had told me that they didn't go begging; so I realized that the Jews hiding in that field could only be strangers.

It took me quite a while to reach the mill. I had to be very careful when walking in broad daylight. I walked at the edge of the fields and whenever I saw people even from far away I dove into the field until they were out of sight. I had noticed the mill before, but I had to retrace my steps several times before I finally found it.

I stood still for a minute, trying to plan how best to handle the situation. I had to guess which was the field that the men had talked about. From where I stood, the nearest field looked undisturbed. But when I came near it and circled around its edges, I saw the revealing crushed wheat stalks. I went down on my hands and knees and crawled into the field. As I moved through the stalks I realized at once that these people knew nothing about hiding in fields. They had not parted the wheat but had trod it down. They had not moved in a zigzag fashion or started false trails. It was easy to track them, shockingly easy.

As I went farther into the field it occurred to me that the sound of my approach would be frightening to people who were hiding to save their lives, and that I should somehow let them know who I was. So I began to recite the Hebrew prayer every Jew knows. I repeated the words over and over again softly: "Shema Yisrael—Hear, O Israel, the Lord our God; the Lord is One." It was the first time I had thought of the prayer since the death march outside of Kopechince. I had recited those Hebrew words instinctively in the face of death.

Eventually I could see dark shapes ahead. There, in a tiny clearing they had crushed down, were a woman and two children. A little girl was clinging to her mother and the mother was holding her tightly in her arms. The child could have been about six years old. At the mother's side was a boy, younger than myself, holding her hand. The three of them stared at me wild-eyed, tensed, and ready to flee. They looked strangely familiar.

"You heard me recite the prayer?" I asked. The woman nodded her head.

"You can't stay here. You went begging in the early morning in a Ukrainian village. There were Banderovcy in that village and they are coming for you tonight."

They said nothing, only stared. It was a heartbreaking sight. Lost in the fields at the mercy of murderers, three innocent human beings were to be hunted down like wild animals and killed only because they were of a different religion from that of the hunters. They looked so pitiful, so thin, so afraid.

"Where are you from?" I asked.

The woman cleared her throat. "Buczacz," she said.

"I thought so. I thought you looked familiar. I am also from Buczacz."

They relaxed a little at hearing this. I looked at the children's faces. Hunger and fear had left deep circles around their eyes, which seemed to have sunk deeply into their sockets. Looking at them, I felt I was seeing the last remnants of our people, surviving in agony and fear until whatever destiny time would bring.

"I am going to get you out of here," I said. "But first you have to know some things." The woman nodded. I quickly explained how they were to move through the wheat. I even gave a small demonstration, parting the stalks and disappearing for a moment, then working my way back quickly. The woman nodded again. There was no response from the children; I didn't know if they understood or not.

"Now," I said, "when we leave this field we are not going to bother to take care. When they arrive tonight they will see that you have been here; we can't hide that. But when we reach the next field, I want you to do as I have told you, and stay behind me. Don't talk until I say you can." That seemed like a wasted point, the children had yet to say a word.

I quickly led them from the field; we crawled on our hands and knees. I made them wait just inside while I checked the area for other people. Luckily there were none. I hurried them out. I took them around edges of fields, not through them. It was wise not to cross inside a wheat field if it could be avoided, since even with the greatest care some sort of trail would be left behind. So we moved quickly past the fields, bending down all the while to make ourselves less visible.

As we moved along, my mind raced. Where could I take these people? To Wujciu? No. Absolutely not. There were already five people hiding in his tiny kitchen. I couldn't raise the number to eight. Even if I wanted to, Wujciu would never stand for it. What else, then? The ravine? It was fairly safe, but I would not be able to feed them all by myself.

They would have to go begging again or starve. None of them could work. They looked pitiful in their old city clothes and would be spotted as Jews the minute they were seen. Besides, the mother couldn't leave the children alone. At first I thought perhaps I could take the boy along to work in the fields. But it was hard for me to avoid arousing suspicion among the farmers as it was and I looked like a village girl. The appearance of another child out of nowhere would start the farmers talking. There was no way. I knew I had risked discovery just by having left the field that morning. I could never go back there again.

I decided to take them to our ravine, at least for the time being. It would give me time to think, and they would be safe there. At the ravine they immediately clustered together just as I had first found them—the mother's arms around the clinging daughter, the son holding his mother's hand, all three of them staring silently at me. It was unnerving, all that fear and suffering projected at me through demanding, silent eyes. Looking at them hunched together, I realized to my own shame that I was beginning to resent this additional burden. I was getting very hungry, having forfeited the piece of bread I would have normally received had I stayed in the field, not to mention the bread I was going to bring to my mother.

The woman finally spoke timidly.

"Are you sure it is safe here?"

"Where are we safe anywhere in this world?" I answered. "But my mother and I stay here often."

It occurred to me that if the Banderovcy would make a thorough search of the whole area, they could come as far as this ravine, and even as far as Wujciu's house. I had to chase those terrible thoughts away, otherwise I might panic, and that would have been the worst thing to have happened at that moment.

Luckily the woman spoke again.

"Where do you stay now?"

"I can't say."

My quick and negative response hit the woman like a slap in the face, and she quickly looked away. She couldn't afford to anger me; we both knew that. I felt doubly bad for having spoken so sharply.

"I have actually been in this area for a few weeks," I said. "I have found a way to hide with some degree of safety, at least I want to think so. But it has not been easy. I work in the fields for a piece of bread until there is no more strength left in my body, and then I drop off to sleep wherever I can." This was not entirely a lie; I often slept under the stars rather than at Wujciu's.

"I see." The woman nodded understandingly.

"What are your children's names?" I asked. The woman reached for the boy's arm.

"This is my son, Benjamin, and this is my daughter, Rutka. My name is Sarah Hening."

I had not asked after her husband or even how they had come to this area. It wasn't really important. The man was probably dead; that they were still alive was all that mattered.

The problem of what to do with this family kept turning over and over in my mind. I was sure about one thing—our destinies were now linked for better or for worse, and my destiny was linked to that of a dear, angelic old man.

We stayed together all day, dozing on and off, drinking water from the jug my mother and I kept hidden in the ravine. When it became dark I asked them to follow me to a different place. I still hadn't mentioned Wujciu to them. I asked them to wait for me in a wheat field quite a distance from Wujciu's and told them that I would be back shortly. I touched them each gently on the shoulder to reassure them, and left.

My mother met me with a worried expression on her face.

"I was so worried about you, Alicia," she said in a choking voice, embracing me. "Come in, I have some warm water for you. You can wash your hair."

"Thank you, dear Mama, but a little later. Can we go outside and talk?"

Once outside, I told my mother about the family. Even in the dark I could see how touched my mother was.

"You will have to speak with Wujciu about them," she said, but added, "Please do it very gently; he isn't feeling very well today."

"I will do my best," I answered, and we went inside.

The first thing I did after having a couple of slices of baked potato from the stove, a very generous gift from my dear friend Basia, was to offer to delouse Wujciu's shirt. After he put it on I asked him if I could speak with him in privacy in the hall.

"Wujciu," I said, putting my hand on his arm, "I have found three poor people who need your help or they will never survive the week." As I spoke, his benign expression turned to one of a man bracing himself for the worst. He even seemed to sway a little, as though about to fall. I held his arm tighter now.

"Helka," he said, "do you know what month this is? It is the end of July, and next month is August, when harvest begins. People will be swarming all over the fields near our home. And now you want to hide even more Jews? I must have been mad to ever listen to you."

I felt as though he had slapped me on the face.

"Why?" I asked. "What ill has come of this? Don't you have company now? Isn't your laundry and cooking done for you? When you don't feel well, isn't there someone always here to help you? What wrong have we done you, Wujciu?"

He turned away.

"You know what I mean," he said after a moment's pause. "Helka, I could be killed if you were found in my house, don't you realize what that means? I could die for this!"

"What do you mean, don't I realize?" I said, my voice rising a little.

"Wujciu, my entire family has been murdered. What do you think we are doing here? My father was killed shortly after the Germans arrived. My oldest brother was hanged. My second oldest brother was lined up and shot in a work camp. We don't even know what happened to my little brother. Every day I go into the fields I wonder if this is going to be the day I will be caught and killed. Every time I leave my mother I wonder if this is the last time I will ever see her. So don't you—"

"I had nothing to do with any of that!" he cried. "I had nothing to do with that, and you know it. I just wanted to be left alone, and live my life peacefully."

"And then we came along and made things difficult for you. Is that what you are saying? Has life really become more difficult for you, Wujciu? Are you suffering now? Tell me, because my mother and I are willing to leave this minute. We will go back into the ravine. Maybe I can find a barn somewhere. How long do you think we will last then, eh? How long do you think my mother will last during the winter, with no shelter, tell me, Wujciu?" I stopped myself; I realized I was screaming at him.

I could feel through his arm that his body tensed suddenly. He began to cough and stagger a bit, and for a moment I was afraid he was going to have a seizure.

"Let me help you," I said, but he angrily shook off my hand. I ran into the kitchen to get the only chair in the house. My mother followed me back into the hall.

She helped Wujciu to sit down. The old man braced himself against the back of the chair. I sat down on the floor near him and put my head on his still-trembling knee.

"Wujciu, we have no choice but to take these poor people in." I lied, "They know where we are hiding now. We can't turn them away even if we wanted to."

I fell silent. Suddenly I felt something touch my head ever so gently. Wujciu let out a great and deep sigh.

My mother broke the silence.

"Wujciu," she said gently, "we will be able to manage all right. We will share the food as we have done from the start. And there is a young boy who can keep you company." She patted his back lightly and motioned for me to get up and get the family. I did so quickly.

We all filed into the small kitchen, the children staying behind their mother. I introduced them to Wujciu, who completely ignored their presence. I knew this troubled Sarah, but I also knew she had nothing to fear. Wujciu was beaten; I had beaten that sweet old man. Tears welled in my eyes, and I turned and hurried out of the house. Behind me I could hear my mother's soothing voice welcoming the tired family and setting them at ease.

Outside I sat on the ground near the well, silent tears streaming down my cheeks. I had done a low, dishonorable thing. I had forced an old man's hand, overpowered him, taken advantage of him. A noble, lovely man like Wujciu. It is true I had done it only to save lives, but it still left a bitter taste in my mouth.

My mother came out of the house looking for me.

"Mama," I said hoarsely, "I think I will spend the night in the ravine. I don't want to go back in there right now."

She smiled a sad smile and stroked my hair.

"You did the right thing, sweetheart," she said. "Wujciu knows that."

"All the same," I said, "I would prefer to be alone tonight." There was a pause, and then I added, "You know I did not get food today." She put her arm around me and pulled me close. "I have discovered something very interesting," she said. "Now that it is close to harvest time and the wheat is ripe, I have been chewing on the grains. They don't taste bad really, and they break your hunger. You must chew them well, though."

She hugged me again. "Will I see you tomorrow, then?"

I nodded, wiping the last tears from my cheeks. "I will see you after work. Where will you be?"

"I don't know. How about the fourth field from the little brook. You know, the one we used for bathing the other day."

We had started numbering the fields because there was no other way to describe them.

"Please be careful, Alicia. The Ukrainians may still be looking for Sarah and the children."

I smiled ironically. "What could happen to me? I am Helka, the wonder girl of the Poles. I am Slavka, the good Ukrainian field hand. Of course I will be careful!"

August arrived, and with it the harvesting of the wheat and barley. I had acted on my mother's suggestion and had been chewing ripened raw wheat grains for the last week. They weren't bad, actually. After I became used to them, they reduced the hunger that I felt constantly. I thought often about Wujciu and was still feeling uneasy about the old man and the position I had put him in.

In the meantime the new family seemed to be settling in well. Although I had been spending much of my time away from the house, I did manage to talk to the children and all of us gave them food. I offered some of my bread. Basia contributed potatoes, and Wujciu gave them vegetables from his garden. They were still very quiet, but not as afraid as they were when I first saw them. I liked Benjamin very much because he reminded me of Herzl. Each time I looked at him I felt a terrible longing for my brother.

During the harvest I worked long hours, sometimes going to a second field at night after a long day's work just to get an extra chunk of bread for our hungry people. But the group at Wujciu's considered me the lucky one. There I was, out in the fresh air while they stayed cooped up in the little room. With the harvesting taking place so near to them, it was out of the question for anyone except Wujciu to step outdoors during the day. Cooking had to be done carefully, only when Wujciu was in the house, and the little laundry we had couldn't be hung outside.

With September came the potato harvest. This was very hard work, much harder than the wheat harvest. The potato plant stalk had to be grasped firmly, loosened up in the earth, and then pulled out. The potatoes attached to the stringy roots were then pulled off and put in the sack. After pulling out the initial stalk, one then had to dig through the soil with one's hands, feeling around for potatoes that grew deeper than others. After making sure none could be reached by hand, the earth was turned over with a shovel to be sure that all the potatoes were out of the hole. Only then, after digging a hole sometimes as deep as a foot and a half, could one move on to the next bunch of stalks and begin the whole process all over again.

As we worked, the farmer would stroll up and down the rows and check each person's efforts, turning some of the holes over again with his shovel to make sure we had dug deeply enough. I worked hard and was very conscientious, and the farmers for whom I worked seemed pleased with me.

I hadn't been in the potato harvest very long, when I had an inspiration. What if I left some potatoes in the earth, at the edge of the field, to retrieve later? After all, I worked hard every day for only a slice of bread and a cup of sour milk: What would be the harm in taking a few potatoes here and there? Those poor people at Wujciu's—there was barely enough food to keep us from starving to death. If I could bring back a few potatoes, we would slice them thin and bake them on top of the stove. Yes, to deliberately leave potatoes behind and come back for them later was stealing; I knew that. If caught, I would have to pay dearly—a beating, maybe, or being turned in to the police. Yes, the risk was great, but we were all so hungry that I was willing to try.

I began leaving potatoes behind along the edges of the fields, covering them with discarded stalks. That way it looked as though the potatoes were thrown out accidentally and not by design. Then I would come back to look for them after dusk, when everyone else had left the field. Sometimes I would get as many as fifteen or twenty potatoes; other times the glow of a campfire as I approached the field told me I had been beaten to my prize; shepherds from neighboring pastures, bored with nothing to do while grazing their animals, would often light fires, using the dried potato stalks as fuel. They would find my potatoes and bake them in the fire. If the shepherds were young and friendly, I would walk up to them casually and say I, too, was grazing my cows, and could I join them? But most of the time I would wait until they left and then poke through the ashes to look for any remaining potatoes. Sometimes I would find a nicely baked one, soft inside, which I would eat with great joy, but most of the time the potatoes I found in the ashes were burned black; I might as well have tried to eat charcoal. Then I would go back to the field to continue my search for potatoes. Usually I would find a few and bring them back home.

I started calling Wujciu's house "home." My mother was there, and I liked the rest of the people very much, especially Basia, with whom I was becoming good friends. We often talked girl talk and had fantasies about the future, if we lived through the war. Basia told me that someday she would own twelve houses in New York, and I talked about being a doctor like my uncle Kurtz, about being free to go to school and having friends. These fantasies got us through many lonely hours, as did Basia's good nature, which also helped to reduce the tensions that flared up occasionally as a result of so many people being confined in such a cramped space.

Summer was gone and autumn was coming to an end as well. The farmers were plowing their fields and spreading manure for the winter. The fields were empty now, and I had to find another way to get food. I knew it was time to get to know the people in Wujciechovka. There were still cows to be milked and chickens to be fed. Perhaps I could learn how to spin yarn. If I couldn't find work because the farmers were afraid to let me near their homes, I had only one alternative left to me: go out and beg. I dreaded the thought of begging, but if I didn't, we would starve to death. Several times during the summer I had been asked to go to a farm to get some cooked cereal at night, so I was somewhat familiar with the village, and with the fact that most homes had dogs. Later, when I had to walk at night in the villages, I found dogs to be my biggest enemy. They would alert the farmers, who would come out angry, and sometimes scared, to see who dared come to their homes at night.

I could avoid dogs, but I couldn't avoid the weather. It was the end of October, and the nights had gone from cool to cold. I was still going barefoot in the peasant blouse and skirt, which were my only clothes. I would have to take long walks through the village in search of work. I knew I would not last long wearing such meager attire. The people at Wujciu's had no clothes to give me, and I couldn't be so foolhardy as to steal from the villagers. Where could I go for help? This was the question that occupied my mind day and night.

One late afternoon as I was returning from the fields, I sat down at the edge of a dirt road, picked up a wooden stick from the ditch, and started drawing in the dirt. I often did this when I had things on my mind. I was drawing a house with a girl nearby carrying schoolbooks. I finished the drawing and, without thinking, signed it "Slavka." Then it struck me. Of course—there was one person who might still help me, who might not turn me in to the police even though she was a Ukrainian. It was my school friend Slavka, whose name I borrowed when working in the Ukrainian fields. It was Slavka who, when I fell from the tree outside my former classroom, had turned away so she would not see my humiliation. And it was Slavka who told me about Bunio being shot, thinking it would be easier for me if I heard it from her. And it was also Slavka who told me, after we were moved into the ghetto, that she had been told not to see me anymore; that the priest had said the Jews had killed Jesus and that it was God's wrath that was punishing us.

I had mixed feelings about trying to find Slavka. Because I had been away so long, she might no longer care at all what happened to me. She probably thought I was dead. However, she was the only person I could turn to. Then there was the next problem—how to get a message to her? I would have to send someone I could trust to Buczacz. The only person I could send would be . . . Wujciu? How could I ask him for such a favor? I dreaded asking him, but I had no other choice.

The following Sunday morning, after doing an especially good job delousing Wujciu's shirt, I approached him.

"Wujciu," I said, "I have a very great favor to ask of you."

He turned quickly and looked at me wide-eyed. "Not more Jews?"

I laughed. "No, Wujciu, not more Jews."

He sighed in relief. "Thank God," he said. "I wouldn't know where to put them."

"You know, Wujciu, they say in the village that it is going to be a very cold winter, and these are the only clothes I own. What am I going to do? I don't even have any shoes. How can I continue to work if my feet freeze?"

He buttoned his shirt and looked at me.

"Just how do I come into this, dear Helka?" he asked.

I continued. "Wujciu, there is only one person who will give me clothing. I have been thinking seriously about her. She is an old friend of mine who lives in Buczacz."

He snorted. "Buczacz," he said with half a laugh. "How do you ever expect to get to . . ." He realized what was coming next. "Helka," he said sternly, "just what is it you want me to do?"

"I have thought of a plan," I said. "Wujciu, I know it will work. And you know that if I live through the war, I will give you such great rewards that you will never have to worry about anything as long as you live."

"Oh, yes, the reward," he said. "That's all I have been hearing from you since you got here."

"Well, I will reward you if I live. I promise."

"Dearie, if we are not all found out and killed, that will be reward enough. But back to the point. What scheme have you cooked up?"

Quickly I told him of my plan. Every Thursday was market day in Buczacz. Farmers from Wujciechovka and all the neighboring villages loaded up their wagons with produce and traveled to Buczacz. They would leave in the early morning, stay at the marketplace most of the day, and leave again in the late afternoon. Wujciu could beg a ride from one of them.

"Let's assume they give me a ride; what would I say when they asked me why I wanted to go?" he asked. "They know I rarely go into the city now."

"That is easy," I said. "Say that you have decided to get some teeth; that before you go to the Lord you want to chew food again. You might offer them a jar of honey; that might help. Then have the farmer drop you off at the Casa Chora."

The Casa Chora was a medical clinic, and this clinic in particular was not too far from Chechego Maya Street, where Slavka lived. I suggested to Wujciu that he actually stay in the clinic an hour or so and inquire about the teeth so that if someone checked up later, his story would hold true. I even suggested that he get a piece of paper with the price on it for his teeth, something as proof he had been there, for his own protection. Then he could duck out of the clinic, follow the directions I had given him, and go directly to Slavka. There, he should find her and give her the note I wrote on a piece of rag with a piece of burned wood.

I was so carried away with my plan that I was slightly thrown off balance when Wujciu asked his next question.

"What should I say if Slavka asks about you?"

"Don't tell her anything. Don't say where you are from either. It is better not to take the chance."

I didn't tell him about her family's connections with the Banderovcy through her uncle and cousin; there was no point in worrying him. I knew that Wujciu was very concerned about his involvement with us, even though in the entire time we had been with him, people had been near the house only once, and that was during the harvest. The trip into Buczacz was something he would decide on by himself, and I would not press him. It had to be his own choice.

I didn't bring up the issue again, but several times I found him looking at me, especially when I came into the house shivering from cold. On Wednesday night he asked me to give him the note to take to my friend because he had decided to go to Buczacz.

So on Thursday Wujciu, with a jar of honey under his arm, left the house before it was light and went down to the main road to beg a ride from the first farmer who passed by. He had said he was afraid that when these farmers recognized him they would only whip the horses and speed away, but I told him that no one would do that; after all, they all thought he could put curses on people, and no one would risk being cursed. I was very nervous for about an hour, expecting him to come back, but he didn't, so I relaxed a little. I worried all day, imagining all kinds of terrible developments. I pictured Wujciu getting lost and me going to Buczacz to find him; I might then be caught and taken to prison, only to find Wujciu there. Both of us would then be taken to the Fador and shot.

When it began getting dark outside I worried even more. I was becoming very upset when the door finally opened and Wujciu walked in. There he stood, clutching a bundle in his arms, tired but with a big toothless smile on his face and eyes sparkling; probably, I thought, from a shot of vodka. I had to restrain myself from falling over him with joy. We opened the bundle, which contained several slices of white bread, a wool kerchief, a short boy's coat (most likely belonging to Slavka's brother, Bohdan) and a pair of wooden-soled shoes. I quickly tried on the coat; it was a little snug, and the sleeves did not reach my wrists, but it would do nicely. I was very happy to have it. The shoes, though, were another thing. But they were shoes, after all, and I would have to find a way to cram into them. Most likely I would cut the tops open and fill the gap with a rag.

For poor Wujciu the day had been an ordeal. He rode silently the whole way into Buczacz with a peasant family that was clearly terrified of him, only to be laughed at by a nurse at the Casa Chora and advised to forget about teeth and eat mashed potatoes. Then he went to the Chechego Maya Street and met a young girl who went white as she read my note. His entire stay at Slavka's was only five minutes or so; he stood outside the door as she raced through the house, picking up the first things she could find. Then there was the long ride home, again with a family that barely tolerated him but was kind enough to give him a bit of vodka. No wonder the poor man was exhausted.

Just before he was about to lie down to sleep, Wujciu motioned me to follow him outside.

"I should probably be telling your mother this," he began. "But I have decided to let you be the judge."

"What is it, Wujciu?" I asked, my curiosity mingled with dread. "Slavka told you something, didn't she?"

He nodded, staring at the ground.

"Your brother Herzl is dead." I felt my knees go out from under me, and if Wujciu hadn't reached out and steadied me, I would have dropped to the ground.

"I am very sorry, Helka," he said, genuinely grieved. "I had trouble deciding whether to tell you, and now you will understand why I didn't say anything to your mother when I came in.

"Slavka said that your brother was pointed out to the police by his school friend, a boy who knew him well. He was taken to the Fador and shot. She said it happened at the end of May."

Tears sprang to my eyes; I clung tightly to Wujciu, sobbing silently into his shoulder. It was a comfort to have the old man there. At that moment I appreciated him more than he would ever know.

Finally I drew back and wiped my eyes.

"Thank you for telling me, Wujciu," I said hoarsely, trying to regain control of my voice. "I will find a way to tell my mother."

"Of course, the decision is up to you," he said. "But I think you should tell her. She has the right to know."

I nodded and straightened my shoulders. "When the time is right I will tell her." Wujciu returned to the house.

When the time is right! When the time is right! My words kept ringing in my ears, and suddenly I felt such fury I could hardly breathe. When is the time right to tell a mother her fourth son has been murdered?

And then I remembered all the other times I had to tell my mother her sons were murdered, and I sat down on the ground, beating my fists on the hard earth, and howled like a mad dog.

CHAPTER 15

The Bitter Winter of 1943

If only I could have spared my mother the news of Herzl's death. It was very hard, harder surely for my mother, who had lost her children one by one, than for me. My heart ached for Herzl but ached still more for my mother.

She had heard me out, then sat down in a corner near the stove, quiet in her grief. I left her alone because I felt she wished that, and took my own sorrow with me. She sat for a long time. I couldn't bear her loneliness, and once in a while I would go over and hug her, trying to let her know how much I needed her, and how I wanted her to try to live for me. I was afraid that she would give up. I watched her constantly. She still had me; and I loved her very much.

Then one morning, two weeks later, I awoke to see my mother standing near the stove and talking with Basia's mother. I could see the tears running down her cheeks and realized that Mother was trying to come back to life. I wanted to get up and kiss her, I was so relieved, but instinctively felt that this was not the right moment. It seemed to me that talking to a friend, another mother, was what she needed right then.

Now that it appeared my mother would be all right, I could really begin to think about our plans for survival. I needed to find work and earn food, or beg for it if I had to. Our hardest struggle would be to survive the winter months. For one thing, my working schedule would have to be changed. There was no work in the fields, and I could not be seen in the village during the day. This meant working in the evenings.

I was hoping to find villagers who needed help with household chores. I would have to approach them at their homes, not off in some isolated field as I did in summer. This increased the risk for anyone who might be willing to help me, and as I soon found out, there were many who refused. As I had dreaded, I was forced to beg. And even this provided barely enough for us to live on. Only around Christmas-time did the farmers become a little generous—or maybe it was the homemade vodka that warmed their spirit of giving. Sometimes I would get several slices of bread, or a handful of potatoes. Once I even received a slice of pork fat from a farmer for whom I had worked in the summer. That was a real luxury for me. I offered a piece of the pork fat to my mother, but she refused it. Either she did not want to break the kosher laws and eat pork, or she felt I needed the fat to build up my strength. I offered some to Wujciu, and he was delighted with it.

Something besides Christmas cheer was affecting the Polish farmers. While I didn't have much opportunity to hear news of the war, I could sense that something was happening. For one thing, the Ukrainian Banderovcy were stepping up their activities in the Polish villages. I overheard one farmer say to his wife that the Banderovcy used a slogan, difficult to translate from Ukrainian, the gist of which was, "With the Jews we will begin, and with the Poles we will finish. We will eliminate them all from our free Ukraine!" I sensed that with their own homes burning and their families suffering, some of the Polish farmers began to realize that they were next in line. Perhaps they thought it would be better if a few Jews at least survived to occupy the Nazis and the Ukrainians. Maybe those who had betrayed Jewish families were considering this threat to be their judgment. I didn't dwell on it very much. I was too cold and much too hungry.

I learned something else that month, something that may have been happening for quite a while and which, indirectly, was probably helping me.

Early one morning, as I was walking alongside a bush-bordered ravine, I heard voices coming from up ahead, from inside the ravine. I was more than startled; I had never met anyone in the ravines, never. And at this hour? There I was on the other side of the bushes, out in the open. My heart nearly stopped beating when I realized that the language I was hearing was not Polish or Ukrainian but sounded like German. I started shaking, and not from the cold. Germans waiting for me? Had they been alerted to my presence by some farmer, perhaps even by those at the farm I had just left?

Although my heart was now racing from fright, I knew I had to try to hear what they were saying. I needed to know if they had discovered Wujciu's house. So I crept closer and strained to hear. It was then that I realized the language wasn't German at all but something very close to it. It was Yiddish, the language spoken by most of the Polish Jews: Yiddish sounds like German because it originated in Germany in medieval times.

I couldn't believe what I was hearing. Yiddish out here? And the voices were all male. I plunged through the bushes and snow into the ravine, where six guns were trained on me. "I am a Jew," I blurted out, trying not to panic.

"I am a Jew," I repeated again, looking from face to face, making contact with each pair of eyes. When I reached the fourth face, I gasped.

"Ozio Fried?" I cried. "Don't you remember me? I am Alicia Jurman!"

The young man's eyes widened. "Oh, my God," he cried out. "This is the sister of Zachary Jurman! Alicia, little Alicia; I can't believe it."

"Ozio, I can't believe it is you standing here. I thought you were Germans. Where did you get those guns? What are you doing here?" My questions poured out; I felt the kind of excitement one experiences after a taste of danger.

"Hey, wait, Alicia; stop talking!"

Ozio introduced me to his companions, none of whom I knew or who knew me but all of whom seemed to know my brother's name. They told me that they were partisans and that they were patrolling the area. But why, I wanted to know. There were no Germans here. No, not for Germans, they said, for Ukrainians; to protect the Polish villages.

I couldn't believe what I was hearing.

"You are protecting the Poles?" What an ironic turn of events! First they helped the Germans kill us, now we were protecting them.

"Yes," Ozio continued, "we protect them and, in turn, they protect us. We have barns to sleep in and food to eat. These people are terrified of the Banderovcy and, when the Banderovcy hear that there are partisans in the area, with all their bravery, they think twice before burning farms."

"So you see, my dear Alicia," he said with a twisted smile. "The Poles now need us; and we need a way to stay alive until the war ends."

Ozio wanted to know about my family, and I told him about my mother and that several other people were hiding in this area. I did not mention Wujciu.

"Ozio, you will watch over Wujciechovka, won't you?" I asked.

Another of the men called out, "Will they feed us?" and we all laughed. It was good to laugh, good to share even a bitter joke with my own people. It felt wonderful.

I gave two of my potatoes to the fellows. They didn't want to accept them, but I insisted and then said good-bye. They were in a hurry to reach their destination, and so was I. I never met those brave young partisans again. But I often dreamed about them and seeing my brother Zachary among them, he who was among the first of the youth in our town to fight the Germans and the Ukrainians.

I know that Ozio, at least, survived the war; he eventually immigrated to the United States and rebuilt his life in New York City.

I told no one except my mother about my meeting with the Jewish partisans. If we were caught, the Germans would question us about other Jews, and it was better to keep it a secret. I must say I was tempted, because it would have raised the low spirits of the people at Wujciu's, including Wujciu himself. By this time we sorely needed some cheerful news.

One evening I was waiting in a barn in Wujciechovka for the farmer to come and milk the cows; I was hoping to get some work or at least something to eat. But, instead of a farmer, a young girl carrying a lantern entered the barn. She was the most beautiful girl I had seen in a long time and, as she was illuminated by the glow of her lantern, I involuntarily stepped back in awe at her appearance. She was a very slender blond girl. I guessed her age to be about eighteen. She wore wide blue ribbons twisted through her braided hair, with the loose ends bound with lovely bows. Unlike other village girls, who wore rough linens for daily chores, this girl was wearing a beautiful white blouse with colorful embroidery on the sleeves and down the front. She was singing a harvester's song to herself in a clear pure soprano voice, a song I had learned during the summer. Without thinking, I caught the tune and began to sing along.

With the echoes that abound naturally in a barn, the girl didn't hear me until she paused a moment while I continued singing alone. She jumped.

"Who is there?" she cried. "Who is it there?"

I stepped up to her quickly. "I am sorry," I said. "I am very sorry; I didn't mean to frighten you. It is just me."

She quickly crossed herself. "You startled me," she said accusingly.

"I didn't mean to," I said. "I came to ask for work, but you are so beautiful, and you sing like an angel. I couldn't help but sing along with you."

She laughed with embarrassment; then, not saying another word, she picked up a bucket and went over to the cows. I took a bucket and followed her. We washed our hands, wiped them on a towel, and as we began to milk, we continued to hum the harvest song together. After the milking I took the hayfork and changed the straw under the cows while she fed grain to the horses. She picked up a sack of corn and smilingly motioned with her hand that I should follow.

We went into the house, first into a small room, where she set down the corn and the milk, then into a large room that was the main living and sleeping area. It was a lovely room. Against the wall was a large bed with a hand-embroidered cover and large feather pillows. Across the room, under the two windows facing the street, stood a wide wooden bench that doubled as a second bed. Near the stove-oven was a wooden table with four chairs, and nearby stood a spinning wheel and a basket of combed flax waiting to be spun into linen thread. All this I saw by the light of an oil lamp on the table.

I sat at the table and began husking the corn for the chickens while the girl prepared supper.

"I am Manka," she said, smiling. "What is your name?"

"Helka."

"Oh, you are the Jewish girl," she said in a matter-of-fact way, and I could detect no meanness in her voice as she said it. I gasped.

"How did you know that?" I asked stupidly.

"Oh, everyone in Wujciechovka knows about Helka, who works so hard in the fields." Seeing my worried expression, she added: "Oh, I don't think anyone here would betray you; you are much too hard a worker. Besides, everyone assumes you will freeze to death in the winter anyway."

While we were talking, a young man came in carrying a saddle, and, a step behind, an older man. I kept my head inclined over the corn but studied both of the men from the corner of my eye. The younger one—her husband?—walked with a limp. He set the saddle down on the floor near the door and joined the older man, who was washing his hands in a pan. When they were finished, Manka motioned them both over to the table.

"Papa, Stach," she said, "this is Helka. Helka, meet my father and brother."

"I am pleased to meet you," I said, bowing my head and body in kind of a sitting curtsy, thinking that this was the first time in years I had practiced the social manners that I had learned at home. The two men seemed pleased and slightly amused, judging from the looks on their faces. Manka announced that she had invited me for supper and, though I held my breath in anticipation, there were no objections.

We ate potatoes with soft white cheese that night. Manka had set a bowl of potatoes in the center of the table, and we each had a plate. The four of us sat around the table, and one by one took a potato. We picked them up with our fingers, and each took and ate only one at a time before reaching for another. I was fanished as usual; but I ate slowly and gracefully, and tried not to take a potato before my turn came. All that food on the table and more on the stove if we wanted it—would I ever have that again? Would I be hungry the rest of my life?

The evening had been filled with bittersweetness for me; it reminded me of my own happy home, the memories of which stabbed me like a knife. I walked over to the window and looked out at the snow on the ground. The scene outside was so peaceful, so serene, and, what with the warmth of the house and the low voices in conversation behind me, I was moved to tears.

Suddenly I felt a gentle hand on my shoulder and turned to find Manka's father standing next to me. He smiled and wiped the tears from my cheeks with his thumb, then led me back to a chair that had been pulled up next to the bench.

"Let me speak candidly," he said after we sat down. His voice was gentle, not to be feared.

"We know about your unfortunate situation, and we feel very sorry for you. If we could find a way for you to stay here with us, believe me, that way would be found. But, Helka dear, we live in the middle of the village, not out on an isolated farm. People around here know I have only one daughter, and what would they think if her hair were to suddenly change color?" He tugged playfully at one of my braids. This simple fatherly gesture nearly sent me into another flood of tears.

"Even though we can't ask you to stay with us, we want you to know that you are welcome in our home. We ask that you be very careful when you come here and that you separate your visits by several days. As you can see, my son has a bad leg, and we rely on Manka for so many chores. We can always use an extra hand, especially such hardworking hands as yours."

I blushed and looked down at the hands folded in my lap. I then looked at Manka. She smiled at me. Her brother, Stach, listened quietly, and I sensed no hostility from him. Their father ended his kind speech by saying I was welcome to spend the night in the spare room, but I must be sure to be out before four in the morning, when the village awoke. I thanked him profusely for his hospitality, also looking at both Manka and Stach, and promised I would never bring danger to their home.

I was the first one up the next morning. Manka had prepared a small bundle for me: a few slices of bread and a cooked potato left over from the night before. I hurried home to Wujciu's.

Encouraged by Manka's friendship and because I needed to earn food, I decided to visit an older couple whose farm was in a nearby Ukrainian village. I had worked for them several times during the summer and, although they might have guessed who I really was, they didn't seem to mind as long as I worked hard in their field. They told me that if I ever came to their village I should visit their house and they would give me food.

I was hesitating about going into a Ukrainian village, and thought about it all Saturday night. When I awoke to a bright Sunday morning, I decided to visit the farm. I had to time my arrival at the village so that most people would be in church and the roads would be empty.

Moving as quietly as possible so as not to disturb the sleeping people on the floor, I washed my face with cold water, combed and braided my hair, put on my blanket skirt, and wrapped rags around my feet before slipping them into my already too small wooden-soled shoes. Before leaving I picked up the small bundle I had made the night before—two roundish stones the size of eggs wrapped in a kerchief. They were part of the story I planned to tell anyone, if necessary; I was on my way to the village to see the Wrozka, a sort of witch-charmer, to seek help for my mother, who was about to have a baby and was not feeling too well. This story would go well with the superstitious Ukrainians, I knew. Almost every village had some kind of charmer who could cast favorable (or unfavorable) spells, predict the future, or provide charms for a price. My payment would be the make-believe eggs.

This particular village was to the east; I figured a good two hours' walk from Wujciu's, and I was in a hurry to get started. But before leaving the kitchen to go out, I stopped and turned to look at my mother. This had become a habit with me, for even considering the comparative safety of Wujciu's home, I could never be sure that I would see her again. I could be caught or they could be discovered. Indeed, I never left the house without feeling that I might be looking at my dear mother for the last time. Those partings always made me very unhappy; and I was just as glad my mother didn't wake up to see me go.

I wrapped Slavka's woolen scarf tightly around my head and over my nose and throat, put on the jacket, and left, closing the door quietly behind me.

It was a beautiful morning. For all the discomfort it brought, I really loved the snow. It made everything look so peaceful and fairy-tale-like, particularly when the sun was first coming out and the reflections made the ice crystals look like thousands of tiny glittering diamonds. Snow had fallen the previous night, but not enough to cover the sleigh marks on the roads connecting the villages. At this time of day, and especially because it was Sunday, the roads were deserted. As I walked I could hear sleighbells in the distance. People were traveling to church. Thus absorbed in the beauty of the morning and caught up in a kind of dreamlike state, I did not hear the approach of a sleigh until it was almost upon me. I moved over to let it pass. I was prepared to call out my greetings as the sleigh and its occupants passed me, but I choked on my words. There, leaving me behind but slowing down to have a better look at me, was a sleigh full of blue-uniformed men: Ukrainian police.

I felt as though I had been kicked in the stomach. I had to think quickly before they realized that I had no business being on this road on a Sunday morning dressed in rather shabby clothing; they might get suspicious and ask questions. I had to do something.

"Wait!" I cried. "Wait a minute, will you?" Waving both arms, I rushed forward to the sleigh, now slowing to a stop. "Can you give me a ride into the village ahead of us?" I asked while pulling my shawl over my face.

"I am on my way to see the Wrozka. My mother is in labor and having a hard time and my father sent me to get her blessing. Can you help?" I asked, almost crying. I must have sounded convincing to them, because one of them answered.

"You are in luck. I'm from the village, and I know just where she lives. Climb in; we will take you right to her door."

As arms reached out to help me into the sleigh, a shudder passed through my body. For a fleeting moment I saw the madness of my situation. They, thinking me a Ukrainian girl, treated me nicely. They pulled part of the blanket from their knees to my back. Then the fear set in. I remembered another ride on a sleigh, to the prison in Chortkov, and now I really shivered. Although I was able to control my body, I was trembling inside all the time.

It took about twenty minutes to get to the village. The policemen drove me through the village right to the door of a mud house. I thanked them profusely, keeping my head bowed, and one of them patted me on the back and offered words of encouragement about my mother's welfare. They were in a merry mood. I was hoping they would pull away at that point, but they remained to see that I got safely inside the house. So I had no other choice but to knock on the door.

The door was opened by an old woman with long gray hair. She was a homely old woman, missing all her teeth. She really looked like the pictures of "wicked witches" in children's books. I must admit she scared me. I had never before seen one of these women, and looking at her now, it occurred to me that she might be able to see right through my lies and might immediately know who I was. Yet there I stood, clutching my little kerchief with the two round rocks, explaining my mother's supposed problem to her. She gave me one long, piercing look and invited me inside.

There was only one large open room, dark except for the glow of a fireplace. It was an eerie room, and the floor looked as though it had not been swept in quite some time. The woman asked me to sit on a chair by the fireplace, where a large kettle was suspended.

I felt strangely fascinated and curious as I was plunged into an atmosphere of sorcery and dark magic. The woman bustled about the room, her long, raggedy skirt sweeping up little clouds of unswept dust as she searched her shelves for certain herb jars.

"What is your name, my dear?" she asked.

"Slavka," I said timidly.

"And your mother's?"

"Maria." She nodded thoughtfully and spilled a number of different herbs onto the little workbench. She chopped them all together and carried the mixture over to the kettle, which was already steaming. Solemnly she threw the herbs into the bubbling liquid, causing it to give off a mighty hiss and a foul smell. She stirred the kettle with a long wooden spoon. Then, dipping a red rag into the pot, she sprinkled the brew first into the fire, mumbling something as she did so, and then onto me. I wanted to run out of that crazy place, but I remembered the Ukrainian police who might still be outside, so I dropped back into the chair and tried not to breathe in the foul odor. She repeated the sprinkling motion two more times, first on the fire, then on me, redipping the red cloth each time.

"You and your mother shall be blessed," she said.

"God will protect you from all evil men. From vicious animals, bad spirits, and especially"—this last part she drew out dramatically—"from Jews."

Inwardly I gasped, but outwardly my reaction was little more than a slight widening of my eyes. My appreciation for a good joke nearly got the better of me as I fought off the giggles.

"Oh, thank you," I said, stifling the insane laughter welling inside of me.

"Let me pay you for your trouble." I reached for my little bundle and undid the kerchief. This called for a feat of bluffing and acting that would top even the performance given by my hostess. I revealed the two round stones.

"Oh, no!" I cried. "Oh, no! Look what my little brother has done! That bad boy had exchanged my eggs for these stones." I looked at her in horror.

"After the great good you have done me, to not be able to pay you properly. . . . He will get a beating for this, I will see to that!"

The old woman smiled benevolently. "Little brothers can be demons," she said.

"Come back tomorrow with the eggs, or a little flour, perhaps."

"Oh, thank you so much," I said. I was about to start feeling sorry for her and ashamed for what I had done, when I remembered how she had classified the Jewish people with vicious animals and bad spirits. I picked up my kerchief from the chair, mumbled something, walked to the door, and quickly closed it behind me.

I was afraid to meet the Ukrainian policemen again, so I hid in a wooden shack behind the Wrozkas' hut until it was dark, and then found my way back to Wujciu's.

The following Sunday I was back at Manka's. It had been two weeks since my first visit. Manka's father was in the barn milking the cows when I arrived, and he welcomed me cheerfully. I offered to help with the milking, but he said no, that this was his Sunday chore, and that I would be warmer and happier in the house with Manka. When I came in she was preparing breakfast. Stach was there too. Their father came in a few minutes later, and we sat down to a breakfast of corn cereal with sour milk. Then I helped clear the table and washed the dishes while Stach and his father prepared for church.

I watched Manka as she dressed. She was such a pretty girl, and in her Sunday best she looked even more like an angel than the first time I had seen her. She put on a gorgeous embroidered blouse that had once belonged to her mother and a blue skirt, over which she tied a white apron that was also embroidered and trimmed in lace. Finally she twisted her long blond braids into a crown at the back of her head and fastened them securely. Then she brought out a little bundle in a piece of linen and unwrapped it to reveal an exquisite crown of silk ribbons and flowers, formed to fit the head, with the ribbons streaming downward in bright colors. I gasped when I saw it; it was so beautiful and dainty. Manka, seeing my reaction, did a very sweet and unselfish thing.

"Would you like to try it on, Helka?" she asked.

My eyes went quickly from the lovely crown to Manka, but looking at the ground, I said, "Oh, no, thank you, but I couldn't."

"Why, of course you can," she insisted. "Let's see. First we need to arrange your hair."

She sat me down in front of the mirror, quickly undid my braids, and brushed my hair thoroughly. Then she rebraided it tightly, and twisting the braids around and around, arranged them into a crown of hair like her own. The luxury of having someone fuss over me after so long was thrilling, almost like a dream. Manka found two extra hairpins to secure my hair.

"You can keep these if you like," she said. Then she reached for the crown of ribbons and pinned it lightly over my coiled braids.

"There," she said proudly, "you look just like a princess now."

I looked at myself in the mirror and blushed deeply. For the first time since I could remember, I felt pretty. At this moment I could see myself wearing embroidered blouses and ribbons in my hair, and the reflection in the mirror showed my eyes filled with such longing that I had to look away. I think Manka must have sensed my feelings, because she reached out both hands and rested them on my shoulders, giving them a slight pat, and then with one hand lifted my face. We watched our reflections in the mirror together, not speaking.

There was a knock on the door.

"Manka, are you ready?" It was Manka's girlfriend. Manka and I exchanged startled looks, and she motioned me to the side room, following as I hurried in.

"Stay here," she whispered. "I will be right back after church, and we can spend the day together. You won't have to leave until after suppertime. Oh! My crown . . ."

"Take it quickly," I whispered back. "Don't keep your friend waiting." She pulled out the pins and unfastened the crown.

"I'm coming, Franka, I'm coming," she called. "Just let me do one more thing." She quickly pinned the crown to her hair. "Does it look all right?" she asked in a whisper.

"Perfect," I said. She hurried to the door but then stopped, and I could see she was troubled. "Helka . . ." she began softly.

"Go, don't keep your friend waiting," I said. "I will see you later."

"Don't leave," she said, smiling sadly. Then she turned and was gone. For a moment I wondered why Manka was so kind to me, but I could sense that she was beautiful inside as well as outside. I couldn't imagine her being unkind to anyone.

Lying there on the cot in that tiny room, I realized that I couldn't remember when I last had a day like this. I didn't have to get up before dawn to go to work, or at night to work and beg. What indulgence! I thought of the past summer of being dragged through the corn field by cows, of spending hours soaking my feet in cold streams to pull out splinters, of swinging sickles until my arms seemed pulled out of their sockets, and digging potatoes until my back ached. I deserved a day off; yes, I did. I was not going to feel guilty over it. And with that thought I rolled over and indulged myself in what was, for me, an unthinkable luxury: I took a nap on a bed.

I must have been asleep for about an hour, when I awoke with a start, studdenly aware of the presence of another person in the room. I sat up. There, framed in the door, stood a young man, not too tall, dark-haired, and slender, in his late twenties.

"Stach is not here?" he asked.

I shook my head, trying to find the right words. "Church" was all I could think to say.

"Ah"—he nodded—"I should have known. It is Sunday. I have come to check his leg." Then suddenly he raised his hand and pointed at me.

"You know . . ."

I tensed. Was he going to ask who I was? He stepped forward wordlessly, pointing his finger accusingly. I prepared to run. One more step and I would bolt off the bench, knock him down, and head for the door. Because of my weakened lungs, I was not such a good long distance runner, but when desperate, I was a great sprinter. But then he spoke, looking worried. "You don't look good." It took me a moment to understand what he meant, and then I did.

"Well," I said, "that is what a diet of cold air will do for you." He laughed.

"I am David," he said, extending his hand to be shaken. "You must be Helka. Stach mentioned you."

I shook his hand and looked at him more closely.

"You're a Jew, aren't you?" I said, more as a statement than a question. He nodded.

"But what are you doing here in Wujciechovka?" I immediately realized what a stupid question that was.

"The same as you, trying to survive. What else?"

I got out of the bench, put down the wooden cover, and motioned with my hand for David to sit down. I liked him right away and apparently he liked me as well, because in minutes we were talking together like old friends. He told me that he came originally from Krakov, where he had studied medicine. When the Germans occupied Krakov in 1939, he escaped to the Russian side of Poland and stayed with relatives in Lvov until the Germans arrived in 1941. He lost all of his family and, like ourselves, driven by the madness of the Nazis in a mad war, he wandered from place to place until he reached Wujciechovka. He suddenly became very sad, so I quickly changed the subject.

"And how did you meet Stach?" I asked.

"I was fortunate to find a Polish family with eight children. Their farm is somewhat isolated from the village, so they took me in as sort of live-in doctor and teacher."

"But how did you meet Stach?"

"I saw him one day from my hiding place in the barn, when he was walking in the backyard. He was limping badly and seemed to be in a lot of pain. That same night I spoke to my benefactor about Stach and offered to have a look at his leg."

"And . . ." I kept encouraging him. I was interested in his story.

"It was a bullet wound. He had been shot in the knee."

"By whom?" I asked, suddenly feeling worried.

"Well that, curious miss, is a professional secret, but you can ask Manka. Maybe she will tell you."

Of course I wouldn't ask Manka; but I did find out about Stach later, from a most unlikely source—our own very dear Wujciu. The incident was such a great scandal that it even reached Wujciu's ears. Stach, as a young man of twenty, fell in love with a married Ukrainian woman whose husband was serving in the Soviet army. The woman had a baby boy, fathered by Stach. When the husband came home on leave and found out what had happened, he tried to kill Stach. Fortunately he escaped with only a leg wound. But the episode had left him a very unhappy young man.

David and I continued to talk in the little room until the family came back from church. I had a chance to tell him a little about myself.

When the family returned, I could see that Stach was very glad to see David, judging from the way they shook hands. They immediately disappeared into the little room and I tagged along behind Manka like a kid sister as she changed into her everyday clothes and began to fix lunch. I was to have three meals that day, think of it! I, who had managed on a slice of bread or a potato a day. It was a piece of heaven, that day at Manka's.

I helped her with the evening chores, and after supper she offered to teach me to spin linen thread. I was enthusiastic; this would give me yet another skill to use when begging for work. I mastered the technique quickly enough, but I also painfully learned why it is so important to clean the flax thoroughly before spinning it. Little splintery fragments of stem and stalk hide in the flax and, as you pump the wheel and the fibers run through your fingers, a splinter could lodge in your skin. Manka only laughed when this happened to me. She showed me her own hands, which were callused from the very tips of her fingers all the way down to the palms.

Before I left that evening, Manka gave me a small bundle of food and kissed me lightly on the cheek. I felt an emotion I hadn't experienced in a long time, a kind of gladness, and even a measure of happiness. The chilly night air made me tingle with a wonderful sense of being alive, and I realized while walking home that there might be another goal to survival besides seeking revenge on the Germans and their collaborators. I realized that someday I might be able to live without fear and without hunger. I might be able to walk freely, wear pretty things, put ribbons in my hair, and wear an embroidered blouse. Someday girl- and boyfriends would stop at my door. And, as I walked home that clear winter night, the stars seemed to twinkle just for me, like diamonds in the sky.

When I arrived at Wujciu's and opened the bundle, I found that as a wrapper, Manka had given me a pretty white blouse.

I was wearing that very blouse three nights later, when the luck of our little household seemed to run out.

When I look back on what happened, I marvel that I was even home that night. I tried to spend the nights in barns whenever I could, so that I could ask for work from the farmer in the early morning, thus saving me a walk in the cold snow in the dark. But on this particular night, for no special reason, I decided to stay home. I had warmed up a pot of water, and Basia helped me wash my hair while we talked. After washing my hair I toweled it dry, combed it, pinned it up on the sides with the pins Manka had given me, and let it hang loose to dry. With the remaining water I sponged my whole body behind a blanket Basia held up in front of me. I felt really clean. We were settling down for the night, Wujciu nearest the stove for warmth, and the others all over the floor. I lingered near the stove for a while, waiting for my hair to dry before braiding it for the night.

Suddenly there was a pounding on the door. "Open up, you damned Jews!" we heard a voice shout in Ukrainian. "We know you are there! Open up or we will break in the door! We know you are there!"

Inside the kitchen all movement froze, then burst into a sort of frenzy. By mutual agreement, and without words, we all got up and moved to the storage room which was filled with cut straw. Our first reaction was to climb under the straw and hide, to dig in and just disappear into it, and I even suggested in a moment of panic that Basia cover me; but I immediately realized how ridiculous that idea was. In the meantime, there was renewed pounding on the door. I saw only one way to handle the situation.

I went up to my mother, touched her hand briefly, opened the storage door, and closed it gently behind me. I stood for a second in front of the outside door, my heart pounding so wildly that I thought it was trying to escape from my body. With one quick movement I opened the door. A gust of cold air came in, followed by several men, one of them holding an oil lamp high above his head. They were young men, six or seven of them, some wearing blue caps of the hated Banderovcy. One stomped up to me, his eyes blazing.

"All right, you," he said. "Where are you hiding the Jews?" I stared at him, saying nothing. He reached out his hand and was about to push me aside, when another voice spoke.

"Slavka!"

I couldn't believe it. There, coming through the doorway, was Pietro, with whom I had worked when harvesting his family's fields. We stared at each other in shocked silence. In a voice mixed with amazement and outrage, he cried, "What are you doing here with the Jews?"

I swallowed, then spoke calmly but strongly.

"What do you mean, Pietro? You want to know what I am doing with Jews? I am a Jew!"

His mouth dropped open. There was complete silence. I held my head high and proud.

"Have you come to take us to the police, or will you just kill us outside? Why? Because we are Jews?"

I suddenly felt the fear leave me and a cold anger surge through me.

"Yes, Pietro," I said, looking straight at him. "I am a Jew, and I have a right to live, just like you.

"Do you know how old I am, Pietro? Not yet fourteen. I am just beginning to live, and am doing everything to stay alive because, like you, I love life. My heart is breaking to see that you would commit such a crime as killing innocent women and children. You are all young . . ." I motioned to the others, looking quickly from face to face. "Someday you will marry. Someday you will have children my age and then"—I paused—"then you will know what it is to live in fear, because I will curse you all for what you do here tonight!"

I glared at them, my fists clenched, words coming effortlessly from my mouth. "There will come a time when you will know my curse. I swear in the name of my God and yours, I will haunt you from my grave. You won't know a day's happiness, any of you!"

I paused for a moment, looking at Pietro. I saw something in his eyes that stopped me from saying anything more. Suddenly Pietro turned to his friends, motioned them out, and gently closed the door behind him. I stood there rooted to the floor and listened as the sleighs pulled away. A minute later the last sounds of their departure faded away.

I opened the door to the storage room. Everyone was sitting motionless on the straw.

"They are gone," I could barely whisper as my body began to shake. My mother took me in her arms and held me tightly, telling me that they had heard everything that was said.

We decided to leave Wujciu's for the night in case Pietro and his friends got drunk and came back for us. We all separated, going into different barns. Before leaving I told Sarah where she could go for shelter, and where the dogs might be tied up for the night. Basia and her family knew some farmers, and they went there. I wanted to take Wujciu with us, but he insisted that the men would not harm him if they returned; so he stayed home. Mama and I spent a terrible night huddling together in the straw near the cows and then, before daylight, we returned to Wujciu's. We had no choice but to return and hope that what I had said to Pietro and his friends left a lasting impression. Our only other alternative was to freeze to death.

January 1944 was a long and exhausting month for me, physically as well as emotionally. I lived with cold fear for days following the attack on Wujciu's house. I often stayed out at night, listening for any approaching sleighbells and going into the house only when I couldn't stand the cold anymore. When I finally went back to my old routine, something else happened that nearly shattered me.

It all started routinely enough, with my everyday search for food. I had waited until dark, as usual, to approach the farmhouse. This time I decided to try a house where I had been given food once before. Even though this was a Ukrainian village, I had to try. Lately many of the farmers just chased me away before I even had a chance to say a word. Everyone seemed to be nervous. As much as I hated to go into a Ukrainian village, I rationalized that I was going to see someone I knew already. I had worked for the farmer during the summer, and he had been nice to me when I visited him in November.

I hurried to reach the farm before milking time and visited with the cows, talking gently and stroking their sides. Then I went to sit in the straw to wait for the arrival of the farmer. I noticed that the straw had been piled, not directly against the back wall, but about five feet in front of it, so that from the front of the barn it looked as though the straw were actually piled against the wall.

It was while studying this wall, trying to understand the mystery of the straw, that I noticed a narrow line of light along the floor. There was a door there; now I could make it out—a hidden door, only about four feet high. My curiosity was aroused and, since it was still a few minutes before the expected arrival of the farmer, I pushed the door open and crawled inside.

It was a small room, more narrow and tall than wide, with no windows. The only light came from an oil lamp in one corner. Sitting by the lamp, unaware of my presence, was a man with wire-rimmed glasses pulled down low on his nose. He was bent over a piece of animal fur, stitching away with a needle and thread. I cleared my throat.

"Good evening," I said. The poor man started so violently at the sound of my voice that the narrow stool on which he was seated toppled over backward. I rushed up to help him, but he shrank back, shaking with fear.

He then righted the little stool and sat down, pulling the fur over his knees.

"Please don't tell anyone you have seen me here. I beg of you." The way he said it, and the way he rolled his R sort of lightly and not deeply the way the Ukrainians do, made it easy for me to identify him.

"Don't be afraid," I reassured him. "I would never bring you any harm. I am also a Jew." The man shrunk back and eyed me suspiciously. Then his voice turned angry.

"How dare you frighten me so," he said gruffly as he pulled his glasses over his nose. I could sense his embarrassment over having humiliated himself, and needlessly, too, in front of a mere child.

"I am sorry," I said. "I saw the light under the door."

"And how have you survived so long, with your apparent curiosity?" he asked as he picked up his needle and started working again on the fur.

"By my wits," I said smartly. His rudeness was beginning to offend me.

"Look," I said, "let's not be so harsh with each other. How often do you find a friend in these parts?"

"You want to be my friend?" he snorted. "Then don't come around here anymore. Don't attract any attention to me. I have already been in one massacre, for your information, and I hope to avoid any more."

"I have been through a massacre too," I said. "Outside

Kopechince. We were thrown into huge pits. They used machine guns and rifle butts to kill us, and some were even buried alive. I barely escaped." Hearing this, the man softened a little.

"I was hit in the back of this thigh," he said, rubbing high on his leg. "I thought the pain alone would kill me, but I kept running." He fell silent for a moment, and I could see from the look in his eyes that he was reliving the horrible experience.

"Where did all this happen to you?" I asked.

"In Buczacz."

In Buczacz, in Buczacz. I kept repeating the name to myself, suddenly feeling cold.

"Did you always sew furs together like this?"

"No." He smiled crookedly. "I owned a big shop where over a dozen people worked for me. You would think that I should have known better than to go out that day."

My mind was putting all he said together, and memories were coming back to me, but I had to ask him one more thing. I was praying silently for courage to ask this man one special question.

"Are you referring to the day when you went to register after the Germans occupied Buczacz? Did you go with other men, about six hundred of them?" My heart was pounding, waiting for his answer.

"Yes, I went to register." He spoke bitterly. "They took us into prison cells and early the following morning they marched us to the Fador. Enough!" he said, his voice breaking. "I escaped, as you can see."

"Who else escaped?" I asked softly, fearfully. He only shook his head.

"No one," he said. "No one but me." He grew silent seeing the scene, remembering that horrible day. Then: "There was one man that I thought would make it," he said. "He was standing right near me. The German told him to run, but a Ukrainian policeman shot him in the back." He shook his head.

"The poor man," I said sadly. He nodded.

"He had such a good chance. The German, seeing his medal for bravery from the Austrian emperor Franz Joseph, was impressed enough to let him escape, but the Ukrainian shot him."

At the words "medal for bravery" my mouth went suddenly dry. I forced myself to speak. I had to.

"What did the man who ran look like?" I asked.

He threw up his hands. "Who can remember? He was a nice-looking man. Blond? No, reddish-blond hair. Tall, sort of military bearing. I don't know. By that time I was running myself. Then I, too, was shot; but I kept running. Oh, yes, I kept running. But now I can't run so well anymore."

He stood up and walked a few feet, and I could see that it was a major effort to drag his stiff leg behind him.

"So," he continued, "somehow I made it this far. I have given everything I own to these people to hide me—and look!" He picked up the scrap of fur. "I have promised the wife a fur jacket."

I had started trembling because I knew that the man who had tried to escape from the massacre was my father. I felt the room becoming very small, very close, with almost no air. I had to get out of there.

"I am sorry I frightened you," I mumbled. "I will tell no one I have seen you."

"Stay awhile," he said. "To tell you the truth, I am glad for company."

"No, no. I can't. I must leave." I hurried through the low door.

Back in the barn I tried to compose myself, hoping that my trembling would stop. I was so dazed, stunned by what I had just heard, that I didn't even bother to crouch down behind the straw. A woman who had come to milk the cows saw me and gasped.

"What are you doing here?" she cried. It seemed as though I were looking at her from under water. Her image seemed distorted, kind of blurred, and the voice seemed to come at me in a long, slow waver. Finally I was able to pull myself together.

"Don't you remember me?" I asked. "I am Slavka from the fields. I worked for you during the summer. I was here in November, and you said I could come back again. I am sorry if I frightened you. Maybe you have some work for me. I am very hungry."

The woman rubbed her hands together nervously, throwing a fleeting glance in the direction where the man was hiding.

"We have no work today," she said. "Run along." But I only stood there, trying to understand what it was she said.

"Do you have a piece of bread you could give me?" I asked. I couldn't believe I had not yet run from the barn. My legs felt weighted down, as though I were standing knee-deep in mud.

The woman eyed me nervously. "Wait here," she said, and she quickly left the barn. It crossed my mind that I should leave, but I didn't.

She returned shortly with several slices of bread—more than I would normally be given—and a jug of sour milk.

"Here," she said, pushing them into my hands.

"Take these and go. Quickly. Make sure that no one sees you and never come back again."

How I escaped from being caught that night, I will never know, since I walked through the whole village before I entered the fields. I know if I had been stopped I could have offered no explanation to save myself. My feet just plodded on, and my lips kept saying, "I have to get back to Wujciu."

The snow that had been falling most of the day had blanketed the ground evenly, covering the furrows, unturned stalks, and other reminders of the last harvest, and so I did not see the hoe. But suddenly I was facedown in the snow, the bread and jug flying in the air as I tried to break my fall with my hands. The immediate sense of falling and the shock of the snow on my face jolted me back to reality, and I looked around quickly to see what had happened to the food. The bread was scattered around me. The jug was lying on its side, spilling its milk steadily into the snow. I lunged forward and grasped it, trying to save the milk. But it was too late; only a small amount remained. I clutched the jug tightly and cried inconsolably. My father! It was my father who had tried to get away and return to us. I hugged the empty jug to me as if it were human, and cried and cried.

I don't know how long I stayed in that field. It might have been an hour or only a few minutes. But at last I was ready to start for home. I rubbed a handful of snow onto my face and wiped it with a kerchief, pressing back the tears that still threatened to flow. I examined the bread; the slices were a little damp on one side from the snow, but they would do. So with the jug in one arm and the bread inside my jacket, I continued home. It was a bitter night.

My mother sensed immediately that something was wrong.

"What is it?" she asked as I entered the house, my face pure white.

"Alicia dear, what happened?" I handed her the jug silently, my hand trembling.

"I spilled the milk, Mamusiu," I said.

She studied me intently. "There is more," she said. "Something else happened." I shook my head.

She left me alone, and I found a little corner on the floor. Sleep had always been my rescue; in times of greatest crisis I was always able to force myself to sleep, and while sleeping I refreshed myself and gained the strength to face the world again. But on this night sleep was my enemy, filled with fearful dreams. I screamed in my sleep and jerked awake to find myself drenched in perspiration, my mother bending over me, stroking my damp hair.

"Tell Mama, sweetheart," she begged. "What is troubling you so?"

I rolled over and lay my head in her lap, and she wrapped her arms around me and rocked me gently. I decided not to tell my mother what I had learned. She had suffered enough. I felt the tears building within me, but I fought them back. "I am so tired, Mama," I said wearily. "Sometimes I feel this will never end."

"It will one day. Everything that had a beginning must have an end. Besides, we must have faith. Our people have always had faith. This is what sustained us for generations: our faith and our hope." She continued to stroke my hair and, mercifully, I drifted back to sleep.

A few days later I came home to Wujciu's to find my mother and the other people in a state of subdued excitement. I could see traces of tears on my mother's face; I saw that the others had also been crying. And something else was changed in the room. Then I realized what it was. People were talking louder to one another, not in the usual whispers. Then I looked at Wujciu, and his twinkling eyes and broad smile told me that I would be hearing some good news for a change.

"Alicia," my mother said as she reached for my hand to pull me down on the floor, "I have some news to tell you.

"Wujciu came back from the village and he said that the people were talking about the Germans; that they are retreating from Russia; that the Russians are beating them in battle; and that the Russians will be coming back within a couple of months."

She repeated the words "a couple of months" as though disbelieving what she had just said, or perhaps realizing that a couple of months could be a lifetime for us. I was thinking just that. What could happen to us in a couple of months? . . .

I forced myself to show excitement at this good news. Yet I felt strangely distant from the excitement despite the smile I tried to put on my face. I simply could not get too enthusiastic. If I had not been grieving all over again for my father, if I hadn't stopped going to Manka's because I was afraid to endanger her family after Pietro's attack on us, I would have noticed that the farmers were kinder to me and didn't chase me away as often.

But a week later, when a Polish farmer and his wife welcomed me openly and warmly into their kitchen and offered not only bread and milk but a small piece of cheese, I knew something was happening. The farmer made no secret of it.

"Some friends of yours were by today," he said mysteriously, and he and his wife exchanged winks like children who knew something you didn't and delighted in teasing you about it.

I played it safe. I just smiled, and said, "Oh?"

"Yes," the man said, "partisans." I was puzzled. Was he talking about Ozio Fried and his friends? My mind worked quickly. Why was he telling me such things if this was supposed to be a secret? I felt my smile freezing on my face. "Partisans?" I said, a note of confusion in my voice.

"Russian partisans!" he said, nodding dramatically and lowering his voice.

"Russian partisans!" I cried a little too loudly, quite shaken. "Are you sure? How do you know they were Russians?"

"They told us!" he said. "About ten men came to my door wanting food and water. They told me they were Russian partisans. Why would they lie?" I could not quite believe him. The news was too good to be true.

"And," he added, "they told us the regular army won't be far behind. A month at the most, isn't that what they said, Wanda?"

His wife nodded her head. "That's right, a month at the very longest. That's what they told us."

I looked incredulously from face to face. They were so happy, those people, as though they were expecting a messiah. Whenever I thought about farmers I didn't think that they, too, might be suffering from the war. They had their daily chores; they sowed seed in the spring, weeded through the early summer, and harvested in the summer and fall. With the exception of the marauding Banderovcy, their lives seemed free of menace. They had plenty to eat. I didn't really see how their lives had been affected by the war. So it surprised me that these people were so excited about the Russians liberating their villages.

The people at Wujciu's were also very pleased with this news, but I reacted somewhat differently. What immediately went through my mind was that the Ukrainians, fearful of reprisals from the surviving Jews, might want to eliminate every last witness to their murdering and destruction. Pietro and his friends knew about our existence at Wujciu's, and that made me very apprehensive. I stayed at Wujciu's every night, hoping that my presence would somehow keep us safe. The possibility that we could be betrayed and killed just a few weeks before liberation dominated my thoughts during those days. Now that it looked as though we might survive, I had something to lose.

February passed; March came along; the snow started melting all around us. Signs of spring began to show in the meadows through the partially melted snow. Slowly the fear started melting inside me. My spirits began to lift, and the hope of being free started nourishing my soul. When I thought of freedom and trust in people, I questioned: How was one to be free of the pain of the loss of family, the tragic and total loss of those we loved so dearly? But for the time being at least, I was willing to try.

CHAPTER 16

My Mother

March 24, 1944. I will always remember that day. The morning of liberation had been like every other morning, with my getting up early to go into the village. I had already decided on the house I would be visiting; it was that of a farmer for whom I had worked in the summer. I had done good work for him, and he and his wife had already given me food twice that winter. I sensed that they knew I was Jewish, although we never discussed it. They had never been very hospitable toward me, but that would have been too much to expect. It was enough that they gave me a piece of bread now and then.

But on this particular morning the farmer not only greeted me cordially but invited me inside for breakfast. There I was, seated at the breakfast table, Polish children chattering happily around me, the wife singing to herself as she prepared breakfast, the farmer patting me on my back. It was baffling.

Then they broke the news. The Russians had arrived. "Oh, yes, it's true," they said. They had seen the soldiers that morning. They passed right by the house. The villagers had rushed out of their homes to watch the troops move by. The entire area was liberated! The fighting had moved to the west, and the soldiers assured the villagers that the Germans would soon be totally defeated. For others the war continued, but Galicia and its people were finally free.

Excitement didn't prevent me from eating as much bread as they could set in front of me, and when I left they loaded me down with a big jug of milk and two complete loaves. "Stop by the main road and see for yourself," the farmer told me. But I didn't trust the road yet; instead, I picked my way carefully across the fields. I dropped the food off at Wujciu's and then hurried back to the road, being careful to stay in the bushes, just in case.

And there they were, Russian trucks and horse-drawn sleighs moving in an endless line toward Buczacz. I hurried back to my mother. "Mama," I said, gasping for breath, "come quickly, I want to show you something."

"Alicia! What is it?"

"You'll see." I pulled her along as quickly as we could move through the snow. When the road finally came into view, my mother gasped and stared at the passing convoy. Suddenly we were laughing and crying at the same time, hugging each other and jumping up and down. "Praise God," my mother said as she wiped at her eyes. "Praise God." We hurried back to the others, and minutes later everyone was down at the road waving at the trucks and crying. Our excitement was tremendous.

That night we celebrated by opening a jar of honey and eating all the bread I had been given that morning. Wujciu was very happy. "Now you can go back to your bachelor life," I teased him. I wondered what his life would be like now. Perhaps after living eight months with a houseful of people he would welcome being alone—or perhaps he would find loneliness harder to bear. One thing was certain: his life would never again be the same.

Mother and I made immediate plans to return to Buczacz. We decided that I would go first to make sure it was truly safe to make the move back to our city; then, if I had not returned in three days, she would follow. The next morning I said good-bye to the families and Wujciu. I wrapped clean rags around my feet and slipped them carefully into the tight wooden shoes. Spring might be on its way, but there was still snow on the ground, and the air was still chilly. I went down to the road and waved down a Russian sleigh. "Are you going anywhere near Buczacz?" I asked. "It's about thirty kilometers south of here."

"Yes," said a soldier on the sleigh. "We're going right by it. Do you want a lift?"

"Please." They hauled me up into the sleigh and off we went. Along the way the soldiers confirmed what the farmer had said about Tarnopol and the retreat of the enemy. They were happy and excited, flushed with victory and ready to destroy the Germans once and for all.

I could see that the Russians hated the Germans as much as I did, and I felt an immediate bond with them.

All along the road to Buczacz people came rushing up to wave and blow kisses at the advancing army. The journey took several hours because of the convoy's slow, steady pace, but finally in the afternoon the soldiers pulled the sleigh to the side of the road just across from the Charny Most bridge on the edge of the city and helped me get out.

Suddenly I wasn't so excited about going home anymore. After all, the city really hadn't been too kind to me or to the other thousands of Jews who had lived there. We had been pointed out to the Germans and the Ukrainian policemen by our Polish neighbors, many of whom then looted our homes and stole our belongings. Now I was going back to find no home, no possessions, and, most painfully, no family. As I crossed the bridge into the city it was like walking into a fog of shock and grief. All of us, all the surviving Jews, shared this experience when we first returned to what had been our homes.

For so long every bit of thought and energy I had had gone into survival. And now, here I was a survivor, filled with a terrible sense of loss and confusion.

The streets were filled with people. There were Russian trucks everywhere; the army had wasted no time in establishing itself in town. You couldn't look down any street without seeing some sign of the Red Army. There were so many civilians on the streets that I thought there couldn't be anyone still indoors. Because so many people had changed their homes for one reason or another, the only way to find friends and relatives was to wander up and down the streets, searching for familiar faces.

I made my way to Chechego Maya Street and Slavka's house, but there was no one there; the house was empty. Just down the street was the house we had moved into when Papa recouped his fortunes. I crossed the street and passed it without looking up; I think it would have removed all traces of my sanity to see it again, knowing that new people were living there, people who may have been standing by, rubbing their hands together in anticipation as my mother and brothers and I were forced out with the few belongings we could carry on our backs. No, I couldn't be thinking about that now; there was too much to do.

I went back to the business district; I thought that it would be the best place to look for people. I recognized many faces, but most of them were Polish. There were very few Jews. I told myself it would be days, weeks, before those in hiding would come back to town; but deep down I knew that most would not be coming back at all.

As I walked up and down the streets looking at the shop windows, I tried to remember what life had been like just a few years earlier. It was almost impossible to conjure up old memories. I would say to myself, "I know this place; I've been here many times. . . ." And then there was a barrier that blocked off any other memories.

One thing I did recognize, and with a great stab of emotional pain, was a fur coat that had once belonged to my dear friend Sara Kriegel. It was now on the back of a blond Polish girl. It was strange that this memory would return to me, the memory of Sara and the beautiful coat that she received for her birthday four or five years before. All of us in Dr. Ferenhoff's class were so envious, and I remembered how Sara let us take turns trying it on after our Hebrew class. Now here was the coat, on the back of a Pole, and where was my dear friend Sara? Had someone said, "Daddy, the Kriegel girl had a most wonderful fur," and had someone's father made a trip to the police station to point out a Jewish home? I had to sit down and hold my hand over my eyes for several minutes until the young girl moved out of view. My body trembled with outrage . . . and this was only the beginning.

It was not long after seeing the coat that I found Slavka, or, rather, Slavka found me. I was heading up yet another street, not even bothering to search faces anymore but just trying to keep moving to obliterate painful memories. There were all sorts of street noises: trucks going by, people calling out to one another, children laughing as they chased each other. Slavka told me she had called out my name several times but that I didn't hear her, and I could certainly believe that. When I finally snapped out of my daze, there she was, calling my name and heading toward me, waving.

I had been looking for Slavka for hours, and now that I had found her, my first impulse was to turn and run. She had become so beautiful since we had seen each other last; and I was so tattered and skinny in my rags and too-small shoes. I think she wanted to throw her arms around my neck and hug me, but my constrained manner kept her back. As we looked into each other's eyes, discomfort hovered between us. She reached out and patted the sleeve of my coat. "I see you got the coat all right," she said. "Yes," I replied, "and the shoes and the scarf. Thank you so much." She smiled nervously and looked down the street at a sleigh passing by.

It was so painful not knowing what to say, when less than three years before we had been such close friends. I knew instinctively that I would need a base from which to begin again—a place to sleep for a few days, a place for my mother. I didn't want to have to ask a favor of Slavka. But it was most important that she invite me home with her. Luckily, she did.

The Charkovs had been in their new house on Stripa Street by the river less than a month; it had been a Jewish home, as I could tell by the faint impression on the doorpost where a mezuzah had once been displayed. On the way to Stripa Street Slavka told me that her family had moved when the war turned and it looked as though the Russians would be coming back. They had already been through one Russian occupation and remembered, as we did, that the Russians did not take too kindly to signs of wealth. The family was in a precarious position, being Ukrainian. Slavka's uncle on her mother's side was actually a Banderovic and a Ukrainian policeman. That side of the family supported Ukrainian nationalism and helped the Germans. Now that the Germans were out, all collaborators and even sympathizers would soon be feeling the anger of the Soviet forces.

But ironically, and fortunately for them, Slavka's father had a brother who had reached a high rank in the Russian army. It was this relationship, coupled with the move to a more modest dwelling, that they hoped would spare them. I did not know at that time of the atrocities that had been committed by the German army in the Soviet Union, but the Russians were wreaking vengeance on the Germans and their collaborators with a passion even greater than my own.

The house on Stripa Street was nice, not as nice as our old homes on Chechego Maya Street, but worlds better than where we had lived in the ghetto. Slavka's mother greeted me warmly, while eyeing my coat, a ghost from her closet. It felt strange to be in the home of Ukrainians, even though they were friends. For the last few years I had learned to be wary of them; now here I was a guest in their home.

If meeting Slavka had been difficult, it couldn't compare to dinner that night at her home. The family behaved as though they were afraid of me, especially Slavka's brother, Paulo. He and my brother Herzl had gone to school together and had been friends, but he might have been the friend who had betrayed Herzl. I could not bear this thought and forced myself to think of something else.

That night I made a new discovery. There I was, tossing and turning in Slavka's bed, keeping her awake with every shuffle of the covers, every change of position. It took two hours of this misery before

I realized the problem. "Slavka," I said, "do you think you could spare me a blanket? I'd like to try sleeping on the floor."

"What?" She was aghast. "But, Alicia . . ."

"Don't worry, Slavka," I said. "I know it sounds crazy, but I've slept so long on the ground and floors that I know I'll never be able to fall asleep in a bed tonight. Just spare me a blanket or quilt, and I'll be fine." And sure enough, I dozed off in less than ten minutes.

The next morning Slavka and I went to the marketplace to look for villagers from Wujciechovka. I had decided to get a message to my mother right away rather than wait for the three days as we had originally planned. I was able to get a villager to take a note to Wujciu's, and two days later my mother turned up at Slavka's door.

She had ridden in on an army truck with the other two families from Wujciu's, then separated herself from them at the Charny Most. Basia's family stayed with the truck and continued to their own city; Sarah and the children got off with Mother at the Charny Most but went from there in another direction. It had been only two days, but I had missed my mother and was glad to see her. She and Slavka's mother spoke together quietly; they had been such good friends before the war.

Now it was time to act, and Mother took the role of the leader. First she found a three-room apartment on Kolejova Street, not far from the center of town. It was also a former Jewish home, having once belonged to a friend of our family's; a dentist, now dead. She got the key from the superintendent.

There were several beds in the apartment, some cooking utensils, but no other real furnishings. We moved one bed into the kitchen near the stove for warmth at night. Somehow my mother managed to get some money, and we were able to eat. It's possible she may have borrowed from Slavka's mother, although I really didn't know. I was just glad I did not have to beg for food anymore.

Everyone—and by that I mean about two hundred and fifty Jewish survivors—was in a daze, filled with a terrible feeling of loss and pain. I remember waking up several times each night during those first days because the bed was actually shaking with my mother's silent, convulsive sobbing. I knew that she waited until after I was asleep to release her grief and longing for my father and my brothers, and so I pretended to be asleep each time this happened.

I also cried only when there was no one else around. Instinctively I knew that grieving had to be done in private; otherwise, how could we remain brave with one another as we planned for the future?

Like the other survivors, I took daily walks through the streets of Buczacz. It was on these walks that I began to recognize people I had grown up with as well as some whom I had met in the ghetto, Jews who had been transported to Buczacz by the Germans from their outlying cities and villages.

Everyone stared at everyone else, looking for something familiar, something to identify with. The clothing—a combination of peasant discards and our old city clothes—made it easy to recognize others like myself. Underweight and undernourished, we really felt the cold. Yet the realization that we could actually walk on the street and not have to look over our shoulders for fear of imprisonment and death made us bear the chill, or, more correctly, ignore it. Few stayed indoors. There were those who stood on street corners all day, staring blankly. What were they staring at? What were they thinking?

I remember passing our once-beautiful large synagogue, which had not been used for many years now, and seeing a woman leaning against the wall wailing, just crying out in agony. She looked to me like a branch dismembered from a tree, an arm without a body, a mind filled with grief, a bleeding heart, a walking tragedy. I hurried away, afraid of being swept up into her grief.

As far as I could see, very few were able to fully absorb how totally our people had been wiped out; generations and generations of innocent men, women, and children murdered. And their only crime? They had been Jews.

I don't know how it happened, but one day I found myself walking up the steps to the police station, seeking out the very room where I had been processed for death by the father of my friend Olga. Now, in the same room, prisoners were being released. Having been imprisoned by the Germans and now awaiting unknown fates, these people had to wait behind bars until the liberating Russians had time to check their criminal histories. I carefully studied the prisoners' faces. Not that I was looking for anyone. Perhaps I was trying subconsciously to rid myself of the terrible nightmares connected with this place by reliving my imprisonment. It was good to see people being set free.

I came back for several days to watch the prisoners being released. One day on the way out I happened to glance through the window into the prison yard, and saw the police burning stacks and stacks of papers that looked to me like official files. The Germans had kept careful records of all their prisoners. Was it the name of Sigmund Jurman the flames were eating up? Or Zachary Jurman? Or Bunio and Herzl Jurman? Or Alicia Jurman?

During those visits I attracted the attention of the man in charge. He was a young Pole, very handsome, and we began to talk. He told me how he had hidden his Jewish sweetheart throughout the war. They had a son who was now six months old, and soon after the city was liberated they were married. His wife's name was Salka. Every day Salka came to the prison to bring Jozek's lunch, and she often stayed, like myself, and we visited. She was a lovely young woman of about twenty-two with the saddest brown eyes I had seen since our liberation. I could imagine the events that made her eyes look like that instead of being full of laughter and joy.

I did not talk with her much, just as I didn't talk with the survivors I met on the streets. There was a feeling of embarrassment among us, a sense of guilt for having survived. Conversations were always brief. The question, "And who else?" and then heads would shake sorrowfully. We gestured with our eyes, our hands. It was difficult to utter the words. Heads turned away, tears came to the eyes; there was a constant pantomime of tragedy. One person would raise his eyebrows questioningly; the other would spread his open palms in a gesture of futility. These gestures were more powerful than words and told everything.

It was on one of my aimless morning walks that I heard my name being called out by a voice from the past. I turned, and there down the street, running toward me with his arms outstretched, was Milek! I flew toward him and threw myself into his arms. We hugged and kissed and cried for several minutes, stopping only long enough for him to introduce his friend Samuel. I shook hands with the boy, whom I vaguely remembered from our ghetto days.

I invited the two boys home to see my mother, who was thrilled to see Milek alive and well. I had told her how he saved me at the open grave. We had both been convinced that he must have been killed in the struggle. My mother invited them to move in with us, which they would have done, but Milek was leaving the following day to look for relatives and friends in his home town of Stanislavov. He promised to consider the invitation upon his return. I hated to lose him again even for a brief time, yet I knew he had to go.

Milek's sudden appearance and my realization of how deeply I loved him had been just what I needed to begin my climb out of post-liberation depression.

About two months went by; warm weather had arrived and the Jewish survivors began settling down to some semblance of normality. Still stricken with grief, they had no choice but to let events guide them into actions needed for daily survival. The flowing tears were beginning to have their curative effect, to bring back an awareness of life. It was this very awareness that made us sense something unusual. There was something in the air, a certain nervousness, particularly surrounding our liberators, the Russians. It was a feeling one couldn't quite identify, but there was definitely an element of anxiety.

Then it happened, just like that, out of nowhere! Terrible explosions were heard in the middle of the night. It was artillery, shelling in the direction of our city. Our war had begun again!

My mother and I dressed and hurried out into the street to see what was happening. We saw Russian troops moving in all directions in their panic to flee the city. In our terror we, too, wanted to flee, but where? The shelling seemed to be coming from all directions. We had no idea what to do. My God, I thought, what could have happened? The Russians on the sleigh to Buczacz had promised me that the Germans were all but beaten.

After our initial panic we had enough presence of mind to ask questions. What we gathered was that the German divisions that had been trapped in Tarnopol, some eighty kilometers northeast, had managed to break through the surrounding Russian army and were fighting their way back to Germany, right through our city, it seemed. The Germans were coming back, and from all the shooting, it sounded as though they had a strong army. It was a nightmare.

The shooting had begun about midnight, and by early morning artillery shells were exploding inside the city. We knew all too well what this meant. With the return of the Germans, our lives were once again in grave danger. Mother and I began to make our way north along Kolejova Street in the direction of the Zazamec. The Zazamec was an old castle, a remnant of the fortifications built around Buczacz in the fifteenth century.

The nearer we got to the Zazamec, the more fierce the shelling became. The noise was deafening. The roads were jammed with fleeing civilians and Russian soldiers. We pushed through a sea of humanity moving in one direction, only to reach another wave of people going the opposite way. There was a great deal of confusion; it seemed no one knew where to find safety from the invading German army.

We were very near the Zazamec, about a kilometer from our apartment, when a shell landed on the road not far from us. I remember the explosion very clearly, feeling myself thrown back by the impact, the screams coming from all around me. Several people had been hit and some killed by the exploding shell's fragments. I looked up to find my mother gripping her leg, her face contorted in pain. She had been hit in the thigh by a piece of shrapnel and was bleeding profusely. I quickly pulled her to her feet, half carried her from the road into a nearby field, and began ripping at my dress to make bandages. I wrapped her leg as tightly as I could, but she had already lost a lot of blood. Within seconds the bandages were soaked through. That was the end of our flight; our only hope now was to find shelter and plan our next move.

I helped my mother to her feet, and together we began the painful trip back to our apartment, fighting the streams of near-hysterical people flooding the streets. We were able to make it only halfway, when Mother's strength at last gave out. I pounded on the door of the nearest house. "Please," I told the frightened man who answered, "my mother has been terribly hurt. Please let us in for a while, I beg of you." Seeing my plight, he took pity on us. He reached out and took my mother's arm, gently helping her inside. We spent the remaining hours of the night in the kitchen of that home, me tightening and replacing Mother's bandages, she deathly pale and frightened but gritting her teeth against the pain.

Early the next morning there was a knock on the door, and we froze in place, fearing the worst. It was a man, a neighbor of the family. He and our benefactor spoke in hushed voices.

"Did I see you take people into your house?" he asked. "Are they Jews? Then you should be careful. When the Gestapo arrives, the first thing they'll do is look for Jews."

Even with their voices low I could hear the word "Jews" distinctly. My heart beat wildly. With the Germans back and my mother too injured to be moved, what would we do? What would happen to us now? I hugged my mother closely as I watched our benefactor and his wife go into the next room. A few moments later he entered the kitchen, and I knew before he opened his mouth what his words would be.

"I'm sorry," he said sadly. "We can't let you stay here any longer.

You know as well as I what would happen if the Germans found Jews in our home."

"Who says we are Jews?" I cried hotly, desperate to bluff a few more hours' rest for my mother. But Mother waved her hand weakly to silence me. Raising her head, she managed a weak yet gracious smile.

"We quite understand," she said with quiet dignity. "We thank you for taking us in, and we will not burden you any longer."

It was only after we were back on the street and saw the German soldiers that I began to feel the full impact of our desperate situation. We had been freed, and after two months were just starting to live again; now the misery was returning. Mother pulled together the last of her strength, and we struggled back to our apartment as quickly as we could. I helped her onto the bed in the kitchen, and she lay there without moving, exhausted and in terrible pain.

We needed water, so I took two pails and went to the Ratush well to get some. There were German soldiers everywhere. How could the Russians have surrounded those thousands of soldiers and expected them to surrender just like that? The Germans had broken out of the Soviet ring as water through a dam, destroying everything on the way. I stopped to rest a moment near an ambulance. Maybe I could reach in and steal some real bandages for my mother, or some medicine. But what if I were caught? What would happen to Mama? So I gave up the idea and hurried back home, locking the door tightly behind me.

My poor mother was suffering greatly, I knew. She was already feverish from infection. I did what I could to make her more comfortable; I sat on the floor by the bed and held her hand. Hours went by, and I dozed off. Then I heard my mother's voice. "Wake up, sweetheart." Her voice was now weakened to just a whisper. I was groggy from sleep, and at first I thought I must be dreaming when she told me she had decided I must flee the city that very night. "I want you to go back to Wujciu's," she said. "You will be safe there, Alicia. You are a smart girl, and I know you can get there without any trouble."

"You know I would never leave you alone, Mamusiu," I said, squeezing her hand. "I would never even consider it. We will survive somehow."

But my mother looked at me intensely, her beautiful eyes filled with pain. "You must go, Alicia. You must live!" She grimaced in pain and squeezed my hand so tightly that I had to grit my teeth to keep from from crying out.

"I have always known you would survive this war, Alicia," she continued. "I have always felt it in my heart. All the times we were separated, I knew you were alive. Even if I never see you again, I know you will survive. You must survive. You are the only witness to what happened to our family, to our people."

"But you're a witness too," I protested.

She shook her head. "I will not survive this war," she said without emotion. "But you must live, and to live you must hide. You owe it to us all to survive. I want you to leave tonight."

I reached over and stroked her hair gently. Mother closed her eyes, and I saw a tiny tear run down the side of her face and into the hair at her temple. I leaned forward and kissed her cheek, and I put my arms around her feverish body. I never even considered leaving her.

While we anguished behind locked doors, the Germans outside were rebuilding their stranglehold on the city. After the army came the German police and the Gestapo, whose main task it was to round up the remaining Jews and dispose of them as quickly as possible. The Poles and the Ukrainians helped again as much as before and even more. It had been quite a jolt for them to see that a few hundred of us remained alive. We knew that they had moved into our homes and appropriated all of our property and businesses. They had been extremely uncomfortable being stared at by the burning eyes of the remnant who had returned. So, naturally, they aided the Germans as much as they could, pointing out homes where Jews might be hiding again, knocking on floors and walls to find bunkers, anything they could do to wipe the Jews from their lives and their consciences and to eliminate those last witnesses to their part in helping the German murderers.

So I was not really surprised when late one afternoon, about a week after the new German occupation, I heard the familiar shout, *"Juden heraus,"* outside the door. Our good neighbors or the superintendent must have pointed us out. I clutched Mother's hand tightly, but we made no other move. She was so frighteningly weak, and there was no time to do anything, not to get to the cellar, not to hide under the bed, nothing. So we remained there, huddled on that little bed, our hearts pounding, our stomachs tightening.

Suddenly the door was kicked completely off its hinges, and two large SS men stormed in.

"Out! Make it quick, you damned Jews!" one of them shouted. I helped my mother up, and together we struggled out into the street. Except for us and the two SS men, the street was empty.

As we stood there shivering, clinging to each other, one of the SS men stepped back, drew his pistol, and aimed it right at me. Whether it was because my mother was with me, or because I was numb from a week of suffering, or simply because I had no chance to run away from this death, I was not afraid at all. I knew that I was going to die.

What happened next only added to the nightmare. I heard the gun go off, and suddenly my mother lay dead at my feet. She had thrown herself between me and my murderer and had been hit by the bullet meant for me.

As I looked up dumbly from my mother's body I could see the cruel face of her killer, and his gun now pointing at me. He pulled the trigger, but this time there was only a clicking noise. He pulled the trigger again, but again nothing. He had used his last bullet to kill my mother.

I will never know why he did not reload or why the other SS man did not shoot me, but for some reason they decided to take me to prison instead. They called for me to get moving, but their voices seemed to be coming as from underwater; I could not quite make out what they were saying. Their faces began to run also, so all I could see were two ugly blobs with dark spots for eyes and distorted, grotesque moving mouths. I was unable to move until one of them reached over and gave me a strong shove. My poor mother lay so still and alone on the pavement; I really wished at that moment to be dead by her side. But somehow my legs carried me away with the SS to the main street and toward the police station, the very jail where I had stayed before my death ride to the prison in Chortkov, and the very cells where only weeks before I had watched so many people receive their freedom.

The cell I was put into was designed to hold four people, five at most, but it must have contained twenty-five or thirty prisoners. As I worked my way over to rest my tired back against the wall, I began to recognize faces—not people I knew personally, but faces I had seen out on the streets.

One face I did know well. It was Eva Saling, who had been a good friend of my brother Zachary at the music conservatory in Lvov. She had been a beautiful girl, but now, like the rest of us, she was pitifully thin, her face sallow, her eyes rimmed with dark rings. I had not seen her in years, and was surprised to find her alive. But seeing her here, I realized how desperate I was to find a friend, someone with a shared experience.

"Eva," I asked, "do you recognize me? I'm Alicia Jurman, Zachary Jurman's sister." She studied me blankly for a moment, then her face showed recognition.

"Oh, yes," she said somewhat dully, nodding as though drugged, "Zachary Jurman's little sister. You've become so tall." I grimaced ruefully. I had grown quite tall, it was true; in fact, I was nearly five feet six inches tall by that time.

We talked haltingly, exchanging our experiences and despair. Nothing seemed real, yet at the same time it was all too real and too painful. How can one explain what we felt to someone who has not lived through it? I don't think it is possible. I had a feeling of déjà vu— as though I had lived this experience before. And I had. I had escaped then and somehow I felt I must and would escape again.

"Eva, I know what will happen," I told her, holding her hand in both my own. "The Gestapo will probably take us all to the Fador in the morning to be shot. If they do, then I know how you and I can escape."

She eyed me warily. "How?" she asked.

"Remember the hill that leads down to the riverbank? Where the new pine trees were planted? Before the war we used to do cartwheels in the grass. Surely you remember! Once we reach that hill, it takes only a moment to reach the water."

She listened somberly as I continued. "We have got to break away from the group and get to the river," I whispered. "Once we do, I know a place where we can hide." Then I told her all about the hollowed tree in the water that I had discovered years before in my attempts to smuggle firewood down the Stripa. I explained how easy it was to enter the tree by diving down beneath the water's surface. "Don't you see?" I said. "From the outside it looks like an ordinary tree. And since it's in the water, the dogs won't smell us. It's perfect."

Eva nodded. "But what if something goes wrong? What will happen to us if we're caught?"

"Eva," I hissed, "they're going to kill us anyway. What does it matter if we're caught? This is our only hope."

She took a deep breath. "All right," she said. "We'll do it."

"Good. Now I have to get some sleep," I said. "You try to sleep too. We're going to need every bit of strength we have."

"Here," Eva said, "lay your head in my lap. We'll sleep warmer if we huddle together." I laid my head in her lap, and she wrapped herself around me, resting her cheek against my bony hip. I squeezed my eyes shut and forced myself to go to sleep. Thoughts of my mother kept invading my mind, but I pushed them out. If I escaped tomorrow, I might have a lifetime to grieve. The only thing I allowed myself to think about were her last words: "Alicia, you must live."

I woke very early the next morning feeling that there was a dead weight on top of me. "Eva," I whispered, "move a little; you are crushing me." But there was no movement. "Eva, you will have to get off me; you are too heavy." But there was still no sign that she even heard me.

I struggled to free myself from underneath Eva's body, thinking with horror that she might have died during the night.

"Eva!" I shook her. "Look at me. Open your eyes and look at me." Dully she half opened her eyes, and I breathed a sigh of relief. I continued to shake her, and her head wobbled pitiably on her spindly neck. "Look at me!" I urged. "Eva, it's morning. They will be taking us soon. You have got to wake up! Eva!" Her eyes opened a little more, but still not completely, and she stared at me blankly.

Others in the cell were beginning to stir, and from the noises echoing from upstairs, the Germans were beginning to move around too. It wouldn't be much longer now.

"Eva! Wake up! Wake up now!" As I shook her shoulders her head nodded limply from side to side. "Remember me? I'm Alicia, Zachary Jurman's sister. Come on now, Eva; this is very important. Open your eyes!" I drew back my hand and slapped her cheek fiercely. The blow threw her head sharply to one side, and her eyes widened somewhat. "Pay attention!" I demanded. She actually turned and looked at me for a brief moment, but then her eyes half closed again and her head drooped on one side.

It was only then that I realized the horrible truth; that somehow, at some time during the night, poor Eva had completely lost her mind. She didn't want to look at the world again, so she closed her eyes and refused to wake up. I doubted at this point if she was even aware of where she was. I put my arms around her and hugged her to my heart. "It's all right, Eva," I said softly. "Everything will be all right. Alicia will take care of you."

Not long after that the cell door opened and we were ordered to move out. I couldn't be sure, but it must have been about five in the morning. I held Eva's hand in mine as we all walked up the steps and lined up outside in front of the police station. Again I was shocked to see how many people—easily two hundred—the Gestapo had been able to find with the help of our treacherous neighbors. May they all burn in hell, I cursed them.

I knew my fate depended on which direction they would be taking us. To the right was the Fador and a chance to escape; to the left, uncertainty. I was more than relieved when they ordered us to the right.

As we headed up the street toward the Fador, I whispered constantly to Eva. Maybe it would help. Maybe it would not; I didn't know. "Remember the river," I said. "Remember the tree. Run when I run. Don't look back; don't stop until you are in the tree. I will hold your hand." These things I told her over and over, though she made no sign that she heard me.

After a half-hour walk up the hill onto the Fador we finally reached the stopping point, a giant grave carved into the sloping meadow. It was a grave like so many others that had scarred that peaceful place. This one was not wide but was very long. The SS guards ordered the people to line up, side by side, directly in front of it. I had made sure to be toward the end of the line. I had learned that at Kopechince.

When the shooting began, I bolted. But Eva resisted-—and stood as though firmly rooted to the ground. "Come on!" I cried, jerking at her hand. "Run!" But she just stood there holding my hand in an iron grip. Now a new fear hit me—what if I couldn't get loose? Dear God, no! Then Eva loosened her hold, and I was able to pull my hand free, the force of release nearly throwing me to the ground. My brain signaled the message. "Run! Run, Alicia!" And I did run, half bent over and in a zigzag so that if the SS saw me and fired, I would have a chance not to be hit. Others also broke into a run, and I heard gunfire. I didn't look back.

I was weakened from hunger, not accustomed to running, and after a minute my knees wobbled treacherously and I thought my heart would tear out of my chest. At last there were the pine saplings. I was halfway there. My entire body began to tremble, and I was beginning to lose feeling in my legs when I saw the river. I ran briefly along the edge until I spotted the tree and then plunged headlong into the cold water, coming up for air only once. Oh, God, could I last? My skinny arms pulled me heavily through the icy water. Finally I reached the tree, and felt for the underwater opening. Climbing inside, I pushed my way to the surface of the water. As I broke through I gasped for air—the sweetest breath of life I had taken since my birth. I was shaking uncontrollably, and gasping heavily. But I was safe again, if only for the moment.

I knew they would never find me there, unless, of course, someone knew about the tree, which was unlikely. Now it was only a matter of waiting.

I stayed in the tree all day and shivered every minute. Outside I could hear muffled shouts, the barking of dogs, some gunfire. They were probably hunting down the other escapees; I wondered if any of the others had succeeded. Late at night I left the tree, swam over the width of the river, climbed up the opposite bank on the side of the Zazamek, and headed into the forest. I was wet and cold, and I knew that unless I found shelter and something dry to wear, I would become ill. With that thought I headed in the direction of the Zazamek and stopped at the first farm I reached. I stole into the barn, found some potato sacks in one corner, and wrapped myself in them. I spread my wet clothing out to dry and climbed into the loft to try to sleep; but instead I kept waking and dozing off, tortured by terrible nightmares. By the time I heard the first cry of the rooster I had dressed in my still-damp clothing; I had to leave before the farmer came out to milk the cows.

I had decided to remain in the area of the Zazamek. I thought that with so much confusion there, people coming and going, I wouldn't be noticed. Perhaps I could beg for a little food, or find a family to stay with.

There were many people there, Polish and Ukrainian refugees on their way out of town. One day I had managed to get a piece of bread from one kind woman who had several children with her. I was sitting quite close to them so that passersby would think I was another daughter, when I heard my name called. It was a man's voice, vaguely familiar. "Alicia, over here!" I looked to where the voice was coming from and saw Jozek, the young man who had been freeing the prisoners back at the police station.

"Alicia," he said, "thank God you're alive! I heard what happened on the Fador. But where's—" He stopped himself. Quickly changing the subject, he continued. "Listen," he said, dropping his voice so that only I could hear, "my wife and child are in the forest in a bunker. We escaped there with our friends. There are some Russian soldiers with us too."

"What are you doing here?"

"I've come to get food. But you know how it is; I have to be very, very careful." Of course he had to. Even though he was a Pole, someone might recognize him from the police station, and being married to a Jewish woman was far from safe.

Jozek suggested that it would be a good idea for me to know the location of the bunker in case I needed it or the people in the bunker needed me. I followed him into the woods; it was not an area I was familiar with. We had walked quite a distance, when suddenly he pulled me over next to a tree. "It's this way a little farther, and just to the right," he said, pointing. "I hope you understand, but I really don't want to approach it until nightfall. I don't want to take any chances."

"Of course."

"But if you should need me for anything, come to this spot and the lookout will see you. Just give my name and all will be well." We turned and headed back to the Zazamek.

"Listen," he said to me, "I'm going to give you some money. Do you think you could buy food for us? I want to keep an eye out for trouble." He gave me a handful of coins, and walked with me for a while out on the clearing, his arm around my shoulder like a big brother. "Alicia," he said, "I know you are a smart girl. If you've survived this long, you will live to see the end of this war." He gave my shoulder a squeeze and kissed the top of my forehead. "Have heart, my dear," he said softly. We agreed to meet the following day in the late afternoon, and after saying good-bye, Jozek turned once again toward the forest.

But as he went, I saw something Jozek didn't. Two German soldiers had noticed him moving off into the trees and had begun to follow him. Something had to be done to warn Jozek and to distract the attention of the soldiers. But what? There was no time to think, only to act.

So I began to scream. I screamed and screamed, and made whatever other horrifying noises I could. I clenched up my fists and held them close to my stomach and doubled over and screamed again. It worked. The two soldiers turned around and came running in my direction. I pointed to the grass, and using my hands and some German words, I tried to tell them that I saw snakes, large snakes all over the place. They pretended to look around, but only to humor this poor girl, obviously driven mad by the events of the past week. They soon left me, but thank God, not to return to the forest. I sighed in relief. How close had Jozek come to being captured?

This experience left me quite shaken, yet I knew I had to get food for the people in the bunker. I bought bread and cheese from a farmer. The next afternoon I headed for the forest, making very sure I hadn't been followed. Jozek wasn't at our agreed upon place, but I wasn't concerned. I waited for quite a while before deciding to move into the forest and, if need be, to find the bunker myself. It was well hidden, and having seen its possible location only from a distance, I wondered if I would be able to find it. My best chance was to be found by the lookout, who was probably in a tree, and deliver the food to him.

The sudden sound of footsteps stopped me in my tracks. Germans? No, it was a Russian soldier who stood only a few feet away from me. What a relief. Apparently he had not seen me.

"Hey!" I called softly. Startled, he whirled around.

"Don't move or I'll shoot," he commanded, pointing his gun at me.

"Don't shoot," I said in his own language, which I remembered from my schooldays. "We are on the same side, you and I. I'm looking for a friend, you see."

He eyed me suspiciously. "What friend?" he asked.

"Look," I said, "you are a Russian and I am a Jew. We are both dead if the Germans find us." I told him about Jozek and our arrangement. Hearing this, the soldier sighed, and shook his head slowly.

"It's no use," he said. "They're all gone."

"Gone?" I felt suddenly sick. "What are you talking about?"

"I had a bad bout of diarrhea," he explained. "And so as not to bother the others, I left the bunker early this morning. Now I return and find they are all gone. The Germans must have found them; they must have been betrayed." His eyes burned in anger. "They're all gone, the Jews, my comrades, everyone. Gone."

"Oh, God." I felt my knees buckling. The soldier helped me to a sitting position and sat down beside me.

"Did you know them well?" he asked.

I shook my head. "I never even met most of them. I knew only Jozek and his family."

"I had three friends there," he said. "We could not get out of the town; it was Jozek who brought us here. He helped the people who hid here originally during the war. My friends and I were going to stay here a few days, and then head back east. Now it looks like I will have to go alone."

"But the Russian front shouldn't be too far away," I said. "You should be able to reach it in a few days."

"We'll see." He paused for a moment. "What about you?"

"Oh, I don't know. I'll be all right here."

He studied me for a moment. "How old are you, anyway?"

I looked at him wearily. "Very old."

"Well, I guess we should be on our way." He helped me to my feet. "Will you be able to make it all right?"

"Yes, thank you, I feel fine now." I remembered the bundle of bread and cheese. "Look," I said, "I have all this food. Take some; you'll be needing it."

"Are you sure?"

"Absolutely. I have a much easier time getting food than you." I could see tears welling in his eyes.

"*Spaseba, dorogaya dievushka* [thank you, dear girl]," he said, bowing slightly and taking the food I offered him. It was then that I noticed his officer's bars.

"Where will you go now?" he asked.

I shrugged. "I don't really know."

He pointed to the north. "There's a clearing over that way, inside the forest, less than a kilometer from here. Refugees are gathering there, at least a hundred people by now. It would be a good place to stay until you make plans for your next move." He pointed again. "That way, just keep walking straight. You can't miss it."

"Thanks," I said, "and good luck to you."

We shook hands. "And to you too," he said, and smiled.

I headed straight in the direction the Russian had pointed, and found the clearing he had mentioned in less than twenty minutes. It was hundreds of meters long and wide, bordered by the forest on all sides. There were at least a hundred refugees there, gathered in little groups that dotted the clearing. They were Poles and Ukrainians, fleeing from the front lines newly established by the German breakthrough.

The Russian had been right; this was a place where I could stay awhile, gather my strength, and decide where to go next. Becoming a refugee was strange for me, rather like a promotion. From the hunted Jew to the status of refugee. I could see some safety in this situation, although there was a definite drawback: many of those refugees might still point me out as a Jew to the German or Ukrainian police.

When the first campfire was lit for the night, I walked up to it and just sat down. Since I spoke both Polish and Ukrainian, the people around the fire did not appear to suspect me or mind my presence. During the next two days I moved freely from camp to camp, looking for a family I could trust and stay with until the Germans were defeated once more and the Russians returned.

Had I been more alert, I probably would have noticed that these people were gradually realizing I was a Jewish girl. Something was giving my identity away.

Before meals, after meals, when they talked of the dead, of evil spirits, of harvests both good and bad, the Poles and Ukrainians always crossed themselves. I had done this before myself when I worked in the fields near Wujciechovka, but only when there were other workers nearby. This time I really didn't think too much about it. But looking back, I can imagine the refugees getting together and saying, "Have you noticed that girl over there never crosses herself?" Or was it the suffering in my eyes that was so easily detected? Probably a combination of both. Those people had seen the mass murders by the Germans; some had undoubtedly helped by pointing out Jewish hiding places; some even murdered Jews themselves. I thought bitterly, these people could really recognize a Jew. But as yet no one in the clearing had bothered me, and I didn't sense any danger.

One day after I had been with the refugees about a week I noticed a newcomer to the clearing. People arrived every day, but this one was different from the others. A young boy, about twelve years old, pitifully thin, wearing ragged clothes, his face pale and his large brown eyes almost sunken in their sockets. He did not come into the clearing but stood partially concealed behind a tree on the meadow's edge. He stood there for about an hour, watching, not daring to step into the open.

For the first time in a week something stirred in my heart—concern and compassion for another human being. This young boy needed a friend, and I, too, needed a friend. I got up and strolled as casually as I could across the open space to where he was standing. Smiling, I approached him slowly, for I could see that the closer I got, the more apprehensive he became. There was a horse grazing not far from the boy, and as I approached, I caught hold of the animal's harness and led him over.

"Shalom," I said, watching for his reaction. His eyes widened with surprise.

"Don't worry," I went on. "It's safe. I have been here a week and they have done nothing to me." As I talked I stroked the horse's muzzle. This poor lost Jewish boy! My heart went out to him.

"There is food," I continued. "The people share when you ask them. I will tell them you're from my village and that your parents were killed during the last German attack. How about coming a little closer?" He edged forward, eyeing me carefully, until he stood on the other side of the horse. "My name is Alicia," I said. "What's yours?"

"Joseph," he replied timidly.

Joseph! The name was like a knife blade in my heart. Jozek is the Polish name for Joseph; Jozek, my friend, the Polish policeman who was now likely dead. I hoped for the boy's sake I had not reacted too visibly. "Where do you come from?" I asked. He told me he was from a small town not far from Buczacz. I went on talking, trying to reassure him, when suddenly I noticed he had begun to tremble, and was staring over my shoulder at something.

"What is it; what's the matter?" I asked, turning to look behind me. Then I saw what the boy had seen. On the opposite side of the meadow a German soldier on horseback had appeared. I held my breath. One of the refugees, a man, went over to the rider and said something to him. Then he turned and pointed directly across the clearing at Joseph and me.

I felt that old sickening feeling again, and pure hatred for those people. My God, I thought, you people feed me, visit with me, suffer with me for a week, and at the first opportunity you betray me to the Germans. May you all burn in hell, every one of you!

My first thought was for the boy. I quickly stepped in front of him, blocking him from view, and pushed him toward the forest. "Run!" I urged. "Run as far as your legs will take you." He quickly disappeared into the trees, just seconds before the German and his horse reached me. Even if I had time to run into the forest, I could not take the chance, not knowing if Joseph had escaped or if he was sitting, paralyzed with fear, under some nearby bush. Anyway, it was too late now.

I was relieved when I recognized the rider to be a regular army soldier and not an SS man. He wore jodhpurs and riding boots and sat very straight on his saddle. Ah, I thought bitterly, a gentleman.

"Turn loose the horse," he commanded. I did as he said, and the animal moved away. "Now sit on the ground." This I did too. So he's going to shoot me like a dog, that bastard, I thought to myself. And then it struck me. I had known horses since I was a child and had learned even more about them on the farms during the last eight months. I knew how to handle them, and I knew how easily they could be panicked. Suddenly I knew what I would do. The minute the German made a move, whether to pull out his revolver to shoot me or to dismount, I would reach out with my foot and kick his horse in the leg. The horse would rear up, and whether or not he threw the German, I would gain time; perhaps I could still escape. Sitting on the ground, I began to edge closer and closer to the animal. All the time the German looked down at me silently, leaning over the side of the horse, seeming to study me.

I was close enough to the horse to kick him when I looked up at the officer. For a moment our eyes locked. I saw blue eyes, so typical of the Germans; but strangely enough they lacked the murderous glint I had seen so many times. Later I would often wonder what he had seen in my own eyes. But with our eyes still locked and me prepared to strike at any moment, the man suddenly spoke. "You are innocent," he said. "You are innocent." Swiftly he whipped the horse around and galloped back across the clearing and into the woods.

I stared after the horse and rider, now gone, for at least a minute. What do I do now? Should I head into the woods and leave my food behind? No. Straightening my shoulders, holding my head high, I walked calmly back across the clearing, past the campsites and the gawking people, to get my small bundle. After the spectacle they had just seen, I didn't doubt that every pair of eyes in that camp was following me. I was not going to give them the satisfaction of seeing me run.

As I passed the people, there was not a sound, only hands flying to foreheads, frantically delivering the sign of the cross. I looked haughtily down at them all. Why had they betrayed me? It was obvious to me now that the German was just passing by and had stumbled onto the clearing. He hadn't been hunting anyone. Did they think it would please him to get a chance to kill another Jew? I reached my bundle, picked it up without a word, and, looking straight ahead now, I moved quickly past the people and headed into the forest.

CHAPTER 17

Struggle to Survive

In the relative safety of the forest I now began to feel the effects of the events of the last two weeks. Whenever I closed my eyes I saw the two Gestapo men and the gun with which they'd killed my mother; I heard the sound it made when it pointed at me and misfired. I relived my escape from the massacre at the Fador, and mixed with the other images in my nightmares, I saw the faces of the German on the horse and the Jewish boy with haunted eyes.

Night after night these dreams kept returning. The sleep that had served me so well in the past, that had always restored my fighting spirit and my physical strength, was now denied me.

I spent most of my days walking aimlessly around the edges of the forest, feeling completely lost. Even though no bullet had pierced my body, I felt a raw wound inside of me, and an unending pain.

Then one night, exhausted from a day of aimless wandering, I finally fell into a deep sleep. Again I dreamed about my mother, but this time she was not being killed. She was alive, standing near me and holding out both hands as though trying to pull me up from the ground.

"Get up, Alicia!" she was calling to me. "Get up from the ground. You must not lie there and grieve. You must go on living; you must live! You must live, Alicia! Take my hands, sweetheart. Get up and go away from here."

I wanted to ask her why I should leave there and where I should go, to tell her that I had nowhere to go; but as suddenly as she had appeared, she disappeared again. I woke up with a start. It took me some time to realize that I had been dreaming. I looked at my hands. I saw only the pattern of light coming through the trees, but I still felt my mother's touch on them. Then I felt the pain inside me expanding until it became unbearable. I leaned my head against the tree, and my body shook with choking sobs.

I left the forest and found the main road leading out of Buczacz. The road was filled with people, mostly from villages, heading away from the city, all going in one direction—to the west. Many carried bundles in their hands or strung over their shoulders. Some were lucky enough to have their own wagons and horses to carry their families and belongings, but most were walking. They were apparently coming from the villages where there was still fighting between the Russians and the Germans. They had no choice but to head deeper into Poland, where they felt it was safer.

I kept hearing my mother's voice urging me to keep going, so I remained with the refugees on the roads. I would have stayed with them for some time if I hadn't happened to look into one woman's bundle as she was tying it back up. There, on top of her belongings, was the blue cap worn by the hated Ukrainian police and Banderovcy. It must have belonged to her husband.

One look at that cap and I realized that among the people on the roads were not only refugees from the front lines, but also people who had collaborated with the Germans and were now fleeing from Russian vengeance. Their hatred of the surviving Jews was such that if they found out I was Jewish, they wouldn't hesitate to kill me. They now had serious problems of their own, but that would certainly not make any difference; of this, I was sure.

I followed the refugees, but from some distance. I noticed, however, that they began to separate. Some continued walking westward. When they reached a railroad station, others boarded the few freight trains that were made available to civilians. I was with one such group one day at a railroad station outside a small town. I stood among the people, closely observing what was happening near the trains. Some passing trains carried German soldiers, and some trains were filled with civilians. Others were a combination of passenger and freight cars. When the trains stopped, some passengers, mostly young boys and girls dressed in village clothing, climbed out of the freight cars to stretch their legs. I assumed that they were going to Germany to work on farms there. I wondered, as I looked at them, what life would be like for them in Germany. Then I had a crazy thought. What would it be like for me to hide on a German farm? Indeed, a crazy thought. Just the mere sound of the German language, the way it was used by the Gestapo, made me shiver with fright.

But, surprisingly, the idea stayed in my mind. Who would expect to find a Jewish girl on a German farm? Also, I was lonely for people my own age, and those girls on the train seemed friendly to one another.

I quickly put the idea aside and looked again for work in the fields. It was May, and the need for farmhands was great, so I had no problems finding work, especially since all I asked for was bread and a cup of sour milk. I was repeating the same pattern I had followed in Wujciechovka, but with one great difference: my heart wasn't in what I was doing. The need to care for my mother was gone, and with it much of the inspiration for my fighting spirit. All I had left was my basic instinct for survival.

Most of the farmers in the area were Polish, because I was now somewhere near central Poland. The story I used to account for my being alone was that I was a Ukrainian farm girl who had escaped from a train that was taking me to forced labor in Germany. The Poles here hadn't suffered from the Ukrainian Banderovcy, so their feelings against the Ukrainians were not very personal, and they didn't much care who I was. Of course I spoke Polish, trying to mix in some Ukrainian words occasionally, and not always by design either. Sometimes I asked them if they knew someone in a neighboring village that I might pass on my way home to the Ukraine. Usually they were helpful and would give me directions. They would never give me the name of the farmer, but they would give me their own name as a reference.

As I continued westward, I left the Podole, the fertile breadbasket of Poland, behind me. Although the land was fruitful here, too, the earth was not the rich black soil I had known, but was mixed with hard red soil and was more difficult to cultivate. This part of Poland had not been liberated by the Russians so the people had no idea that any Jews had survived, and they would be less likely to guess that I was Jewish. I was careful to choose fields with women and older people, but I was not so afraid. I never stayed after I finished my work, and I never went to see the farmers in their homes. I finished my work, found a hiding place in a ravine or forest, then moved to another field the following day.

I will never understand why I took my next step; blame it on fate and its strange workings.

One morning I found myself in the railroad station of a big city called Sandomiez. The station was on the edge of the city, and I was about to pass through it on my way to the next village. There were two trains in the station blowing smoke and steam into the air, ready to move. The one nearest me was the same type of combination passenger and freight train I had seen before. The doors to the freight cars were open, and nearby stood many village boys and girls, some as young as myself and some older, dressed in what looked like their Sunday best. One of the girls had walked a little distance away from the group and was standing, just looking around. I walked over to talk to her. She was a friendly girl, and she told me that they were from the Ukraine, near the Russian-Polish border, and that they were going to work on German farms. She didn't seem to be unhappy about being separated from her family. Then I remembered that the Ukrainians and the Germans were allies, and she had no reason to fear the Germans. But I couldn't understand why now, when it was obvious that the Russians were beginning to win the war, she would want to leave her village.

I will never understand why I did it; but when the girl left to return to her group I simply followed her. When they started pulling one another back onto the car and a pair of hands was extended in my direction, I let myself be pulled in with the rest. I kept close to the girl, and when she sat down on the straw-covered floor, I sat down near her. Shortly after, the train whistle sounded and the doors were closed from the outside. I felt a terrible panic. Suddenly I remembered another train pulling out of Buczacz in 1941, and my heart began beating violently. I looked around me fearfully, but was reassured by the presence of all those young people. Still, the fright that had settled around my heart made me feel cold all over and did not diminish.

I must have had a premonition of trouble, because the train hadn't gone far—perhaps a couple of hundred meters—when suddenly I heard a loud explosion. Our car shook violently and the train stopped.

The door to our car opened, and a man cried out for us to leave the car and run for cover to the nearby ditch. We caught up our bundles and ran as fast as we could. As I was running to the ditch, I was thrown to the ground by another blast. I felt a searing pain in my leg and buttocks, but I continued to run. Once I was safely in the ditch, I examined my leg. It had been hit by a fragment from a grenade or mortar shell. One small fragment had shot deeply into my buttock. I was bleeding a little, but not badly. Another fragment, a small one too, was sticking out of my shin. Stabs of pain moved up my leg and made me feel weak, but I grasped the piece of metal between my fingers and continued to work very carefully until I pulled the whole piece out. There was an ugly, torn wound, not large but bleeding profusely. I used my kerchief and bandaged my leg with it, hoping it would stop the bleeding.

Those who had reached the ditch with me were now peering over the edge, trying to see what was happening. The explosions and the shooting had stopped, but there was a lot of screaming and shouting. Some of the travelers were lying dead or wounded along the cars. Then my heart nearly stopped beating as I saw SS men running alongside the tracks with their guns drawn, shouting in German to the people to get away from the train.

After a while the SS men turned in the direction of the passenger cars and disappeared inside. All this action around me looked as though some people had deliberately attacked this train because they knew that the SS men were on it; and they might do it again. Then suddenly the locomotive sounded a piercing whistle and the train started moving. I watched as it quickly picked up speed. Only the passenger cars were running; the freight cars were left behind. I was greatly relieved when I realized that the SS men had disappeared with the train, but also regretful that the mission to destroy the train which carried the SS murderers had failed.

For the time being I stayed close to Tania, the girl who had befriended me. She seemed in shock, as were the rest of the people in the ditch. After a while a man who was apparently in charge gathered us all up and walked us to the station. There we were put into basement rooms and were told to wait until morning and then continue our journey. The man in charge was very reassuring and told us not to worry and that everything would be all right. One of the boys asked him why we were locked up like prisoners. The man said we were not prisoners, but that the train was attacked by Russian partisans who were now being rounded up by the police. The police wanted to make sure that no one in our group had had anything to do with the attack on the train. This suspicion brought fierce denials from those present and caused a lot of resentment, but eventually we all settled down. Those who had some food took it out of their bundles and shared it with the others who had left everything they owned on the train.

What appeared only a possibility when I thought about it in the ditch was now a real danger. I knew now that I must get out of there before we were questioned by the police.

"Tania," I said to my friend. "How are you feeling? Are you afraid to get on the train again?"

She looked at me thoughtfully and then said, "As a matter of fact, I think we all are, but we have to continue. It won't be so bad once we get out of Poland. Don't you think so?"

I really should have given her moral support, as I would have under other circumstances. Also, before we were locked up I would have ordinarily gone to the train and helped with the other wounded. But I now had to consider my own survival, so I told her a story I improvised:

"I am ashamed to tell you, but I am petrified to get on that train, even more than I am afraid of the cruel stepmother from whom I ran away. She used to beat me and my little brother every day. I shudder to think how my brother must be suffering right now because I ran away. I think I will go back home. Could you help me? Please, Tania, will you help me?"

I pressed on and on. "Maybe this is a sign from God that I should not leave my village."

Tania looked at me strangely. I didn't know if she believed my story, or whether she was still upset enough over what happened that she was willing to help me without giving it too much thought.

"What do you want me to do?" she asked.

"Do you know someone who would be willing to help you lift me up to the window? I could get out in seconds and be gone before you even knew it."

"Well, there is a boy over there in the corner. I will go over and ask him."

"Thank you, Tania, you are a good friend; if you ever pass my village, you are welcome in my house."

"No, with that cruel stepmother of yours, I would rather not," she said, and she smiled at me.

I had a moment of anguish as Tania talked with the boy, but they returned together. I was lifted up on the boy's shoulders while Tania held my legs. It was hard to open the window, but it finally gave and, with a strong push from the boy, I was half outside. Slowly, so as not to break the glass, I pulled myself out completely, caught my bundle from Tania, and gently closed the window.

As I was crawling away along the building wall I passed another window and looked inside. I could see men on the floor and heard what sounded like moaning. I realized that they were probably wounded partisans who had been caught by the police. They will certainly be shot, poor men, I thought, probably after being tortured. I felt such compassion for the men in that room that I made up my mind to try to help them.

I tapped on the window until I got their attention. Soon a bandaged head appeared. I motioned with my hands that I would pull them out. It happened very quickly. They opened the window, and I reached my arm in as far as I could and braced myself against the wall so that I wouldn't be pulled back through the window. A hand grasped mine. I pulled with all my strength and was able to help the fellow pull himself far enough so that he was half free, arms and waist on the outside, legs dangling into the room below. I held the collar of his uniform and tugged as hard as I could. He was very weak, probably from loss of blood, but finally he was out far enough so that he could pull himself the rest of the way. Wordlessly he turned and reached back through the window, and soon we were pulling out a second man. Then a third and fourth. Altogether we managed to free about seven men, all within a very short time. I felt exhausted from all the pulling and I was all sticky with blood. Those men were badly wounded, but I thought at least they now have a chance, if not to live, at least to die free men.

Now we had to move away quickly. There was a half moon out, and that gave us enough light to see where the forest was. The partisans helped one another to walk slowly away from the building. When the last man was about to leave, I stopped him.

"Take me with you," I pleaded. "I speak Russian and perfect Polish and Ukrainian. Please take me along; I want to help you fight those murdering dogs."

"How can we take you?" he said in a sad voice. "We had to leave some of our own comrades in that room, knowing that they will be dead by morning. You are a girl, and I can see you are wounded yourself. I am very sorry. We are very grateful for your help."

He touched my shoulder and was gone. I hurried after him; not to follow him but because the forest was the only place where I, too, could hide.

It was summer now and warm outside, and the woods were beautiful. This forest reminded me very much of the one I had lived in when I walked from Kopechince to Buczacz after I escaped from the grave. I followed the same pattern this time. I would find a field to work in during the day, get a piece of bread and sour milk, and return to the forest for the night. I had a new story to tell the farmers, which was partly true: I had been wounded in the attack on the train on the way to Germany and, since I was wounded, they wouldn't take me to Germany but told me to return to my village. I had lost everything I owned on the train, so I had to earn some food as I made my way home. This time I really had a feeling that they believed me. Some had heard of the train sabotage, and those who didn't just shook their heads at the news.

There was another reason why I stayed in the forest. I was hoping to find the Russian partisans I had helped save in Sandomiez. This time I wanted to convince them to take me along. My leg was healing, thanks to the application of babka leaves which drew out the pus and left the wound clean. It still hurt a little, but not much. The piece of shrapnel that lodged in my buttock didn't bother me at all. So I thought I was now ready for the long walks that might be necessary; maybe they would think so too.

One Sunday morning, as I was lying in my hiding place in the forest looking through the branches that hid me and trying to catch a glimpse of the sky, I was startled to hear voices. They were coming from far back in the forest, but as I listened I could hear them more clearly. The voices became louder and louder as they came nearer to my hiding place. Soon I was able to recognize the language they were speaking. It was Russian. My heart leapt with joy. Could it be that the people coming toward me were Russian partisans? Was it possible that among them would be some of the partisans I had met?

I sat up, grasped the branch that was obstructing my view of the trail, and waited with great anticipation to see who came. I really would have liked to go out and meet them, but some instinct stopped me. It would be better to wait until I could see them. As the voices came nearer I could clearly hear a man saying, "They will shoot you if you refuse to fight on the front." Before I could understand what he meant by this, two men wearing German army uniforms appeared on the trail. I nearly cried out, I was so shocked. Luckily the cry froze on my lips, because they passed very close to where I was hiding. It took me several minutes to believe what I was seeing, and then I thought I understood. The partisans were disguised as Germans in order to move around freely. What a splendid idea, I thought, those partisans are really clever. I got up and followed them to see where they were going.

I was very careful not to be heard and, as soon as they left the forest, I climbed up on a tree to get a good view of them. What I saw from my hiding place in the tree made my mouth go dry, and my heart beat violently. The meadow that had been empty only last night was now filled with German Wehrmacht soldiers. Some of them were resting on the grass, some were working in what looked like a field kitchen, and others were currying their horses. There were perhaps a hundred men. I looked on horrified as the two disguised partisans walked straight into this trap. I took a firmer hold of the branch I was leaning on, bracing myself to watch a terrible scene—shooting and fighting just as at the railroad station. I had a fleeting thought that I might be struck by a bullet in all this shooting and that I had better get down from the tree, but my eyes would not leave the partisans. Then to my great bewilderment I saw them walk up to the kitchen, pick up two cups, and pour something into them. They carried their cups to the grass and sat down to drink. One of them must have said something funny, because the second man laughed loudly.

That did it. I snapped out of my shock and started to think. Slowly I realized that the men I thought to be partisans weren't partisans at all. They were Russians, of that I was sure, but Russians serving in the German army. What other explanation could there be? I felt myself getting very angry when I realized that they were traitors: Russian traitors. I had learned by now what the Germans did in Russia, and here were Russians fighting against their own people. My God, I thought, imagine what will happen to them when they are finally captured by the Red army.

And I had almost run into their arms.

I returned to my hiding place to think. The episode had upset me, but it had also given me some insight into the progress of the war. I understood now what one of the Russians had meant when he said:

"They shoot you when you don't want to fight at the front." I knew who was supposed to do the fighting, but who was doing the threatening? I wondered if perhaps the SS was pushing those Russians to the front, but then they would have to be there to do the pushing, and I couldn't picture those murdering cowards at the front. My only experience with the SS was when they bravely faced defenseless Jewish men, women, and children. How well I remembered that. Well, whoever was doing the threatening, I could feel no pity for those who collaborated with the Germans.

I quickly dismissed all that from my mind and concentrated on getting out of the forest as quickly as possible. The Germans would probably be coming into the forest, especially when they discovered the sweet blueberries that grew wild not far from my hiding place. Besides, it was time to look for a place in the village. The potato harvest was soon to begin and with it would come colder weather. It was true that the war might end soon, but I still had to eat and keep out of the cold. It seemed to me that the same cycle of misery I had experienced in Wujciechovka when the cold weather set in was about to begin for me all over again.

As I was walking farther south, I noted the change in scenery. Gone were the villages, with their endless stretches of fields. Instead, I came upon valleys surrounded by low mountains. The air was crisper, especially in the morning, and the soil of the farms became harder. The farmers spoke a Polish dialect of their own. I could remember from childhood that the Gurali might have spoken that way. What amazed me most were the roads. They were wider than usual village roads, which made it easier for the wagons to bring in the harvest. At the same time they had a drawback; they brought the German army into the villages. Everywhere I looked I could see Germans; the whole area was literally crawling with soldiers. The people in the village where I finally settled believed that the front was not far away, but since we didn't actually hear shooting it was hard to be sure. I was not really worried about the German soldiers. They were now fighting for their own lives and were much too preoccupied to go looking for Jews. It never occurred to them that the scrawny girl they saw in the fields and herding cows was a Jewish girl, at least I hoped not.

As for the farmers, I told them the usual story, that I was a Ukrainian orphan. During most of my time in this village I worked and lived on the farm of an elderly couple and their family. There was one daughter about sixteen and twin boys about eleven. The girl, named Paula, resembled Manka from Wujciechovka, but in looks only. Manka had been a sweet and generous girl, whereas Paula was just the opposite. She was beautiful, true, but she was lazy and very mean. She certainly fooled her parents, but she didn't fool me or her twin brothers. This situation created a friendly bond between the twins and me.

Paula would leave me barely any food after I came back from milking, cleaning the barn, and bedding down the animals for the night. Sometimes she gave me a small piece of bread, or one boiled potato. If it wasn't for the kindness of the twins, Tomek and Tadeush, I would have had to leave the farm. They often saved me some food from their supper and sneaked it into the loft where I slept. They were sweet boys, and I was grateful to them.

The twins and I had our best moments when Paula was away from the farm. She always said she was visiting her cousins in the neighboring village, and she did so at every opportunity, often staying overnight. I thought that might not be where she really was, but I kept quiet. It was none of my business. When Paula was gone, the boys would take out their schoolbooks, and we would study arithmetic. We always counted with cows and horses. Once I laughed hysterically when Tomek, pleased with his number of horses, became confused and remarked that there would be none left for him after Paula took her dowry out of the farm when she got married. He was sure that his parents would give everything to Paula. I covered my laughter by hugging him to my heart.

Even though Paula was mean to me I liked that farm, and I liked her parents. They were kind, and so to please them, I offered to take Paula's place when German soldiers came into the house and asked Paula to come with them to the school and help peel potatoes for their field kitchen. Lately the Germans used village girls to do this chore. I happened to be in the house when they came one morning, and I could see that Paula's parents were very frightened. Their daughter was a beautiful girl, and they had all heard horror stories of Germans raping girls. I could have told them that in many cases the girls willingly met with the Germans, from what I had seen in Buczacz.

I must admit that it wasn't all consideration for the farmer that made me volunteer for this job. I was also hoping to get some more food. Despite all the help from the twins, I was constantly hungry. I was hoping to get the potato peels, so that when out in the pasture I could hold them over the fire, bake them, and have a good meal. But when I arrived at the German kitchen and was given a small knife and a sack of potatoes, I was cautioned to scrape, not peel, the potatoes. I was shown how by one of the girls who was already there. I was disappointed, but held on to the fact that I had done something for Paula's parents.

However, eventually I did find a source of food at the kitchen. The potatoes that we peeled were thrown into a huge kettle, along with meat, to be boiled into a thick soup. Tightly sealed aluminum cans were filled with this soup, and German soldiers came to the kitchen and took the cans away. Some of the soup was served at the kitchen. At the end of every meal the huge kettle had to be scrubbed clean. On the first day of my potato peeling I was nominated by my coworkers for this job because I was the skinniest girl and could fit easily inside the kettle, and also because my clothes were already so shabby that they couldn't be damaged very much. While cleaning inside, I discovered delicious vegetables on the inside of the rim stuck to the wall of the kettle. I would scoop them up with my fingers and then sit inside eating every bit with great relish. Then, of course, I would scour the kettle, which was a difficult and messy job. I would return to the farm wet and dirty but at least not hungry.

One afternoon, as I was sitting inside the kettle eating my vegetables, I heard soldiers talking. They had filled up their cans with food to take back to their comrades, but also took some extra food for themselves, and were now eating and talking.

I stopped eating when I heard the voices and sat very quietly. If they heard me and found me hidden inside the kettle, they might think I was spying on them, and Lord knows what trouble I might be in then. They were talking about finally finding someone; someone hiding in the woods close by. They were speaking at a normal conversational level, and I had to strain to hear them. Who were they talking about, I wondered. What poor unfortunates were hiding this time? I wondered if they might be Jews. Why was the Wehrmacht looking for Jews, when they themselves were in such trouble?

I listened carefully as the voices continued to give more details. They talked about Ukrainians who helped them locate the partisans, and how the partisans were giving them a lot of problems.

"Before the end of the day those damned Russian dogs will all be dead," one of the soldiers growled.

So that was it! The Russian partisans again! I wondered if they were the same partisans I had helped save months before. The voices also mentioned Ukrainians who were with the German army, probably the

Banderovcy. That really put fear into me. Would they start burning Polish farms again? Would they burn our farm?

Finally the voices were silent. I sat a while longer, then climbed out of the kettle, and as quickly as my legs could carry me ran back to the farm and into the barn. I put a rope around the horse as though I were going to lead him to pasture, mounted, and leaning low over the horse's neck, I galloped toward the forest. The sky had become dark with rain clouds, and there were signs that a storm was coming. Once in a while I could hear distant thunder. I dismounted at the edge of the forest and led the horse inside.

Once in the forest I had no idea where to go. I was hoping that the partisans had lookouts stationed all over and that one of them would hear me. In the meantime I was going deep into the woods. Just as I had hoped, one of the partisans found me. It seemed as though the man pointing a rifle at me had stepped out of thin air.

"Put your hands up or I will shoot," he said in Russian. "What are you doing here? Who sent you?"

"*Ya Yevreika*, I am a Jewess, and would not hurt you," I said in Russian. "I overheard the Germans talking. They and the Ukrainians know where you are. You must leave the forest immediately. I have to get back."

The partisan thanked me, saluted, and was gone. All this took no more than a minute. I turned my horse around and led him back toward the forest edge. It had started raining and thundering, and the horse seemed very unhappy. I was just coming out of the forest, when suddenly I was surrounded by German soldiers and Ukrainian police.

"What were you doing inside the forest?" the Ukrainian demanded. I began to cry, partly as an act, and partly because I was very frightened.

"This terrible horse," I cried, and slapped the horse's muzzle. He jerked his head up, startled. I spoke in Polish.

"He is going to get me into trouble. He ran away and the storm could have killed him. I found him just in time. I will probably get a beating from my father anyway. He beats me often, you know. On top of that, I haven't even milked the cows. I hate this horse!" I cried, striking the horse's belly this time; he nearly reared up.

The Ukrainians only laughed, and I could hear one of the Germans asking, "What is she saying?"

"Oh, nothing," said the Ukrainian, "she is just a crazy village girl. Be gone from here!"

When I brought the horse back into the barn I brushed him down.
I put my face near his and we looked at each other, my eyes begging
forgiveness, and his looking at me with what I hoped was understanding.

About a month passed. We could now hear distant firing, and each
day it came closer to our village. I was afraid that the front was getting
near us and that our village might be evacuated. I slept very poorly and
kept alert. I kept my belongings nearby, and was ready to leave at a
moment's notice. I sensed the same tension throughout the house. We
were all waiting for something to happen. And then, all of a sudden,
the Germans were gone, and the Russian army was there. I could see
them traveling through the village roads when I was out in the pasture
with the cows. Once I caught a glimpse of them as they came out of
the house carrying what looked like jugs of milk. But I didn't come
close to them or talk to them. I wanted to, but my instinct told me to
wait. I was afraid that they might just be passing through, the way they
did in Buczacz. The painful memory of what happened in Buczacz
had never left me. So I went about my chores as usual and waited to
see what would happen next.

One day I was out in the pasture with the cows, when Tomek came
running for me.

"Slavka," he called, trying to catch his breath. "They want you at
the house."

"Who wants me? Your father? Or Paula?"

"No, no. Soldiers. The soldiers want you."

I was alarmed. "What soldiers?"

"What soldiers?" he repeated after me. "What's the matter with
you, the Russian soldiers, of course. Father said for you to hurry.
Hurry! I will keep an eye on the cows."

But he didn't; he followed after me. I was wondering why the
Russian soldiers wanted to see me. It couldn't be that they were now
hunting down Jews. What a crazy idea. I remembered from Buczacz
that they were friendly toward us. Maybe they needed someone to peel
potatoes for them? All these thoughts kept running through my mind
as I came near the house. Just the same, as I walked I straightened out
my head kerchief and smoothed out the wrinkles in my skirt as I let it
down from my waistline. I always kept my skirt tucked in so that it
would not get dirty.

At the house there were two Russians. One was obviously an
officer. The second wore a plain uniform without officer's shoulder

boards, but he looked like an officer, the way he stood there. All this I could see as I entered, and I also saw that the farmer and his wife were quite frightened. No one in Poland was quite sure what the Russian army had in mind for them. The Russians had appeared at the door and asked if a young girl lived there. The farmer thought they were asking for Paula, but they said no, they were looking for a tall girl about fourteen years old with dark hair and dark eyes.

I stood there silently as the Russians studied me.

"Is this the one?" the high-ranking officer asked. The other one looked at me and said, "Yes, she is the one."

Something in my memory was surfacing. It occurred to me that this man looked vaguely familiar. Why, I thought, if it isn't the man from . . . I couldn't quite remember.

"*Dievuchka*, will you please come with us?"

I swallowed hard and nodded. How could I refuse? Meanwhile the farmer and his family looked worried. I could see that Tomek was edging toward me as though he were going to step between me and the soldiers. I really loved that sweet boy. I looked at the farmer and his wife wordlessly, wondering if they were as frightened for me as they were for themselves. Then I left with the Russians.

They took me to the army's headquarters, the same school building where the Germans had set up their kitchen. But there wasn't a kettle outside that I could see. I did see many soldiers going in and out of the school building; they seemed to be settling in permanently.

The young man, the one who seemed familiar, asked me to have a seat when we entered one of the rooms. He offered me a cup of tea, which I politely refused.

"You speak Russian well," he commented. "Where did you learn it?"

I shrugged nervously. "I sort of picked it up here and there. It is useful."

He laughed out loud. "I should say it is. You don't remember me, do you?"

I looked at him, trying to identify his face. I thought I remembered it, but I wouldn't admit it; instead, I said, "I do, but I don't. Does that make sense?"

"It certainly does. That last time we saw each other I am afraid you couldn't see my face, and the time before we were both in a bit of a hurry. As a matter of fact, we met three times."

He was just about to explain, when the door opened and a soldier motioned us to follow him. The room we entered didn't look like a schoolroom anymore, but seemed more like a living room. There were various chairs scattered all around the room. We were shown to a corner, where a group of men were sitting in a sort of circle with a little table in the middle. On the table were bottles of vodka and plates filled with food.

"Sit down, girl, have something to eat!" one of the officers cried out as he got up to offer me his chair. "Here, have some of this meat. It is from America and is very delicious."

I sat down, but just folded my hands in my lap. I was wondering why they had brought me there. As I looked around, I could see several high-ranking officers, and the rest wore uniforms without any insignias at all. That was strange, particularly in the Russian army. They had one thing in common, they were all young, and to me, looked very beautiful and brave.

Then one of the officers got up, raised his glass, and said: "Comrades, let's drink a toast to a very brave girl who helped our men here." He swept his hand toward the others in the group. "She risked her life at the train station, and not very long ago, right here in this village. Let us drink to our country, to Stalin, to our partisan leader General-Major Kalpak, twice Hero of the Soviet Union, and to our young friend here, our new hero!"

Someone put a glass in my hand and urged me to drink. I could smell the vodka. I just touched the rim of the glass with my lips but didn't drink it. They toasted several more times.

"What is your name?" the man sitting near me asked.

"Alicia Jurman," I answered. "You can call me Alicia."

"Alicia." He turned the name on his tongue. "Alicia is not a good name for a brave girl like you; I will call you Anusha. That is a good Russian name. To your health, Anusha."

The man who just gave me my new name got up and lifted his glass.

"Comrades, comrades, silence for a moment! As you know, we brought Anusha here for a purpose—to thank her and to give her this." He pulled a box from his pocket, opened it, took out a medal, and pinned it on my shirt. "It says here on this medal *Za advahu*—For bravery. Let's drink to that, and to all of us, the heroes of this war!"

Then they proceeded to toast one another, calling out all their names. This was how I learned the name of the soldier who had brought me here. His name was Kola. He toasted with the rest but didn't throw the vodka down his throat like the others did.

"Well, Anusha, do you remember me now?" he asked. "It was I who stopped you in the forest, and it was I who was digging your potato field."

He started telling the others his story. I had caught him harvesting potatoes from our field one early morning when I brought the cows to the pasture. There he was, pulling the stalks and digging potatoes out with his hands. When I asked him what he was doing, he didn't answer, just shrugged his shoulders, picked up the sack of potatoes, and left.

But apparently he didn't leave, staying hidden to see what I would do next; and what I did brought a tremendous gale of laughter from the listeners. Even I burst out laughing. He certainly was a vivid storyteller. I had tried to repair the potato field by putting the discarded potato stalks in their former places to make it look as though the field had never been touched. It sounded hilarious now, but at that time I thought it a good idea.

This story made everybody even more friendly toward me, and some of them were coming up and tapping me on the shoulders. The frequency kept increasing, and my shoulders started hurting; besides, my new friends were getting drunk, and it was time for me to leave.

"Kola, I would like to get home now. I had a good time; thank you very much." I got up to go.

"Just one moment longer, there is someone else who wants to see you. Would you please follow me." I nodded my head. Why not, it was nice to be made a fuss over. I was a free person now. I could choose to go or not to go. But I would have to leave soon, I thought, because the twins must be worried by now. I shook hands with my hosts, thanked them for the honors, and hurried after Kola.

The room we entered was bare except for a wooden bench under a window, where an older man, apparently a high-ranking officer, sat. He had a military pouch on his lap, the kind officers wore slung across the chest and hanging at the hip. He was putting a map into it with one hand and with the other he was trying to locate something inside.

"Zdrastvute, dievushka—greetings, girl. Please sit down."

He motioned me to sit on the bench next to him. "What is your name?" he asked.

"My name is A—Anusha." He was talking to me while he was still organizing something in his purse. He had his head down, and I couldn't see his face clearly.

"Thank you, Kola. Please wait for us outside." Kola saluted and left the room, closing the door gently.

After a few seconds he put his purse aside and lifted his head. When I looked at him I was shocked. He was crying. I could see tears rolling down his cheeks into his uniform collar. He just sat there, not even blinking, staring at me with such sorrow that I had to look away. I felt tears in my own eyes, and inside me I felt a terrible ache. There we sat silently crying together; this man, a total stranger, an officer in the Russian army, and I. I looked at him again and saw the pain in his eyes, a pain I knew so well. Then I understood who this man was. Gently I reached out for his hand and brought it to my lips.

When I came out of the room where I left the crying man, Kola was waiting for me. His expression told me that he understood what had happened inside the room.

"What will you do now, Anusha?" he asked gently. "What can I do for you?"

"I would like to go back to Buczacz," I said. "I have things to do there. I want to make sure that my mother is buried according to Jewish law. Could you find transportation for me as far as Turka Nad Streyem? I passed the city on my way here. From there I will find my way home. Could you, Kola, please?"

"Of course. I will pick you up about six tomorrow morning; please be ready for me." We shook hands and parted.

On the way back to the farmer's, I took off the medal. For some reason I thought it might be wisest not to let them know that they had been harboring a Jewish girl for almost two months and one who supported the partisans at that. There are no secrets in small villages, and I was sure that some of the Ukrainians were hiding in the forest now and would eventually return home. They might even kill me if they heard about me. Also, the family might be punished for hiding a Jew. So I went back to the farmhouse and told the people there that the Russians had found my family and were going to send me to them. I don't know whether they believed me or not, but the farmer's wife gave me a clean blouse and skirt and wrapped up a little food for me to take along. I kept the food but left the skirt and blouse in the barn. They were Paula's, and I didn't want to use them.

The most difficult moment came when I had to say good-bye to the twins, especially Tomek. There was something about this sweet boy that reminded me of my brother Herzl, and apparently without realizing it I had transferred some of my love for my brother to him. Something inside me cried out with pain at our parting. I am sure he felt the same about me, because he cried when we stood hugging each other in the barn. Tadeush saw his brother cry and started crying too. It was really too much for me so, using a rather stern tone of voice, I shooed them out of the barn.

Kola came for me the way he promised, even a little earlier, but I was ready. I had hardly slept all night. We had barely left the farm, when Kola stopped me.

"Anusha, I have something for you. Here, take it." He handed me an envelope and a small bundle. "Open the envelope first; it is from my father, and the bundle is from all of us, the Kalpak partisans."

"Here, take it," he urged when I made no move to do so.

"This envelope is from your father? Your father?" I repeated, not quite understanding.

"Yes, my father. The man I left you with is my father. Anusha, we are Jews like yourself. When I told my father about you, he wanted to see you, especially when I mentioned that you spoke Russian and that you were about my sister Tanya's age. You see, my father and I were in Moscow when the Germans attacked Russia in 1941. My mother and my two sisters were in Kiev. They were trying to bring my grandparents to Moscow to live with us. They couldn't get back, and they were all killed by the Germans."

His voice dropped and began to tremble, and I was afraid he was going to cry, but he continued. "The rest you know. You bear a remarkable resemblance to my sister Tanya."

Now I understood why Kola's father had reacted like that when he saw me. Had he hoped I might be his daughter? Poor man. And I had left him alone with his grief. Perhaps I should have stayed. But his tears were breaking my heart, and I knew if I stayed I would have broken down completely.

When I tore off the top of the envelope and shook out its contents, a letter and several bills came tumbling out. I let the money lie on the ground where it fell and unfolded the letter. I could hardly believe my eyes. The letter was written in Hebrew.

Shalom, dear daughter Anusha, I read. I couldn't go on reading. My whole body started trembling. Kola took the letter from me and started reading. He read the Hebrew and translated it into Russian. I didn't even have the strength to tell him that I understood Hebrew, I was so upset. Next, he read the two documents that were attached to the letter. One identified the medal that had been given to me; the second stated that I was on my way to Moscow to become a student at a medical institute of which the director was Dr. Eliosha (Elyahu) Yaarov, the same name as the signature on the Hebrew letter.

"All the documents are stamped and signed," Kola said, looking at the documents and the money he had picked up. "These will see you safely home." He stuffed them into the bundle I carried and took my hand as we hurried to the school.

A big military truck stood in the schoolyard with its engine running.

"Vasily," called Kola as we came near the cabin, "are you ready to go? Turn off the engine, I want to talk with you."

A young soldier about Kola's age, twenty or twenty-one, with a big smile on his face, came near us.

"This is the girl who will be traveling with you. Take good care of her; you know what to do. Make sure to tell them that she is to travel inside the cabin when they put her in a truck again."

Vasily nodded his head and went back into the cabin. Kola turned to me.

"Listen, Anusha, listen carefully to what I am going to tell you. You are all right, aren't you?" Kola asked, looking anxiously into my face.

"I'm all right. Don't worry; and I am listening."

"You asked me once to take you along, remember? Near the window?"

"You? You?" I gasped. "You were the one with the bandaged head?"

He nodded. "I couldn't do it. But I will do it when the war is over and I come to Buczacz to pick you up. I know Buczacz well. I passed there in February with the partisans.

"If I live, I will be back to pick you up, I promise you! I will come, just wait for me!" Kola repeated.

Vasily was getting impatient and was calling to us. Kola lifted me up into the cabin and impulsively I threw my arms around his neck and hugged him. I suddenly realized that I didn't want to leave.

CHAPTER 18

Return to Buczacz

I had not completely accepted the fact that we had been liberated from German occupation once again, this time perhaps permanently. But the events of the last forty-eight hours finally made the liberation real to me. My liberation, yes; but meeting Kola and his father and hearing how their families had been destroyed by the Nazis in Russia reminded me of how little the liberation meant to my family and all but a remnant of my people. Our liberators, the Russian army, had come to free us. But they came too late.

I sat next to Vasily as he steered the truck over the mountain roads leading to Turka Nad Stryem.

"Vasily, thank you for your kindness to me," I said, trying to smile at him. "Please tell me about Kola and his father. Have you known them a long time?"

Vasily didn't need much urging, and from the tone of his voice I could sense that he had a special feeling for them. He told me that he and Kola had been medical students at the Institute of Medicine in Moscow. Kola's father was a professor of surgery there. When Kalpak was organizing his special unit of partisans to fight behind the German lines, both Kola and his father volunteered, and he, Vasily, just followed them.

"You know"—Vasily lowered his voice—"they are both *Yevreye*, Jews, but they fight like lions." I froze for a moment on hearing the word "but." Vasily was a young man who was raised in an enlightened society based on the equality of all men, but the way he referred to his

212

friends who were Jewish revealed the attitudes and prejudices of the old Russia. Their concept of equality apparently didn't acknowledge the existence of brave Jewish men. I thought that perhaps I was expecting too much and quickly pushed those thoughts out of my mind.

"You know, Anusha, Kola was wounded three times during attacks on the Germans, and he could have been discharged from the unit, but he insisted on staying on to fight and help the wounded. He acted as though he were driven by the devil himself." Here Vasily stopped and took a drink from his bottle of vodka. I wanted to tell Vasily that it wasn't the devil that had driven Kola, but the desire to destroy the Germans who had murdered his mother and sisters, to destroy the Nazi evil. That was what had driven poor Kola. But I kept quiet. Ours was a private grief.

About thirty minutes later we arrived near a lake. We parked on the side road. Vasily helped me out of the cabin, and as I stood outside breathing the fresh air I became aware of the beauty of the day and of our surroundings. The sun was shining brightly, warming the earth with a parting generosity, perhaps as a sign of regret, or as an apology for the wintry weather soon to follow. The month of October is the month of color in that area; the sky, the lake, and most of all the brilliant leaves on the ground and those remaining on the trees sparkled in the sunshine. The lake surface reflected the sun's rays and was smooth except for the slight ripple caused by passing swans. I was completely enchanted by my surroundings. I looked up at Vasily and saw him standing quietly with his eyes closed, his face turned to the sun.

Soon we were busy getting our meal ready. Vasily pulled a blanket out of the cabin and spread it on the grass. He put a basket filled with food on the blanket. I watched with great interest as he opened a can of what looked like American ham, the same type I was offered the day before. Next he pulled out a large loaf of bread and cut generous slices, putting each slice on a piece of clean linen. Then he unwrapped a piece of white cheese and placed it near the bread. To all this food he added two large red apples: A magnificent feast. Now it was my turn. I took out the bundle that Tomek's mother had given me and added my two boiled potatoes and one slice of thinly cut bread. It was a pathetic contribution to such a fine meal, but it was lucky I had this food because I couldn't have eaten the rich food Vasily set in front of us; my shrunken stomach would have revolted. But I did enjoy the apple, which was sweet and juicy. Vasily did not have my problem and ate heartily, washing the food down with the remains of his vodka. After he finished he stretched out on the blanket and fell asleep.

I covered him with his jacket and walked off to have a look around. As I crossed a nearby ravine I recognized the area, particularly the orchard and the house nearby. I had been there before on my way south. I remembered passing the orchard, looking longingly at the winter pears still on the trees and wishing I could pick some but not daring to do so because the people from the house might catch me. Then I had seen what looked like two German military cars and a motorcycle parked near the house and quickly left the area.

But now I didn't notice any signs of life. The house looked deserted. The sidewalk leading to the front door was covered with undisturbed fallen leaves. The flower beds looked as though someone had ridden over them, the stems broken and the flowers wilted. I went to the back door of the house and stood listening. But I heard nothing. Impulsively I tried the doorknob, and to my great surprise the door opened. Again I listened for voices. Not hearing any, I entered the house.

The inside of the house was very lovely; it was fully furnished. It looked as though the occupants had left in a great hurry. The living room was clean except for the ashes spilled outside the fireplace and some scattered newspapers. I hadn't seen a newspaper for a very long time, so I picked one up and saw that it was printed in German. This and the vehicles I had seen parked in front of the house indicated that the last occupants of this house were Germans.

A shudder passed through me. I was still terrified of the Germans. As I continued to explore, I saw a pantry, or storage room, that had an assortment of items on the shelves. A suitcase stood near the wall and several coats were hanging on hooks. I went back to the living room and sat down on the beautifully upholstered chair. It felt unreal. It had been so long since I had been in a living room. Suddenly it struck me. Why hadn't the people taken their coats with them when they left? And to whom did the suitcase in the storage room belong? Could it be waiting for someone? I went into the storage room and examined the suitcase. It was locked and quite heavy. I also admired the lovely wood paneling on the walls and moved my hand over it. I don't know what made me look behind the hanging coats, but I did and I found that the coats had covered a door. I opened the door, then lit a candle and went down the steps it disclosed. What followed next was really incredible.

The steps led down to a cellar, which like the storage room had wood-paneled walls. Even by the dim light of my single candle I could see that the cellar was very large. The right side of the wall was covered with suitcases and boxes of different sizes. I opened some of the boxes and nearly cried out in surprise when I saw their contents. The cellar contained a store of every conceivable garment a man or woman could use! Everything was completely new. Hah, I thought, fate wanted me to have something to wear instead of my shabby peasant clothing.

I pulled out two old leather suitcases and filled them up with dresses, sweaters, underwear, and beautiful shawls, the kind Manka from Wujciechovka wore on Sunday. Next I looked and found a complete outfit for Wujciu, including a fur hat. I picked up a box with thread, but I dropped it and it spilled, revealing hidden jewelry. I took a small watch and put the rest of it back in place.

I took only things I would need or would give as gifts to people who had been kind to us, like Wujciu and Manka. I tied the suitcases with leather belts and brought them upstairs. They were too heavy, so I put on some of the clothing, one article over another. Just before leaving the house I thought of leaving the suitcases and just taking what I was wearing, but I changed my mind. Someone, most likely the owner of the coats, had accumulated all the things I saw in the cellar. Maybe he stole them, or they were burglarized from Jewish homes, or perhaps the goods were ransom payments for someone's life. Maybe some of the things even came from my own big family. Whatever the truth might be, I felt that I was entitled to take what I so desperately needed.

I half carried, half pulled the suitcases back to the truck. I thought that Vasily would certainly be surprised to see me changed from a skinny girl to a plump one in such a short time. I would have to explain to him how it happened, and I didn't particularly look forward to that. But when I returned to the truck, Vasily was still fast asleep. I put the suitcases and a sleeveless lamb jacket I had also taken into the back of the truck and went to wake Vasily.

Vasily did not show any reaction to my considerably changed appearance until he tried to help me back into the cabin and my peasant skirt lifted, revealing all the layers of clothing underneath it. He dropped me on the grass and burst out laughing. He laughed so hard that tears were running down his cheeks. I didn't see anything at all funny in all this, but I realized that I would have to take off some of the clothing before we arrived in the city.

Perhaps the most remarkable thing about this entire incident was that Vasily never asked about my new clothing or about the suitcases. Either he knew, or didn't want to know.

Vasily and I were sitting on a bench outside the army headquarters in Turka Nad Stryem. We were waiting for an army truck that was going to Stanislavov on the way to Buczacz.

"Well, Anusha." Vasily turned to me. "This is where we part. You will be going home, and I will return to the village. I see you are now a person of property." He gave my two suitcases a sweeping glance. "But before I go I would like you to look at the bundle Kola gave you. It contains a gift from us, the Kalpak partisans."

I picked up the bundle lying on top of the suitcases, and with slightly trembling hands untied the four knots in the kerchief. The first thing I saw was a leather hat, the kind pilots wear, with earflaps that closed under the chin. It was used but in excellent condition. I stroked its soft brown leather as though it were a living thing. Next I saw a military shirt neatly folded and all buttoned up to the collar. Inside the shirt was a rolled-up leather belt. I touched the lieutenant's insignia on the shoulders. There must be some mistake, I thought as I picked up the shirt.

"Vasily," I said, turning to him. "Kola made a mistake. He gave me the wrong bundle. Will you please take this back to him?"

Vasily smiled and patted me on my shoulder.

"No, Anusha, Kola didn't make a mistake; it is his shirt and hat. He wanted you to have them. The lieutenant's rank is honorary. You may still have to earn it; but you can wear it now. It says so in your documents."

I was deeply touched by this beautiful gift. The shirt was brand new. I felt tears gather in my eyes, and it took all my strength not to cry. Next I took off the officer's insignia and gave it to Vasily.

"Please give these back to Kola. I will keep the shirt and hat." I unbuttoned the shirt and put it on. It was a little big but possible to wear with a belt around my waist. The length was right, and the hat was perfect. I had a very strange feeling, wearing those clothes. They were especially dear to me because they came from Kola. I could see that Vasily, too, became very emotional, because he got up and hugged me to his chest.

It was getting late in the afternoon and Vasily was getting restless. He had to get back. Before leaving he introduced me to a sergeant who promised to take care of me and see me on my way as soon as there was a truck going in the direction of Buczacz.

I had planned to return to Buczacz as quickly as possible, but when we approached Stanislavov I surprised myself by asking the driver to stop the truck inside the city. I had recognized the park where I had played as a child while visiting my uncle, Dr. Kurtz. Then I saw my uncle's white house, and I felt my heart begin to beat violently as we passed it. I asked the driver to back up, park across the street, and wait a few minutes for me. He acknowledged my request with a smile. He was a friendly young soldier who treated me with respect even though he didn't understand who I was or why I was dressed so strangely.

The house looked just the way I remembered it from my last visit in 1938. The garden in front of the house still had a white fence. The walls were white, setting off the beauty of the intricately hand-carved door, a special gift from grandfather Kurtz. As I lifted my hand to knock, it felt like lead, and my heart pounded so loudly that I thought its sound alone would open the door. After what seemed like a long time but could have been only a minute, the door was opened by an old woman wearing a head kerchief and a long peasant dress.

"I would like to see Dr. Kurtz, please," I said politely. "I am his niece." The woman's brown eyes became very large and she cried out loudly.

"*Pan doktor!*—Mr. Doctor!" Then, before my eyes, she appeared to fold into the floor and lay there motionless. I immediately bent over her, untied her head kerchief, and put her head on my lap, but as I looked at her closely I suddenly felt like screaming myself. I recognized her. I knew her well. She was Aunt Rania. We called her "aunt" although she was actually my grandmother's servant. She was one of the orphans my grandmother had given a dowry so that she could marry one of the village men. Aunt Rania was very devoted to my family, especially to my uncle, and when he opened his practice in Stanislavov she and her husband went along to keep house for him.

"What's going on here, and what is the meaning of all this noise?" called an angry voice from inside the house. A man wearing a doctor's white jacket appeared in front of us.

"This poor woman has fainted, *Panie doktorze*," I said. "Could you please help me lift her onto a sofa or bed?"

"There is no need to bother with her." He pulled Aunt Rania out of my arms, dropped her on the floor, and, holding the door with one hand, he pointed with the other for me to leave. What an ugly man, I thought as I stood up. I was getting angry at this monster for his treatment of the old woman, but I controlled my voice when I spoke to him.

"I am looking for Dr. Kurtz; I am his niece. Do you know where he might be?"

The man gave me a startled look, and I could see his face go pale. The hand holding the door shook.

"There is no one living here by that name and no one ever lived here by that name!" he spat out. "You had better leave before I shoot you." He pulled a revolver from his white jacket and pointed it at me.

I don't know why I didn't just leave quickly when faced by that angry man with the gun. I was probably almost insane with rage and frustration, and with the realization of still another painful loss.

Instead, I stood facing this man and screamed at him.

"You murdering Pole, this is my uncle's house! Get out of here before I kill you with my bare hands. Tell me, what did you do to get this house? Did you betray my uncle to the Nazis? And you call yourself a doctor!"

My screams must have been heard all over the neighborhood, because suddenly the Russian driver of my truck was beside me, his pistol pointed at the Pole. He stepped between us.

"What's going on here? Why is this man threatening you with a gun?" he asked me. The doctor was trying to close the door, but the Russian had his foot there.

"This is my uncle's house," I sobbed. "Now I know he must be dead!" I said this in Russian. The driver nodded sympathetically and asked, "What do you want me to do?"

"What can you do? What can I do? What can anyone do?"

I turned to face the doctor. "I will return one day and throw you out of my uncle's house. Remember that!" Then I did something I had never done before. I spat in the Pole's face.

I said I would be back, but I knew I never would. I tugged at the driver's sleeve. We quietly returned to the truck.

I was very shaken by this encounter and cried for a long time as we drove on. When I told this story later to some of the Jewish survivors I met in Buczacz, I found out that encounters like mine often ended in tragedy, and that my Russian driver had probably saved my life. I was told that the Jews who tried to reclaim their homes or other property simply disappeared, never to be seen again.

* * *

My driver had to turn back immediately. He said that I wouldn't have any trouble getting a ride to Buczacz, and he was right. Within half an hour a military truck picked me up. The driver checked my documents and, satisfied, helped load my belongings and drove on to Buczacz.

I dozed off and on, waking up every few minutes to see where we were. But finally I fell into a deep sleep, thus missing our entry into Buczacz. I was awakened by the driver when we stopped in the middle of the city. We were in front of a restaurant on Chechego Maya Street. I was back. The driver suggested that we have a cup of tea, and I gladly followed him. He was kind to me and put my suitcases inside the restaurant, then went to order the tea.

When the kind Russian soldier brought me my tea I couldn't even drink it; I was fully aware of where I was now, and my throat was choked with memories. I didn't even notice when he left.

I don't know how long I sat there in my chair thinking and remembering before I realized someone was telling me that the restaurant was about to close and asking whether there was anything I needed.

The voice sounded familiar. I looked up and there, standing in front of me with her beautiful red hair, dressed in an embroidered peasant blouse, a white apron tied over her skirt, wearing red boots with a whip stuck into one boot, was Bella. Our dear friend Bella from the ghetto, Rachel's sister and little Hanale's and Danny's mother.

It was Bella, I could see, yet not quite the same Bella I remembered from the ghetto. She had changed. The once-beautiful blue-green eyes, which had always been filled with courage and joy of life, were now sunken in their sockets and filled with heartbreaking sadness. It took all my willpower not to cry. Then those sad eyes widened as she recognized me. She didn't say anything but took off my leather hat, pulled me to my feet, and, putting her arms around me, held me tightly to her heart.

I was very fortunate to have found Bella. She took me to a Jewish family named Siegel who lived in the same building she did. The family consisted of a mother, a daughter about ten years old, and a niece of fourteen, my own age. I later found out that there had been a father who also survived, but he went back to his small town to reclaim his flour mill and was murdered by its new owners. The family was destitute but lucky to have Bella as a friend.

They offered to let me share the bed with the niece, but I decided to sleep on a straw pallet on the floor. This was a wise choice because the girl had terrible nightmares and cried most of the night. Poor tortured soul, I thought as I finally fell asleep just before dawn.

When I awoke in the morning it took me a while to realize where I was. My straw pallet was in a room that looked like a kitchen. There were people sitting around a table, eating breakfast and talking in Yiddish. There was a smell of chicory in the room. I still had a sense of unreality and closed my eyes, thinking that perhaps it was a dream; but when I opened them, I was still there. I was in Buczacz, living with Jewish people.

As I became fully awake I remembered meeting Bella in her restaurant, so I dressed quickly and went to see her. I also wanted to see her children, who I remembered so well from the ghetto. I felt a pang of pain as I also remembered Rachel. The restaurant wasn't open yet but Bella let me in. She was alone with her son. I recognized Danny immediately. He had grown in the two years since I last saw him, and was now a very good-looking boy. He greeted me shyly, shaking my hand. I looked for Hanale. She wasn't there. Probably with the maid in the house, I thought. Danny saw my look and understood that I was looking for Hanale, but he didn't say anything. I offered to help, but Bella suggested that I sit down and have breakfast first. Bella looked up once in a while from her work and must have read something in my face, because she soon came over and sat next to me.

"Alicia, you have something on your mind which I can see is troubling you greatly. Can I help you?"

"I have to find my mother's grave and bring her to the Jewish cemetery, to Kever Israel." With a voice filled with tears I told her briefly how my mother had died. I had never seen Bella cry before, but she cried then.

"I really loved your mother, Alicia. She was a great lady, a loving human being. I know a man who might be able to help you. He will be here soon. He eats breakfast here every morning."

That was how I met Mr. Rosenthal once more. I knew him well, and his daughter had been one of my friends. We had gone to Hebrew school together. I had played in her house many times. My favorite place there was Mr. Rosenthal's furniture workshop. We had had several pieces of furniture in our house that were made by him before the war. All this was past. Now Mr. Rosenthal was the only survivor of his whole family.

Bella set plates of cooked cereal in front of us with a cup of chicory for Mr. Rosenthal and a glass of warm milk for me. It was strange to sit there and eat with him. We kept looking at each other. The poor man was probably thinking of his daughter, and I was wondering if I was right to ask him to help me with my mother after all he had been through already. Would he have the mental strength to help me bring my mother to Kever Israel for a proper Jewish burial? I hoped he wouldn't break down and cry. I really couldn't bear it when grown-ups cried: I felt as though the whole world were being shattered around me.

One would expect that Mr. Rosenthal would start the conversation by asking me first how I was, but he didn't; none of us asked this. We all knew how we were; we were all lost. We were all drifting in a world of bitter memories, trying to hold on to sanity somehow and not to give in to despair.

"Alicia dear," he said softly, "I feel there is something you wish to tell me. Please don't hesitate; we are old friends, right?"

I told him about my mother. He listened, and when I finished, he asked me if I wanted him to help me find out where my mother was buried. I thanked him and told him that I would do it myself. As he got up to go, he said that he would immediately begin the preparations necessary according to Jewish law. Before he left he put his hand on my head, and I felt his hand tremble.

As I suspected all along, it was the woman superintendent of the house where we lived on the Koliova street who had betrayed my mother and me to the SS men. She was very frightened when she saw me at her door and kept crossing herself, calling on the Holy Mother to save her. She was afraid that I was going to strangle her when she saw the fury and hate in my eyes. I was just waiting for her to lie and deny her treachery. Then I might have killed her, so insane was I with grief, but she didn't. She walked out of the house and silently pointed to my mother's grave. It was in the backyard of the house, where people buried their dogs.

I had lived through some horrors in my life, and I thought I could handle the pain, but I wasn't prepared for the anguish I experienced the following day. Even Mr. Rosenthal broke down when he lifted my mother out of her shallow grave and wrapped her body in a white sheet. We put her in a wooden box which we placed on a wheelbarrow, and brought her to the Jewish cemetery. I had taken my mother's little box out of its hiding place in the wall of our house the night before and placed it unopened in the grave by her side. I threw the first handful of earth over her. Mr. Rosenthal recited the Kaddish, the memorial prayer, and I repeated the words after him.

El malei rachamin, God of Mercy. The words repeated themselves over and over in my mind. Poor God, poor Mother, poor Zachary in his grave near Mother, poor Rachel . . . poor Alicia. . . .

I didn't hear Danny until he took my hand, and I couldn't see him because my eyes were blind with tears, but I felt his hand in mine. We stood there for a long time.

It was here, standing over the graves of the people we loved, that Danny told me what had happened to Hanale. He cried as he spoke, but he needed to talk. They had left Buczacz soon after I disappeared. Beniek and his friends had a bunker near Drohobich, and they were hiding there. They were betrayed by the people who had supplied them with food. While the search for the bunker was going on outside, Hanale had started crying. Someone put a pillow over her face to muffle the sound, and she suffocated.

The bunker was discovered in the end. Beniek and his friends fought for their lives. They killed some Germans and Ukrainian policemen, and the rest ran away. Six Jews, including Hanale, were killed. The survivors moved away from the forest, but first they found and killed the people who had betrayed them. Poor little Hanale; poor Danny, too, for having witnessed such a tragedy. No wonder Bella had such pain in her eyes.

It had started raining, but we still didn't move. I don't know how long we had been standing there, when finally Danny pulled my hand and we left the cemetery.

"Alicia, do you think there is a God? Do you really think there is one?" Danny suddenly stopped and asked in a pleading voice. "Please tell me if there is a God. I have to know."

I looked at him in surprise. There was an urgency in his question. Then I remembered that I had had a similar need when I was Danny's age, eleven. I had gone to Reb Srool with my question, and while I respected the answer he gave me, I could not quite accept it.

We sat down on the stone fence of the cemetery, under a big tree. It was still raining, but not very hard.

"I have always believed there is a God," I said to Danny. "I was brought up that way. I always prayed to Him, and the sweetest memories I have of my family are all connected with our Jewish traditions, and with God."

I tried to remember the words Reb Srool used when I had asked him almost the same question, but I wasn't wise enough to explain during the years when we were being hunted down and murdered by the Nazis. Many times I had heard adults say, "If there is a God, how can He be silent at our cries of anguish? How come He doesn't punish murderers?"

"When I heard people say that, Danny dear, do you know what I thought? I thought that God was ashamed of the people on this earth and was shocked by what they were doing to one another, but that He couldn't do anything to help us.

"But look, do you see those raindrops? They could be tears falling from the skies. Maybe God is crying with us, for He has lost so many people He also loved. I don't know whether you should believe in God or not. You will have to decide for yourself. But everyone should believe in something or somebody, and right now, the way I see it, God needs us to believe in Him. He is as alone as we are, and as lost as we are. Somehow we will have to prove to Him that people aren't all evil, that they are capable of love, love of one another and love of Him; unconditional love. We will have to do good deeds, to have God respect us and thus regain our self-respect. We will have to fight evil with good; we really must."

As I continued talking I realized that if I were to survive at all and escape from the swamp of anguish and despair, I would have to reach out to people, to those who survived like myself, and perhaps sometime in the future, to all people. I would not be able to continue to hate, because I knew in my young heart that hate could eventually destroy me.

But I would always remember what had happened to my family and to my people and would never be able to forgive those who committed the crimes. I didn't have the right: Jewish tradition decrees that only the victim can forgive sins committed against himself. Most of the victims were dead and could not grant forgiveness—could I forgive in their name? Sins against God could be forgiven by God. Perhaps the wholesale murder of God's creations was also a sin against God. Then let the murderers answer to God in some future existence. Perhaps He would forgive them. I couldn't speak for anyone but myself, and I could never forgive. I was silent for a moment, stunned at the implications of my thoughts. I expressed much of this to Danny.

"Did I answer your question?" I asked. Danny just looked at me, bewildered, and didn't say a word.

"Danny, you know I love you very much," I said, and I bent down and kissed his face. I could taste his salty tears on my lips.

After the seven days of shiva, the traditional mourning period, I took a walk outside. Over a week had passed since I had returned to Buczacz. It was market day, and the city was bustling with wagons coming from the surrounding farms. I joined the crowds of people at the marketplace in spite of the memories the place brought back. I was determined to find what I was looking for, so I continued to walk about, carefully examining each wagon's occupants. Finally I recognized a farming couple from Wujciechovka. I had worked on their fields several times during the summer of 1943, and I hoped that they would recognize me as well and would help me contact my old friend Wujciu.

Before I even had a chance to greet them the woman called out in a loud voice, "Helka, how nice to see you again. How are you?" I was taken aback a little because she didn't seem surprised to see me. But then I remembered that many of the people in Wujciechovka knew my identity, and by now they probably all knew that I was Jewish.

We greeted each other and talked for a while. They seemed happy now that the Germans were gone, and the Banderovcy with them. They could sell their produce to the government or on the open market, whichever way they chose. The harvest was good last year, and it looked as though this winter would not be severe. I thanked them for being kind to me in the past, and finally I worked the conversation around to the purpose of my visit to the marketplace.

"Do you know the beekeeper who lives alone in the little house outside the village? You know who I mean?" I asked, addressing myself to the woman.

"I know who you mean, the one who kept the Jews in his house," she said. "Don't be surprised. We knew all along that something was going on in his house."

"Well, that is all in the past." I interrupted her rudely because I was afraid that she was going to say something unkind about Wujciu and then I would get angry, which would defeat my purpose. I needed her help.

"I would be grateful if you could bring him with you to the market next week. Could you do this, please?"

The woman hesitated. "I don't know if we will come next week. I'll have to see."

But I knew that she didn't like the idea of riding with Wujciu. She also believed in the rumors that Wujciu could cast spells on people and that he was possessed by evil spirits.

But I persisted. "Look, I know it is difficult to decide now, but could you please give him this letter. And this is for your trouble." I held out to her a letter and four hundred rubles, which I took out of the money Kola's father had given me. She understood what I wanted her to do, looked at her husband, and they both nodded their heads. I put the money in her hand and smiled.

"I will be here next Thursday morning. Don't forget!" I said as I waved and turned away from their wagon.

I never considered the possibility that the farmers would not keep their promise to bring Wujciu. It had been about eight months since I'd said good-bye to him, and I wanted very much to see him again. But at the same time I was unhappy about it. I thought about my mother and how we had planned to reward Wujciu for saving our lives. We even hoped that in time we could have him live with us. I was glad I could help him now, but it was not the same without my mother.

I had included some very nice clothing for Wujciu in the selection I had taken from the cellar. I would have to get shoes for him somehow when he came to Buczacz. Bella promised to help me sell some of my shawls to Russian soldiers, who were buying them to send home to their families. The shawls were very much in demand and were bringing in as much as two thousand rubles each. I sold some right away so that I would have enough money to do all I was planning to do for Wujciu and Manka.

I lived in great suspense all week, waiting for Thursday. On Thursday I was the first one at the marketplace and watched the first wagons arrive and open for business. The place was filling up quickly and was already bustling with people, but there still was no sign of the farmer's wagon and Wujciu. I was beginning to worry that perhaps Wujciu was ill or perhaps, God forbid, had died, when I finally saw him. He was sitting in the front seat of the wagon with the farmer. My heart leapt with joy at the sight. I truly loved that dear old man. He saw me, too, and smiled a toothless smile that lit up his whole face. I felt I couldn't wait another moment but had to get to him right away. I nearly pulled him off the wagon, so eager was I to touch him.

I will never forget that day as long as I live, and I believe Wujciu didn't either. I had everything planned for us. We went immediately to Bella's restaurant and had breakfast there. I was so choked up with emotion at seeing Wujciu that I couldn't eat. I could see that Wujciu was only picking at his cereal; he probably felt the same way. Only after Bella gave Wujciu a glass of wine' did he relax a little.

Bella had agreed to let us use her galvanized iron bathtub. Danny was already in the kitchen and had prepared hot water. I was afraid Wujciu would object when he saw what we were planning for him, but he was delighted and later I could hear his ohs and ahs of satisfaction from the kitchen, where we had installed the bathtub.

While Wujciu was bathing, I sat in the bedroom-living room sewing. I was sewing money I had gotten for the shawls into Wujciu's jacket. I had thought of giving the money to him but changed my mind. Suppose the farmers gave him something to drink on the way home and he lost it. It was safer inside his coat lining. I also put a letter to Manka into Wujciu's jacket. The letter told her about myself and begged her forgiveness for not seeing her for such a long time. I told her about Pietro and his friends who had come to kill us at Wujciu's and what happened. I ended my letter wishing her good luck in life and hoping that she, her father, and her brother would use all the gifts I was sending her in good health. I remember that I cried when I wrote the letter. I was so very happy I could do all this. I had used up a whole suitcase of clothing and shawls, but the thought that I could share something with those wonderful people made me very happy.

I had just finished my task and was sitting hugging Wujciu's jacket to my heart, when Danny called me to the kitchen.

I will always cherish the sight of my dear old Wujciu as he stood there, dressed in a white shirt and brown woolen pants, wearing the new boots, with his bald head shining and still slightly wet. His blue eyes sparkled with gladness. I thought I saw tears in his eyes as he smiled his so familiar toothless smile.

Oh, God, how was I going to part from this dear man whom I loved like a grandfather? In my heart I knew that he belonged in his home and village, and I belonged . . . where did I belong?

Wujciu and I spent the rest of the day together. We went to the cemetery, and there we prayed for my mother. I showed him my brother Zachary's grave and Rachel's grave and it was only thanks to Wujciu's strong moral support that we were able to continue the day with some measure of joy at our reunion. He showed himself to me in a new light, that of a man of learning and knowledge of social graces. We had lunch at Bella's. I could see that Wujciu was very taken with Bella, who couldn't help but succumb to his charm.

It was getting late, so we went to my home and picked up the things I was going to give him. There was a basket with a cake and tea and many goodies I thought Wujciu would enjoy, as well as the gifts for Manka and her family. I had a new military blanket for Wujciu and two new white sheets. I explained about the money and letter inside his coat. He lowered his eyes but didn't say anything.

The farmers were glad to see us that afternoon, especially when I handed the man the vodka and the woman a package containing tea and yeast. They had not sold all of their produce. Their potatoes were of the finest quality, blue potatoes, and they had wanted to get a good price for them. They also had some cut-up wood left over. I don't know why I did what I did next, but I asked them how much they wanted for all they had in the wagon. I had enough money to pay for it. I paid their price and asked them to unload the things at Wujciu's house. Wujciu tried to object to this transaction but, as usual, I won.

"I know, Helka dear—or should I call you Alicia now?—you always win."

"I am sorry, Wujciu, or should I call you . . ."

"Wladislav Chernicky at your service, Miss Alicia." He bowed gallantly. I stared in astonishment. Gone was the old village man, and in his place stood a Polish aristocrat. Even his Polish sounded different as he introduced himself. I had always suspected what was now evident. Wujciu was not a peasant. I could not guess what circumstances had reduced him to the life of a lonely beekeeper, but they must have been very unusual.

When I looked at the farmers I could see that they, too, were taken by surprise at Wujciu's unusual behavior. It occurred to me that perhaps they would now treat him with some measure of the respect that he so rightly deserved.

The day that had started with such joy was coming to an end, and I knew in my heart that I would never see Wujciu again.

The moment I dreaded so much had come. Wujciu and I had to part. The farmers were ready to leave.

"Alicia, dear child, remember who you are and act accordingly," he whispered into my ear as we stood hugging each other. I was afraid I was going to cry, but I took courage from Wujciu, who expected me to be brave.

I stood watching until Wujciu's wagon disappeared, and then, because I didn't have to appear brave anymore, I allowed my tears to flow.

I felt let down after Wujciu's visit. I thought about him often and worried about his welfare. Winter was coming and I pictured him all alone in the little house. I only hoped that Manka would visit him after reading my letter and make sure he had enough food and firewood. She was a kind girl, and I was sure that she would put the money I sent her to good use.

In the meantime I continued living with Mrs. Siegel, her daughter Rivkale, and her niece Tamar. But I was spending a lot of time with Danny. We sort of adopted each other. I took him with me when I finally went to look for Slavka and her family. The house where she had lived when I visited her in March after our first liberation was empty. When I asked the neighbors about the family, all they could tell me was that they had left, and no one knew where they had gone. One neighbor, however, remembered seeing a high-ranking Russian officer come to their house several times. Now I understood. The officer who had visited them was probably Slavka's uncle, her father's brother. They had probably left with him.

I was terribly sorry not to see her. But then I remembered that they had had connections with the Ukrainian police and the Banderovcy during the German occupation, and was glad that they had left town. I didn't for a moment doubt that the Russian NKVD secret police would eventually look for all those who had collaborated with the Germans. I hadn't forgotten what the Russians did to my brother Moshe when he ran away from school, and how he never returned from the prison in Chortkov. Perhaps one day I will see Slavka again, I thought, but I wasn't planning to look for her. I also remembered her brother Pavlo's strange behavior the last time I was in their home, especially when I mentioned my brother Herzl.

As days passed, I began to notice differences between life after the first liberation in March 1944 and now. The city had been liberated for several months, and during my walks with Danny on Chechego Maya Street, I should have met some Jewish people, but I didn't. Most of those who had survived in March were killed in the massacre on the Fador when the Germans reoccupied Buczacz, and the rest were probably shot where they were found.

When Danny and I weren't looking for Jewish survivors, we spent our time visiting the cemetery. Mr. Rosenthal gave us pieces of wood, and we made *matzevot* (memorial plaques) out of them for my mother, Zachary, Rachel, and for an unmarked grave nearby. We carved their names in Hebrew and placed the *matzevot* on the top of the graves. Sometimes I brought fall flowers from the marketplace or made strings of colorful leaves to put on the graves. I seemed to remember that it was against Orthodox Jewish tradition to put cut flowers on a grave, but to me flowers meant love, so I did anyway, and we also put small stones beside them.

The cemetery became the main focus of my life. As I recited the memorial prayer daily, I also included the unknown person who was buried nearby. I couldn't understand why I was always drawn to that grave, but I was. I even asked Danny about it, but he turned away from me and wouldn't say a word.

Bella apparently questioned Danny about how we were spending our time. He probably told her that we spent much of the time at the cemetery, because one day she suggested that I help her in the restaurant and also teach Danny Hebrew, math, and everything I could remember from my schooldays. I had considered the possibility of returning to our school but in the end decided against it. I couldn't face the memories of my friends Sydia Katz, Netka Lebhart, and Reika Reich, who were all dead. I also didn't want to see my former friend, Olga, whose father had hit me at the prison. But I did not want to study, so I followed Bella's suggestion and started teaching Danny at home.

I didn't have Hebrew books, but I borrowed Mr. Rosenthal's prayer book. Sometimes at night Bella would be sewing while listening to our lessons and would correct me, and sometimes she would even tell us stories from books she had read. Bella was an educated woman and a wonderful storyteller. But most of the time she just sat and watched us in silence. I caught her watching me one night and saw such sorrow in her face that it took all of my willpower to finish the lesson with Danny.

I was much more successful in teaching Danny than with helping Bella in the kitchen. I was always in a state of shock when I saw all the food on the kitchen table. My mind kept wandering back to the ghetto children, and I couldn't stop thinking of how many children I could have fed with this food. It was wrong of me to think that way, but I couldn't help it. Bella finally realized that I was useless in the kitchen, so she suggested that I help out in the dining room by serving and cleaning tables.

Most of the customers at the restaurant were military people, plus a few occasional Jewish survivors, who ate at their own table. Bella served the survivors herself, and I noticed that they never paid for their food. Dear Bella, she hadn't changed much, I thought. How well I remembered the soup she had served me when I visited Rachel. I am sure I would have starved to death if it weren't for Bella. And now she was again so generous to people who had no source of income, people who had lost all they had during the war.

Among the regular military customers was a young Russian sergeant who ate his noon meal in the restaurant every day. Sometimes he ate by himself, other times some of his friends joined him. They often had some vodka with their meals. Then one of his friends would urge the sergeant to sing. He would start slowly and quietly in a beautiful alto voice and would increase the volume of sound gradually. His voice would seem to envelop the whole room. Those present would stop eating and would listen, enthralled.

I loved two of his songs and had him write the words out for me. One song told the tragic story of a partisan who lay dead under an oak tree at the edge of a forest. He lay there as though in a deep sleep. The wind blew his golden curls. Over his grave stood his mother, crying. "I have given birth to you, my son, but could not protect you; and now your grave will be here." Years later this song was translated into Hebrew when Jewish sons died for their country in the deserts of Israel and Jewish mothers cried over their sons' graves. This song had always touched me deeply.

The second song told the story of a young girl, Anuta, who sold flowers in a flower shop. She sang as she sold her flowers, explaining that flowers are stronger than words, and invited customers into her store. And when they bought from her she showered her customers with additional flowers, especially soldiers, because her sweetheart was also a soldier, a captain, and she was waiting for him to return to her. The song ends with the invitation "Please come in. Buy flowers." It was a sad and very romantic song; somehow it made me think that I, too, was waiting for someone. Deep inside me I was hoping to see the one person I had loved all my life, a boy who went away to look for his family in Stanislavov just before the Germans broke the Russian lines and reoccupied Buczacz. The boy who had saved my life in Kopechince. I was waiting for my friend Milek.

I learned those two songs and often sang them in Bella's house. Bella encouraged me and complimented me on my sweet soprano voice and on the feeling I was putting into the words. She said that it was good to sing the sorrow out of my heart. And she was right. I always felt better when I finished the songs.

Bella was always right, and she was so very kind to me. I felt, though, that I contributed to her sadness. It was clear to me that I reminded her of her sister Rachel, whom she missed very much. At such times I wished Rachel were there in my place. I was beginning to experience the same feeling which, I learned later, was shared by most survivors: a guilty feeling about being alive, that I didn't deserve to be the one who survived, and that any one of my brothers was more deserving. I kept those thoughts to myself during the day, but my nightmares always included them.

One month had passed since my return and it was now late November 1944. I continued to help Bella in the restaurant, study with Danny, and make my daily visits to those I loved in the cemetery.

But one evening when I was about to leave and go back to Mrs. Siegel's for the night, Bella called me aside.

"Alicia, I have a favor to ask of you. Please sit down."

She spoke in such a solemn voice that I was suddenly gripped by fear. I was afraid that she had some bad news; perhaps she was leaving Buczacz, or was ill.

"Alicia dear, I remember that Rachel once told me that you wanted to be a doctor. Do you still want to be a doctor?" I shrugged my shoulders. "If you do, here is your opportunity to find out."

Then Bella told me about a sixteen-year-old Jewish boy who had stepped on a mine and lost half of his right leg. The remaining half was healing slowly, and while he needed a lot of care, he would eventually be well. But his soul was not healing. He had no will to live and needed help.

Bella continued. "He lives two houses from here. Here is his address. An old nurse is taking care of him, but she is not able to reach him emotionally. I thought perhaps you . . ." I nodded slowly and took the address.

And that was how I met Benjamin, who eventually regained his will to live but indirectly caused me to lose mine.

I was eager to serve Bella and curious to see if the idea of reaching out and helping other survivors like ourselves might also prove to be the solution to my own loneliness and despair. I would find out if what I had told Danny at the cemetery were empty words or whether they could be put into practice and give me a purpose in life, a reason to exist. With these thoughts I presented myself at Benjamin's door early the following morning.

The woman who opened the door smiled as though she had expected me. And Benjamin was prepared for my visit. He was sitting fully dressed on a chair near a table. I sat down on the chair opposite him. He was of medium height, with light brown curly hair, rather long in the back, and brown eyes. His eyes were sunken, with dark circles under them. They were eyes that had seen terrible events, eyes of an old man who had suffered a great deal.

I had seen many such eyes before, but I was more distressed by the signs of resignation and indifference in his whole face. These signs were also familiar. I knew them well; I had felt them in myself after my mother was killed when I had lost all will to live. I certainly was faced with a challenge.

I could see that Benjamin was deep in his own labyrinth of darkness and despair, and I could understand why. To have lived through the horrors of the German occupation and then, after the liberation, to be crippled by a mine at the age of sixteen was more than his mind could accept. I wondered if Bella had been right to send me here to help Benjamin. But Bella had always been right before, so I assumed she knew what she was doing this time as well.

I could see that the nurse took good care of Benjamin. His room had two large windows and a rug on the floor. There were pictures on the walls and books on the bookshelf. Benjamin's clothing was clean and pressed. The shirt he wore was snow white. We sat silently, looking at each other and through the window that faced a backyard. We watched together as the wind tore off the last fall leaves, twirling them around until they rested on the ground. The smell of freshly baked bread came from the kitchen. The nurse brought us tea, bread, butter, and marmalade. Benjamin didn't touch his food. I drank the tea but couldn't swallow the bread. We didn't talk much during the first visit. I left after about an hour, promising to visit again the following afternoon.

It wasn't until my fifth visit with Benjamin that we really talked, or rather, I talked and he listened. I started telling him about the weather outside and then, somehow, I began telling him about my childhood in the Carpathian Mountains. I told him about nearly drowning in the river when I tried to recover the shoes that I had let float while pretending they were ships, and I related other incidents from my happy childhood before the war. I was so absorbed in my storytelling that I was startled when I heard Benjamin cry out.

"Alicia! My God, you were a pain in the neck! You should have been given a good spanking." And he began to laugh.

"Oh, I was, Benjamin. I was, but what do you expect from a daughter of a father like mine. Let me tell you, listen. . . ."

Suddenly I was transported into my family's past. I spent the next hour telling an enraptured Benjamin one of my favorite stories.

My father, Sigmund Jurman, came to Galicia because of my mother. Father was actually born near Vienna in Austria. The son of a rabbi, he had a passion for learning and for horses. His heart was set on joining the military academy in Vienna, and he was eventually accepted during a time when prejudice against Jews was severe. After graduation he became an officer in the Austrian calvary. Father was quick, brilliant, and very charming. It was very likely that his looks were just as important as his abilities: He was tall, had a regal bearing, and his reddish-blond hair and clear blue-gray eyes were certainly an asset at a time when there were few Jews among the higher ranks of the army. Because he spoke Polish and Russian as fluently as his own German, he was sent to the Russian front when the First World War broke out.

My father was not a man to shout out his accomplishments. But he was never without the gold medal given him personally by the Austrian emperor Franz Joseph, a high honor presented for bravery. Father always wore it on a chain around his neck. He was given it for saving the lives of thirty Austrian officers who had been captured by the Russians. Father's regiment had known that these men were being held under guard in a small synagogue in a nearby town. The original plan to save them involved a surprise attack and a sudden getaway on horses. But the planners realized that the Russians had horses just as swift as their own and might easily have outrun and captured them. Then my father introduced a plan that was accepted, and he volunteered to go out on the mission alone. Dressed as a peasant, he tied a keg of vodka onto his saddle and rode to the Russian camp. He stunk of the stuff, having splashed it over himself and gargled with it, and carried the alcohol into the compound singing and staggering, announcing loudly that he had come to honor the Russian victors. The soldiers accepted Father's story; at any rate, they certainly accepted his vodka. All night long they passed the keg around the campfire, filling their tin cups again and again. Father drank enough to cast off suspicion, but since he had seemed drunk to begin with, the soldiers were pleased when he insisted they take most of the liquor themselves.

When the last drop had been drunk and the last soldier lay snoring in a drunken stupor, Papa hurried to the synagogue, broke off the lock, and freed the prisoners.

"Just like that!" Benjamin called out, surprised.

"Oh, no, Benjamin, he had to knock out a couple of guards. But listen. . . . Then, after 'borrowing' the Russians' horses, they made their escape."

"Yes, quite a father," Benjamin commented.

"Yes, quite a father," I repeated after him. "But when he had to face Grandmother Kurtz, that was a different matter," I said, and burst out laughing.

"Well, what about Grandmother Kurtz?" Benjamin wanted to know. So I told him the story.

My grandmother Kurtz had loved to tell how my parents met. Grandmother Kurtz was a shrewd woman whose maternal instincts extended beyond her own large family to the entire Solotvina community. At that late stage of the war many men from the area were missing. Some were off fighting, some dead, and their women and children often fell victim to the murdering Cossacks who were part of the invading Russian army. They had been known for generations as fierce Jew-killers.

When a handsome young Austrian cavalry officer appeared one day with a detachment of soldiers to commandeer a number of horses and wagons for the war effort, Grandmother gave them over gladly, but she also persuaded the young officer whose name was Jurman to escort some of the local women and children several hundred miles west into Czechoslovakia. My father agreed, and ended up leading thirty-five wagons into Prague! The people in the city must have thought it was an invasion.

Later, when asked why she had trusted the young man to return her property, Grandmother Kurtz would say, "The way he looked at Frieda, I knew he'd be back." And she was right; one look at my beautiful mother, then only sixteen, with her dark curly hair, creamy white complexion, and violet eyes, and my father was completely smitten.

But at the war's end, when he returned to Galicia to court my mother, Father received an awful shock. Oh, the Kurtzes liked him well enough, very much in fact. But he was poor and they were rich, and Mother was one of Grandfather's favorites. They wanted her to marry someone who would provide for her in the style to which she was accustomed.

The situation could have ended tragically, with the young lovers never being allowed to marry, had my mother's older brother not stepped in. Knowing it had long been Grandfather's dream to provide medical care for the poorer people in the community, my uncle flatly refused to continue medical school unless his sister were allowed to marry Sigmund Jurman. In the end Mother was allowed to marry Father and my uncle finished medical school.

"Well, quite a story, Alicia, quite a story," Benjamin kept repeating.

From that day on we talked and talked during my visits. Bella always sent over some cookies or apples, and we ate as we talked. Sometimes we played chess. I remembered a little chess from my brothers, and now Benjamin was teaching me. Sometimes we just sat and read. I stayed almost two hours each time and began to really look forward to each visit. One day Benjamin told me that he was going to Eretz Israel (then Palestine), to settle there. It pleased me to hear him making plans because that was a sign that somehow I was reaching him and helping him think about the future. When I told Bella about Benjamin's plans she was very happy.

Benjamin had many books, and he let me borrow some. Because they were all written in Polish I had no difficulty understanding them. They opened a new world for me. Since my education had been interrupted, there was so much I wanted to know. Whenever I visited Benjamin I would always wander over to the shelf near his bed and see if he had any new books. I almost missed seeing one. It was open and I couldn't see the title. When I picked it up I was surprised to see that it was a biology book, a textbook used at the gymnasia, the Polish high schools.

"Benjamin, where did you get this biology book?" I inquired, turning to him. He didn't answer.

"Where did you get this book?" I repeated my question again.

"It belonged to my friend." His voice was abrupt and filled with bitterness. "He was always collecting science books. It was while we were on our way to get some books from Professor Korngut that we stepped on the mine on the bridge. He was killed and I . . . Milek always talked about becoming a doctor."

"Milek?! Benjamin, did you say Milek?" I heard myself asking in a voice that didn't belong to me. "Was he a boy about sixteen with blond hair and blue eyes?"

"Yes."

Benjamin's answer felt like a bullet to my heart. It pierced my body; I felt a terrible coldness and then I felt nothing.

"Alexander, are you sure she will be all right? Can't you do something to help her?" I heard the voice as from a distance. I thought I knew the voice.

"She will be fine. She got it all out of her system; but I never expected such anguish and fury from such a young girl. I am a doctor, and I have seen many things, but this. . . . Who is she anyway?"

"Oh, it is a long story, going back to the ghetto. I love this girl like a daughter. She and my poor sister Rachel were friends, you know. As a matter of fact, they both loved the boy who was killed. Children can feel. Poor Benjamin; she certainly frightened him. Thank you for coming so quickly, Alexander; I don't know what I would have done without you."

"Now you see, Bella, you need me. Come to the Crimea with me. You and Danny can take the girl and even Benjamin along. I can provide well for all of you. Besides, my mother will be very happy to care for young children again. Please, Bella, think about it. That girl should leave this place."

The voices faded to a murmur. I lay there, only semiconscious, repeating the same thought in my mind over and over.

"I must wait and see if he is alive."

Bella had moved all my belongings to her own home, and now all three of us slept in the room that served as both bedroom and living room. Bella insisted that I help in the restaurant and I did. I didn't go to visit Benjamin. I remembered a voice there saying that something terrible had happened. I knew now that Milek was dead. Once in a while I thought about Benjamin, but I couldn't bring myself to see him.

Then one day, as I was setting the table for lunch, I saw Benjamin sitting in the corner where the survivors usually sat. I wasn't really surprised to see him, although I remembered that he had refused to use his crutches during the day, claiming he wasn't yet ready to be seen in public. But it was daylight, and he had come to the restaurant.

He looked terrible, poor boy. Just the way he did when I first saw him. I sat down at his table.

"Did I hurt you, Benjamin? Did I?" I asked, looking searchingly into his sunken eyes. I was afraid of what his answer might be, but I needed to know.

"No, Alicia," he said in a quiet voice. "Please forgive me. I didn't know you knew Milek, or what he meant to you. I am deeply sorry.

"Will you come for a walk with me, only for a short while?" he asked, looking at me anxiously. "I am sure Bella wouldn't mind."

I was glad to get away from the restaurant. The sergeant was due for his noon meal soon, and I didn't feel like listening to his songs at that moment.

Benjamin was using his crutches more and more expertly as we walked slowly down Chechego Maya Street. Both of us cast brief glances at the homes where the ghetto used to be. They looked like empty shells but were still able to bring back painful memories.

We passed the big Polish church and turned onto the road leading to the Jewish cemetery. I hadn't been there for several days and felt guilty about it.

When we reached the cemetery Benjamin pointed to Milek's grave. I looked at it in shock. It was the grave of the unknown person that I had tended together with the graves of my loved ones. I had been drawn to it by a strange force without knowing why.

My mother, Zachary, Rachel, and now Milek were all buried close to one another under the only remaining tree, and a part of me was buried with them.

I stood there with Benjamin and recited the Kaddish in a voice choked with tears. And I realized that the time had come for me to leave Buczacz.

CHAPTER 19

In a Russian Prison

I had mixed reactions to leaving this city so full of my past. Buczacz held memories that were dear to me—of my parents, my brothers, of my entire family as we had lived before the war. It contained memories of that portion of my childhood which could be called happy. But in Buczacz there were also too many reminders of the tragic war years. The city was drowned in the blood of my family and thousands of my people.

And yet it was painful to leave. Buczacz was the only home I knew, and throughout the war I had always tried to return to that place. I felt somehow that that was where I belonged. If I left I would be truly homeless. Also, I had become attached to Bella, Danny, and Benjamin.

But a few days after Benjamin showed me Milek's grave, something happened that made it clear to me that I should not delay my departure.

I was at the cemetery putting a new *matzeva*, with Milek's name on it, on his grave. After reciting the Kaddish, I sat down near the grave on a blanket. It had started snowing, the first snow of the year, gently swirling in the air only to dissolve quickly as it hit the earth. I folded the blanket over myself and lay back over Milek's grave as I watched the falling snow. As time passed, the volume of the snowflakes increased. Now they came down thickly and piled up on top of one another, while still keeping their identity as individual delicate and beautiful stars. They fell upon Milek's grave and upon me, covering us with a soft blanket. I closed my eyes and lay there peacefully in the whiteness of the earth.

Danny wept later when he told me what had happened. When it became late and I hadn't returned from my daily visit to the cemetery, he came looking for me. He nearly missed seeing me because I looked like another grave covered by the snow. It was almost dark and it was hard to see, but some instinct told him that I must be there. When he saw me he pulled me up and practically dragged me home. I stumbled along, stiff and shaking with a chill that seemed to have penetrated my bones.

I was really disturbed by what had happened. I didn't remember thinking about anything except how peaceful it was and how close I felt to Milek as I lay there under the snow. I was sorry to have caused Bella and Danny such anxiety. Bella and I talked for a long time that night, and I began to realize that while I felt I couldn't live without those I loved, neither could I die with them. If Danny hadn't found me, I might have frozen to death! Bella explained that according to our tradition, one had to let the dead rest. I was not able to do this in Buczacz, so I had no choice but to leave.

Bella made arrangements with one of the Russian army truck drivers to take me as far as the marketplace in Chortkov. She gave me a letter of introduction to friends who lived near the market. She was sure that I could stay with them, and since they were planning to leave Chortkov, I might be able to travel with them. At that time I had no ultimate destination or plan; I was just leaving Buczacz.

But I was parting from people I cared for and this, like all my partings in the past, was excruciating. As I sat in the cabin of the military truck on the way to Chortkov I felt the pain inside me and tried with all my willpower not to cry. So many partings, so many good-byes; it seemed I was always bidding farewell to those I loved, or to their graves. And now once again it was time to move on, time to leave the place I had looked upon as home but which was now only a ghost town of sad remembrances.

I tried to forget the memory of my most recent trip to Chortkov, the journey by sleigh to the Chortkov prison, and thought instead of my childhood visits to the rabbi for his blessings. My father also had cousins there, and I wondered if any of them had survived. Perhaps the

Golds were still alive, that kind and wonderful couple who had saved my life in the winter of 1943, almost a year ago.

The driver stopped at the marketplace. I left the truck and, taking my two suitcases, I began to look for the address of Bella's friends.

A market is usually a busy and noisy place, and I normally would not pay much attention to individual voices, but as I passed a stall I heard a cry that was like that of a wounded young animal. It was a pitiful voice, and I turned to look where it was coming from. I saw a very pregnant woman pulling a crying and screaming five- or six-year-old boy by his arm. As she pulled him, she talked to the boy, but he only cried louder. But to me, the remarkable thing was that the woman was speaking to the boy in Yiddish.

Suddenly she pulled his arm strongly, and, dropping the basket she was carrying, seemed about to hit the boy with her other hand. I jumped quickly and caught her arm, holding it firm with all my strength. I knew that what I was doing was wrong; I had no right to interfere, but I couldn't stand by and watch a child being hit. I had seen too much of that! The woman swore in Yiddish and released the boy's arm. He promptly sat down on the ground and embraced her leg.

I stood there expecting more curses and a strongly worded instruction to mind my own business. Instead the woman, who apparently was the boy's mother, took a deep breath and explained in Polish.

"Moishele is afraid of people. He was hidden in an underground bunker for two years and now he is afraid to be outside even when he is with me. May the Germans rot in hell for what they did to us!"

People were beginning to gather around us, so I handed the woman her basket.

"Take your son home," I said. "I will follow you. Now, go quickly before the people gathering start laughing at us. We should not attract too much attention." At my use of the word "we," the woman looked at me closely, then nodded.

I wasn't invited to stay with the Taubs; I just stayed. It seemed natural for me to follow the pregnant woman and the frightened little boy to their home. When the father came home later in the day and saw me, he didn't ask any questions. Nor did he ask questions when he saw me standing over the stove preparing corn cereal while his wife lay in bed resting. Things just happened. It was natural for me to stay and help the family just as it was natural for Moishele to get out of his bed at night to come and sleep with me. It was also natural for me not to say a word when Moishele, who I learned was six years old, wet himself during the night.

By now I was used to sad children, but this six-year-old tore at my heart. I felt great compassion for him and he, sensing this, clung to me as though to a lifebuoy. Perhaps I also clung to Moishele in the same manner. Whatever the reason, we soon became very good friends. We went outside together, but whenever the streets were crowded with people, Moishele would shake with fear and we would have to turn back. We didn't go to the marketplace but tried to find deserted streets to walk through. I knew it would take some time for the child to stop being afraid, and I was willing to wait patiently. But I also realized that he could not continue hiding in the house, and that he would have to learn to live normally as soon as possible.

While on my walks with Moishele I located the house where Bella's friends had lived, but they were gone. There were other survivors living in the house now. This is how it was. People would live somewhere and then would leave without a forwarding address for the simple reason that they didn't have one. They were driven from a place where memories threatened to destroy them and where they could no longer put down roots. I understood that well.

The Taubs were originally from Chortkov and knew the city. I asked Mr. Taub if the Chortkov rabbi had survived or if he knew of anyone living by the name of Jurman or Gold. He told me that he was sure that the rabbi hadn't survived. He told me that he remembered a young woman named Jurman whose little girl had been torn out of her arms and killed by SS men before her eyes in the marketplace. He had heard of a lawyer by the name of Gold in the ghetto but didn't know him personally. As far as he knew, none of the people I mentioned had survived. But he said that one could not be absolutely certain that a missing person would never return. It was not likely, but sometimes a person presumed dead would reappear.

Mr. Taub was kind enough to go with me to the area of the city where the ghetto stood. I didn't know what I was searching for, because I couldn't have recognized the house where the Golds had lived. It was a shattering experience for me, especially when I saw the Chortkov prison again. I never wanted to return to that part of the city again.

The place I frequented most was the public well, where I drew water every morning. Mr. Taub was away most of the day working, and the pregnant Mrs. Taub had little strength and needed a lot of rest. I would take Moishele with me. I carried a pail in one hand and held his hand with the other; he also carried a small pail. He enjoyed this daily ritual as much as I did. He loved the running water, and many times he would spill the water out of his pail and then fill it up again just to see the water flowing. It apparently had a soothing effect on his disturbed mind.

For me the well was a new place to meet people, especially survivors. Since the only language Moishele spoke was Yiddish, and I always answered him in a combination of Yiddish and Polish, any survivors waiting to draw water knew immediately that we were Jewish and spoke to us. We met some very nice people that way and invited them to visit our home. It was on one of our trips to the public well that I met Sabina. We had been fellow students in public and Hebrew school, and we had a very emotional reunion. She told me that she had been in Chortkov for some time and was staying with a cousin of her mother's and his young son because she had lost all of her family. Sabina invited me to her home, and we spent an afternoon making noodles. I was amazed and a little envious to see her prepare a dinner, since I could not cook at all.

Sabina told me that the Kleiners—another family I had known since childhood—were living in Chernovtsy in what was then Russian-occupied Romania. I had known the daughter Dora but not well; she had gone to school with one of my brothers. Sabina also informed me that there were other survivors from Buczacz whose names she didn't know but that Dora would be able to tell me, since her home was a gathering place for Buczacz people. Sabina was also interested in knowing more about these survivors and suggested that since it was quite easy to get to Chernovtsy, I should visit Dora and return to tell her all about it. All I had to do was walk up the hill to the Chortkov-Buczacz junction and ask for a ride on a military truck going past that junction in the direction of Romania. I could stop on the way in a small town called Zalescheke, where a Jewish family kept a hostel, sleep over there, and then take another truck on its way to Chernovtsy.

When I think back on that conversation, I wonder at the way fourteen-year-old girls talked and planned. The proposed trip involved hitchhiking on military vehicles that might or might not be available and that might or might not agree to take riders, and traveling long distances across a national boundary to a strange city. But in the first year following liberation, with thousands of people displaced from their homes, people were constantly on the move trying to rebuild their lives; there were no standards of normal behavior for travel.

For us the constant search for other survivors was more important than consideration of boundaries, distances, and dangers; we looked for the friends and relatives whose existence could give meaning to our lives once more.

I sold two more of my shawls, leaving me with four. Now I had enough money to live on for the next month or so. I chose a nice sunny day and walked up the hill to wait for a ride.

While I was waiting, I saw a group of Russian soldiers marching in my direction. They were singing; it was a nice sight to see. All those young men! My eyes traveled over the group and over their uniforms. Then my attention was caught by a pair of boots walking on the right side of the group, those of the drill leader.

The toes of those boots had become disconnected from the soles, and were opening and closing like hungry mouths as the soldier walked. Probably to avoid having them "eat" a stone, the marcher performed a kind of dance with each step, landing on the heel then gliding forward as he let each toe gently down. I thought it was terribly funny and started to laugh.

Then I looked up at the owner of those boots, and I recognized him. It was Dudek, a Jewish boy I remembered from the Buczacz ghetto. I was so shocked that I let the group pass, but then I ran after them.

"Dudek, Dudek, wait for me, wait for a moment."

He turned in surprise, then, recognizing me, he put his finger to his lips to signal that I should not call out again. He called out something to the troop. The soldiers continued marching and singing, but Dudek stayed behind.

We talked for a while, exchanging information on families and friends. Dudek told me that he had been conscripted into the Red Army after the liberation but that he hoped to be out soon. As we talked, he saw me looking at his boots, and I could see that he was embarrassed. I took part of the money I had received for the shawls, enough to buy new boots, and gave it to him. Dudek smiled gratefully and thanked me. He promised to look for me in Chortkov, then ran to join his troop, which was waiting patiently down the road. I was very pleased to be able to help a friend.

✢   ✢   ✢

I followed Sabina's instructions and arrived in Chernovtsy the following afternoon. After a short search, using the German language, which was widely understood in Chernovtsy, I found the Kleiners.

It had been at least four years since I had seen Dora Kleiner. We had both changed a great deal. I had grown from a child to a teenager, and she was now about twenty years old. She was very pleased to see me and knew her father would be also. She had a girlfriend with her, a girl closer to my age named Bronia, whose family lived in Chortkov. Bronia seemed nice and was very friendly. While we waited for Dora's father to return, Bronia offered to show me the city. Dora elected to stay home.

Chernovtsy was a big and very lovely city. As we walked I noticed its cleanliness and the apartment houses, none higher than three stories, which harmonized with the single homes scattered among them. We walked past the marketplace and could smell freshly roasted chestnuts. In little stalls people were selling bread, eggs, chickens, butter, and fresh fruits. It felt as though the war had never touched the city.

Suddenly we were approached by two Russian policemen, members of the NKVD.

"Excuse me, girls," said one. "May we see your documents please?"

I was puzzled; they had not seemed to pick us randomly but had walked directly to us. I looked at Bronia, who seemed very nervous. I handed the policeman my documents, the certificate I received in Buczacz under my own name, and the papers the Kolpak partisans gave me under the name of Anusha Jurman. I could see that the policeman was surprised when he checked my documents. Then he put them, together with Bronia's, into his side pouch.

"Will you please come with us," he said politely, and we did. I tried to think of a reason why the NKVD would want us but couldn't. It occurred to me that perhaps Bronia might have some idea, so I leaned over to her and whispered.

"Do you know what's going on?" She shook her head stiffly. I realized that she was frightened.

"Think," I whispered again. "Don't you have any idea what could be the matter?"

"No." But I could see she had become very pale. She knew something and wasn't telling me.

When the door of the police station closed behind us, I had a strange feeling that I was reliving part of my past. I was in a police station, arrested again. Before, I had been detained by the Nazis because I was Jewish, but why now by the Russians? What was my crime this time, I kept asking myself. I was separated from Bronia and led to a small office, where I found the man who had brought me to the station. We sat facing each other across his desk.

"I see that you have two different first names on your documents. Which one is the right one?" he asked.

"My real name is Alicia, but your comrades thought that I deserved a good Russian name, so they named me Anusha. Don't you believe I deserve a good Russian name, Comrade Commandant?" I asked.

He looked up at me in surprise. I thought I saw the beginnings of a smile, but I could have been wrong. When our eyes made contact I felt a shudder pass through my body, but I didn't look down. I had nothing to fear, I told myself; I had done nothing wrong.

"You are a Hero of the Soviet Union, so your documents say. Therefore, I can't understand why you have participated in such despicable acts."

I was stunned. What was he talking about? I was about to object to the words he was using, when he suddenly became angry and cried out: "I want you to tell me where you got the stuff! And tell me why you are trying to protect those parasites." Then he lowered his voice. "All you have to do is tell me where you bought the stuff and I will let you go."

I thought at first that he must be crazy, but when I finally realized what he was talking about, I began to understand what had happened. He believed that I had bought something, but I didn't know what. I was supposed to have bought it on my arrival in Chernovtsy. The only place I visited was the Kleiners, and the only person who could have sent the police after me was Dora. Unless, of course, the police were really looking only for Bronia and I was arrested only because I was with her. Bronia might very well know what all this was about, but I knew then that I was in big trouble. My arrest was somehow connected with an illegal market in something, but I didn't know what. I had seen all the food, and clothing as well, sold freely in the open market. What else could a person need? What could young girls like Bronia or even Dora be involved in? Certainly not heavy artillery. I nearly burst out laughing at the thought.

The policeman asked me more questions. How long had I known

Bronia and where was I staying. I told him that I had just met Bronia, that I had just arrived in the city, and that I didn't know where I would be staying. He now spoke in a rather friendly tone of voice, and I answered him truthfully. I also told him that I didn't know what he was referring to and that I wouldn't want to hurt the Soviet Union, especially not the people whose lives I had saved, as he could see from my documents. I rather thought that I had given a smart answer, and I saw that he thought so, too, because he smiled.

"Well, you had better join your friend now," he said.

He brought me into a room that looked like a prison cell where I was reunited with Bronia. There were two chairs and nothing else. Bronia was sitting and crying. Apparently the police had treated her badly, and she seemed to be very frightened. I felt very sorry for her, but I had to know why we were arrested.

"All right, Bronia, calm down now and tell me the whole story. Next time they question me, they will not be so polite. I have to know!"

Slowly Bronia started talking. The items that the Russians believed I had purchased, she said, were matches and yeast, rationed items. The suppliers were Dora and her father. Mr. Kleiner bought these products from people who worked in the factories and then sold them in units of ten kilos of yeast and one hundred boxes of matches. Bronia and others bought them from the Kleiners and brought them to Chortkov, where they were sold on the black market, making a twenty-five-percent profit. Those were the only earnings she could depend on to support herself, her mother, and her younger sister. This was how they and many Jewish survivors lived. They had lost everything in the war and had no land or property. Bronia continued her sad story. Yes, there were others she worked with. Most of them lived in Chortkov. As many as ten young boys and girls and a few older people helped transport and sell the products.

I listened attentively as Bronia talked. Although, in most countries, this would be considered a normal business transaction, the illegal purchase and resale of controlled items was, to the Russian police, a crime labeled as black marketeering and punishable by imprisonment or exile to Siberia. The more I thought about it, the more frightened I became because of what might happen if the police learned the names of the people who were engaged in this business. After having already suffered during the Nazi occupation, they would be imprisoned once more.

Whatever the outcome of our arrest, I was certain of one thing, and that was that Bronia must never reveal any names or admit that she even knew anyone connected with the Kleiners. She would have to be very firm in her denials. I really didn't know Bronia, and I had no idea how she would stand up under questioning by the NKVD. But I hoped that she remembered the bitterness of being betrayed by friends and would keep that in mind when questioned.

Bronia was sobbing. "I don't know what will happen to my mother and sister if we stay here a long time. I don't know what I will do."

"Bronia, I am very sorry it turned out so badly for us, but remember"—and I was now voicing all my thoughts—"you must never admit anything or reveal the names of the people who bought the yeast and matches from Dora. I know how angry you must be at her or at whoever gave your name to the NKVD—so am I. Perhaps she just panicked when she saw the police. That happens sometimes. Perhaps she will get us out of here tomorrow. We must wait and see what happens."

"That's easy for you to say!" Bronia cried. "But what will happen to me and my family if she doesn't help us? How will we survive?"

We were on the verge of an argument, and I knew that would accomplish nothing, so I didn't answer her. But I had to make it very clear to Bronia that as long as I was around, I would not let her name names. It occurred to me that my friend Sabina's cousin, who regularly visited the Kleiners, might also be involved in this business. If his name were known to the police and he were to be convicted, what would happen to Sabina and her cousin's son?

We were in a great deal of trouble, but at least I now knew what we were accused of. We sat through the night, and the following morning we were interrogated again. I was asked the same questions over and over, and I denied any involvement or knowledge of illegal activities.

After that I was afraid every time they came to question us that Bronia would tell all she knew. Although she was fifteen years old—a year older than I—she was in many ways less mature, and the NKVD men could be very frightening. I had the advantage that I really hadn't been involved, and it is easier to tell the truth than to lie. I wasn't sitting in judgment of her. But I felt a responsibility for the people she might involve, so every day I would hold her shoulders and threaten her with all kinds of punishment if she disclosed any names. I would send her into the interrogation trembling. I hated to scare her, and I could imagine what mental agonies she was suffering behind the closed door of the NKVD office, but I felt I had no choice.

The NKVD apparently realized that I didn't know anything, because on the fourth day, after the usual questions, the policeman handed me my documents.

"You are free to go home, Anusha Jurman." He stood up and extended his hand to me. I stood stunned. It took me a minute to realize what was happening, and by that time the man had withdrawn his hand.

"Thank you, Comrade Commandant," I said. "With your permission, I will wait for my friend Bronia, and we will leave together."

"Your friend Bronia is not free to go; she will be detained for more questioning. But you had better leave right now."

And suddenly the old fear that I had hoped I would never have to feel again was back with me.

"But I can't leave without my friend. Certainly you understand that; she is a stranger here and she needs someone to look after her. She went through hell under the German occupation, and now—"

"Stop right there, girl, do you realize what you are about to say? Are you implying that . . ." The Russians were very sensitive to any comparisons with the Germans.

"I am not implying anything. I am just trying to tell you that I can't leave without my friend. Please don't misunderstand me. All I am asking is that you let her leave with me, because I can't go without her. Surely you can see that."

"Then stay with her!" He snatched the documents out of my hand and pointed in the direction of our cell. "Get in there before I really get angry!"

And thus, instead of leaving for freedom I returned to the cell I shared with Bronia.

The next day we were transferred from the police station jail to the big city prison. It was on Market Street, I remember; but there was no market there. It was a cold winter day in December and snow was falling heavily. Even though it was a short trip, it was long enough to bring back memories of my imprisonment in Chortkov in 1942. When I entered the prison gate I was raging inwardly against the injustice of my fate.

My imprisonment under the Soviets was a most unusual experience. Bronia and I were put in a cell that should have held a maximum of four people but was already occupied by six middle-aged Romanian peasant women. I later learned that they had escaped from a Russian labor camp somewhere in Siberia, were searched out in their homes, imprisoned, and would eventually be returned to their labor camps. They told us in the little Russian they had learned that if they were sent back, they would try to escape again, because it is in the nature of human beings to seek freedom.

Theirs was actually a very simple case, and in a way I envied them. Where Bronia and I were concerned, the only way we could gain our freedom, our interrogators told us, would be when we delivered the names of some poor Jews who were now classed as "Enemies of the Soviet Union." Our freedom in exchange for theirs.

We couldn't do that, because we knew those "Enemies of the Soviet Union" only as Jewish survivors of the Nazi terror, people who had passed through hell, came out destitute, and were only trying to support themselves the best way they could in a world where no one really cared if they lived or died. I considered it a shame that anyone should put labels on these people, and hated those who did. There was an evil force behind all this, I felt, and I was trying to fight it in the best way I knew how.

Soon Bronia and I fell into a daily routine. We were awakened at six A.M. by the guard who brought us what was called coffee but was actually brewed chicory, and one small piece of stale bread. At noon we received a tin cup of soup and in the evening another slice of bread with hot water, which I usually used to wash my face. Even though I was accustomed to near starvation, it took me some time to get used to the lack of food again. I am sure we would have eventually become ill from malnutrition and lack of fresh air and exercise if the kind Romanian women hadn't taken pity on us and shared some of their food. Their families delivered food packages to them every other week. Although half of the contents were taken out by the prison guards, the remainder was still enough to give them the nutrition needed to keep from starving, and since they pooled their food, they even had enough to share with us. I wouldn't go so far as to say that they actually invited us to eat with them, but when they finished eating and saw us sitting there all alone and hungry, they would give us some bread, a piece of sausage, or a piece of cheese. Just enough to keep body and soul together.

Bronia and I were very grateful for their kindness, and we tried to learn enough Romanian to thank them in their own language. Some of them probably had children of their own, I thought, because I caught them looking at us sometimes with sadness in their eyes, or perhaps they knew that if we were sent to Siberia, our chances of staying alive were minimal. Whatever their thoughts were, I was grateful for even this small sign of caring, because as the days passed, I became convinced that Dora Kleiner was going to let us rot in prison without telling a soul.

As hard as the days were, the nights really presented a challenge. A wooden platform stood on one side of the room, covering half the floor area. We all sat on it during the day and slept on it at night. When we stretched out at night, our bodies fitted together like sardines in a can. Our Romanian cellmates wore sheeps'-wool-lined coats with the hide on the outside and the warm wool fleece close to the body. At night they would take these coats off and use them as blankets. The coats overlapped a little from one person to the next. Bronia was wearing a light cloth coat when the NKVD arrested us, so we shared the fur coat I had borrowed from Mr. Taub and tried to huddle close to the Romanian women, pulling a little of their covering over us.

Thus, the nights were spent in constant pulling and turning, because when one of us turned, the whole row had to turn as well. Many times I chose to sit on the indoor toilet on top of the lid, shivering from the cold and dozing off occasionally. The communal tossing and turning wasn't the only reason I did this. Those little bloodsuckers, lice, had made their home with us. Nestled in all the wooly lambskins, and with the lights too dim to permit us to hunt for them, they had the upper hand, leaping from one person to another and all getting fat on our blood. Even though we were allowed one shower in lukewarm water every week, we had to put our dirty and lice-ridden clothing back on. No matter how hard we shook, the lice couldn't be dislodged. Of course, our poor nutrition didn't help either.

Our daily ration had little food value. Several times I suggested to the jailer that he scrape the bottom for some solids when he poured the soup into the tin cups, but he ignored me. I had the feeling that he was actually selecting Bronia and me for some kind of personal vengeance and was punishing us by giving us only the liquid of the soup. Perhaps he was a patriot who hated political prisoners. But any idiot could see that we were just two starved young girls, and his treatment of us made me blow up in anger.

One day I watched as he deliberately skimmed the top of the soup and poured the clear broth into Bronia's cup. He did the same when my turn came.

"What is the matter with you?" I demanded. "Why can't you mix the soup so that we get some of the vegetables for a change? I'm going to starve to death on this water."

"If you don't like it here," he sneered, "you can cooperate with the authorities and get out." Suddenly something inside me snapped. I lifted the tin cup holding the hot soup he had just poured in and threw it in his face.

"That's the only cooperation you will get from me, you crazy dog!" I shouted. He gasped and sputtered, trying to wipe the smelly soup from his eyes.

"You're going to be very sorry you did that!" he cried.

"I doubt it!" I snapped. One thing I didn't doubt, though, was that I would be punished for what I did. I was still angry and wasn't at all sorry that I had taught that man a lesson. The joke was on me, however, because I was soon to learn a bitter lesson myself.

There was complete silence in our cell after the jailer slammed the door shut. We all waited in suspense for something to happen.

Bronia offered to share her soup with me, but I wasn't hungry anymore. I still didn't regret what I did, but I was very worried about the consequences that would probably follow.

"Bronia," I said rather sternly. "I don't know what will happen to me, but if for some reason we are separated, please remember that you are to repeat your pleas of innocence, just the way you have done until now. I imagine that the last two times they questioned you since we arrived you have done so." She nodded her head. "I did the same. I have a feeling that soon something will be decided about us. We have been here one month already. How much longer can they keep us anyway? I don't know what they will do with me now, but I want you to know something."

I told her what happened at the police station and how I had refused my freedom unless she, too, was freed. I knew Bronia might have hated me because she might feel that I, by insisting she withhold names, was responsible for her remaining in prison. But now, after my explanation, I could see that she understood what I had been asking of her, and I sensed a change in her. I hoped she finally understood my commitment to stand by those unknown people, not dwelling on the treachery that brought us there but trying to make the best of a terrible situation. I hoped that what I now saw in her eyes would make her act with dignity and silence in the face of NKVD interrogation. I knew that the NKVD could force a confession out of us if they really wanted to. But I had the feeling, after my last questioning, that they saw us for what we were—two young, half-starved girls—and thought that our problem would eventually solve itself. We would become ill and die. Hadn't they done the same with my brother Moshe?

I was about to talk some more with Bronia, but the door suddenly opened and the jailer called my name and asked me to follow him. I looked briefly at Bronia and saw tears in her eyes. Poor girl; I was sorry I had treated her so harshly at times. But when I returned, if I returned, our relationship would, I felt, surely be more trusting.

I was locked up all by myself in a small room, without food or water, for two days. It was a small, cold cell, and I shivered all day and all night. If someone were to ask me if I regretted throwing the soup in my jailer's face, I would have still said no. Sitting there all alone, the soup became a symbolic weapon against injustice. After all I had gone through, I couldn't let myself be degraded once more or be treated less than a person. I felt I was doing the honorable thing—but this did not prevent me from also feeling miserable.

I didn't know it then, but this act marked a new beginning. I was entering into a new phase of my life in the postwar "free" society where I would have to fight at almost every step to exist. For myself and others who survived, this struggle would be a daily task. We still had to carve out a place for ourselves, to fit in somewhere, where we could live in dignity and freedom, like other human beings.

Bronia had apparently done some thinking during my solitary confinement. When I was returned to the cell she went out of her way to be very kind to me. She had saved some water for me and helped me wash. The women gave me more food than usual. I was grateful for their kindness. The relationship between Bronia and me began to develop into friendship. We discovered that we both could speak Hebrew and conversed in it often. We taught each other new words as we remembered them.

I had developed a bad cough in the solitary cell and was afraid that my lungs were making me ill again. After Bronia learned that pork fat could help me, she begged pieces from the Romanian women. It was helping me now as it did in the ghetto, when Rachel fed me some. The only thing that didn't change was the frequency of our interrogation and the apprehension I still had when Bronia was led out of the cell for that purpose. I wasn't called as often as Bronia, but in my case the questioning had taken a new direction.

"How can you, a Hero of the Soviet Union, turn traitor on us this way?" the NKVD man would ask.

"I have not betrayed you," I would counter. "I haven't done anything to hurt you."

"You are keeping the identity of those people from us. Those speculators are ruining the economy. How is Europe to regain a stable economy with speculation rampant?"

"I know of no one who is speculating. I was in this city less than one hour when your police picked me up."

"How do you know the Kleiners?"

"I have told you about this several times. Dora went to school with one of my brothers. And you know that my family was murdered by the Germans."

"How long have you known Bronia?"

"For less than an hour when you picked us up."

The interrogator beat his fist sharply against the table. "How can you do this?" he cried. "We honored you for your loyalty to the Soviet Union. How dare you turn your back on us when we need you?"

This man was making me very angry. He was trying to make me feel guilty and called me a traitor. Before the words were out of my mouth I realized that I should have kept my temper, but it was too late.

"I was given these documents because I risked my life twice to help people who were in need," I answered fiercely. "It had nothing whatsoever to do with my feelings for the Soviet Union. As a matter of fact, I felt betrayed by the Soviet Union when no one told us about the possibility of a German breakthrough and a second occupation of our city in the spring of 1944. Someone should have told us! I lost my mother. The Germans murdered her in front of my eyes. I hated and still hate the Germans and, at that time, I was thinking only to save the partisans. To me they were human beings; that was all. I did it the second time for the same reason, and I am glad I did. Both times I could have been caught. Now I am in the same situation. Do you think if the Germans or the Ukrainians caught me and questioned me about the partisans I would have betrayed them?

"I don't know the speculators you are after, but whoever they are, they can't possibly be your enemy, just as I am not your enemy or a traitor to the Soviet Union. But if you want to imprison me for life, there is nothing I can change, absolutely nothing." Suddenly I felt so tired that I was on the verge of crying.

"You are being foolish," the NKVD man said.

"Perhaps," I whispered.

I told Bronia about my outburst and cautioned her about the new tactic they had used on me. I expected each day to be called for further questioning, but strangely enough I wasn't, and neither was Bronia. This new turn of events worried me greatly, and I wondered day and night what might be the reason. I thought of only one. The NKVD had completed their investigation and now would sentence us. I kept these thoughts to myself, but whenever the door opened, I expected to be taken away. There were also changes in our cell. During the last two weeks four of our Romanian women were moved out and new inmates substituted. I didn't know what happened to those who left. I was afraid that they were being returned to the labor camps from which they had escaped.

Three months had passed since we were imprisoned. It was the beginning of March. A whole winter had gone by, a whole season without our being outdoors once. It felt like an eternity. I had not completely given up hope of ever seeing the outside again, but the thread of hope was wearing very thin. I had expected some change after they stopped questioning us. Anything would have been an improvement, I thought, preferable to remaining forgotten forever. Dora Kleiner, the one person who could have helped us, had not. At times I thought of cursing her, and then I remembered that she was already cursed with a guilty conscience.

This was our mental state when after three and a half months in prison the door opened one morning and Bronia was handed a package. She stood there in shock, holding the package tightly to her heart and crying "My brother, my brother!" over and over again. "I knew he would come." This was the first time I had heard her mention a brother. I felt tears gather in my eyes too. When I think about the expression "manna from heaven," I am always reminded of the package Bronia received from her brother that morning in our prison cell. When she quieted down enough to open it, we all stood around her, watching. The package contained bread, cheese, marmalade, peanuts, and two pairs of silk panties. Bronia and I were stunned when we saw them. Some woman must have packed that parcel, a loving human being.

According to our prison tradition, we shared our food with the other inmates and finished everything within two days. I had a terrible stomachache, but it was worth it. Two more packages arrived within one week's time. But I could see that Bronia was worried. Although she was sure the sender was her brother, who must have returned from

Russia, there weren't any letters in the packages, not a word. Maybe they were taken out of the packages because letters weren't allowed, but someone cared enough to send a piece of soap, two towels, two undershirts, everything in twos. I was deeply touched because I felt someone was thinking of me as well. Bronia shared all these things with me, and I was embarrassed by her generosity. Now that she knew someone cared about us, perhaps she realized that I had been right to impose silence on her. It was still too early to say how things would turn out.

Then one ordinary afternoon about two weeks after our first package had arrived, the cell door opened and the guard called our names. He told us to take all of our belongings with us. We had expected to be called eventually and were mentally prepared, but when it actually happened we became so frightened we could hardly move.

As we followed the guard, I was thinking, my heart pounding wildly. Were they transferring us to another cell? No, we were being led away from the cells. Were they sending us to Russia or to a labor camp in Siberia? I felt my stomach tighten with fear. That was what we were afraid might happen to us. We were led upstairs and escorted into what looked a courtroom. So we were being sentenced, I thought bitterly.

In front of a desk near a window stood a big, tough-looking woman. Near the desk to her right stood a tall blond young man who was wearing a Polish military uniform. I could hardly believe my eyes. I hadn't seen a Polish uniform since the war had started in 1939. I thought for a moment that I was hallucinating. But no, there he stood. Suddenly I felt Bronia gripping my arm as she whispered. "It is my brother David. It's my brother." I heard Bronia but didn't turn to her, for my eyes were glued to the fairy-tale prince standing near the window.

Suddenly the woman addressed us in Russian.

"Bronia Valevska and Alicia Jurman, you have been found"—we held our breath—"innocent of the charge of conspiracy to speculate. This court rules that you shall be released today. Please come to the bench." We went to her. "Sign here," she said, "and here, and here." We did. She handed me my documents. For a brief moment I thought of tearing them up. But I remembered that at the beginning in the police station, the NKVD man had wanted to set me free. To be truthful, I was in prison of my own free will. She didn't return the money that was taken from me when I was arrested, and I didn't mention it. Bronia, too, was given her documents.

"You are free to go," said the woman judge. "The Soviet Union is your friend." I wanted to say something to that, but I knew it would land me right back in the cell. So I kept quiet and we were allowed to leave with Bronia's handsome brother.

Once we were out on the street, Bronia flew into her brother's arms, she crying and clinging to him, he hugging and kissing her cheek. I thought to myself how awful it would be if any of Bronia's lice got on his handsome uniform. The scene made me want to cry, first with happiness at their reunion after three years of separation and then also because I realized with overwhelming sorrow and pain that Bronia's brother David resembled my brother Zachary, and that had my brother lived, he would have been the same age. It could have been me being hugged and kissed by Zachary. It was at times such as these that I really felt the pain of my loneliness. In the midst of their happiness I was unhappy, wishing I could have had at least one surviving family member to belong to.

David probably knew the story of our imprisonment, but I wondered if he knew how harshly I had behaved to his sister and why. As we walked, David explained that he had returned to look for his family, and to his great happiness he found that some had survived. He found out that three and a half months had passed since Bronia had disappeared, and it took some gentle pressure on the NKVD to find her. As soon as he learned what had happened, he began to work on her release. When he found out there had been another girl with Bronia, his work became doubly hard, but he never considered freeing just one and not the other. At this point he turned to look at me, gave me a knowing smile, and continued his story.

It took him a week to raise the forty thousand rubles he had to pay in order to compensate the authorities for all the troubles we had caused them. To speed up matters, David gave the judge a beautiful gun that had been given to him by the famous Polish commander Wanda Wasilewska. Yes, David continued, the judge's eyebrows really shot up when she heard the name. Wanda Wasilewska was a great hero to the soldiers of the Polish units she had organized: She had united Polish exiles in Russia to join in the fight against the Germans. Many Polish-Jewish boys served in those units. Here David stopped dramatically. "And these soldiers, dear girls, contributed the forty thousand rubles that freed you from prison." The fight to free us was a strictly military operation in which several Russian-Jewish officers also participated. I was deeply moved by David's story. What a splendid young man! And when he smiled one of his radiant smiles I was ready to die for him.

"Well, let's hurry, dear girls," he cried, and, taking our hands in his, we walked to his friend's house.

If I wished to describe heaven, I would tell of my next three days. David's friends were a family of three: a father, mother, and a beautiful eighteen-year-old daughter with the very romantic name of Orleanda. To me they all seemed like angels. I was given a big sunny room with a very comfortable bed. I thought it belonged to the daughter, but I found out later that it was a guest room, and the house, which had belonged to them before the war, had eight equally lovely rooms furnished with the most handsome furniture I had seen in a long time. For families in Romania, unlike in Poland, it was possible to reclaim property.

A maid led me straight into a little room, where I soaked for a long time in a hot bath. I was given a pink flannel nightgown trimmed with pink lace, and after a light meal I went straight to bed. The same day a doctor came to check me because I was still coughing. I couldn't quite get rid of the cough that had begun during my solitary confinement in prison. The doctor gave me a thorough checkup and asked many questions about my family, my illnesses, and my imprisonment. He as well as David's friends were Jews. We talked for a long time. He gave me some medicine but mainly told me to eat properly and stay in bed until I was fully rested. When he left he kissed me on my cheek, and I could see that he had tears in his eyes. Mine weren't exactly dry, because his gentleness and sympathy reminded me of my poor uncle, Dr. Kurtz.

David, Bronia, and Orleanda were gone most of the day, shopping, sight-seeing, and just enjoying the freedom, I assumed, but I stayed home and just slept and ate all day. The maid constantly brought me small quantities of soup, fresh fruits, and cookies, and I ate all I could, slept, and was beginning to feel much better. I was out of bed the third day and presented myself in the living room wearing a nice blue skirt and Kola's shirt, which the maid had washed for me. All my underthings were new, a gift, the maid said, from Miss Orleanda. There was a jacket to match the skirt waiting for me in the closet. Mr. Taub's lamb coat was wrapped up in a bundle, cleaned up as well as possible. It was a little unreal for me to sit with all those strangers in a beautiful living room after what I had lived through in the prison. I hardly recognized Bronia in her new clothing, which was also probably a gift from the lovely and generous Orleanda, who it seemed to me had also fallen victim to David's charms.

The following day, very early in the morning, we were traveling in a covered military truck back to Chortkov. Bronia and I sat inside the cabin, and David and two hitchhikers traveled in the back. When we arrived in Chortkov we went directly to Bronia's home and had dinner there.

Back in her home Bronia treated me rather coolly. But her brother was wonderful. He introduced me to his lovely Russian wife, Valeria. Bronia told me later that they had been married while he was recovering from wounds at a hospital where she was a doctor. But even meeting Valeria didn't stop me from thinking of David as my knight in shining armor, my Prince Charming. We had a chance to talk in private, and I told him the whole story of our imprisonment.

"Bronia doesn't realize all that you have done," he said. "She is thinking only of herself. But I know, and others will know too. On behalf of our family and our people, I thank you, Alicia."

He took my hand and kissed it lightly, and I thought I would faint from joy. He was so dashing. I didn't think Bronia deserved such a wonderful brother. Shortly after, I said good-bye to Bronia and her family. As I was leaving, Bronia came up to me and gave me a hug and kiss.

"Thank you, Alicia," she whispered softly.

That same evening I returned to the Taubs, the family I had lived with before I went to Chernovtsy. They were shocked to see me, almost as if I had been a ghost. After the shock lessened they welcomed me into their home. Moishele shied away from me when I tried to take him in my arms, and I couldn't really blame him. I had promised that I would return in three or four days. Then I just disappeared without a word. I cared for him deeply and hoped that in time I would be able to explain and that he would forgive me. The baby I had hoped to see born had arrived and was a darling tiny girl. She was called Feigele, which means "little bird" in Yiddish. She was a sweet pink baby with a squeaky little voice, and she immediately captured my heart. She was the first Jewish baby I had seen since the SS man shot the two babies in

Kopechince. My hand trembled when I took her little hand in mine. Silently I prayed for her.

I wasn't the only one who had fallen in love with Feigele. Moishele was her slave. The way he rocked her crib with his two small hands, and the way he looked at her astonished me. He seemed so much more grown-up since I had last seen him. I was hoping that little Feigele would bring Moishele the joy he rightly deserved.

Although at first everything looked the same, I noticed changes as I sat at the kitchen table. The Taubs seemed nervous, and I saw two suitcases open near the wall as though someone had been packing.

"Are you going somewhere?" I asked Mrs. Taub.

Mr. Taub answered. "We are leaving Chortkov and going to Lodz in central Poland. From there we are going to America. I have two very influential brothers, and they will bring us over to Boston, where they live. I have to get in touch with them in Lodz."

"Since you are leaving, do you mind if I stay in the apartment a little while?"

"Not at all. You are most welcome," said Mr. Taub.

"By the way, where are my suitcases? I don't see them anywhere."

"Your suitcases? Yes." He looked at me and then at his wife. "Where are Alicia's suitcases?" he asked her. Mrs. Taub paled visibly. "Er, I think in the cellar," she said slowly.

I went down to the cellar and brought up the suitcases. As I carried them I felt that something was wrong. When I opened them I saw that they were almost empty.

"Where are my things?" I asked, trying to keep my voice calm.

"What do you mean?" asked Mr. Taub. "That was all you brought with you."

"Oh, no, it's not," I cried. "I am missing four shawls and other things."

Mr. Taub looked away, not able to meet my eyes. I looked straight at him.

"Do you think it is possible that some of my things may have accidentally been packed away with yours?" I went to their suitcases, lifted some of their clothing, and there lay my own things, neatly folded inside. I took them out and put them on top of my suitcases.

"Let's forget all this and have some tea," I suggested calmly, as though the episode were closed. But Mr. Taub thought otherwise.

"What do you want from us?" he snapped. "You have been gone

for three and a half months. You said you would be back in three or
four days. How could we have known what happened? We thought
you were dead. Besides, you had our fur coat. Should we have left
your things in an empty apartment to be looted?"

He challenged me with his look. "Where have you been anyway?"

"I have been in prison for the last three and a half months," I said
stiffly. "I was nearly sent to Siberia. I assure you it has not been a party
for me."

I was rude, and I knew it; I felt betrayed by those people. How
could they have given me up for dead? But had I thought with my
brain instead of my heart I would have recognized that they had acted
logically. Three and a half months was a lifetime during the postwar
days.

"Please, let's forget all this." I didn't want to argue anymore. "You
are going to America, and I wish you the best of luck and a mazel tov
with Feigele." I gave Mrs. Taub a pair of the stockings that I had
received in Chernovtsy, and she accepted them with lowered eyes.

Mr. Taub watched me as I repacked my suitcases.

"Maybe . . . maybe we could take you with us," he said
hesitantly.

"What?"

"To America," he said. "You resemble one of my nieces very
much. We could tell my brothers that their niece survived, and they
wouldn't know the difference. They are very well off; you would have a
good life."

I looked at him stunned. He wanted me to take the place of an
unfortunate girl who had been murdered by the Nazis. To use her
name, to make her family in America believe that she was alive. He
wanted me to take that poor girl's place in exchange for a good life? I
remembered that there was someone else who had hoped I could take
another's place, and I felt sick inside. I had not allowed myself to think
about Kola and his father while I was in prison, but this conversation
brought those memories back.

I tried to control the turmoil inside me and answered as politely as I
could.

"Thank you, Mr. Taub, for your kind but most unusual offer. I am
not ready to go to America or anywhere else right now. And whenever
I go, I will use my own name which, as you know, is Alicia Jurman.
Thank you again."

Even though I told Mr. Taub that I wasn't ready to leave Chortkov,

I had been considering doing so for some time. The Hebrew conversations that Bronia and I had had in prison started me thinking about Eretz Israel. Our talks had brought back painful memories of my family, which had always been Zionist. Eretz Israel were household words in our home, and I thought of Hebrew as my second language, so it was natural for my plans to turn in that direction.

One evening shortly after my return there was a knock at our door. When I opened it I found about twenty people standing outside carrying plates of food and bottles of assorted drinks. Someone had brought a balalaika (a Russian guitar). I recognized some of the people. Most, especially the people in Polish and Russian uniforms, were strangers to me, but all were Jews. They had come to celebrate my freedom, they declared, and to thank me, as some of them were or had been involved in the supposed black market and others were their friends.

I invited them in, embarrassed by all that attention, but soon I entered into the party spirit. It was wonderful. The food was delicious. The man with the balalaika played an assortment of Yiddish, Polish, and Russian songs, and everybody sang. True, most of the songs were sad but were songs nevertheless. People were called to sing. I don't know how it happened, but I found myself standing and singing the song of the flower girl Anuta. I started slowly, just as I remembered the sergeant had in Bella's restaurant, then gradually increased the volume of my voice and poured all my emotions and lonely heart into the song. There was complete silence when I finished. Soon people came up to hug me and shake my hand and thank me for everything. Some had tears in their eyes. I was rather bewildered to receive so much affection.

The highest point of the evening came when they cleared a circle around me in the middle of the room. A man stood next to me, holding a long narrow sack. One by one, people stepped up and put money in the sack, again and again, until the sack filled to my height with rubles. I was stunned. There were thousands of rubles there. Tears welled up in my eyes as I looked at the man who was tying the sack.

"Alicia dear, this gift is a token of recognition of what you did for some of us in Chernovtsy. Money may not make you happy, but it will keep you from being hungry." Then, raising his glass of vodka, he called to us all to drink, *"Lechaim."*

* * *

I was determined to make friends with Moishele before he left Chortkov. His parents were waiting for Feigele to cut her first tooth and quiet down a little before they departed. She had been very cranky.

I suggested to Moishele that we make kites and fly them in the nearby park. He thought it a good idea, and while we walked we talked. I told him what had happened to me. I talked to him as I would talk to a grown-up, and I could see from the expression in his eyes that he understood what I was telling him. We sealed our renewed friendship with a hug and were soon on our way to the park. We spent a lovely time together, and I was very happy to hear Moishele laugh. His laughter was contagious, and I was also laughing as I leapt about and ran after my kite. It was a lovely day indeed.

When we returned home we found a girl about fifteen who had come to live in our house. Her name was Rivka and she seemed to be friendly. She was the only survivor of her family, except for some distant cousins who lived in Krakow.

Shortly after the Taubs left I, too, decided to leave. When I told Rivka about it, she said she would go with me. She planned to join her cousins in Krakow, and she was sure that if I needed to stay for a while I could. I thanked her for the offer but told her that I intended to go to Bielsko, to find the factory where my father and Mr. Ekerberg had been partners. I wanted to know this place that had been so much a part of my father's life. Besides, Bielsko was, I hoped, on the way to Eretz Israel, the land I had heard so much about as a young child. I decided that it was there, in my homeland, that I belonged.

In April 1945, in the early morning, Rivka and I boarded the train to Lvov. From there we would transfer to a train to Krakow, and I would continue on to Bielsko. I was excited when I sat down on the bench and lifted my two suitcases to the overhead rack. Suddenly I realized that I was also afraid, and when the whistle blew, I was shaking inside. I remembered other train rides: memories, always memories. I realized that I would have to start thinking of the future and suppress thoughts of the past that always threatened to overwhelm me.

The train started to move. I got up to stand in front of the window. I unbuttoned the pocket of my shirt, took out the letter Kola's father had given me, unfolded it, and gently pushed it through the slightly opened window. It hung there for a moment, suspended in the air as though waiting for someone to reach out and grab it, then it fluttered away until I couldn't see it anymore.

CHAPTER 20

My Orphanage

When we arrived in Lvov, the station was filled with travelers. I wondered where all the people were going. Most of them had a great many bundles, as though they were moving permanently rather than traveling to visit someone. Although I didn't know it then, this was indeed the case. Even before the war ended, the Russian authorities in eastern Poland were encouraging Poles to leave for the west. Later, that section of Poland was annexed to the Soviet Union.

Although I had never been in Lvov, several of my uncles and their families had lived there, and it was in this city that my older brother Zachary had gone to school. For a fleeting moment I thought that perhaps I should stay in Lvov for a few days to find out if any of my mother's family had survived. But then I remembered my bitter experience at the house in Stanislavov that had belonged to my uncle, Dr. Kurtz. If anyone had survived, I hoped they would leave Lvov and that eventually we would find each other. But the truth was that I no longer had any hope that any of my mother's side of the family, Kurtzes or Halperns, were still alive.

That same day we boarded the train to Przemysl, where we transferred to a train going to Krakow. I felt rather good about being a normal traveler, with a real train ticket and luggage. Although I was a little frightened by this new experience, I tried to act as though I were a seasoned traveler. I carried my two suitcases with a sense of purpose and with great care. They held all my worldly possessions—my clothing and the rest of the money that remained from the generous

263

gift I had received in Chortkov. I could describe myself as a person dressed for traveling. I wore Kola's military shirt gathered up with a leather belt, a green woolen skirt, and a pair of black leather boots. Tucked under my arm I carried a brown woolen jacket, which I didn't have to wear since spring had arrived.

After settling in our seats on the train to Krakow, Rivka and I relaxed and watched the scenery through the window. The train stopped at little towns along the route, picking up passengers each time. Some stops were only five minutes long. At other times the train would stop for as long as twenty minutes. There were stalls along the train stations, and people frequently stepped off the train long enough to make a quick purchase or just to stretch their legs.

When we stopped at the city of Tarnow, Rivka decided she would like a cup of tea. She didn't want to go alone, and I felt that I could use a little leg stretching, so I asked an elderly couple to watch our suitcases, and we went out together. We left the platform and went down a corridor to the station room where the tea stall was located. The line was long and as the minutes went by I became nervous about returning to the train. But we were getting closer and closer to the counter, so I said nothing.

We were finally able to buy the tea and I hurried Rivka back to the tracks just in time to see our train pulling out.

"Wait!" I cried, and broke into a run, but the train had already picked up speed, taking all of our belongings with it.

Rivka caught up with me. "Alicia, what are we going to do now?" she asked, shocked.

"What can we do?" I said. "The train is gone."

Strange as it may seem, it never occurred to us to tell the stationmaster that we lost our luggage on the train. Perhaps he could have done something about finding it for us. But we never thought to ask. We were too young, and had become accustomed to losses—they seemed a normal part of life.

"Do you have any money with you, Rivka?" I asked her.

"Just a little. I am planning to stay with relatives in Krakow."

I had put some rubles in one of the front pockets of my shirt, but now, as I unbuttoned the flap, I noticed that my fountain pen had leaked and stained the pocket and its contents: eight Russian rubles. Luckily my documents and my train ticket were in the other pocket. When I held the stained rubles in my hand, I realized that no one would accept them as cash and that I was literally penniless.

We finally decided to find a conductor and see if we could continue on another train. He looked at our tickets and told us that another train for Krakow would be arriving in an hour. The train stopped at many stations, so we did not reach Krakow until the next morning.

Rivka and I parted in Krakow, she to join her relatives, I to see a little of the city before going on to Bielsko. I left for Bielsko a few hours later on what was becoming my way to travel—a military truck. Bielsko wasn't far from Krakow and by noon we arrived at the Russian military headquarters. Since my imprisonment in Chernovtsy I had tried to stay away from the Russians, but I now had little choice in the matter since I had no money and was very hungry. I showed my documents to the soldier on duty and told him that I had lost my luggage and my money. He was very understanding and told me that I could eat there as long as I needed to; he would try to find a place for me to stay. I had lunch and went to look for the marketplace.

When I arrived there, I spoke with a woman who was selling fruit. She told me of a Jewish family named Sharf who lived on the second floor of an apartment building where her friend was the superintendent. She wrote the address on a piece of paper and gave me general directions to the house in the center of the city.

The Sharfs turned out to be very nice people. There were two brothers. The younger brother, Ben, was about thirty years old and newly married, but Herman, the older, was about forty and had lost his family. He was a sick man and stayed in bed most of the time. They received me very warmly, and Mrs. Sharf told me that I could stay with them as long as I wished if I was willing to help with cleaning the house and the daily shopping. Soon I felt like a member of the family.

The apartment was very large. It had eight rooms. I had a very lovely room with a bed and wardrobe, overlooking the busy street. I didn't mind the noises of city life during the day, but I worried about what sounded like distant cannon fire during the night. When I questioned the older of the two brothers about it, he told me that the war was still going on, and that the Germans and the Russians were still fighting. In order not to dwell on this I kept very busy.

In addition to cleaning the house and shopping for food I liked to help Mrs. Sharf by doing all kinds of little chores for her brother-in-law, Herman, who was ill with tuberculosis. After I cleaned his room and changed his bed linen I would often stay in his room to talk if he wasn't too tired. He told me that he had been born in Bielsko and had practiced law there before the war.

He told me that most of the Jews who had lived in Bielsko before the war had been killed by the Germans. Only a very few had survived and returned to the city.

One day I told him about my family and about my father, and why I had come to Bielsko. He listened with interest, but I could see that his face clouded when I mentioned the factory and Mr. Eckerberg. When I finished we sat silently for a long time. Then Mr. Sharf took my hand in his and looked at me thoughtfully.

"Alicia, you may as well know there isn't a chance in the world for you to recover anything from your father's former business. If I were you, I wouldn't mention this to anyone. I can understand that you would like to see the place. Well, you can do that. As a matter of fact, I know exactly where it is. But before I tell you, you must promise not to talk to anyone you may meet near the factory. Do I have your promise?"

"I promise," I said solemnly. "You are right, Mr. Sharf. We had the same problem in Buczacz. As a matter of fact, some people who went to claim their property were actually killed by the new owners."

"So you know what is happening. You are a big girl and you will be careful." He wrote the address on a piece of paper and gave it to me.

The same afternoon I went to see the factory. I stopped people along the way and asked directions. It took over an hour for me to find it. It was a tall building, part of a group of buildings. I could make out a faint printing ECKERBERG FABRICS on the side of the wall. I took a deep breath and started to cross the street. But, strangely, the closer I got, the more uneasy I became. Was it just that I would have to face more memories of my father bringing fabrics from this factory home to my mother? Or Father telling my mother and us about his business trip?

I stood facing the building, my heart pounding, my mouth dry. I had not expected the intense feeling of danger. It was like being back in the war again, when I couldn't let anyone know I was Jewish because I would have been killed. I felt the same way now, because I couldn't let anyone know that part of this factory had belonged to my family.

As I watched the factory I thought that I would wait until the war ended to put in a claim for the part that had belonged to my father. But then suddenly it didn't seem to matter anymore; the money wasn't important. I couldn't reach out for my father this way. I would have to close this chapter of our family's past. I turned around and walked away.

It was nice to return to the Sharfs, especially since after seeing the factory I was very sad. I went to talk with Herman, as I always did whenever I returned from my walks. I would describe the weather and tell him about life outside. He encouraged my daily walks, asking me to take a little walk for him too. He told me that Bielsko was a very interesting city, and he was right. Bielsko was really quite beautiful. There was a large park not far from where we lived and wide streets with lovely buildings. I walked aimlessly through the streets, looking about me and at the sky, listening to the birds and smelling the flowers. Sometimes I would go to the bank of the river to watch the clear blue water. I would sweep my hand against the current and feel the water's cool freshness. Other times I would walk into the woods at the edge of the city and watch the birds as they pecked, looking for worms. It was spring and nature was in its full glory. I was learning to be free again.

But among the people on the streets I began to notice some children who didn't seem to belong somehow. They were dressed poorly and were pitifully thin. This in itself was not too unusual, although most people in the streets seemed to have a purpose. They were going somewhere or doing something. These children walked hunched over, their faces to the ground, as though they didn't want to be seen or to look directly at people. They seemed nervous and, if approached, would shy away in fear, as though expecting to be struck.

They had the bodies of small children but the faces of teenagers and, when you could see them, very old eyes. I felt, somehow, a kinship with those children and was waiting for a chance to talk with them.

The opportunity came one afternoon when I was resting on a bench at the edge of the woods. I was sitting and listening to the life around me, thinking about my three weeks in Bielsko. Then I heard someone crying: short, painful sobs. I recognized that kind of crying. It was filled with such pain and sorrow that I couldn't remain sitting there but went to find out who it was. Behind some large bushes I found two teenage girls. It was hard to fix their exact ages from their physical appearance. When the girl who was crying saw me, she tried to stop, but her body could not stop shaking and deep moans continued to escape from within her. The older girl, who had been consoling her in what sounded like German or Yiddish, looked up at me angrily.

"I'm sorry; I didn't mean to interfere," I said, "but can I help you?"

The girls exchanged glances but did not answer. I was just about to turn away, when the oldest looked up at me doubtfully, then said in Polish, "Yes, you can help us. Can you give us something to eat? We haven't eaten anything for two days, since we came back to Bielsko. Just a piece of bread will be fine."

God, I thought, how well I remembered my own pleas for just a piece of bread. It was hard to keep my voice from trembling.

"Yes, yes, you shall have food. But you must come with me."

I had decided to take them to the Sharfs. There was enough space in the apartment, and I knew that Mrs. Sharf was a generous soul. I had no right to do this, but I had the feeling that she would have asked them to come if she were with me.

When we reached the apartment, Eta Sharf took one look at the girls and, without saying a word, led them to seats at the kitchen table and brought out food. After they had eaten, she took their clothes to be washed. The girls had baths and fell asleep together in one of the bedrooms.

These were my first two orphans and my first real contact with the reality of what had happened to the Jews in German concentration camps. Up to this time I had only heard rumors. To me, reality was the murder of my people in their homes, in prison courtyards, and in front of mass graves in the meadows of Poland. I hadn't thought much, or known much about the German camps. I knew people were taken away in trains; I was on one such train. But where did they go? To what fate? I could only guess.

Now here were two children who had been in a concentration camp. Herman Sharf had also been liberated from such a camp. Until I brought the children to his home, he had never mentioned this. But when he saw the children, perhaps to help me understand them, he told me about the camps and what Hitler and his SS men had done to the Jewish people there. He told me what had happened in other parts of Poland and all over Europe wherever the Germans and their collaborators had been in power—what might still be happening in the lands under Nazi occupation. He had not talked about these things earlier, but now he could not stop.

I sat near his bed, and as I listened, each sentence fell upon my heart and soul like a searing iron. I started crying because my young heart couldn't accept more anguish and pain.

I was very careful not to ask the two girls, Stefa and Bronin, any questions, but I now knew enough to understand that the other strange children I had seen on the streets were Jewish orphans who had survived the concentration camps, and that they were in great need of food and shelter. They needed to belong to someone. They had been freed, but there was no one to look after them. The Russians were otherwise occupied, and the Poles didn't care.

The following day Stefa, Bronin, and I started looking for those other children. We walked city streets, went near the river and into the forest. Within a week we had collected another eight children. We brought them to the Sharfs, who didn't say a word when their door opened and they saw new arrivals. The empty rooms began filling up quickly and, with all the eaters, Ben Sharf was very busy getting more food, and his wife and several orphans were constantly busy in the kitchen. Suddenly we were a big family. It occurred to me that I couldn't continue imposing on the Sharf's generosity indefinitely; yet I had no money of my own. I started thinking. Maybe if I opened an orphanage I could get help from the city officials. I talked to Herman Sharf about my idea, and he looked at me strangely.

"Alicia, do you know what you are undertaking? These aren't ordinary children. Do you realize what the nights will be like for you? I can hear you now as you get up to quiet them when they have nightmares. It has been only one week, and look at the dark circles under your eyes! Are you sure you want to get involved in all this, you, a young girl and an orphan yourself?"

I understood what he was saying. I remembered the responsibilities I had assumed as breadwinner for my mother, brother, and others during the war, but I had already promised myself that I would do everything I could to help those orphans.

"I have to, Mr. Sharf. I can't let them just wander in the streets, not after all they have lived through. I understand how they must feel; I felt like that for years during the war, and I still feel homeless and orphaned right now.

"We can't stay here, because then we are limited by the size of this apartment and the limits of your generosity—and surely there must be limits. Yet I am certain that there must be more homeless orphans in this city. First we have to find a larger place to live, and then I will try to get help from the authorities. Do you know a home or an apartment that formerly belonged to Jewish people and was later taken over by

Germans? The Germans would have left when the Russians occupied the city. Can you think of a house like that, please, Mr. Sharf?"

"Well, as I can see that you are a determined girl, I will ask Ben. He may know of a house you can use."

The following morning Herman Sharf gave me the address of a large apartment in Biala, which was part of Bielsko. It had six rooms and a kitchen and had belonged to a former colleague of his who perished in the concentration camps with his whole family. There was only a maid acting as caretaker there now. Herman told me that I was a very smart girl to think of such a house, and that his brother had promised that he would help us as much as possible. The orphanage seemed to him to be a good idea after all. He was, however, worried, or, rather, skeptical about the possibility that we could get help from the Polish officials, but said it was worth trying.

The next day I put on a new dress that Mrs. Sharf had given me, fixed up my hair as best as I could, pinning it up to make myself look older than almost fifteen, and went to the Bielsko city hall. I asked to speak to the man in charge of welfare, especially orphanages, and was shown to a waiting room where a few other people were sitting awaiting their turn. As I sat I rehearsed my little speech.

Finally I was called in. My heart was pounding and I realized that I wasn't at all happy about going to a Polish official for help. But I had no choice, so I put on a happy face as I entered the office. The Polish official sat in a huge leather chair behind an ornately carved desk. He asked me to sit, pointing at a chair in front of his desk. The man was middle-aged, with graying hair. He had the kind of face one couldn't read.

"What is your name, miss?" he asked.

"Alicia," I said.

"Are you from Bielsko, miss?"

"No, sir. I am from Buczacz originally. I have been in your city a little over two weeks."

"Ah." He folded his hands across his stomach, leaning back in the huge chair.

"And what can I do for you today?" he inquired.

I took a deep breath and began my little speech.

"You see, sir, we are a small group of Jewish orphans who—"

"What!" He slammed his hand down on the desk so fiercely that I jumped. His face changed abruptly and became red and ugly. His eyes narrowed into little slits.

"You Jews still survived?" he cried. "You cursed Jews survived?"

For the briefest moment this reaction immobilized me entirely. I sat in my chair, my mouth open, staring at the ugly face, not quite believing what I had just heard. But I didn't stay that way for long. In an instant, rage surged through me like a forest fire. I leapt from my chair, came around his desk, and, swinging my right hand back, smacked him in the face with all my strength.

"You mad Polish dog," I cried, and ran out of the room and into the street as though I were being chased by the devil himself. I was crying bitterly in frustration and anger and didn't care whether anyone saw me or heard me. I was furious and I was scared. How could I have been so stupid as to forget how much the Poles hated us; even now he might be sending the police after me and they might shoot me down on the street. But I was glad I had slapped him, and I would do it again. He deserved even worse treatment from me!

I finally stopped running and leaned against a building. My sobs had stopped too, but the tears were still rolling silently down my face. I looked around to see if there was a policeman coming after me, but I couldn't see any. Directly across from me, parked against the curb, was a Russian truck. There were two men there, a driver and another, who I could tell by his uniform and all the medals was an officer. He was standing outside the truck, one foot on the running board, eating from a tin. They were watching me.

"Hey, what's the matter?" the officer asked. He put down the tin and came over to me, reaching out to wipe the tears from my cheeks with a handkerchief he pulled out of his breast pocket.

"What is the matter, *dievushka*," he asked softly. I burst into tears all over again. He led me to the truck. I sat down on the running board and because he was kind to me I sobbed out my story. I could see his face cloud up with fury. For a moment I regretted involving him in my problem, but he had seemed so sympathetic and I had to talk to someone. We sat silently for a moment and then he handed me a tin of meat loaf and urged me to eat, saying that it was from America and very tasty. I took a couple of bites just to be polite, but I could hardly swallow because I was still very angry.

"Let's see how your problem can be solved," he said. "Come with me to the back of the truck.

"Here are some sacks of clothing and all kinds of things you can use." He pointed inside the truck. Next, he unbuttoned the pocket in the front of his shirt and took out a bundle of Polish zlotys and handed them to me. "This will help, for the time being."

I was so astonished by his generosity that I couldn't move. "Here, take it," he urged, and he pushed the money into my hand. "You don't need those Polish dogs. My friends and I, we will help you. We all have good Jewish hearts." He smiled. "Some of my friends are Polish Jews serving in the Russian army, crazy fellows but good soldiers. I am a Russian Jew from Leningrad. We will adopt you. Don't worry. My name is Mesha. What are you called?"

I wanted to say Anusha, just to please him, but instead I said Ala, short for Alicia. "You can call me Ala. And thank you very much, Officer Mesha, the Jew from Leningrad. God bless you for your kindness to us." I said the last words in Hebrew, but he didn't understand.

"Where would you like to go now, Ala?" he asked.

It occurred to me that it would be a good idea to see the apartment Mr. Sharf told me about. I had the address with me, so we traveled to Biala. I had no difficulty finding it, and when we rang the bell an older woman who looked like a maid opened the door. Mesha told her that we were moving into the apartment, and that we knew the former owners, who were Jews. She nodded her head. She apparently had been expecting someone to come and live there, because she was ready to leave within half an hour. Mesha gave her some money, and she gave us the key to the apartment.

The apartment was all I could have hoped for. It had five bedrooms, a large living room, and a large kitchen-dining room. I could see traces on the doorpost where a mezuzah had once been placed. I thought about the Jewish family who had once lived there, and I felt a deep sorrow. I looked around the apartment. The Germans who had lived there during the occupation had not had time to remove all the lovely china, crystal, and carpets. The beds and the bedding were all in very good condition, and I thought how nice it would be for the orphans to live in this house. There was indoor plumbing in the bathroom—a toilet, a sink, and a tub—but there were no pipes leading to the tub; it had to be filled by hand. In the kitchen there was another faucet which delivered only cold water. But none of these small problems took away from my joy. What pleased me most was the huge stove in the kitchen. Not only did it have a large griddle area, an oven, and plenty of storage for firewood, but there was a tank built into the back of the stove to store water which was heated whenever the stove was in use. It couldn't have been more perfect.

Mesha and his driver unloaded the sacks of clothing from the back of the truck, and we drove to the Sharfs to get the children and bring them to their new home.

Mesha had to go back to his army unit, but he promised to visit again in a few days. I asked him to be there on May 9 because that day was my birthday, and I was going to be fifteen years old.

All of us loved our new home. We spent our first evening eating American K rations which Mesha had given us, and examining the contents of the sacks. We separated the clothing into piles and sorted out the items that we could wear and those we would sell in the market. I was about to become a businesswoman again on that memorable day of May 6, 1945.

The following day Stefa and I put some of the clothing into a suitcase we found in the house and carried it to the market, which was not far from our apartment. We sold all of the clothing quickly and cheaply, and with the money we bought bread, cheese, butter, milk, fresh fruits, and three live chickens. It was Stefa's idea to buy the chickens. She wanted to make chicken soup. But when we got the chickens home and put them on the kitchen floor, we all stood around looking at them and didn't know what to do. Stefa and I knew that we couldn't cook live chickens, and none of us was prepared to kill them. So we picked them up, took them outside, untied their legs, and set them free. I rather suspect that some of our neighbors watched us freeing the chickens and caught them, because when I looked out the window a short while later there wasn't a chicken in sight.

I was very busy settling into our new home, so I didn't have a chance to visit the Sharfs during the next two days. When I finally managed to go to their house in the late afternoon of May 8, I had a wonderful surprise waiting for me. Mr. Sharf told me that the war had ended. The horrible war in Europe had ended! All over the world nations were rejoicing. I thought about Kola and his father; about Mesha and David, Bronia's brother, and I was grateful that they would not have to fight anymore.

But we, the orphans in Biala, sat in silence while the world celebrated. We were thinking of our murdered families, and we wept. For us the end of the war had come too late.

Mesha returned as he promised, on May 9, and brought us more sacks of clothing and also two of his friends. They were both Russian Jews whose families had been killed by the Germans, and they wanted very much to help us. We celebrated my fifteenth birthday, and Mesha gave me a gold and ruby necklace. We had a good dinner and sang songs. I sang the partisan song and the song of the flower girl Anuta. I must have sung well, because I received many hugs and kisses. That same evening I showed Mesha the documents the Kalpak partisans had given me, and he said he understood now why I cried when I sang the partisan song. I didn't tell him that this song reminded me of Kola, and I sometimes wondered if Kola had gone to Buczacz to get me as he had promised.

We had a surprise waiting for Mesha and his friends. I had purchased two Omega watches and five bottles of vodka for Mesha and his driver, and we gave them to him. I also promised to have more vodka and watches waiting for him when he and his friends returned, because we felt they should be compensated for the things they brought to us. We had a very nice evening. This was the beginning of more visits by my adopted brothers and their friends, who regularly supplied us with clothing they "liberated" from abandoned German houses. They no doubt remembered how the Germans had looted Russian homes when the Nazis invaded the Soviet Union.

In the meantime, our number was growing. The orphans who lived with us brought others from as far as Krakow and Lodz, and soon there were twenty-four of us, ranging in age from ten to fifteen years old. I was sure that ours was the only Jewish orphanage in the whole area, something I thought we could be proud of. At the same time, our used-clothing business was booming. We had enough food and clothing; we had people who cared about us, we had all the physical comforts; but what we didn't have was peace of mind. Each day was fully occupied by such activities as shopping, cooking, cleaning, reading, taking walks to the Bielsko forest, visiting the Sharfs, or just enjoying the beautiful spring days. But when night came, everything changed. All the horrors we had lived through under the German occupation were coming back in the form of terrible nightmares. I don't remember sleeping through one night peacefully.

We had other minor problems. One of them was that some of the children were hiding food. I couldn't really blame them, remembering how hungry I used to be. But there was no need for it now. We had plenty. But I let it pass. I never brought up this problem, although Stefa and I searched the house every day because rats had started coming into the apartment, and that terrified me. Since the time I had been in prisons I was terrified of rats.

We also had a serious problem with the hot water tank. Someone had made it a hiding place for their bread. The bread was attached to a string that was lowered into the tank just above the water level. That would have been all right, but we had a rule that whoever drew hot water had to replace it, and when this was done, water was poured over the string and the bread dissolved, and so we constantly had muddy water. No one ever found out who it was that hid bread in the water tank. We just learned to live with the problem.

One day in the marketplace we met two young Jewish men who bought clothing from us. They told us that they were from Lodz and were buying things in Bielsko-Biala, where they were cheaper. When they returned to Lodz, they resold the goods at a nice profit. They bought from us several times, and it occurred to me that if they could buy all of our clothing, we could sell it to them at a low price and wouldn't have to stay in the market every day. They agreed to take our whole stock from us and paid us well. Our Russian friends brought more used clothing the next day.

Indeed, our business was prospering and we had suitcases filled with money. Often I would ask the orphans to take some of it and go out and buy whatever their hearts desired, but their answer would always be the same. They had all they needed and couldn't think of anything they wanted. The only time they would take money was for traveling, because like all of the survivors they were driven to look for relatives or friends. But I thought it a good idea to save some money for them. I talked about it with Ben Sharf, and he suggested that I bring the zlotys that we didn't need to live on, and he would buy us American paper dollars, gold twenty-dollar coins, or Russian gold coins called "little pigs." He would save an equal amount for each of the original twenty-four members of our orphanage. And each time one of us left, he could go to him for his share. We all liked this arrangement and agreed that Ben Sharf was the right person to handle all that for us. He told me that he had been in the jewelry business before the war and now he was dealing in foreign currency and gold coins. He was becoming a very wealthy man, he told me. I was happy to hear that because he was a good brother to Herman, and he was kind and generous to us.

I do not wish to give the impression that we lived in some kind of utopia with everyone loving one another. That would have been impossible. We had our share of disagreements and fistfights, especially among the boys, whom we would have to send to the Sharfs

to cool off, but Stefa and I handled most of the problems as they came
along. These, we called ordinary problems. More difficult to handle
were cases of heartache such as in the case of Dina, a fifteen-year-old,
who had found her ten-year-old sister in a convent and brought her to
stay with us. At the convent, the sisters had changed her name from
Ruth to Maria, and when Dina called her Ruth, she refused to answer.
I moved Dina and her sister to my own tiny room to give them some
privacy and I went to sleep with Stefa, thereby adding a fifth person to
an already crowded room. It was very painful for Dina to see her sister
constantly crossing herself and kneeling down to say her prayers before
going to sleep, and often I would hear crying coming from that room. I
felt a lot of sympathy for Ruth-Maria. She only vaguely remembered
her parents and her home; she knew only the nuns and the convent
where she had been hidden during the war years.

Finally I suggested that Dina talk to the Mother Superior and seek
her advice. And so it turned out that both girls spent some time at the
convent and some time with us. Finally Dina decided to leave Bielsko
and go to live in Krakow. The day they left I gave Ruth-Maria a silver
Star of David which she attached to the same chain as her cross. One
of the symbols was going to possess the little girl's soul someday, but
truthfully I couldn't predict which symbol it would be.

CHAPTER 21

The Brecha

Two months had passed since the day we moved into our new home and started our orphanage. Time passed quickly; it was June 1945. We were busy all week with our daily chores, but managed to rest on Saturday and Sunday. On Saturdays we visited the Sharfs and observed the Sabbath by dressing in nice clothing and just relaxing. Several times I tried to welcome the Sabbath by lighting candles on Friday at sundown, by saying the blessing in Hebrew, and by singing the hymn of welcome to the Sabbath Queen, but this evoked such painful memories for all of us that I had to stop. To us children, the lighting of the Sabbath candles brought back images of our families, especially of our mothers. It brought back a time in our lives that was still painful to remember and too hard to forget. We couldn't accept our losses yet, and our longing for our families was so great that anything reminding us of them was unbearable.

We often picnicked in the woods, as on this occasion. We spread out blankets in a clearing, took out the food the girls had prepared under Stefa's supervision, and had a wonderful time. As I ate I looked around me. It was amazing to see the change in the orphans. They looked much healthier physically, and no wonder. The amount of food they ate was unbelievable. But what made me really happy was the change in Stefa. Her body had filled out and she was beginning to look like a girl. Her hair, which had been chopped short and of an indefinite color, was long now and the color of golden honey. Today she had gathered her hair up in the back with a blue ribbon to complement her blue summer dress. She was remarkably different from the girl I had first met in this very forest only two months earlier. The only thing about her that hadn't changed were her large blue eyes. Although they often smiled now, they retained their deep sadness. I also noticed differences in the rest of the girls, which pleased me greatly. Perhaps I had also changed.

Unfortunately I couldn't say the same about our ten boys. They, too, looked healthier since they came to us, but they were listless and sad. Having had four brothers, I thought I understood boys, so I paid special attention to them. There were times when I thought that I had reached them through the sheer force of my love and devotion to them, and they appeared a little more cheerful, but at other times I felt that I hadn't touched them at all. They were like turtles, pulling back into their shells when anyone came near them. Sometimes I was so frustrated that I wished I could break their shells and force them out into the open. Then I felt ashamed to have had such thoughts, realizing that it was those very shells that had enabled them to live through the horrors of the concentration camps. So all I could do was continue to love and guide them.

What the boys really needed was direction, a purpose in life. They should have been going to school, where they would be busy with homework and sports. But after six years of absence they wouldn't fit into any normal classroom. They simply didn't have the knowledge or the necessary identification papers. As a matter of fact, not one of us had any kind of legal status or documents. Poland was trying to return to normality, but we didn't exist.

I thought we might hire a private teacher and had already mentioned this to Herman Sharf. It would be a splendid idea to have a teacher come to our home. We could all study with him. Once we started such a school, I would be able to teach Hebrew. I would renew my own knowledge of the language and teach the basic words to the others.

In the meantime we depended on Herman Sharf to be our spiritual teacher. He reminded me of a man in a story our Hebrew teacher had told my class before the war. The story was about one of our biblical sages, Rabbi Akiva, who had been imprisoned by the Romans. He was known for his great wisdom and willingness to give advice to those who sought it. Jewish people used to stand outside under the window of his prison cell and talk with him. I thought of Herman Sharf, imprisoned by his illness but always ready to give advice to those who needed it, which we certainly did.

On this beautiful summer day I left the picnic to take a peaceful walk in the forest. I was wondering how long we would stay together and where we would go from there. I knew that we couldn't stay in the building we occupied indefinitely. Sooner or later someone would ask us to pay rent. Our adopted brothers would be going back to their homes soon, some to the Soviet Union, and those who were born in Poland would probably leave the country after their discharge from the army. When they left, our means of support would leave with them. As a matter of fact, I believed that all the Jews who survived should leave Poland. We were no longer part of Polish life. The Poles not only didn't want us; many hated us. I had been convinced of this by the way the Polish official had reacted to my plea for help. It was not illogical. Before the war, one out of every ten Poles was Jewish; now the Jews were almost all gone. Every one of us who survived was a reminder of Polish indifference at the best, often betrayal. Would the Polish occupier of a Jewish home or the proprietor of a former Jewish business wish to give it up to Jewish survivors? I thought not. My orphans could not expect to reclaim their families' property. Lately the question of our future occupied my thoughts more often than I cared to admit.

Had I known that fate was working on our behalf, I would have relaxed and been satisfied just to enjoy that beautiful summer day in the forest. When I think back, I realize that I was actually ready for a change. What surprised me, though, was the unexpected direction from which it came.

It happened the day after our picnic in the forest. We had completed another sale of our goods to the two men from Lodz. Usually they would leave our home with a promise to return soon. This time they didn't leave, but asked permission to stay overnight. They said they wished to speak to me in private. I was a little surprised at this request, and curious to know what they wanted.

They had stayed over at our house once before, early in our business association. They had been skeptical of our ability to supply them with enough merchandise to make it worth their while to come more often to Biala from Lodz. At that time I showed them my documents in order to convince them that they could trust me, as others had trusted me in the past. Perhaps, being a young girl, I just wanted to impress them, but anyway, I could see that they were impressed and my qualifications were never mentioned again.

Now I waited to hear what it was they had to say to me. To have privacy in our home was almost impossible unless one took a bath. And that was where the three of us went. We brought in chairs and sat down in the bathroom to talk.

When I looked closely at those two men, I realized, to my great surprise, that they were very young, perhaps twenty or twenty-one. I had always thought of them as older. It was just that they acted old. I nearly laughed out loud as I thought that I hadn't acted very young either. After all, I was responsible for the lives and well-being of our household.

"Why don't you start, Izio," said one of the men. "You are a better talker."

"Well, I don't know where to begin. Hmm. Alicia, have you heard of a Jewish organization called the Brecha? The word means 'to smuggle.'"

"No, I haven't heard of a smuggling organization called the Brecha, and to be very honest with you, I don't really want to hear about anything that has to do with smuggling. I had enough trouble in Chernovtsy, and that is a story I don't want to go into right now." I started to get up.

"Wait, wait, let me finish! My God, Alicia, you certainly have a temper!" cried Izio. Then he continued.

"The Brecha is an organization that smuggles Jews out of Russian-occupied countries such as Latvia, Poland, Czechoslovakia, and Hungary. Yes, I know what you are thinking, Alicia, you are thinking that all those countries should be happy to let us leave because they don't want us as witnesses to their disgraceful behavior toward us under the German occupation, but it isn't that simple. We have to use all kinds of tricks to actually cross the borders to the west. But what I want to talk about now is a young woman called Tzivia. We call her Tzivia, the Warsaw Ghetto Fighter, and she deserves that name. She is an outstanding young woman and you, Alicia, are a little like her. I say a little, because there is only one Tzivia." Izio then took my hand in his and smiled into my eyes. "Just as there is only one Alicia."

I blushed deeply. That flatterer certainly had a way with words, I thought. I would have to be careful with him because I could sense that he wanted something from me.

"Tzivia is a very courageous woman," Izio continued. "I heard said about her that she dressed herself in a German SS uniform and used counterfeit documents to free some of her friends from Gestapo headquarters. A very brave woman indeed. A real fighter. When one looks at her slight build and innocent brown eyes one can hardly believe her capable of such courage, but when you speak with her she literally hypnotizes you and you are willing to do anything she wants you to do. And her friend Helek is also quite a man. They make an excellent team."

"Look, Izio," I replied, "why don't you come to the point? What is it you want of me? And how can I possibly be connected with such great people?"

"As a matter of fact, my dear girl, you are already connected with Tzivia, Helek, and the Brecha. All the clothing I have been buying from you, and I must say very cheaply, too, has served our organization very well. Most of it went for the use of the people whom we smuggle out of Poland. We sell the rest for a good price.

"But I will get to the point now. I told Tzivia about you, and of course I mentioned your documents from the partisans, and that you speak Russian and several other languages and get along well with people. I must admit that we have other people with those qualifications, but your greatest asset to our organization would be the combination of those assets and your deep commitment to your people. Something is driving you, Alicia, some inner force, and we need that energy."

He was beginning to analyze me, and I didn't like that at all. "Just one moment, Izio," I interrupted. "What do you want from me?"

"Tzivia wants to see you in Lodz, and she asked us to bring you there as soon as possible, like tomorrow. She just wants to meet you, Alicia. That's all."

That was certainly not all Izio had in mind while telling me all about Tzivia and flattering me, I thought. I might go, but what about the orphans? I had never left them alone. It wasn't that they couldn't manage without me for a couple of days, but I would worry about them and about the business. And why should I get involved with all this? Why should I come running when a person I had never met asked me to come, literally commanded me to come? Yet I knew I would go to Lodz, and I knew why. Tzivia sounded fascinating to me. She sounded so adventurous, so appealing, and so devoted to the Jewish people; and she was doing something very important. She was directing Jewish survivors toward some kind of future. I was interested in that future. I had been worried about us, and Tzivia might have an answer for me. Besides, I was flattered by an invitation to meet such an important person.

We sat there in silence for a minute. Then I looked at Izio and nodded my head.

Upon our arrival in Lodz we went straight to Piotrkowska Street, number 28. The building, a former apartment house, now served as a center for the remaining Lodz Jewish community and for Jewish survivors who lived there temporarily, or were just passing through the city. It was a busy place, with people coming and going all the time. At the entrance hall I noticed a large bulletin board covered with pinned-up notes. I stopped for a moment to read some of them. They contained names of survivors searching for their families. Some wrote on their notes that they were leaving Poland and hoped to get to Palestine. There were notes that started with pleas of "Have you seen my son? My daughter? My mother? My father?" then included a description of the person sought and the dates they were taken out of the Lodz ghetto and transported to concentration camps. I was deeply shaken by those notes. For a moment I thought that perhaps I, too, should put up a note, but I decided against it. I doubted that any of my family had survived.

Tzivia was not in her office when we arrived, so I went back to read some more of the notices. I began a conversation with a girl about my age who was also checking the board. Her name was Peppa. She and her cousin's family had arrived in Lodz a couple of weeks before from the city of Grodno, in Latvia. They lived a couple of streets away. We became quite friendly, and she invited me to stay with her and her cousin, who had just had a baby.

I returned to wait for Tzivia in her office. Finally she arrived. She strode briskly into the office with people swarming about her.

"Would you authorize this, Tzivia?"

"I couldn't reach Jordana, Tzivia. Do you want me to keep trying?"

"Tzivia, Michael was here. He said it was urgent."

All this time I tried to read the expression on the face of that young woman, who seemed so calm in the middle of the surrounding frenzy. The office gradually emptied of people until only Tzivia and I remained. She seated herself behind her cluttered desk, picked up a piece of paper, and then looked at me. She was a nice-looking young woman with very warm light brown eyes and light brown short hair.

"Your name is Ala Jurman," she said, reading from the paper. "Is that your real name?"

"Actually, my name is Alicia."

"That's such a pretty name," she said, "Why did you change it?"

I shrugged. "Ala is short for Alicia, and when I am called Alicia it brings back memories of my family."

"Hmm." She paused for a moment and then continued.

"You are the sole survivor of your family?"

"Yes."

"And you're fifteen years old?"

"Yes I am."

"Izio told me that you have a certificate of heroism awarded by the Soviet army. And he told me that you received the certificate for saving Russian partisans from a Nazi ambush. Is that true?"

"Yes."

"Did you know any of the partisans?"

"No."

"Then why did you do it?"

"I didn't want them to be killed."

"Is that why you risked your life, to prevent strangers from being killed?"

"Was it so wrong of me?"

She smiled, and took a sip of tea she had brought with her. "No, I don't think it was wrong," she said. "But was that the only reason to take such a risk?"

I thought for a minute. "They were fighting the Germans," I replied. "I would have helped anyone who fought the Germans."

"Hmm." She took another sip of her tea, then studied the sheet of paper again.

"You are running an orphanage in Biala?"

"Yes."

"Without adult supervision?"

"In a way, but we have adopted older brothers; and the Sharfs keep an eye on us."

"How many orphans live in the house?"

"About twenty-four."

"Hmm." She took another sip of her tea.

"Why did you do that?" she asked.

"What do you mean?"

"Why did you start an orphanage?"

I was beginning to become annoyed and angered by all this

interrogation. I didn't care how important Tzivia was. She was asking too many questions.

"Well, I don't see what concern it is of yours whether I want to run an orphanage or not!" I said hotly.

"Please don't be angry," she said. "I only want to understand why a young girl like yourself, free of obligations, should tie herself down with so much responsibility."

"Those children needed a home. Many were living in the streets. Most of them were begging for food. All of them had lice. I didn't see anyone else offering to help them."

"Hmm. I also understand you are running a business out of your home with the help of the Russians."

"Yes, we trade with them. It is perfectly legitimate."

She smiled and took another sip of her tea. "I wouldn't care if it were entirely illegal," she said. "But tell me, how did you get the Russians to help you?"

"Actually they are mostly Russian Jews. They adopted us and are our brothers. They just like helping us."

"I know many young girls your age who are terrified to go near the Russians. Why aren't you?"

"Why should I be? True, they are Russians, but they have Jewish hearts. Besides, I don't think those Russians would deliberately hurt me. They have also suffered from the Germans. Then I can always show my documents." It was my turn now to smile.

"Ala," she asked, "did your family speak Hebrew?"

"Of course. Everybody in Buczacz spoke Hebrew."

"Do you remember any of it?"

"Oh, yes."

"Then you know what 'brecha' means."

"It means to smuggle. It comes from the word *lehavriach*."

"Exactly. Now I will tell you; we are an underground organization called the Brecha, and we smuggle Jews out of Poland."

She brought out a sheet of paper and drew a rough map of Europe.

"Look, here we are; there is Germany; there is France, down here is Austria; there is Czechoslovakia. Here is Russia. Now," she said, "do you know how the Allies have divided Europe?"

She drew a slash down in the middle of Germany and between Austria and Czechoslovakia. "There. Everything on this side"—she indicated France, Italy, and other countries to the west of the line—

"enjoys the protection of the Americans and the British. But everything over here"—now she tapped the pencil directly on Poland—"has fallen under Russian domination."

"So?"

"Alicia, how old were you when the Russians first occupied eastern Poland?"

"Nine."

"Then you should have been old enough to remember."

I sat silently for a moment. I did remember.

She took another sip of her tea, then continued. "And that's not all of it. Do you really think because the war is over the problems of the Jewish people are over? We already know of two pogroms that have taken place since the end of the war."

I looked up, outraged but not really surprised. I myself felt uncomfortable among the Poles. I told her about my experience with the city official in Bielsko who had been furious when he learned that I and my handful of Jewish orphans had survived the war. She nodded vigorously.

"Of course, of course," she said. "They hated us before the war, and you know how many of them cooperated with the Nazis where we were concerned. Now that the war is over, does anyone really think those people are ready to be our friends?"

I shook my head. "Where do the Jews go after they leave Poland?" I asked.

"You mean where does the Brecha bring them? They are left in Linz, Austria, and from there they are distributed to various DP camps, camps for displaced persons. Those camps are managed by the UNRRA, the United Nations Relief and Rehabilitation Agency. There they wait until we can get them to Palestine. Some may be reunited with their families in America, Australia, England, or other countries. Most hope to go to Eretz Israel."

"You can arrange for people to get to Eretz Israel?" Now I was really interested.

"Why, is that where you want to go?"

"More than anything."

"More than taking care of the orphans?"

The question jolted me, and she could see it. "Let's not worry about the orphans for the moment," she continued. "If you were free of responsibility, would you want to go to Eretz Israel?"

"Yes," I whispered.

"There are two ways to enter Eretz Israel these days—legally and illegally. There are problems with both. Legally the British are allowing a very small number of Jews to enter Palestine. Only those who get affidavits from their families there and those who receive one of a limited number of affidavits made available to the Jewish Agency. Those who get affidavits from the Jewish Agency are usually people very much needed in Eretz Israel and those who earn it by working with the Brecha. The majority of the survivors, unfortunately, will have to try to get to Eretz Israel on illegal ships. We call this route Aliyah Beth."

"What would I have to do to get an affidavit to go to Eretz Israel?" I inquired.

"Oh." She laughed lightly. "We can't just hand them out, you know. We try to save them for our transport leaders. Ala, we want to train you to be such a leader."

"What?" I gasped. "Why me?" I realized that this was a stupid question to ask after all Tzivia had already told me. But somehow I was still surprised by her suggestion.

"Because you are smart; you can take care of yourself and others; you are willing to take risks to help other people; and you carry documents stating you are a Hero of the Soviet Union."

"So that's it," I said. "You want the documents."

"Of course we want the documents," she said. "But we don't want them without you."

There was complete silence in the office. I knew I had to say something. I wanted to please Tzivia, but instead I said, "It is quite impossible; I can't take on this responsibility right now. I have to take care of my children in Biala."

"What if we guaranteed you safe passage to Eretz Israel?" asked Tzivia.

"No, I'm sorry."

"Hmm." She nodded thoughtfully. "Do something for me, will you, Ala?" she asked. "Don't say no right away. Think about it a little. Do you have lodgings for tonight?" I nodded yes. "Good. Then will you come back tomorrow morning? I want you to see a little more of how we work before you make up your mind. Will you do that for me?"

"Certainly."

"Let's say around half past nine in this room." We shook hands and smiled at each other.

"Shalom, Alicia, until tomorrow!"

I felt my hand tremble when I closed the door to Tzivia's office. The way she said "Shalom, Alicia" in Hebrew reached into the depths of my soul. How well I remembered those two words, said to me so often by my family and friends. It seemed like a lifetime ago. Also, I felt that I had walked into a new world. If I joined Tzivia, I would be starting a new phase in my life.

In the past year or so I had been quite independent. I had made my own decisions, and right or wrong, I was responsible only to myself. Here was an organization managed by a very capable young woman who would expect those associated with her to accept her decisions. If I should join that organization I would be responsible for the welfare of other people based on orders given by someone else. I would have to learn to trust strangers, to follow instead of to lead. And there undoubtedly would be much else I would have to learn.

On my way out I found Peppa still in front of the bulletin board. She was busy helping people fill out their notes and pin them on the board. I went home with her and was invited to stay with her family for as long as I wished.

The next morning I returned to Piotrkowska 28. I had thought seriously about what Tzivia had said, but I hadn't changed my mind. There had been too many times throughout the war when I had been responsible for the lives of others, and I knew how difficult it was. Even now, managing our household and my many sleepless nights had placed dark rings under my eyes. If I worked for the Brecha I would have to lead groups of people through frontiers of several countries. How would I possibly do that?

Yet there was something about Tzivia that I couldn't resist, something about the way she had looked at me when I had said no.

When I arrived, there were a lot of people milling about, just as the day before. Izio, the man who brought me to Lodz, was standing in front of the bulletin board. He came over when he saw me.

"Good morning, Alicia!" he said cheerfully. "It's good to see you. I'm glad you came. Let's find you a seat." He led me down a hallway to a large room filled with rows of chairs, with people sitting in the first few rows. In front of the chairs was a table where Tzivia, a young girl, and a young man were sitting facing the people.

"What is the reason for this meeting?"

"This is a transport briefing. All the people in this room will be leaving for the West tomorrow morning."

The briefing began. Tzivia explained, step by step, how the people would be traveling on the way to Linz in Austria. They would ride mostly on trains, she said; much of this train travel would be in boxcars. They would cross the river in small boats at the Czechoslovakian-Hungarian border because the bridge had been destroyed. They would rest along the way in houses operated by the Jewish Agency. The rest stops would be Krakow, Bratislava, Budapest, Vienna, and Linz. The entire trip would take about a week at the most. Tzivia advised the travelers to bring along some cash and food that wouldn't spoil, like bread and cheese.

She introduced the girl who was to lead them. Her name was Ursula and she was only a few years older than I. The entire briefing took about an hour. Afterward, people crowded around Tzivia and Ursula with all kinds of questions. I sat looking at the people. The majority were adults, with only a few children. There were over thirty of them. To help conceal their identity, they wore a combination of Russian shirts and peasant clothing. To me they looked like people who had lived through the war in forests or bunkers, just as I had. I wondered for just a moment what it would be like to be with them for a whole week under difficult conditions. I was much younger than they. Would they listen to me?

Tzivia and the young man came over to my seat.

"Ala, this is my friend Helek. He is the head of the Brecha." We shook hands. I had been very impressed by Helek when I saw him sitting at the table, and I began to realize that the Brecha was a very serious organization run by very competent people.

"Let's take a walk, Ala," Tzivia suggested. As we were leaving the building, people clustered around her asking various questions.

"All those people crowding around you every moment," I asked, "don't you ever get tired of that?"

"Oh, yes," she replied. "Sometimes I think to myself, can't you all leave me alone for just a minute? Just one minute of peace, that's all I ask!"

"Why do you do it, then?"

"Why do you run an orphanage?"

I thought about this for a moment. "You understand why I must continue with the orphanage."

"Oh, yes, certainly. I quite understand."

Her answer surprised me, and for a while we said nothing. Then she continued.

"Tell me, Ala, what plans do you have for the orphanage? Will you relocate to a larger place? Izio told me that you are very crowded in your present home."

"I don't know; I am so busy with day-to-day affairs that I haven't had a chance to think about it."

"What about school?"

"You know they can't go to regular school, but we are planning to get a private teacher."

"Have you considered what will happen when your adopted brothers go home? How will you live then?"

"That's a nice question to ask a former ghetto rat, or, as I prefer, a ghetto lion."

"What about medical care for the orphans?"

"Well, that must be some kind of joke. After what they have lived through, they have probably already had every possible illness." This was not a very adult reply, but all those questions were beginning to annoy me. Still, I knew I had to keep my temper because Tzivia evidently had something on her mind, and I would have to wait for her to tell me.

"You know, Ala," she said, "we could arrange for your orphanage to be managed by the Jewish Agency. The children would get an education, medical care, and there would be adults to look after them. Then when the time is right, we would send every one of them to Eretz Israel. What do you think of that?"

"And in return I join the Brecha; is that what you are suggesting?"

"Not necessarily. But since you would suddenly have a lot of time on your hands, it would give you something to do."

We both laughed. I liked her. We passed a tea shop and she suggested we go inside. There we continued our conversation.

"Ala, you said yesterday that you wanted to go to Eretz Israel more than anything," she said. "Were your parents Zionists by any chance?"

"Oh, yes, my father even had a brother who went to Palestine as a pioneer many years ago."

She nodded. "My family weren't Zionists, but I am one now. When the last transport leaves Poland, I will be on it. Say, have you ever thought about America? A young girl like you could be adopted by a nice Jewish family in America. You could have a very peaceful life there."

"My family almost moved to America once, many years ago," I said. "Yes, I would love to go to America. But I would rather go to Eretz Israel."

"Why?"

"Eretz Israel is our land. It is the land God gave to Abraham and his people, and besides, Eretz Israel needs all the people it can get."

She looked at me seriously. "So does the Brecha."

I squirmed uncomfortably. "Please," I said, "I have told you I can't join the Brecha. The responsibility for all those adults frightens me right now. Besides, I have done my share and I am still doing it."

"You have done your share?" she cried out. "Ala, what makes you think there is such a thing as a share? Look around you; how many Jews do you see? Haven't you noticed how few of us are left? Ala, over ninety percent of all Jews in Europe have been murdered, and the murderers are still living all around us! No, there is no share. We can never do enough to keep one another alive. Those of us who are strong, who can be leaders, who can keep our heads when in danger, are needed more than ever. For us there can be no 'share.' You are needed, Ala. Are you really going to say no to those who need you? You helped before; won't you help now?"

I looked down at my teacup.

"That's not fair," I said softly.

She smiled sadly. "Isn't it? Tell me, tell me, when did life ever treat you fairly?"

Suddenly she reached across the table and squeezed my hand.

"Don't come back with me to the office. Walk around, see Lodz, think things over, and come to see me tomorrow afternoon. Shalom, Ala." She put some coins on the table and was gone.

I walked up and down the streets of Lodz for the rest of the day. I sat in a park, threw stones in the little lake, and thought seriously about Tzivia and the Brecha. She was right. We had to leave Poland. All of us, we should all leave Europe: It was just one big Jewish cemetery.

I thought about the people at the briefing, and I was worried that they might object to me because I was too young to be entrusted with such responsibility. Yet Tzivia didn't think I was too young. I thought about the possibility of entering Eretz Israel on an affidavit and beginning my education, because I still wanted to study medicine. Now, after visiting my uncle's house, I felt a deeper commitment than I ever had before. I also wondered what it would be like to cross all those frontiers. And as I thought all these thoughts, two things became clear: the future of the orphans and the good care they would be given by the Jewish Agency, and the trust that Tzivia evidently had in me.

Well, why not try it? Suddenly I felt relieved and curious about the new adventures ahead of me.

I didn't wait until the next day, but that afternoon I went to Piotrkowska 28 and told Tzivia that I would join the Brecha. Helek was there. He shook my hand, welcoming me to the organization. I told Tzivia that I would return to Lodz within ten days and would report to her office. She assured me that she would send people to take the orphanage over from me before I left or soon after.

"We will see you soon," Tzivia said as we shook hands.

"Shalom," I said, and turned to leave the office.

"Oh, and, Ala?" she called.

I stopped and turned around. "Yes, Tzivia?"

"Helek and I are glad you are with us."

"Thank you."

Saying good-bye to the orphans wasn't going to be easy for me, I thought as they crowded around me in the living room. From my seat in the only chair in the room, they looked to me like a bunch of colorful flowers that I wanted to gather up in my arms. I was already feeling the first pangs of separation, and I knew it was going to be difficult to leave. The hour was late, but I had decided to meet with the children on the same day I returned from Lodz instead of waiting for the next morning. They knew that I had something to tell them, and there was no need to let them worry all night.

I swallowed hard a couple of times, trying to dislodge the lump I felt in my throat. Then I told them about the Jewish agency and the Brecha. I described the wonderful work Tzivia, Helek, Ursula, and Izio were doing, leading people out of Poland. I told them that Tzivia had promised me that the agency would take over the home and that they would probably be moved to a bigger place, where everyone would have his own bed. There would be classrooms, and life would take on a definite direction and purpose. God willing, we would all meet again in Eretz Israel. I told them that I agreed with the people in Lodz who thought that there was no future for the Jews in Poland, or, for that matter, anywhere else in Europe.

We must start our lives all over again. But it would take time to accomplish all that, and in the meantime everyone could continue looking for relatives who might still be alive. The last sentence I spoke in a very low voice, because that was only wishful thinking. I changed the subject by telling the children how wonderful they were and how I had enjoyed living with them. True, I said, I hadn't lived through the horrors of the concentration camps, but I had my own horrors and terrible dreams. If they would let me sleep through one night, I would give them a chance to hear my nightmares. Some laughed when I said that, but most were silent. And at the end I told them how much I was going to miss them.

There was total silence in the room. I must admit I was hoping that some of the orphans would speak up and tell me that they would miss me, too, but no one did. They retreated into their shells, yet they couldn't take all of their feelings with them, and I could see that some had a sad look in their eyes, and others a look of worry. Although their harsh lives had taught them to handle separations, still I could see tears in some eyes. It did not really matter whether the tears were for me or for themselves: What mattered was that they felt something, and that, I knew, was necessary if they were to live normal lives again.

Saying good-bye to the Sharf family, especially to Herman, was also heartbreaking. He still hadn't made any definite plans to go to Switzerland to be cured of his tuberculosis, and I suspected that his illness was too advanced anyway.

I repeated my conversation with Tzivia and told them what I had seen in Lodz. They listened carefully to every word. I could see that they approved of my decision to join the Brecha and were very pleased that the Jewish agency would take over management of the orphanage. Herman Sharf, that wonderfully perceptive man, sensed that I was worried about what people's reactions might be to my age, and suggested that since I was a tall girl, about five feet seven inches, I didn't have to advertise how young I was. When asked, I should use the talmudic method of answering a question with another question.

"After all," he added with sadness in his voice, "you never really had your teenage years. Did you, Alicia?"

"No, not really."

Things seemed to be working out well, as well as could be expected under the circumstances. Mesha and his driver arrived one evening with a big load of clothing and various other items. I was surprised at the number of sacks he brought and commented on it.

"My dear little sister," Mesha said as he hugged me. "I have some sad and some happy news for you. Which do you want to hear first?"

"The good news first, please, Mesha. It will soothe my aching heart, and when the blow of the bad news comes, it will not be so painful."

"I have fallen in love, my little dove. I have fallen in love with the most beautiful girl in the world!" he declared with a big smile. "And I am going to marry her as soon as we are both discharged from the army. She is an army doctor and she, too, is from Leningrad. Yes, she is a Jewish girl. She even knows a few words of Hebrew which she promised to teach me."

"Hey, *golubchik*! Don't look sad. If I hadn't fallen in love with Tania, I would have waited for you to grow up. Honest I would have; you are a very pretty girl and someday will be a very lovely woman, believe me! Now don't be sad. Smile for me, please. Share in my happiness, little sister."

God, what a splendid man, our Mesha; lucky Tania, I thought.

"I am not sad because you are in love. I am happy for you and Tania. It is just that I can guess the bad news, and that is that you are leaving us. Am I right?"

"Yes, I am. I came to say good-bye; but I will come by again in a couple of weeks to say good-bye to the Sharfs and will try to stop over again. But my friends will continue to help you all for the time being."

Then it occurred to me that it wouldn't be a good idea, with Mesha and myself gone, to have the trucks drive up with goods and have the people from the agency deal with them. The best thing would be to discontinue our business. If our brothers needed something, they could get it from Ben Sharf. He could supply things directly to them instead of through us. We had enough money now to last for six months, and besides, the Sharfs would never let us starve. I explained my thoughts to Mesha, and he agreed with me. We kissed and hugged and cried when we finally said good-bye. Just before he left, Mesha said to me, "Ala, if I ever have a daughter, I will want her to be just like you." Then he turned and was gone.

My next step toward my departure was to take the suitcases from under our beds, put in the money for the sales of the sacks Mesha had brought us, and add up all our assets. We had a very substantial amount. I gave part of it to Stefa, to keep for emergencies. We bought a lot of food, mostly things in tins, and the rest I took to Ben Sharf to keep for us. After I gave him the money, Ben Sharf asked me into the office.

"Well, Alicia, when are you leaving us?" he asked.

"The day after tomorrow if all goes well."

He went to his safe and took out a package, unwrapped it, and handed it to me. It looked like a white linen belt with many small pockets on the outside. I had never seen a belt like that one before and was wondering why he was giving it to me and how I was supposed to wear it.

"I can see from your expression that you aren't familiar with this kind of belt. This is a money belt. It contains your share of the money and a little extra. I hope you will use it in good health and will be able to get a good education in Eretz Israel. Now, guard it well because there is a small fortune in it, nearly eight thousand American dollars. There is paper money and gold coins, both American and Russian." He saw the shock on my face and hastened to add: "It is your fair share, I assure you. The extra is from Herman. He thinks of you as his own daughter. You want to become a doctor; maybe you can take care of people who—" And here he nearly broke down. I knew Ben loved his brother very much, and now to my great sorrow I understood that Herman Sharf would never get well. At that moment I wished I could stay and devote my time to caring for him, but I knew he would never allow it. Whatever he had to face, Herman Sharf would face alone and with courage.

"Now, Alicia, pull up your shirt and I will show you how to put your belt on. Please don't be shy; just around the waistline."

It fit perfectly. Since I was still very skinny, it was impossible to see that I had something under my shirt.

Mr. Sharf looked satisfied after I tucked the shirt back into my skirt.

"You must never let this belt out of your sight, please promise me," he urged me. I promised.

Next I took off my necklace and handed it to Mr. Sharf.

"Sir, could you please do me a great favor and give this to Mesha when he comes to see you. He said he would come again to say good-bye to you. He gave me this necklace for my fifteenth birthday in May, and I really love it. But he is getting married and this should be worn by his future wife."

Mr. Sharf took the necklace, wrapped it up in a piece of black velvet, and put it in the safe.

"You have made a very wise decision, Alicia. I saw you wearing this necklace and admired its beautiful rubies. I wondered whether you would realize that the rubies were real, but now I see that you knew they were all the time.

"Truthfully speaking, I wasn't sure until I saw the way you were looking at me when I wore it the first time." Suddenly Mr. Sharf burst out laughing.

"Oh, I will miss you, Alicia. I will really miss you very much. God be with you always," he said as he hugged me and kissed my cheek.

I really dreaded parting from Herman Sharf. He was sitting in his favorite place, near the window, where he could look outside toward the park. The sun's rays were streaming into the room through the open window and made his face look sort of golden—to match his heart, I thought.

He was smiling when he extended his hands to me, but I felt them tremble.

"Well, so you are off on a new venture, Alicia. I am sure you will do a good job. Just remember to keep your temper in check. A little bit of spirit is good for the soul, but too much can be harmful." He winked as he said that and invited me to sit near him.

"You saw my brother?" he asked. I nodded, and he continued. "You have nothing to worry about now. You have enough to become anything you wish. Just try to get to Eretz Israel as soon as possible."

I pulled up my shirt and showed him the belt. He opened a few buttons and looked inside. That gave me my first look at what the belt contained. I was deeply touched by his generosity and began thanking him. But he stopped me.

"Well, my dear, you had better go now. I am beginning to get tired." But he didn't fool me, because when I bent down to kiss his cheek, I could taste his tears.

CHAPTER 22

Lodz

My departure was very unceremonious; in fact, several of the orphans weren't even home. I shook a few hands, kissed and hugged some of the children, and asked everyone to cooperate with the agency people. But there were no cries of "We'll miss you" or "Can you take me with you?" Stefa wanted to come to the train station with me, but I talked her out of it. I carried my suitcase and handbag and walked there alone. It wasn't a happy day for me.

I arrived in Lodz the same afternoon and went directly to Peppa's, where it had been agreed that I would stay. The next morning, promptly at nine o'clock, I reported at Brecha headquarters, Piotrkowska 28.

Tzivia welcomed me warmly and assigned me to Ursula, whom I had met before at the briefing. She was to teach me how to lead transports. We left the following morning. I traveled as a Greek-Jewish refugee from a concentration camp, acting like one of the thirty-three people in the group who were also supposed to be Jews returning to Greece. I remained close to Ursula as she explained every step we took along the way.

Our first step was to take a train to Krakow. After we arrived in Krakow we went to a synagogue and spent the night on the second story sleeping on our blankets on the floor. The next day Ursula, dressed in a Russian army uniform, went to the city hall to get our travel permits. I accompanied her inside the building but didn't go with her into the office of the Polish official whom she bribed to provide the documents, at two thousand zlotys per person.

On the way back to the synagogue Ursula ordered and paid for a freight car that was attached to a train. The next day all the people in our group except for Ursula and myself boarded the freight car. The irony of putting those people in a freight car was not lost on me; some of them must have remembered their nightmarish travel to concentration camps. I felt bad about it, but it couldn't be helped. We had to keep a low profile and stay out of sight of the Poles, and the Russians as well. The Poles weren't friendly to us, and a highly visible group of Jews could have tempted some of them to verbal or even physical abuse. If provoked I doubted if the Jews would have remained quiet. Any possibility of confrontation had to be avoided even if painful memories were brought back. Anything that might alert the authorities to the existence of the Brecha could be disastrous. Luckily it was summer and the freight car door could be kept open.

At the Polish-Czechoslovakian border, in Zebzedovitcy, Ursula showed a list of the people and the travel permits to the officer in charge, and he let us continue into Czechoslovakia to Bratislava. At the Bratislava station we were met by two Czech-Jewish youths who took us to the local Brecha headquarters in a school for our second overnight stop. Every day those young men escorted dozens of people—for ours was one of several transports traveling on any given day—to the school for food and a place to rest.

As soon as we arrived at the school we were given soap, buckets of water, and some scrub brushes; before we could lay our blankets down on the floor, we first had to wash it. As tired and nervous as the people were, no one said a word. There were rarely any complaints in any of the transports I was eventually to lead, because the people knew they were lucky to be leaving Poland at all. I learned that each city on our route had its own Brecha headquarters and resting point.

We stayed overnight in Bratislava, and then trucks rented by the Brecha took us to the river which was the Czechoslovakian-Hungarian border. As we waited to be loaded into the small boats that would take us across the river, Ursula seemed slightly nervous. She explained to me that this was a Russian military checkpoint and a sensitive place for the Brecha. I watched every move, standing close to Ursula, and stored everything I saw or heard in my memory for future use. On the Hungarian side we were met by a member of the Hungarian Brecha and traveled by tram to Budapest, to the Brecha headquarters located in a former Jewish hospital. Ursula delivered the people, with their documents, to the Hungarian Brecha and shook hands with each one of the group. Ursula and I slept overnight in Budapest and started back to Lodz the following morning, retracing our route. We were now traveling as Poles who were returning from work camps in Hungary.

A few days later I accompanied Ursula on another training trip, and this time we went as far as Vienna. This was a painful experience for me. My paternal grandparents had lived in Vienna; my father had been born there; and all of my family who had lived there had been killed by the Nazis. The railroad station was bombed out. For the first time I saw the ravages of aerial warfare. The small cities and villages I had known in Poland had not been important enough for mass bombing.

We brought our people to the Vienna Brecha headquarters and started back for Lodz the same day.

After what had been two intensive weeks of traveling, Tzivia suggested that I rest for a few days. I was to lead the next transport by myself. She promised to contact me as soon as a new group was organized.

I took full advantage of the lovely summer days. I stayed once again with Peppa and her family, where I would always rest between transports. It was a new experience to wake up in the morning, fairly rested, and not have to go to the market to shop for huge quantities of food. But old habits die hard, and whenever I entered a bakery my eyes looked for the baskets of rolls that we had ordered from the bakery in Biala. Everything I used to buy was times twenty-four. So, as a compromise, I began to buy for Peppa's family as well as myself. Nearby I found a small restaurant run by a Jewish mother and daughter who, like myself, loved chicken soup, and I had my dinners there every day. Peppa's cousin had invited me to eat with them, but she cooked a lot of cabbage and beans and other heavy dishes that my digestive system couldn't handle.

A week passed and I still hadn't heard from Tzivia, so when Peppa suggested that we take a trip to Breslau, a city near the Polish-German border, to see how bombed out it was, I agreed to go with her. I was really shocked at how most of the city had been leveled. There was the marketplace, a building that apparently housed the Polish police, and a Russian flag was flying over the building next to the police station where the Russian military was stationed. But the rest of the city was just streets without buildings. Everything was rubble. I saw the skeleton of one building still standing, and when I looked closer I saw the name of a bank on one wall.

Peppa and I decided to poke around and see what we could find in the bank, which had been opened up for our inspection. I didn't expect much, but I could see that Peppa hoped to find riches in open vaults just waiting for her. It was silly, of course, but it was a beautiful summer morning, and why shouldn't two young girls be silly for a change? We walked around the building, marveling that its walls could still be standing, and then I went off to investigate inside. Suddenly, accompanied by a loud splintering noise and my own shrieking, I felt myself falling through the air. The floor had given way under me. I had fallen into the cellar of the bank, which apparently had also served as an air-raid shelter. Luckily I landed on some mattresses and other bedding which had been left behind. I stared dumbly at the hole in the ceiling through which I had fallen and at the feathers floating down all around me. It wasn't until I heard Peppa's frantic calls that I snapped back to attention and burst out laughing. It was such a bizarre thing to have happened, and since I wasn't really hurt, I thought it very funny indeed. I was laughing so hard it brought tears to my eyes. Luckily the steps leading up to the street level were still intact. But that definitely ended our search in the bank.

There were a few hours left before we had to board the train back to Lodz, so we decided to visit the marketplace. We separated; Peppa went to look at clothing while I walked about the food stalls. I still felt as though I had to feed someone.

When I met Peppa again I could see that she was very upset. I asked her why, and she told me that she had met Beniek Katz, a boy about our age whom she knew from Lodz, and while they were standing and talking, the Polish police came and arrested him. She was sure they had taken him to the Polish police station, and knowing how the Poles were still treating Jews, she was afraid that he would just disappear, never to be seen or heard from again. Peppa asked if there was anything I could do, since she knew I was now with the Brecha. I said, of course, that I would try. I remembered my own arrest in Chernovtsy, and I was angry at the way we still had to suffer, even after the war had ended.

I knew from my past experience that it was pointless to try to deal with the Poles. Since I always had my partisan documents with me, I felt that my only chance to free this boy would be to get help from the Russians.

I told Peppa to wait for me and I went to the building with the Russian flag. Inside, I stopped a Russian officer who was walking in the hallway and proceeded to tell him what Peppa had just told me but added that the boy was my cousin. He listened politely but didn't seem particularly interested. So I took out my documents and showed them to him. I could see that he now looked at me differently, but to ensure his help I told him that my cousin was just a young boy of fifteen and hadn't done anything wrong. Would he please go with me and help me free him?

Perhaps it was the way I pleaded with him, or simply because he was a good person, but he asked me to write down the boy's name, and followed by Peppa, we went to the Polish police. When we arrived I let the Russian officer do all the talking. He demanded the immediate release of Beniek Katz. I don't know if the Polish policeman on duty understood Russian, but he heard the name and within a few minutes a boy of about fifteen looking very frightened was brought out and released to us. To convince the Russian officer that we were indeed cousins, I put my arms around the boy's neck and kissed him on the cheek. A very surprised boy looked at me, but he was smart enough to kiss me back, and we all left the police station together.

"My advice to you is that you get out of town as quickly as possible," said the officer. "The Poles aren't very friendly here." We didn't need much urging, and after thanking the officer for his help the three of us hurried to the train station and returned to Lodz.

The following day I was on a train going back to Breslau. I was tired and all I wanted to do was close my eyes and let the motion of the train rock me to sleep. But I couldn't do that because I was not alone; I was traveling with Peppa's friend Alexander. We were going back to the Breslau Polish police station to try to free Alexander's friend Olek, who was in jail there.

It seemed like only minutes earlier that Peppa had roused me out of a deep sleep to tell me about Olek who, like Beniek Katz, had been arrested in the Breslau marketplace by the Polish police. This was very bad news and woke me up quickly, as I suddenly realized that something was very wrong at the police station in Breslau. It seemed that they were deliberately singling out and arresting Jewish boys. The Gestapo had done this during the war, and I was very upset to hear that this was happening once more.

"When was Olek arrested?" I asked Peppa.

"About a week ago."

"How come Alexander didn't do something about getting him out of there?" I asked angrily, now fully awake.

"He just found out yesterday what happened to Olek. As a matter of fact, he told us when I visited David and Dora after you went to sleep. Naturally, I told them how we got Beniek out of jail, or rather how you and the Russian got Beniek out."

"And you suggested that I might do it again for Olek? Is that right, Peppa?"

"Wouldn't you, Alicia?" she asked softly.

Of course it never occurred to me to say no. Because of my own arrest not so long ago, I felt a great deal of empathy for Olek. Olek's release from jail wouldn't be as simple as Beniek's. He had already been in prison for a week. I would still need the help of a Russian officer, but I might have to do the talking and most likely the bribing. I was thinking about this as I sat looking through the window.

Suddenly I became aware of Alexander, who was staring at me openly. I wished I could have dared stare back at him, because as troubled as I was, I couldn't help noticing that Alexander was an exceptionally handsome young man. He was perhaps twenty or twenty-one years old with longish dark blond curly hair and gray eyes that seemed to look straight through me. I tried to concentrate on what was going on outside but couldn't help glancing at him occasionally from the corner of my eye. He, I could see, didn't have my problem and kept his eyes glued to my face. A short time later the woman who sat next to me left the car and Alexander moved into her place. He started talking about Lodz and about the weather and our mutual friend, Peppa. I answered him but continued to look out the window, trying to fight down the strange new nervousness I was beginning to feel as a result of his nearness.

"Ala, can I confess something to you?" he asked softly. I turned around, but before I could ask "What is it?" he leaned toward me and kissed me full on the mouth. I was so taken by surprise that I just sat there without moving. I have always loved kissing people and being kissed by them, but this kiss was entirely different from anything I had ever experienced before. It felt as though Alexander were trying to swallow my lips. When he finally stopped kissing me I was completely flustered, and I felt myself blushing furiously.

I expected an apology. After all, he was a well-brought-up man and we were in a public place. Instead, he just smiled at me and leaned forward again. This time I saw him coming and pushed him firmly back. He looked hurt.

"What's the matter?" he asked. "Don't you like to be kissed?"

"Not by a stranger," I said. Could I tell him that this was the first time in my life that anyone had kissed me like that? Of course I couldn't. I had lost the growing-up years when I might have had my first taste of normal boy-girl relationships. Romantic love does not thrive in an atmosphere of sickness, hunger, and fear. I was fifteen years old, but as far as experience with the other sex was concerned, I was at best twelve.

Alexander smiled again and continued.

"How can any of us be strangers, after all we have lived through together? How—"

"Look, Alexander the Great," I said. "I am coming with you on a rescue mission. Don't take advantage of it."

He shrugged and leaned back in the seat. "Whatever you say, but can I just put my arm around your shoulders?"

Ordinarily I wouldn't have minded having his arm around my shoulders. In our orphanage we often put our arms around each other, drawing warmth from this innocent show of affection. We even walked on the street that way.

But having Alexander's arm around me was different. He was older, experienced, and he might sense that truthfully I wouldn't have really minded if he kissed me again. But I said that I didn't want his arm around my shoulder. I guess I was acting like a young girl who sometimes says one thing but wants another.

We rode the rest of the way to Breslau in near silence. I dozed on and off with my head leaning on the window. I was very careful not to let my head roll onto Alexander's shoulder.

In Breslau we went directly to the Russian headquarters near the Polish police station. I told the sergeant on duty that I was looking for a captain and gave his description, but the sergeant was new at the post and didn't know which officer I meant. I was just about to show him my documents and ask his help, when suddenly the door opened and in walked the very man I was trying to find. It took all my willpower not to run to the Russian and throw my arms around him, that was how glad I was to see him. He smiled when he saw me and evidently guessed immediately that I needed his help again. After I introduced Alexander I told him how the Polish police had arrested another of my cousins. I told him that it had happened a week ago, but I had just found out about it from Alexander, who was my cousin's friend.

"Another cousin?" the captain asked, raising his eyebrows. "How many cousins do you have?"

"Just two, that is all," I said firmly, but I crossed my fingers.

We were a strange trio facing the Polish policeman on duty: one young girl, one Russian captain, and one handsome fellow. The Russian stood next to me, and Alexander stood behind the Russian. I took out an envelope I had prepared and gave it to the policeman.

"This is the name of our cousin who was arrested a week ago." I put the emphasis on "our" to give the impression that we were all related and were all Russian. "It must have been some kind of mistake, as you have probably realized by now. Since we are here, we will take him home. This is how he spells his name."

The envelope contained thirty thousand zlotys. I felt my hand shake and the trembling was slowly spreading all over my body, but I continued to talk.

"Our train leaves in an hour and we have reservations for the city of Lodz. Isn't that right?" I turned to the captain for confirmation. He nodded his head, and then I realized that I had spoken in Polish instead of Russian. That captain was a very intelligent man. Thank God we had him with us. The Poles might have arrested Alexander and me, but I didn't believe they would do that in the presence of the Russian.

The policeman looked in the envelope, then at our Russian officer. He didn't say a word, only raised an eyebrow slightly. Then he shrugged and left the room.

We sat on a bench and waited for what seemed like a long time, but it was really only about twenty minutes before Olek appeared followed by the policeman. His and Beniek's arrest reminded me of the Gestapo all over again. I was boiling inside, but all I could do was pray that those Poles would someday be treated by others the way they were now treating us, Jewish Poles who had lived for generations in that country.

Alexander and I thanked the Russian, promised never to come to Breslau again, and took Olek back to Lodz.

Some say that important things come in threes. Perhaps my friends would have involved me in some new mission, but when I returned to Peppa's house I found a message from Tzivia. I was to come to her office the next morning.

When I met Tzivia she greeted me warmly, as usual.

"Alicia, I have good news for you. I have sent three people from the agency to take over your orphanage. Izio went with them. They are being moved to a bigger house in Bielsko, and this will be formally recognized by the authorities as a Jewish orphanage. Izio told me that the people who took over were amazed to see the children so well dressed and with money to buy food and anything they could possibly need. The children send their love to you, especially Stefa." I felt like a proud mother.

"Well now, I trust you had a good rest during the last two weeks and are ready to lead your first transport without Ursula. I feel you are ready," she added with confidence.

"Thank you, Tzivia," I said, and found myself blushing. I had suddenly remembered Alexander's kiss. It was just as well that I was leaving now, I thought, because somehow I couldn't get that first real kiss out of my mind.

The people in my group were Polish Jews, mostly survivors of the concentration camps, with a sprinkling of Latvian Jews, some of whom had been partisans. I did everything just as Ursula had taught me, with one exception. The traveling documents were waiting for us in Krakow. Ursula had brought them for us on her return from Vienna. I was very pleased because I hadn't looked forward to dealing with the Polish officials.

All went according to plan. We made our connections with the Brecha in all the countries we passed through, and I delivered my group of thirty-three people to Vienna. On the way back I traveled with two boys who were members of the Brecha and returning to Lodz. I felt very confident when I reported to Tzivia and Helek, and rather proud of myself. However, I was very tired from the tension and the eight days of travel.

The third transport had been as uneventful as the first two. But my experiences before and during my fourth transport more than made up for what the first three had lacked in risk, narrow escapes, and unwelcome adventure.

It all began with a toothache. One particular tooth had been troubling me for years, ever since I had been kicked in the face by a Nazi in Buczacz. I had spit one bloody tooth out and several others were loosened. I was lucky not to have lost them too. In time they seemed to reroot themselves and, except for one tooth, gave me no trouble. Now that tooth had become very painful, and my gum was swollen. I was worried about leading a transport while in constant pain, and confided my worry to Peppa.

"Look," she said. "I know where there is a dentist. If you have it taken care of now, you will probably still have several days for recovery before Tzivia calls for you."

I was very grateful for this suggestion and we immediately went to the dentist, whose office was only one block away. The sign on the door read simply DR. PISARSKI, DENTISTA. Because it hurt me even to talk, Peppa explained the situation to the man in the office, who quickly seated me in a dentist's chair.

"Oh, yes," he said, "your tooth looks very bad indeed. I'm afraid it will have to come out right away. One moment, please, I have just the thing here." Peppa and I exchanged glances as he rattled instruments inside a drawer. "Oh, yes, this will do."

"All right, miss, let's have a look again."

"But aren't you going to—"

"No talking, please," he cautioned. "This will be over in a minute."

Suddenly, without further warning, he pulled the tooth. I screamed in pain, and kept screaming. The pain was unbearable—it shot through my body and made me tremble. A wave of nausea began to move up to my throat. I was afraid I would vomit. In the meantime my mouth was gushing blood all over my chin and down the front of my dress.

"Don't worry, miss, this is to be expected," the dentist said as he placed a piece of gauze into my bleeding gum. "Here, take these with you, and apply pressure on your gum." He handed me additional pieces of gauze. Peppa paid him, and we returned home.

Peppa applied cold water compresses to my cheek and I changed the bloody gauze, but the bleeding didn't stop as Dr. Pisarski had told us it would. It wasn't severe as long as I kept the gauze pressed down, but whenever I removed the gauze the bleeding began once more. I spent a sleepless night applying pressure with gauze after gauze, and when there was no more I used pieces of a cut-up handkerchief. Toward morning I finally dozed off, exhausted. Peppa, seeing me asleep, felt it was safe to leave me and went to the Brecha to notify Tzivia that I had had a tooth pulled and was recovering.

I felt very weak when I got up, and the bleeding started all over again. I knew then that I had to get back to the dentist as soon as possible. I pulled myself together and somehow managed to get out of the apartment. Unfortunately I had forgotten all about the three flights of stairs from the apartment to the street.

Slowly, weakly, I made my way down each flight. I thought I would make it all right, and I did get all the way to the first floor. Then I became very dizzy and stood motionless, clinging desperately to the stair railing, for fear I would fall.

As luck would have it, a Polish air force officer was climbing the steps, and since I was on the wrong side of the steps, he ran into me.

"What in the name of God is the matter with you?" he asked. I was afraid to open my mouth. I just looked at him mournfully and shook my head. I pointed to my swollen jaw.

"Oh," he said, "you have a toothache. Well, I know a wonderful dentist. Let me take you there."

I opened my mouth to explain that I had already been to a dentist, when what I feared would happen did happen. Blood shot from my mouth, spraying the front of his uniform as well as my dress.

"Blessed God!" He jumped back, horrified. "How long have you been like this? Wait; don't say anything." He pulled a pen and a small notebook from his jacket pocket. "Here, write it down."

I sat down on the steps and in a few short sentences wrote down what had happened. He read the note, then reached down and gently took my arm.

"Come on," he said. "We are going to see that dentist right now."

He took me back to Dr. Pisarski's and, with one arm supporting me, rang the bell. When the man came to the door he seemed not to know me at all. But it seemed that he and the officer had known each other for some time.

"Vic Kurtz!" the man said excitedly upon seeing the officer. "How are you? It's good to see you again!"

"Thank you, Heniek, it's good to see you again too. And how are you?"

"Oh, we are very fine. How long have you been back in Lodz?"

"Not very long," said Vic Kurtz, "but tell me, Heniek, where is your wife?"

"Why, she is in the hospital. She just had a baby boy."

"In the hospital?" the young officer asked, puzzled. "Then who pulled this girl's tooth?"

I would have fallen to my knees right there if Vic hadn't been supporting me. My tooth had not been pulled by Dr. Pisarski, but by her husband.

Vic had a few things to say about that, but it was obvious that I needed immediate treatment. The two men rushed me to a surgeon, who stitched up my gum. Then Vic took me back to Peppa's, where I was a very sick girl for several days.

It is strange to think that a bleeding gum was responsible for finding part of my family. When I told the Polish flyer that my mother's maiden name was also Kurtz, and that her name was Frieda, he gasped. "Cousin Frieda? Where is she?" I was so shocked at his statement that I began to cry.

We compared family relationships and soon realized that his cousin Frieda was, in fact, my mother, and that we were second cousins. I told him of our years in hiding and my mother's death. I told him everything, my words tumbling over each other hysterically—I had never expected to meet any part of my family again.

Finally he wiped the tears from my eyes and told me about himself and his sister, Sofie. He had been in the Polish army when the war broke out in 1939 and was taken prisoner by the Russian army and sent to Siberia. Then after Germany invaded Russia, Polish divisions were organized. He became a flyer. He searched for his family after the war, but the only surviving member was Sofie, who was blond and blue-eyed. She had obtained forged papers that identified her as a Christian Pole.

Sofie was now operating a restaurant that had belonged to their family before the war. When Vic saw the frightened look in my eyes he understood and explained that Sofie employed two bodyguards who were with her at all times. Without these it would have been dangerous to have reclaimed the restaurant. As the country returned to normal, they expected that the bodyguards would no longer be necessary.

Cousin Vic came to visit me each day for three days; then on the fourth day he brought a message. He and his sister had been talking it over, he said, and they wanted me to come and live with them, at least as long as it took to complete my recovery. Since I was grateful to Vic for helping me with the dentist, and since they were my cousins, I accepted the invitation. I regretted it almost immediately.

Cousin Sofie was an overwhelming lady. She was about the same age as my mother. Vic was ten years younger and had been the baby of the family. She told me many stories about her youth in Sweden, and about my mother when she was my age and younger. Her father had been a twin brother of my grandfather's, but he had been in the restaurant and manufacturing business, while my grandfather had continued in the lumber business that had been in the family for as long as Sofie could remember. She also told me that there was another brother who had lived in Holland or Denmark, she didn't remember which. He had been in the shipbuilding business and was also an art collector who would buy paintings for the whole family. These stories were enlightening but also very painful to hear. It might have been comforting for me to learn about my family, but the stories only reminded me that they were gone. But she was a sweet and beautiful lady, and I was sure she meant well.

I had no doubts that she was a Kurtz when I saw how she had organized her home and business. She lived in an exquisite house that had belonged to the family before the war and kept a staff of servants who doubled as bodyguards. Even if Vic had not told me, I would have guessed that they were former military men. I learned later that they were Jewish veterans of the Polish army who had been wounded fighting the Germans.

My cousin Sofie was a lovely person. I wished only that she would pay less attention to me. I loved attention, but I wasn't quite ready for what followed next. My wardrobe, which suited me perfectly and which consisted mostly of skirts and blouses, knee-length socks, and simple sport shoes, was found unsuitable by Cousin Sofie. She immediately engaged a dressmaker and had me measured for the sort of clothes she thought Frieda's daughter should wear. The only change I really liked was the new hairstyle that made me look older; I thought it would improve my image with the Brecha people.

But Cousin Sofie wasn't through yet. Oh, no! Within a few days she was interviewing tutors, determined that I should return to school and to the specific grade I would have been in had I not been separated from my studies for the last four years. Then there were the lessons in table manners—which fork for this, which spoon for that—plans for piano lessons, and, most incredible, lessons in etiquette. Cousin Sofie was determined to make a lady out of me and to do it all, it seemed to me, in one week. Of course, she declared, my obligations to the Brecha no longer existed.

No daughter of Frieda's, and certainly none of hers (because this is how she said she now thought of me), should have anything to do with bribery and smuggling. No, she said, work with the Brecha was absolutely out of the question. She would be very happy to supply them with all the money they needed to find someone to replace me. Anyway, she had been donating money to the Jewish agency since she had reclaimed her property.

My cousin Vic was very amused that his sister was organizing my life. He was happy for his sister. She had lost all her family, her husband and two children, and having someone like me to love was really a godsend to her. I understood this and couldn't help but respond to that kind lady. At the same time I had made a commitment to the Brecha that I couldn't possibly break, even though staying with my cousins would have given me a wonderful life.

I had to make up my mind quickly before I was caught up in the web Sofie was so skillfully weaving about me. One night, after I had been there ten days, I packed my suitcase, left a long letter of explanation for Sofie and Vic, and quietly slipped out of the house. It took some planning because of the bodyguards. I was nearly caught by them, but I managed to leave and return to Peppa.

I should have known better than to think that my letter would satisfy Cousin Sofie. She sent her brother to Peppa's house to bring me back. Poor Vic came three times during the following two days, and twice I actually had to hide from him. It was difficult for me to hear his voice and keep hidden. I really liked my handsome cousin and would have loved him deeply, given time. I think Vic understood me, but he was a devoted brother so he did what Sofie asked him to do.

I was even more ashamed of my behavior when I opened the package that Vic left for me on his third visit. Sofie had sent all the beautiful dresses her seamstress had made for me. Inside the packages was also a big envelope with fifty thousand zlotys and a short note saying, "Dear Alicia, we should have known. You are a true Kurtz. Your cousins who love you, Sofie and Vic."

All my bravery suddenly deserted me, and I burst out crying. I just couldn't stop. For hours I just lay in my bed and cried for my parents and brothers, for my cousins, and for Alicia, who deep inside herself was afraid to love again.

I was glad when after three weeks Tzivia finally sent for me. I was to lead a transport of thirty-three people the following day. The briefing was to be held immediately, and I would be able to meet all those I was to help. I went early and sat in the back of the room to watch the people as they came in. I saw some differences from previous groups immediately. Most of them looked like people from my part of Poland or from Latvia. When I heard them talk, I recognized their Yiddish accents and knew for certain they were Jews from Latvia. I knew then that most of my group spoke Russian well, since both eastern Poland and Latvia had been occupied by the Russians. That was good, since my Yiddish was very elementary. Some of the group I knew had been partisans. Having people like that was a great asset.

Tzivia and Helek soon came in and motioned me to come and sit with them at the front table facing the people. Tzivia talked about the route they would be taking, and when she finished she said: "And now I will introduce Alicia to you. She will be your guide. Believe me, you are lucky to have her. So far she has led several transports. All the transports passed well without any problems."

"Surely you are joking," one of the men sitting nearest the table called out. "This young girl? Surely you can't send us with her!"

This was the first resistance I had ever encountered, and frankly, I was hurt. I realized that I was now dealing with a different kind of people than on my previous transports. These people could more easily assess the danger of our venture, and the men didn't hesitate to object to a young girl leading them. My response was to pull out my partisan documents and hand them to the speaker.

"I was given these papers for helping a group of partisans escape from a prison cell while my leg was wounded. On another occasion I rode to a forest on horseback to tell the partisans to leave the forest and was caught by the Germans and Ukrainians in the process. I had many other escapes from death and learned to survive in the woods and fields. I understand your fear, but believe me, I have been through this trip several times. I know the dangers far better than any of you and I am telling you that we are all going to make it through safely." Then I said something that could really have backfired.

"If any one of you doesn't want me to lead this transport, please speak up now and I will step aside. I must have your complete confidence or I can't lead you. Now, who doesn't want me?"

My confrontation startled them into silence; not one spoke up. Next to me Helek had held his breath, and I heard the hiss as he let it rush out. He turned to me and smiled.

"Now, what did Tzivia tell you?" Helek announced to the group. "Didn't we get you the best leader possible?"

After the meeting I met each of the thirty-three people. When they left, Tzivia briefed me. She told me that we were going to travel as Greeks. We would be Greeks who were returning to Greece, but we would get new documents in Budapest changing our identity to Polish Jews in order to get to Linz in Austria. I don't know why. It had something to do with our travel permits. She also told me about three young Russian Jews in our group who had not been formally discharged from the Soviet army. This worried me a lot and I told Tzivia so, but she told me that they would be dressed as women and that they knew exactly how to behave.

"I hope so," I said to Tzivia. But I wished that they could have just traveled as colorfully dressed civilian men. Tzivia, however, was the boss and hers was the final decision.

In the early morning we boarded the train for Krakow. We were a strange assortment of "Greeks," including three women who were dressed in layers of clothing and walked like men. I would have to do something about their walk, I thought.

We arrived safely in Krakow and had just settled into our usual first stopover place, the synagogue, when a Brecha agent appeared and asked to speak with the group leader.

"Look," he said to me, "I have news for you. Please don't say anything to the people." He came straight to the point. "I am afraid you are going to have to spend a few days here, perhaps as long as a week, but hopefully less."

"Why?" I asked, worried.

"There was a pogrom in Krakow yesterday, and Jews were killed by the Poles. I don't know if it will continue today, but we have several men posted outside watching the synagogue. And the Russian authorities have been notified, so we hope all will be well from now on. I will bring food in the evening. Don't worry, you will be safe," he added reassuringly.

I felt my knees go weak: a pogrom again. I suddenly remembered that Tzivia had mentioned to me that there had been pogroms elsewhere since the end of the war. And now in a big city like Krakow!

"And we are supposed to be free," I thought out loud. The man looked at me ruefully.

"Is it so shocking to you? You know the Poles. After five years of hunting us and helping the Germans kill us, did you really think they would be so willing to stop?"

To a Jew from Eastern Europe, and especially from Russia, the word "pogrom" brings back memories of Russian Tzarist Cossacks who would storm Jewish villages and neighborhoods, slashing and spearing anyone in sight. Babies were thrown into the air and caught on spear tips. Men and women were murdered and trampled under horse's hooves. Homes were set on fire, livestock was slaughtered. All this murder and destruction was justified—because the victims were Jews.

And here it was 1945; after the Germans had murdered most of the Jewish people, some Poles were trying to kill the rest. I was sickened but not at all surprised. This, after all, was why the Brecha was smuggling Jews into Western Europe as quickly as possible. There, at least, they had the protection of the American and British armies.

"What should I tell the people when they ask me why we aren't leaving Poland as scheduled?" I asked the Brecha man.

"Tell them that due to delay in getting our travel documents we have to stay here a few days. But they are not to leave the building under any circumstances. Keep the doors of the synagogue locked, and be alert. If you wish, you can take some of the men into your confidence. In case there is trouble you know what to do."

Yes, I know what to do, I thought to myself. I was so angry that I almost wished it would happen, that the Poles would come and we could fight them. None of my people traveled without some type of hidden weapon. But I realized that the Poles would probably have guns and some of us would be killed. Please, God, I thought, don't let anything happen now, not after all we have lived through during the terrible war years.

I called the people together and told them that we would remain a few days; that our documents couldn't be processed immediately—which was half the truth—and that we would have to stay indoors because we didn't want the Poles or the Russians to see a large group of Jews in one place. I stressed again the importance of not letting anyone know that there was a group of Litvaks (fierce forest fighters) in the city, and I smiled as I said that.

"For a young girl, you're all right," said the man who originally objected to my leading the group, and he gave me an affectionate pat on the back that nearly sent me rolling to the other end of the room.

Not long after my little speech one of the Russians masquerading as a woman came up to me.

"I am sorry to trouble you," he said, "but I don't know what I am to do about food. I don't have any money, and I brought only enough food to last me through today. I may starve before we reach our destination."

I knew who this young man was. He was twenty-two years old, nearly six feet tall, and had fought in the defense of Leningrad. He was one of the Leningrad "rats" who had defeated the Germans in 1943. He said he was afraid to starve; what a story!

I looked him up and down in mock sternness. "I bet you eat a lot too." He laughed, and so did I.

"Don't worry," I assured him. "You will not starve. I have arranged for food for all of us. There will be plenty to eat."

I liked this young man and wondered how he had decided to go on this transport. I looked for an excuse to continue talking with him.

"What is your name?" I asked.

"My Greek name or my Russian name?" This time it was I who laughed.

"Your real name, please."

"Sasha Davidovich. How do you do?" We shook hands. "Well, Sasha Davidovich, let's go and find some food for you to eat."

"Your name is Alicia, Ala for short. Is that right?"

"Yes, that is right."

He suddenly became very serious.

"Tell me truthfully, Ala, why are we being detained here?"

The earnestness of his question took me by surprise. "As I told you before, it is a matter of paperwork on our documents," I said.

"It isn't paperwork, Ala. I have been in the war too long to believe such stories. Don't you think I can smell trouble? Tell me the truth; I will not tell anyone. If I do," he said, grinning, "you can withhold my food."

I couldn't resist this charming, handsome fellow with blue eyes that reminded me of my brother Zachary's. I felt I could trust him.

"All right, Sasha, I will tell you. But you must promise not to tell anyone about this, not even your two fellow Russians."

"I promise," he said.

"I was told by a member of the Brecha that yesterday there was a pogrom in this city."

His eyes widened. "You are kidding!" he cried out. "A pogrom! Here in Krakow? Are you sure?"

"Why should I lie about a thing like that?" I asked.

A change suddenly came over Sasha. I watched his face turn an angry red. There he stood, a young Russian Jew many of whose ancestors were butchered in Russian pogroms, and he was facing a similar situation. His fists were clenched, ready to fight. I could guess what was going through his head. He was going to show those bloody Poles.

"Relax, Sasha. The Brecha is patrolling the place, and soon we will know more about the situation. I am expecting a Brecha member any minute now."

"You know, Ala, I have to tell my comrades. They also fought on the front and know how to handle themselves. The three of us can keep an eye on things. The rest should not know. You are right about that, and they should keep inside."

"That's a good idea, Sasha. I am lucky to have you with us. If something should go wrong for me, you must take over." He nodded his head.

"Have you ever been in a pogrom, Alicia?" he asked. I stiffened.

"What do you think the last five years have been?" His face flushed a deep red as he understood the unfairness of his question.

"I am sorry; how stupid of me."

"It is all right. Don't worry about it."

"Do you think we will get out of here alive?" he asked.

"Yes, of course. I always get out alive. Perhaps a little bruised, but alive."

"That's good to know," he said, smiling.

"Thank you for your help. I am now counting on you, but meanwhile, let's get you some food."

Sasha proved a wonderful, if always hungry, friend that week. I had only one problem with him. A father and daughter from Grodno in Latvia were in our group. Sasha, while still in the army, had met and fallen in love with the daughter, and I rather suspected he had followed her and that was why he was on this transport. The father didn't approve of the romance at all. At one point he found the couple sitting and talking on the steps leading to our second floor, screamed at Sasha, and seemed about to hit him. I felt a lot of sympathy for Sasha because I remembered how my brother Zachary had been in love with Lena and how he had suffered when she was killed. But I had to maintain peace, so after this outburst I insisted that Sasha stay near me at all times and even sleep near me. That night, when I thought he was asleep, I took off my belt, gently slipped it around his foot and then around mine, tying our feet together. Sasha, however, wasn't fully asleep.

"It feels like being tied up to a board," he said angrily, and turned around, pulling my foot along. I was very hurt at being called a board, because I was sensitive about my late development. I felt like crying, but I didn't. I remembered that Cousin Sofie had told me that the

Kurtz women were late bloomers but when they bloomed they were very lovely indeed.

I felt a hand on my foot untying the belt.

"I am sorry, Ala, I didn't mean to hurt your feelings. I will stay here, my word of honor. It's just that I am crazy about Sheindl, and that father of hers doesn't even let us talk."

Of course, I forgave him.

The following day the Brecha man brought us more food and told us not to worry. The Russian army was patrolling the streets together with the Polish police, but to be safe we still would have to wait a few more days.

Then, one early morning, a week after our arrival in Krakow, I went out to get the documents. Just as I had on my last transport, I wore the khaki Russian shirt that Kola had given me, with a khaki straight skirt. On my head I wore my pilot's hat and had a military pouch at my side. I looked like someone connected with an army. This and a confident air brought me through the doors of offices in the city municipal building, where my contact for the documents was located. He was a little nervous, perhaps due to the pogrom, but he filled in the names on the travel documents and I handed him the envelope containing sixty-eight thousand zlotys, which I had carried in my pouch. Next I went to the railway station, talked to the stationmaster, paid for a freight car, and returned to my people. Within an hour we were on our way to Zebzedovice.

Usually, when the train stopped, I would present our documents to the border police, they would call out our names, and we would continue on the same train to Czechoslovakia. This time an officer asked us to get out of the train and go into a waiting room. I didn't like this at all, and I told Sasha that we might be in some kind of trouble. We had discussed this possibility before, and he thought that we might have to run across the border. Minutes after we were brought into the waiting room a policeman came in.

"Who is in charge here?" he asked. I said I was.

"Would you please come with me," he said.

I signaled to Sasha with my eyes and followed the policeman. My heart was beating violently, but I knew I had to keep my head and act calm. I was brought to an office. The Polish border officer who had asked us to leave our freight car was sitting behind a desk.

"You are Greeks going to Greece?" he asked.

"Yes, sir, as you can see from our documents."

"Hmm. You don't look very Greek—and your Polish is very good for a Greek."

"I had to learn in the work camp."

"You are the leader of this group, are you not?"

"Yes, sir," I said.

"You know, there is that tall young woman who walks like a man—perhaps I should have a talk with her."

My God, I thought as my heart continued to beat wildly. If he had a good look at Sasha, he would immediately know who he was, and then we would really be in trouble. Sasha would not let himself be taken by the police and neither would the other two Russians.

I caught his eye and, without any preliminaries, asked: "How much?" Suddenly I became very calm, just as I had been when I faced the Ukrainians at Wujciu's.

"All you have with you," he said.

"Do I have your word as a Polish officer and gentleman that you will immediately let us go across the frontier?"

"Yes, you have my word," he said, smiling.

Suddenly I had a great desire to wipe that smile away with my fist, I was so angry, but instead I lifted my blouse, untied the belt I carried around my waist, and handed it to him. He reached out for it. As he held one end of the belt and I the other, we looked at each other. He probably saw what I meant him to see—that I would kill him if he betrayed us—because he took the belt quickly, opened one button and then closed it at once. I could see the shock on his face as he realized the extent of the fortune he had just taken from me.

He stood up and motioned for me to follow him. He talked to two of his policemen while I stood waiting in the rain that had begun to fall heavily.

"You can all leave now; just hurry and get into the train," one of the border policemen said. The officer had disappeared. Soaking wet, we climbed back into our freight car, and the train continued to Bratislava.

Sasha knew that something had happened inside the office. But he didn't ask me about it, and I didn't volunteer any information. He would have felt miserable had he known that he might have been the reason I lost all my money and the chance for an education. As bad as I felt—and I felt miserable—I was glad I had this money with me to be able to buy our freedom. If the Sharfs knew, I thought, they would surely approve of the way I had acted.

As far as I was concerned, the chapter was closed. I planned, however, to suggest to Tzivia that the crossing point into Czechoslovakia be changed immediately; that officer had a taste for money, and he would expect to receive money from now on, especially after what he had taken from me.

In Bratislava we were met by two Brecha boys who complained about having to wait all week for our arrival. When I told them the reason, they were very upset. They accompanied us to a school where we were to spend the night. I was glad to have the Brecha man there take charge after such a hard week, and after we washed the floors, we went straight to sleep. The following day we rested and walked down the hill to a kitchen that was run by the Jewish agency. We received very good meals there and regained our good spirits. It was lucky that the Brecha fed us, because I was again completely penniless.

The following morning after breakfast we traveled by trucks to the Hungarian border. As on previous occasions, we had to be ferried to the Hungarian side. The crossing was made in small boats with the help of Russian soldiers. I noticed several Soviet officers nearby, and that worried me greatly. In contrast to the previous transports, we now carried very precious cargo: our three Russian Jews. If they were caught by the Russians, they would be severely punished, probably shot. After I showed our documents to the Russian in charge, our people started immediately for the boats. They walked in pairs, with Sasha dressed in a long dress and with a shawl wrapped around his face, being supported by a man in our group. It was my idea to pair the people up. As I stood watching them, I remembered the story of Noah's ark and thought what a strange bird Sasha would be if the ferryboat were really the ark.

I was sighing with relief as the boat carrying Sasha and his two friends left the shore, when another problem presented itself. As I stood watching the boats, a high-ranking Russian officer came over and quietly stood near me watching the people getting into the boats. I was still worried, but with the three Russian Jews on the way, I relaxed a little.

I shouldn't have. The next couple to pass included Moshe, a completely irresponsible sixteen-year-old boy who had a reputation as a pest and a smart aleck. I don't think he realized the danger we were in. To him, the entire transport appeared to be a game. I don't know his history or how he survived. Perhaps God provides extra protection for the weak-minded. At any rate, as he came up to the Russian officer standing near me, he looked up with a smirk on his face and said in Hebrew: *"Lecha dodi likrat kala."* Those words are from the Hebrew prayer book and, loosely translated, mean "Let us go welcome the Sabbath."

"Moshe," I hissed at him frantically. "Move!"

"Pney Shabbath nekabla" came a clear answer in Hebrew from the Russian officer. "We welcome the Sabbath." And then in a very quiet voice he added, "Do as she says quickly if you don't want my fist in your stupid face!"

The boy was so startled that he stood with his mouth open, hardly breathing.

"Move now, quickly!" I cried, and he finally ran to the boats.

The Russian officer turned to me, smiled, saluted, and walked away. I felt a warmth spreading all over me and wished I could have really thanked him. I understood now why he was there. He was not watching us; he was watching over us. I was wondering if he, like the Pole, had sensed that Sasha was a Russian. I never found out why he came to stand by me, but I was grateful to God for sending us His guardian angel, that proud Russian Jew. It seemed that beginning with Kola and his father, then with Mesha and his friends, and now with this man whose name I didn't even know, I was to incur debts of gratitude that I didn't know how I could ever repay.

I had no problem getting to our destination, the Elizabeth School in Budapest. We stayed overnight. I had to caution my people not to eat the highly spiced Hungarian soup that was served to us unless they wanted their insides to be set on fire. I had made that mistake on my first visit. We ate bread and cheese and had the tea, which was very delicious. There was always enough food at all of our stops for ordinary eaters, but I arranged a little extra for my dear friend Sasha.

As we left Budapest we were joined by another group. They were Hungarian Jews, and their leader spoke only Hungarian and German, so unfortunately we had to communicate in German. We spoke very quietly so as not to offend the rest of our group. The last thing they wanted, I was sure, was to hear the German language. We were met at the station in Vienna by two Brecha members and went to our regular stopover in a school. We planned to leave early the next morning.

I kept tossing and turning half the night, and when I finally woke up I was sick. I felt hot, then cold, and very weak. I remained awake the rest of the night drinking water and running to the toilet. When I got on the train in the morning I felt a little better, but I started to cough. By the time I arrived in Linz my fever had returned. I had just enough strength to deliver my people to the Brecha at Linz, and then I collapsed on a mattress and shook with chills.

The rest was like a dream. Someone lifted me up and carried me, all wrapped up in a blanket, and I remember being cold and hot. I vaguely remember someone giving me a pill to swallow and having cold compresses put on my head. Someone was talking and talking, and then I slept. I was sick for four days with a high fever; on the fifth day I started to feel better. I found myself in a small hospital set up in a DP camp, a camp for "displaced persons." It was here that I met my first American. He was a doctor who was attached to the UNRRA, an organization for displaced people that seemed to me to be run by the American army but which I later learned was part of the United Nations.

I liked the sound of the English language but understood very little of it. I did, however, understand when the doctor pointed to my chest, and I became very frightened because I immediately thought that my lungs had become infected again. As soon as I could, I spit into my hand. The sputum was clear and I was greatly relieved. I had a low fever and continued to stay in the hospital.

This incident turned out to be not so bad after all. I received many visitors who brought me all kinds of little gifts. The people with whom I had spent ten very hard days showed their affection for me and I was very touched. I was told that Sasha nearly began a fistfight with the American doctor when he wasn't allowed to see me at the beginning of my illness. I had to laugh when I thought of my Russian bear confronting the American cowboy. Both dear to me, both caring for me.

But, I thought, I had to get well and leave Linz. I was postponing my decision about whether or not to continue with the Brecha until the doctor could check me again and say I was recovered. Although I had worked for the Brecha for only three months, the last transport had shaken my self-confidence. I hadn't realized how much of a feeling of security my money belt had given me. With it, I felt I could buy my way out of any trouble. Without it, what would I do if I encountered another such border crossing?

About a week and a half after I entered the hospital, with the nurse translating for the doctor, I was told that I had pneumonia in my right lung and that I would be sent to a nice resort town in the Austrian Alps to regain my health. The name of the town was Badgastein, and the air there was just what my lungs needed. Although it took a little time to admit to myself, I think I was also relieved that the decision to return to Lodz had been taken out of my hands.

I wrote a long letter to Tzivia explaining what had happened on the border and suggested again that she try to find a different crossing point. I enclosed my partisan papers, asking that she use them whenever she needed to and that she return them to me in Eretz Israel. I also enclosed a letter to my cousins, and to Peppa. I gave the letters to a Brecha member who was returning to Lodz. I felt very sad to part with my documents, but if they could be used to bring people out of Poland, then they would have served us all well.

I was still in the hospital when my people came to say good-bye; they were leaving for their next destination, Italy. From there, hopefully, they would travel to Eretz Israel. Had I been well, I could have gone with them, I thought, but most likely I would have gone back to Lodz to take another transport out of Poland.

Within a week after their departure I was on my way to Badgastein with other DPs who, for various reasons, had been sent to this special place. I now had a new identification. I was a DP, a displaced person.

CHAPTER 23

The Badgastein DP Camp

The city of Badgastein was all the American doctor in Linz had said it would be. It had a very healthful climate, with fresh mountain air, and looked like a picture postcard of an Alpine fairyland on a clear September day.

The main street of Badgastein was lined with hotels, each standing attractively on its hilly foundation with easy access from the roadway. The street passed over a bridge, beneath which ran a stream with a beautiful waterfall. The water under the bridge was shallow and foamed as the stream made its way over its rocky bed down the hill, where it disappeared into a small green meadow.

The permanent residents of Badgastein did not live near the main street but in numerous small homes that were scattered all over the hills on which the city was built.

I saw all this from the UNRRA truck that brought our group of fifteen people from Linz to Badgastein. The truck stopped near the bridge to discharge the people who had been assigned to the Hotel Austria. I was going to the Straubinger Hotel, which was only a few meters farther across the bridge.

The UNRRA had rented four hotels and converted them into dormitories for displaced people. After seeing the beauty of the city and its surroundings, I had expected our hotel rooms to be pretty and welcoming as well. Instead, they had been stripped bare, then equipped with bunk beds, two high. The beds were made of plain wooden boards, which posed a constant splinter hazard, and were put together in such a way that they creaked when one sat down on them and moaned when one got up. The floors and the walls were bare of carpets and pictures, and the rooms looked lonely and unloved. It was as though the owners had expected some kind of subhumans to occupy their hotels and had emptied the rooms of any trace of beauty and warmth that could have been there to welcome us. To me, at least, this was an indication of what the Austrians thought of us. I had no intention of becoming friendly with any of them anyway, since I knew that many of them were Nazis and had welcomed Hitler. But it was the land where my father had been born, and even if I didn't choose to admit it, I was curious about the country.

I did not want to allow the bad first impression to bother me, and decided to make some modifications in our sleeping arrangements. I was assigned to a room that was already occupied by one other single girl and a young couple. I took off the top bed and put it near the window. The couple had draped a blanket around their bunk bed for privacy, but they stayed only overnight and were replaced by two middle-aged ladies who followed my example and separated their beds as well. As a result we had a room filled with wall-to-wall beds.

But what was lacking in our rooms was more than made up for by the UNRRA, whose members appeared to be part of the American army. They were kind to us, very hospitable, and cared deeply for our welfare. This became more evident as time passed.

Our meals were good and sufficient to keep us from hunger but generally left us with the feeling that we had not had enough to eat. The bread, for example, was white and so thinly sliced that one could blow a hole through it. It disappeared from the table very quickly. There was a lot of table talk each day about calories; some of us suspected that part of our calories always remained in the kitchen with the Austrian staff.

The fresh air and my daily walks were slowly helping me recover. I soon found out that the hotel had very fine bathing facilities in its basement, and I used these daily and sometimes more often. The tiled bathtubs were built like small swimming pools. They were square and could easily accommodate two people. One person, if alone, could even splash about as though swimming, which I often did. These facilities, as well as towels, were available to all of us without charge, but later I drew my ration of cigarettes from the UNRRA store and gave some to the Austrian attendants. This made me a welcome bather.

Residents could avail themselves of various services. Young children and teenagers could register for the school which was scheduled to open in the Hotel Victoria. Medical and dental care was available at the Gadstein Hotel. The doctors were Jewish survivors of concentration camps and forests, and treatment was free. And when fall changed to winter, an announcement appeared about clothing; it was made available to us at a special store established by the UNRRA. The clothing was donated by people in the United States.

I spent several hours each day wandering from hotel to hotel, sitting in the lobbies and observing people. I was hoping to find someone I knew, but I didn't. I also took long walks into the forests that grew in the surrounding mountains. The countryside reminded me of my childhood in Rosulna in the Carpathian Mountains, and I spent hours just walking and listening to life in the forest. When I would reach a high point I would sit down and look with fascination at the breathtaking view below. I would often meet other residents of the hotels on the forest paths. We always greeted one another, and sometimes we would stop and talk, exchanging information about other particular spots that were worth seeing.

As the weather grew colder I decreased my solitary walks and began looking for friends. Since none of us had assigned seats in the dining room, we often met new people at our tables. I soon met a very lovely girl named Vanda and her friend Lora, both of whom lived in the hotel with Lora's mother. The three lived in one room, only a few doors down the hall from mine. They were from Vilno, survivors of concentration camps, and like myself came to Badgastein to rest up and wait for eventual resettlement to a permanent home. I soon learned that they had family in America with whom they had already communicated. They were waiting to get papers in order to join them. Even though we were going in different directions, this didn't prevent us from becoming good friends. I was especially friendly with Vanda who, like myself, had no one left of her family. She was a very sweet girl, and as she got to know me better she introduced me to her circle of friends, for which I was very grateful.

I was also reunited with my friend Peppa. She had received the letter I had sent her from Linz, in which I had told her that I would be going to Badgastein in Austria. Her cousins were going to join their family in the United States. Although Peppa was expected to go with them, she decided to come to Badgastein first to see me and then make her final decision as to where to go.

I was very happy to see her. She gave me news of my cousins. Vic had been transferred to Warsaw, where he hoped to be discharged from the air force. Peppa had regularly visited my cousin Sofie. She told me that I had indeed been an idiot to have left Sofie, who missed me very much. That comment brought back guilt feelings over the way I had left my cousins, and for a moment I wasn't sure that I was glad to see Peppa after all.

Peppa had been assigned to the International Hotel, and I tried to have her transferred to my hotel, but wasn't immediately successful. When I eventually obtained the permission, Peppa had already established herself in her hotel. She had made new friends and wasn't any longer interested in moving. Besides, she said, she hoped that all the steps she had to climb up to her hotel room might make her grow.

"Look how you have grown, Alicia," she said, looking me up and down. "Look at the waistline of your dress!" Peppa was right about my growth. My waistline was about an inch higher than before.

Until now I had never paid much attention to my height. I had always been the tallest girl for my age wherever I was, and I accepted this as a fact of life. But in our small hotel community, people took more notice of one another, and with little else to occupy themselves, they became involved with one another's affairs.

My growth, I decided, was a relative matter. It wasn't that I was growing so tall, but that those around me weren't growing at all. Due to lack of food during the war years, illnesses, and the horrors of the concentration camps, most of the young people, especially the boys, were short. I thought it was possible that some of them would eventually grow taller, certainly I hoped so, but at that time I was, on the average, almost a head taller than the boys in my age group.

This difference in height was especially noticeable when, upon Vanda's urging, I went with her to a dance given in our public library. I liked dancing and music, and I looked pretty in one of the dresses Sofie had made for me, but I remained a wallflower during most of the evening. My dance partners and I felt very uncomfortable when we danced; their heads usually came up to my chest, making conversation impossible. I tried going to other dances but finally gave them up.

Also, on several occasions when people asked my age, I could see their concern. Some would look at me and say, "Oh! You are still growing?"

So it was quite natural that I looked around for tall people when out walking, and those I noticed were usually among our benefactors, the American soldiers who worked for the UNRRA. I liked to watch the way they walked. They would walk gracefully and confidently, as though the street belonged to them—or the whole town, or the whole world. Indeed, in the winter of 1945–46 it seemed to me that the world belonged to the Americans, because the whole world to me at that time was Badgastein.

I remember that one time I walked past the main street into a residential area and stood watching an UNRRA jeep driven by two Americans slowly following two young frauleins down the street. The soldiers were calling out to the young women in a combination of German and English. The women kept turning their heads toward the Americans and laughing. I stood with my mouth open, watching this wooing with interest until the men came close to me. The jeep finally stopped and the frauleins were helped into it.

Suddenly one of the Americans called out to me in broken German. "Hey, fraulein! Watch out, a bird might fly into your mouth!"

"I am not a fraulein; I am a Jewish girl," I said. Then I burst out laughing.

"Is that so?" he said. He winked at me and they drove off.

That was the only time I received any personal attention from the Americans. I continued to watch them because for some unexplainable reason I felt very drawn to them. I attended English classes conducted in the Hotel Victoria, and I loved the language. I studied hard, and even though I spoke it very hesitantly, my vocabulary was increasing daily. It was while attending the English classes that I had the chance to visit the other classes being held in the Hotel Victoria. Some of the students were in their early teens, but some were closer to my age. I began thinking once more about my education.

Until then, I had pushed thoughts of school out of my mind, but as I watched the students I began to think of myself as one of them, and the idea took root. Then one morning I arrived early to see the principal, whose name was Mr. Zohar.

I spoke to him in Hebrew, gave him my name, and told him that I would like to be a student there. He looked at me, a tall girl of five feet eight inches, and smiled.

"How old are you, Ala?" he asked.

"I am sixteen years old, and I would like to attend classes in your school."

Mr. Zohar looked at me thoughtfully. "Aren't you a little too old to sit in the classroom with all those children?"

I had always been too young, and now suddenly I was too old! But I had expected this question.

"Mr. Zohar, you are a teacher and you probably know the story of our sage, Rabbi Akiva. He was a simple shepherd and forty years old when he first began to study, and look what he became!"

Mr. Zohar burst out laughing. "Well, well. A girl who knows the story of Rabbi Akiva, and knows when to tell it, deserves to enroll in my classes."

And this was how I became a student, the oldest student in our classroom of ten boys and girls. I was the most diligent of them all and the most frustrated as well.

I soon found out that the classes were conducted solely in Yiddish. My own knowledge of the language, although barely adequate for oral communication, was nonexistent as far as the written word was concerned. As a result I had difficulty understanding the teacher and could not take adequate notes. I wrote in Polish or Hebrew, hoping that when I got home I would be able to sort things out, but when I tried to read back my notes I couldn't find one sentence that made any sense.

This went on for a whole week. It wouldn't have been so bad if the classwork hadn't involved answering questions. There my classmates really had fun. They rocked with laughter as I struggled with my Yiddish, breaking periodically into Polish and Hebrew. In desperation I even used Russian. They must have seen me as a tall idiot, and if I weren't a Kurtz-Jurman, I would have given up. But I was determined to stay in the classroom. After some inquiries into the secrets of written Yiddish it was suggested by one student that if I added "alef" and "ayin" to my Hebrew words, they might read like Yiddish, but of course, they didn't. I finally settled on using the Polish alphabet to write down the sounds of the Yiddish words.

What I lacked in general studies I more than made up in my English and Hebrew classes. There, of course, I excelled, which soothed my bruised ego.

My friends Vanda and Peppa thought I was regressing to childhood. Especially Peppa, who knew me when I was an "intelligent adult." When they kidded me about it, and they were sometimes quite irritating, I tried to smile. I couldn't explain to them that the classroom was for me only the first step into a new world, the world of the written word. I felt like a thirsty traveler who had come out of a dry desert into a lush oasis surrounding springs of cold water. I read everything I could beg or borrow: Polish, Hebrew, English, and even Russian books. I understood only half of what was in those books because I read few of those languages well. I spent hours in the public library reading, or just looking through the books with what was a kind of worship; I was beginning to appreciate how much knowledge and wisdom they contained.

After about two months in Badgastein I was feeling better—but decided to stay on. Where else could I go? I had no money and here, at least, I could study.

One day as I returned to my hotel from classes to have lunch, I noticed two young boys, about seventeen or eighteen years old, standing in front of our hotel. Most of the people had gone in for lunch, but these boys just stood there. I was about to go in, too, but instead I went up to the boys and invited them into the lobby. I excused myself and went into the office to ask for two lunch tickets.

During our lunch together I found out that one of the boys, the blond, blue-eyed one, was named Heniek and came from Lodz and that the darker boy with the warm brown eyes was named Beniek and that he came from Krakow. They were both survivors of concentration camps and lived in a pension especially organized for young people with lung illnesses or general malnutrition. The pension in a town called Bad Ischl, housed about twenty boys and girls from fifteen to nineteen years old. The actual number of people varied due to sudden deaths and occasional new arrivals.

As we talked, the boys assured me that they were well now and that they had come to Badgastein to look for friends who might have survived. They were very polite and interesting and we soon became friends. They left to return home in the afternoon but promised to visit again.

A few days later some of their friends came looking for me. Within one month I had made about a dozen new friends, all boys, all very nice, and some as tall as myself. Sometimes they stayed overnight when I could get them a place to sleep, but most of the time they stayed for lunch and left in the afternoon. I would have to skip my afternoon classes, but I showed them Badgastein and we talked, walked, and had a very pleasant time.

After some of the visits I began receiving letters, and that was really lovely. I was corresponding daily with a dozen friends all in Polish, with one exception. Beniek knew Hebrew, so we wrote in Hebrew and Polish. I loved to receive and answer letters. The letters were very informative, mostly about their lives, sometimes about a book they had read, or telling me of a book that I would receive on their next visit. The letters were bare of emotional content. The closest they came to expressing any feelings for me would be to say they missed me. Yet, when we talked I could sense that some of the boys felt more than friendship for me; but no one said or wrote a word.

Heniek remained my closest friend. I knew that he liked me very much and given time he would have probably loved me as well. But we maintained a beautiful friendship through correspondence and occasional visits. My writing in Polish improved considerably, and I received many compliments.

My friendship with both Heniek and Beniek was beautiful. I think, frankly, I needed only one close girlfriend, or two at the most, and I found them in Vanda and Peppa. I had always felt more comfortable with boys than with girls. I wasn't a coy girl; I was extremely honest. I had had a wonderful experience with my father and brothers, and I respected men. My friends knew they could trust me; I didn't gossip. They knew that when they came to Badgastein they had a combination friend and sister in me.

Soon I had another reason to be happy in Badgastein. I joined an organization called PaChaCh.

It happened in a very strange way. Our teacher had asked us to write an essay on the subject "something you wish always to remember." I wrote about Kola, his father and the Kalpak partisans. The teacher gave me an A for my essay. Then he told me about PaChaCh and asked me to join.

The name of the organization was derived from three different words. Those who had fought the Germans in the forest, ghettos, or fields were called partisans. Those who helped the partisans survive while endangering themselves in the process were also entitled to the name partisan. Those who fought in the army were called *chayal*, soldier, and those who were ready to go and work in Eretz Israel were called *chalutz*, pioneer. *Partisan chayal chalutz*, abbreviated to PaChaCh.

I was eligible to join and considered it an honor to become a member. We had meetings once a week in the Hotel Victoria, and I attended faithfully. The meetings usually consisted of sharing the news of the world and discussions about our future. Until then I had been busy with my own survival, then the orphans, and later the Brecha. In this organization I was part of a group that concerned itself with the survival of all of our people everywhere in the world.

We were standing by, ready to go to Eretz Israel. But I soon learned that that wasn't so simple. We now had a new enemy who was preventing us from reaching our goal. His name was Bevin, and he was Britain's foreign secretary.

Eretz Israel, which the world knew as Palestine, was governed by England under a mandate from the old League of Nations. Bevin had issued a "white paper" that drastically limited the entry of Jews into Palestine despite the fact that the English government had, in its Balfour Declaration of 1917, promised that a Jewish homeland would be developed there. The reason for this was that England desired to pacify the Arab world, which strongly opposed such a Jewish homeland. At the rate this "white paper" was allowing immigration into Palestine, we would have to wait ten years to get there, and this was, of course, out of the question.

In addition, it was becoming clear to us that even now no nation in the world wanted to let us into its country. Oh, yes, there were expressions of sympathy, and some families and orphans were even admitted to America under the sponsorship of the Jewish organization called HIAS, but the majority of us had nowhere to go. We were stranded in DP camps, with the painful knowledge that the land of our ancestors—the only place that wanted us desperately—was being denied our presence by Bevin's "white paper," which he draped over the gates of our land like a white shroud of death.

I learned all this at our meetings, and I also discovered that Bevin was in for a surprise. There was nothing in the world that would stop us from reaching Eretz Israel. We were desperate people, the few who were not cruelly murdered by the Nazis, and we would storm the gates of Palestine if need be. To help us do this, the Jewish population of Palestine and the survivors in Europe had by 1946 created a new movement called Aliyah Bet. The word *aliyah* in Hebrew means "going up" and was used in ancient times to refer to the pilgrimage of

Jews up to Jerusalem to pray. In our times the word *aliyah* is often used to describe the immigration of Jews to the Land of Israel. The word *bet* is the second letter of the Hebrew alphabet. Just as Aliyah Aleph then referred to legal immigration (legal under British mandatory law), Aliyah Bet referred to illegal immigration, the smuggling of Jewish settlers past British naval and land blockades into Eretz Israel. Tzivia had first told me about Aliyah Bet when she was encouraging me to join the Brecha.

The more I heard about Aliyah Bet, the more I became convinced that we would reach Palestine. I was very proud to belong to an organization that was part of this movement. I often thought about our brothers in Eretz Israel, so far away, reaching out for us across the ocean with love, devotion, and determination to sacrifice their own lives, if need be, to bring us home. Some of those valiant people were now in Europe organizing ships to bring survivors into Palestine under the very noses of the British. The immigrants would then be taken to kibbutzim, communal farms, where they could be hidden from British patrols.

All we could do for now in Badgastein was demonstrate in the streets against the White Paper and try to call world attention to our plight. We were forced to become accustomed to the idea that getting to Eretz Israel was going to involve a long and dangerous journey.

In the meantime I was busy with my studies and with my friends. It was June of 1946, and although I had been in Badgastein only nine months, it felt as though I had left Poland a long time before. I still thought about Tzivia and the Brecha and wondered who was carrying my documents and using the name Anusha Jurman. I hoped that she was having better luck than I in her work. At times I thought I would like to return to work for the Brecha, but mostly I was glad to be out of Poland and in the second stage of reaching my destination. I was trying to push my experiences in Poland into my subconscious and think only about the future, but I soon realized that that was impossible. Memories of our past followed us wherever we went.

Occasionally I went to the store nearby and stood on line to await my weekly ration of goods, which the UNRRA provided in addition to food and lodging. We stood in line and gave our names to the clerk, who consulted his list and gave us what we asked for; we had a choice of cigarettes or chocolate. One day the clerk was in the process of giving me my chocolates, when suddenly someone pulled me by my arm, turned me around, and cried out, "Little Alicia, is that you?"

I was startled. I couldn't place the middle-aged man who had called my name. Did I know him? He looked only vaguely familiar to me. But there was something about the voice that I recognized.

"Alicia, don't you remember me? I'm Dr. Feldman."

I remembered a Dr. Feldman who had been my uncle's colleague and had helped him with the patients in his hospital.

"Are you the Dr. Feldman who worked with my uncle?"

"Yes, yes, of course. Please, Alicia, can we go somewhere and talk?"

After I took my chocolates, and he dropped out of the line, we walked together to the lobby of the Hotel Austria, where he was staying. We sat down on a sofa. His excited face suddenly became serious and a little sad.

"I have something to tell you, Alicia," he said. "But first, tell me, are you all alone, or have some of your family survived?"

"I am all alone," I said rather curtly. Here we go, I thought. If he starts asking questions about my family, I am just going to pick myself up and leave. I couldn't stand any more sympathy right now.

He must have read my thoughts, because he said immediately, "I'm sorry, but there is a reason for my question. Are you a strong girl, Alicia? Are you mature enough to hear about someone you loved?"

"Yes, yes, I am. You know we are all old, all of us children who survived." At this point he just took my hand and held it gently in his.

"I recognized you, little Alicia, because I remembered when you visited your uncle in Stanislavov. I was the one who became angry when you cut up a sheet to make bandages for your stray cats." He stopped for a minute, making an attempt to smile. "I know you wanted to be a doctor like your uncle, and you will be; you are still young. Your uncle thought you would make a fine doctor. He loved you very much, you know. What you are going to hear now will hurt, Alicia, but you should hear it."

I was beginning to feel a chill creeping into my heart. This man holding my hand obviously had a need to talk and to unburden himself. His pain was so obvious that it seemed to flow through our joined hands straight into me. He continued to talk.

"Your uncle continued to work at the city hospital after the German occupation. Not legally, mind you. They used to bring him in secretly. He was the hospital's only heart specialist, and they needed him. He had to leave his home because one of our colleagues wanted his house. He then moved into the ghetto."

I felt as though someone had stabbed me. I had been right about the man who now lived in my uncle's home.

"Are you listening, Alicia?" Dr. Feldman said, pulling my hand patiently.

"Your uncle was asked to operate on a sick SS man. He refused. But he talked to me about it, and we decided to do it after all, in return for the release of four hundred Jewish children who were being held in a mill. The children had been gathered up in this mill, and the SS men were murdering them in the most cruel way. We were hoping that we might put some of them in the homes of our former patients. The Nazis agreed, and the children were brought back into the ghetto. The operation on the SS man was successful. We checked our patient daily as is normal. On the sixth day after the operation, following our examination, the SS man pulled out a gun and shot your uncle through the heart."

At this point Dr. Feldman started to cry. It broke my heart to see him so upset, but I was not able to say one word to him. I had known my uncle was dead, but the knowledge of how he was killed overcame me. I remembered my visit to his home on the way back to Buczacz, and then I, too, started to cry. We were sitting together in deep misery, when suddenly a girl's voice called.

"Here you are, Father; Dov and I are looking for you. We have to start packing. We are leaving in the morning! Please hurry!" When her father didn't answer immediately, the girl became frightened and asked tensely, "What's the matter, Tatusiu? Are you sick?"

"No, no, I am fine. Please forgive me. Here, Anna, meet Alicia, Dr. Kurtz's niece. Please, sweetheart, go to your brother and tell him I will be up shortly. I have to talk to Alicia. Please." She turned and left with a final look at her father.

"Alicia, listen to me," I heard Dr. Feldman say. "I have affidavits for our family. We are going to Palestine. We are leaving tomorrow and are returning to Salzburg. Now, this is what I want to do. I want to leave my daughter Anna with my cousin there and I want to take you in her place. Then, when I am in Palestine, I can bring her there as my second daughter. It can be done. I just can't leave you here all alone."

I was shocked when I heard what he was planning to do. I could see from the expression on his face that he was very serious, and I realized that he must have loved my uncle very much. I wasn't really surprised that my poor uncle could command such love. Of course I couldn't accept such an offer. But I had to think of a response. Then I remembered. A couple of days earlier an UNRRA official had come to our class at school and registered all orphans who wanted to go to the United States, where some might have a chance of adoption or would be placed in foster homes. I don't believe we really understood what he was saying, but we always registered for everything. I imagined it was a way in which the UNRRA remained aware of the number of people it had to support. Anyway, when my friend asked me if she should put my name down, I said, "Sure, why not?" Now I saw a way to refuse without hurting Dr. Feldman's feelings.

"I am very touched by your offer," I said with a trembling voice. "But I can't accept it. I am registered to go to America, where a family might adopt me. Besides, perhaps my uncle told you that he had a sister in America."

As I said that I flushed deeply. He looked at me with such sorrow that I nearly started to cry again. He knew I was lying then. But it was time for him to go. He hugged me and kissed my cheek. When he offered to give me money, I politely refused, but I promised that once I reached America I would look for him through the Jewish Agency for Palestine. I nearly said "when I reach Palestine." This slip probably confirmed me in his eyes as a liar, but he only smiled sadly and kissed my cheek again. I wished him a good journey to Eretz Israel. As he walked away, he called out softly, "I want you to know that the SS man did not leave the hospital alive."

The minute I walked into the PaChaCh meeting room I sensed the excitement of the people who were already present. There was a complete hush when Mr. Taft, the manager of our organization, opened the meeting. He came straight to the point.

"My friends, I have the opportunity to select ten people to leave for Aliyah Bet. They will go to Belgium, and from there to Eretz Israel. I was instructed to make this offer to those who have worked for the Brecha, and to those who have been here the longest."

I was overjoyed to hear this announcement. I qualified in both instances. When I gave my name I was put on the list without questions. There was a lot of excitement after the meeting, but I left quickly to share the good news with my dear friends Vanda and Peppa. Vanda was leaving for her aunt's home in America, and she gave me her address. Peppa was waiting to go to Eretz Israel and was a little envious of me. I wrote letters to my friends in Bad Ischl and, within a week, I was on my way, feeling very happy that I was finally going to my homeland.

An UNRRA truck took us to a DP camp near Salzburg. We arrived there in the afternoon and were brought to a large room to wait for further travel instructions. The manager of this DP community, a middle-aged man with graying hair, came to welcome us. He was the father of a school friend of mine, in Buczacz. The family had a shoestore on the Hala Targova, and I would often walk home with my friend after school and leave her at her father's store.

He must have sensed that I was watching him, because he turned to look at me. His eyes lingered on my face for a second, but he continued to talk, telling us where to go for our supper. Then suddenly he stood in front of me.

"What is your name?" he asked in Polish.

"I am Alicia Jurman, and I am from Buczacz."

"Of course, I thought I recognized you. You came to the store with Gina. Wait for me a few minutes. I will be right back. Will you have dinner with me, please?"

I hesitated for a moment. I knew it was going to be very painful for both of us, but I said yes, and thanked him. He was back in ten minutes, and I followed him to his home. We had dinner in a room that served as both living room and bedroom. A woman brought in the food and served it on a table set for two. The table was covered with a white cloth and set with lovely chinaware and silver. The food was delicious, but we couldn't really enjoy it. Even the cake which he had apparently ordered in my honor was left untouched. I couldn't eat because there was a lump in my throat. After dinner we remained seated at the table, and he told me that he had lived through the war in Russia. He was a soldier with Wanda Wasilewska's unit. When he returned to Buczacz, he found no one from his family.

"Alicia," he asked softly with tears in his eyes. "Did you see Gina? Can you tell me anything about her?"

I just shook my head. I didn't trust myself to speak. He understood.

"Alicia, must you go with this transport? Could you stay here a little longer? I will send you on the next one, and you can stay with our people from Buczacz. Please think about it, and in the meantime would you like to meet a few landsmen? Come, I will take you to them." He took my hand and pulled me up from my chair.

As we walked I reached out for his hand and held it tightly. Was I pretending that he was my father, or he that I was his daughter? He gave me a sad smile and held my hand in his until we reached the living quarters of the people from Buczacz. He left me there, promising to see me the following morning. I spent the evening with these people, some of whom I remembered. All of them knew my family. We talked about all kinds of things, but mostly I wanted to know who else had survived. When the name of my father's first cousin was mentioned, I was very happy. His name was Israel Katz, and he was now in a DP camp in the English zone. When I asked how he could be brought to Salzburg to be with the community, they told me that they knew of someone who could smuggle him out, but money was needed. I didn't have any money, but I had saved up forty packages of cigarettes, which I gladly gave to the man who knew the smuggler. I didn't stay long enough to meet my father's cousin.

I didn't sleep well that night and was up early. I packed my things and sat waiting for everybody else to awaken. I couldn't stop thinking about my poor friend Gina and about her father. What could I do? I couldn't be his daughter; his daughter was dead. Poor man.

Soon everyone was up, and we went to have breakfast. Then we all walked to the gates of the compound, where the trucks were waiting to take us to the train. I searched for and found Gina's father, who was organizing our departure. I went up to say good-bye to him. He didn't ask me to stay again but took me in his arms and hugged me tightly.

CHAPTER 24

School in Belgium

Our group of ten people was joined with another thirty coming from various other DP camps and we were brought to the train station in Salzburg. I watched with professional interest as our group leader, an American soldier from the UNRRA, did exactly what I used to do when I worked for the Brecha. There was, however, one difference. We had tried to leave Poland secretly, and we entered Austria openly. We were now leaving Austria openly and entering Belgium secretly. It was important that the British not learn about our presence in Belgium. They would know that any organized group of young Jews could have only one purpose, and that was to get on a ship for Palestine.

The American was a very nice young man with a very funny accent, which I learned later was the way people spoke in the Southern United States. He traveled with us inside our freight car and made sure that we had a chance to get off and stretch our legs and could use the station toilets whenever the train stopped. It was summer now and hot inside the car, so some of the boys took off their shirts to keep cool. The older men and our American didn't do this and sweated profusely. We had to keep the door closed and got fresh air only from a little window near the car roof. I hadn't slept well the night before, so I dozed off. When I woke up I became very frightened because I had forgotten where I was. I broke out in a cold sweat. Luckily the American who sat nearby reassured me.

At the train station in Brussels we shook hands with the American

336

and thanked him for his care. I could see that he had tears in his eyes, and I learned later that he was one of the first American soldiers to enter a concentration camp after the liberation. This explained many things. We knew that the UNRRA and the United States army could not be officially connected with Aliyah Bet. But, as individuals, many Americans must have helped.

In Belgium we came under the care of the "Joint," the American Jewish Joint Distribution Committee. They had trucks waiting for us and we were brought to a town with a name that sounded like Ongen, but could have been Enghien, not far from Brussels. Our temporary quarters were in an abandoned monastery. We entered through a wide gate and were told to go into the larger of two buildings, where we would find beds, tables, and food. It was a very gloomy place. The buildings were neglected. Their walls were peeling inside and outside and everything looked dry and sort of dead, including the little green pond. Surrounding the yard were thick stone walls that shut us in from the world outside.

Our living rooms were combination bedroom, dining room, and, later, classrooms. Some small rooms that opened into the large room were assigned to married couples, and the rest of us slept in the large room. Since it was summer, we kept the windows open and didn't drape blankets about our beds for privacy; we lived just like one big family. The women took up one side of the room and the men the other. Most of the time, particularly in the evenings, the young people stayed outside near the little pond. We listened to tales told by some excellent storytellers and sang Hebrew songs in low voices so as not to let the people outside hear us. I was sure the townspeople knew that we were there, but I didn't believe they cared very much one way or another.

Since we expected to stay only a few days, we didn't really mind the conditions, but when many days went by and we didn't leave, we began to worry. On our tenth day there a meeting was called by Leon, a Belgian Jew, who was in charge of our group. We listened carefully as he explained why we were still there. The original plan was for us to join the Jewish brigade from Palestine that had served as a unit of the British army during the war. This group had been in Antwerp and had been given permission to take relatives who had survived the war back to Palestine with them. Unfortunately something had gone wrong, and the ships had sailed a few hours before our arrival. Now we would have to remain hidden until new arrangements could be made for our departure via Aliyah Bet. Leon told us that we weren't the only ones stranded. A group of teenage orphans who had come from Czechoslovakia had also missed the ships.

So, the man concluded, we might as well make ourselves at home. We had plenty of food, courtesy of the Joint, and "une grande chambre," he said, waving his arms at our large room.

If we hadn't been walled in, it wouldn't have been so bad. We began Hebrew and English classes but actually spent most of our time outside near the little pond just sitting and talking.

After about six weeks I began thinking of ways to get out. I asked Leon if he could arrange for me to join a group of Jewish teenagers he had told me about. They had been stranded in Belgium some time ago and now lived in an orphanage. I wanted to study with them.

Two days later I left the monastery for the orphanage-school in Marquain, near Tournai. This move began an important phase of my life.

I fell in love with Marquain from the first moment I saw it. After the rundown monastery, the three-story building in front of me looked like a castle, white and shining in the late August sun. Surrounded by green fields and orchards, peaceful and inviting, it struck a note in my heart that made me want to run on the dirt country road leading to the building. I felt immediately welcome, a feeling that was reinforced when I met Yosef and Rivka Valk, the couple who had come from Eretz Israel to teach and guide children who had survived the Nazi terror. I became very emotional when we shook hands, and they greeted me warmly in Hebrew. Touching them was like touching Eretz Israel. They were my link with the land I hoped to see soon.

I was assigned to a room with three other girls. A large hall had been partitioned into a number of rooms that served as sleeping quarters for the girls. We each had a bed with a night table, a small desk, and a lamp. There was a map of Eretz Israel and a picture of the famous Rabbi HaRav Kook, hanging on the walls of our room.

The teaching staff included Rivka, Yosef, and two young men who were Belgians by birth and had survived the concentration camps. They were going to Eretz Israel with us. The director of the school was a Christian Belgian named Bogards, a retired university professor who was the formal representative of the school to the Belgian authorities. He was always addressed as Monsieur Bogards. I was later told that the school was registered with the government as a Jewish orphanage for

Belgian children. Those of us from Czechoslovakia, Holland, Denmark, and I, the only one from Poland, didn't exist as far as the authorities were concerned. But since we were supported by the Joint and not the Belgian government, the authorities didn't check closely as to who lived there.

Sometimes when I thought of the number of languages we spoke, the school seemed to be a small Tower of Babel. For me it was especially difficult because, except for a few words in Czech, I couldn't understand any of the students. Yosef and Rivka were very wise to insist that only Hebrew be used in the classrooms. I was grateful to my parents for many things, but now particularly grateful that they had sent me to Hebrew school. I joined the ninth grade where I belonged because of all my reading and studying in Badgastein. This was also the oldest group of students and included about twenty boys and girls, ages sixteen to eighteen, of which I was among the youngest.

Here, in this lovely place, I became part of a movement called Youth Aliyah, which in English means "youth immigration." The founder of this movement, Rivka told us, was a great lady named Henrietta Szold, who began rescuing Jewish children from Hitler's Germany during the early thirties and had been able to save thousands and send them to Eretz Israel. There they were enrolled in special schools to be educated and cared for. Youth Aliyah was and is strongly supported by Hadassah, an international but mostly American Jewish women's organization. After the war ended, this movement was very active in caring for surviving children such as myself. I was indeed fortunate to have become a part of this movement. I have remained grateful all my life, and still support that organization in its continuing work. Even now there is no lack of Jewish children in need of help.

I fit well into our class. Although the other students had a better knowledge of the Hebrew language and the Bible since they had already completed one and a half years of regular studies, I made up for this by storytelling. I knew many stories about our traditions and folklore, and, using some gestures and my best Hebrew vocabulary, I always had the attention of the class when I talked. Once in a while I would be carried away by my rhetoric and plunge into Polish. When this happened, I would send the class into gales of laughter.

It was a friendly classroom. Yosef insisted that we call him simply "Yosef" and, a little reluctantly, we did so. He had his own ideas about our names, and he gave some of us new ones. I was one of them. Yosef decided that Alicia, or Ala, was a Polish name, not suitable for a

Jewish girl who was going to Eretz Israel. So he changed it to "Ada," which was closest in sound to Ala. Once more I had acquired a new name. But actually I found myself with three names. Yosef and Rivka called me Ada, the students Ala, and Monsieur Bogards, who was not only the director of our school but also our English teacher, called me Alicia.

One would think that with all those lovely names I would be accepted into the inner circles of the students from Czechoslovakia, Hungary, and other countries. Not at all! To them I was a Pole, and the students associated only with their own countrymen.

Socially I remained an outsider, so I concentrated on my studies and was greatly praised by Yosef and Rivka, especially by Rivka, who taught us hygiene and biology, my favorite subjects. Later, when I began to study English with Monsieur Bogards, I also found him a wonderful teacher and friend.

The otherwise perfect Monsieur Bogards had only one fault. Since most of the children were shorter than I, I had developed a stoop from constantly having to bend down. This apparently bothered Monsieur Bogards, and whenever he saw me, he came up behind me and gently tapped me on my shoulder. I was too shy to ask him to stop this habit, which annoyed me. Eventually I learned to smell his aftershave lotion and straightened up before he could reach me. Once, when he changed his aftershave, I received a couple of pats. I must admit my posture improved.

I learned to walk more erect but this, in a way, was a mixed blessing, since now my classmates accused me of walking with my nose in the air. It was, of course, unavoidable, as in a community of children, that everyone received a nickname. Some were very national, like mine. I was called "Landze," which in Hungarian means "a Pole." At first this bothered me, because I felt again like a duck in a lake of swans. But after a while I adjusted to the idea and didn't pay it much attention, although I continued to feel excluded.

About three months had passed since I'd left Badgastein, and I really missed my friends from the DP camp. I wrote often, but my letters were never answered. I suspected that this was because they had already been moved to their next point of departure for Eretz Israel. So I decided to return to the monastery Enghien to try to convince Tamar, a girl my age, to come to study with us in Marquain. She had some knowledge of Hebrew, and with some help from me, she might be able to fit into our class. I talked about her to Rivka, and she readily agreed to come to Enghien with me to get Tamar.

When I entered the monastery I could see that nothing had changed during the six weeks since I had left. It was the beginning of November, and the little pond in the yard was covered with leaves from the nearby tree. Otherwise the surroundings were as depressing as ever, especially when compared to Marquain.

We were lucky to find Leon in his office. I let Rivka do the talking, which she did in French. I don't know why I interrupted to ask Leon if anyone had inquired about me; perhaps it was force of habit dating back to the bulletin boards in Lodz and Badgastein. To my surprise he went to his desk, pulled out an envelope with my name on it, and handed it to me. It was an open envelope and contained a single American one-hundred-dollar bill. I just looked at him, thinking it was some kind of joke. He explained that a man by the name of Kurtz, who said he was my uncle, had been there. He had left the money for me, and a message that he would be in Antwerp on the American ship, *Liberty*, waiting for me. Leon apologized for not having been there when my uncle came, since he could have told him where I was. He had intended to bring the envelope to me the next time he was near Marquain. All this had happened only three days ago, Leon said, and I might still be able to catch the ship.

I was very upset by what Leon had told me. I sat thinking while he and Rivka went to talk with Tamar. I tried to remember which one of my five Kurtz uncles it could have been and decided that it might have been my mother's youngest brother, Efrum, who had been called up into the Polish army in 1939 before the war broke out. We hadn't heard from him during the two years of the Russian occupation and didn't know what had happened to him. My grandparents had tried to find out if he was killed, but some people who knew him had said that he was seen alive when Poland was occupied by the Germans. I remembered him from my childhood, because he was very close to my mother and to my brother Zachary. He was a gifted violinist and an affectionate uncle, very devoted to all of his nieces and nephews.

Apparently he was alive and had managed to track me down. Perhaps he found our cousins in Lodz, who directed him to Tzivia, who then sent him to Badgastein. He must have put some pressure on the people there to get my address, because our presence in Belgium was a secret. I reasoned out all this while casting an occasional glance at the money in my hand to reassure myself that I wasn't dreaming.

But I couldn't understand why, after going to all that trouble to find me, he hadn't returned to the monastery to talk with Leon.

Rivka returned without Tamar. She had chosen to stay with her brother at the monastery. I had completely forgotten about Tamar, and instead of going to talk to her, I urged Rivka to take me directly to Antwerp to look for my uncle. She couldn't leave immediately, but the following day we traveled to Antwerp.

Rivka knew her way around the city and went directly to the port master to inquire about the *Liberty*. Yes, the ship had been there, the port master said, but it had sailed two days ago for America. There must be some mistake, I cried to Rivka when she told me about the ship. Surely my uncle would not leave me after trying so hard to find me. Perhaps, I suggested in desperation, he was waiting in some hotel. Rivka made inquiries while I waited at the pier. No one by the name of Kurtz was in any of the hotels she called. I pulled out the envelope and looked at it again. I would have thought it was some kind of bad dream if I hadn't been holding the hundred-dollar bill in my hand.

My rational self tried to reason that my uncle might not have willingly deserted me, that he probably had had no choice but to sail with the ship; but another part of me, the part that contained my battered soul, felt betrayed and very unhappy. I didn't want to go to America and I had no intention of going with him, but that was not the point. He was my uncle! Not to wait for me, not even to leave a good-bye letter after finally finding me! This was the ultimate hurt. After my tears stopped I felt a terrible uncontrollable anger, and I swore on my mother's grave never to see my uncle again as long as I lived. When I told Rivka about my promise she was aghast.

"Swearing on your mother's grave is a very serious matter, Ada," she said. "Only a rabbi can now help you to cancel such a serious pledge." That made me even more unhappy, and I cried silently all the way home.

On the way home from Antwerp I had also considered destroying the money, but I didn't, because I knew instinctively that it would help me eventually face reality—I could have imagined my uncle, but the money was real and, besides, it was all the money I had.

Rivka and Yosef were very kind to me and went out of their way to talk to me. When I told Rivka that I believed I had another uncle, my father's brother, in Eretz Israel and when, after some coaxing, I told her his name, she wrote to her family asking them to find my uncle for me.

*   *   *

The winter of 1946–47 passed quickly, and one day I noticed the first signs of spring. The trees began to put out buds, and flowers began to appear in the fields. Everything that was awakening around me increased my restlessness. I was getting impatient and wanted to start on my journey to Eretz Israel. Adding further to my impatience was the letter I had received from my uncle Pesach Jurman, whom Rivka's family had located in Haifa. It was a short and rather strange letter. It was written as though my uncle were in shock. And no wonder, he probably had learned from Rivka's family that I was the only survivor in his whole family.

Then the day finally came. One Friday night we were introduced to two young men from Eretz Israel, Avi and Amiram. They spent Shabbat with us and, on Sunday morning, Yosef called a general meeting. He spoke first. In a trembling voice he told us that being with us had been one of the most rewarding experiences in his teaching career, if not in his life. He would always remember us and had faith in us all. We were the future of the Jewish people; we were the treasure those two young men Avi and Amiram were going to guard and bring safely to Eretz Israel.

Rivka, too, spoke to us with tears in her eyes. I looked up at Monsieur Bogards, who was sitting nearby. Although he didn't understand Hebrew, he had certainly been told that we were going to leave: His face was very sad. He was going to miss us as much as we were going to miss him. I had learned to love that old professor very much. Perhaps someday he would come to visit us in Eretz Israel. Or perhaps someday I would come and visit Marquain once again. More students would be taking our place, I was sure. Would there be another tall girl like myself for Monsieur Bogards to teach, and would he also correct her posture?

CHAPTER 25

Coming Home

"Good-bye, Monsieur Bogards." I shook the hand of the man who had been like a father to me for so many months. "I will miss you and Marquain very much."

At that moment I had already begun to miss them. For the first time in years my life had been peaceful. I had no longer been responsible for the welfare of others. I did not have to hide, or beg for food, or deal with black marketeers. Those times in Poland seemed long ago, but their memories were still strong.

At Marquain it was I who was looked after, and it was at Marquain that the healing of my battered soul had begun. I had been a schoolgirl once again. While there was sadness in my heart, there was also great joy. If all went well, within a month I would be in Eretz Israel. I would be home.

I knew that my decision to go to Eretz Israel had been the right one. I had also been given the opportunity to go to the United States, and this had been very tempting: I wanted to be a doctor, and I knew that in America I would be able to go to medical school. In Eretz Israel, maybe not.

But I wanted to be part of a family again. Being something of an outsider during my stay at Marquain had convinced me of that. Like most sixteen-year-olds, I dreamed of a happy ending, and for me that meant a home and family in Eretz Israel.

Of course the realist in me, the old, old lady who still existed inside me, knew otherwise. Eretz Israel was still governed by the British;

344

Jewish immigration had been heavily restricted. To me and the thousands of other surviving Jews who wanted to leave Europe, this was bitter injustice. There was no way we could ever live again with those who had tried so fiercely to destroy us, yet we had to use illegal means to get away from them. Many Jews had already immigrated to Australia, the United States, and Canada. But it was a different story for those of us who wanted to go to the land of our ancestors. The British would not let us in; rumors were even circulating that illegal ships heading for Palestine ports had been torpedoed and sunk. It was a tense time for us because we had been through so much already.

I believed then, as I do now, that if the Jewish people had the right to live, then they also had the right to live in their homeland. With so many illegal ships already captured and the British concentration camps on Cyprus becoming more crowded each day, I knew the danger was great. But I had decided that if my people were ever again in danger and had to fight for their right to exist, I would fight with them. I knew my parents would have been proud of my decision. When my mother told me that night in Buczacz, "You must live, Alicia," I knew she also meant, "Even if you have to fight to do it."

On this gray morning in March 1947 the dirt road leaving Marquain carried a convoy of trucks. Six trucks, each loaded with ten children, had already moved out, one by one. Now, preparing to board the seventh, I turned for one last look at what had been my home for eight months. My eyes burned with emotion, and try as I might, I couldn't swallow away the painful lump in my throat.

"Good-bye, Alicia," said Monsieur Bogards, gripping my hand tightly. "May God be with you." His eyes, too, were wet, and his taut smile was betrayed by trembling lips. Too emotional to speak, I nodded my farewell and climbed aboard the huge truck. I found an empty spot, tucked my duffel bag and satchel under the bench, and sat down. I straightened and took a deep breath, trying to maintain my composure.

After the tarpaulin was adjusted and secured over the back of the truck, the engine was started up, and we began our trip to Marseilles, where we would sail for Eretz Israel. Everyone was quiet except for one young girl sitting next to me. Twelve-year-old Naomi was whimpering softly, her cheeks wet with tears. I reached for her hand and gave it a gentle squeeze. "Don't worry, *chavivati*," I said. "All will be well. We will reach Eretz Israel safely." She managed a brave little smile and wiped her eyes. Together we watched through the opening in the tarpaulin as our school became smaller and smaller and finally disappeared into the distance.

Making only one brief rest stop, the trucks drove through the night. Shortly after midnight we passed Paris, a city I had heard a great deal about. Watching its twinkling lights as we moved along the highway, I thought about all I had heard about what was done to the French Jews during the Nazi occupation. Paris was quickly reduced to another part of Europe I longed to leave forever.

About noon the next day we finally arrived in Marseilles, tired, achy, and rather cranky from jostling so long on narrow wooden benches. We stopped in front of a school and were ushered into a large room, where we were given hot tea and rolls and told to relax and wait for further instructions. Many of the children used their bundles as pillows and curled up on the floor to try to sleep. But after traveling in a truck all night, I, who could usually fall asleep anywhere, felt wide awake and restless and preferred to keep moving.

As I paced around the large room, sipping my tea and stepping gingerly around sleeping bodies, I thought of all the schools that had served as hotels along the Brecha route. There was the Bratislava school in Czechoslovakia, the Elizabeth in Budapest; and then the school in Linz, where I had stayed when I became too ill to return to Lodz. It was funny really. All those schools, and where was my formal education? But I had indeed been educated—in the art of survival.

My body was weary, but I felt too agitated with thoughts of the past and of the future to rest. Looking across the room at the Frenchmen in charge, I suddenly noticed that they were wearing the berets we "Greeks" had worn during my last transport for the Brecha. We had tried so hard to dress in clothing that would look like an authentic Greek costume; it wasn't until later that I learned Greeks didn't wear berets at all and that they were part of the French tradition. Fortunately most Poles were as ignorant as we were.

In the late afternoon we were told to leave all our luggage behind and to carry only pictures, documents, and just a few pieces of clothing with us. I wasn't happy to leave some of my nice things, but those were our orders. The auditorium looked like a used-clothing market. I was rather sad to see all this, so I was glad when we left.

We were loaded into trucks again and driven to a pier, where we waited. I could hear an argument in French coming from a small boat anchored nearby. It was very loud, and I could understand only a few words, but one of the Belgian boys translated for us. The Frenchman, obviously an official of some sort, wanted more money to let us board the ship. He said he was taking a risk by letting us sail. When told that the ship must leave at once, he asked why, saying, "Why hurry? In this leaky scow the poor bastards will probably drown anyway!" From the sarcastic way the boy translated the bargainer's words, I gathered that the child must have suffered greatly during the war.

Then: "Okay, friends." A man speaking in Hebrew had come around to the back of the truck. "Let's move quickly now. Quietly, please." We did as we were told, hurrying up the ship's gangplank. I didn't know much about boats, but even I could tell this was not a passenger ship.

We all moved together down the narrow and already stuffy hallways, down steps and into one of the storage holds that had been converted into dormitories. Suddenly I stopped dead in the doorway. Before my eyes, all I could see in that dimly lit hold were coffins! "Oh, no," I said. "No, you don't. I didn't spend five years running, hiding, and starving to wind up sleeping in a coffin. No, thanks, this is not for me!"

I turned and forced my way back up through the crowds, back up the steps and onto the top deck. With all the confusion I had no trouble climbing unnoticed into one of the lifeboats, where I proposed to stay for the entire journey. There I huddled, hidden, listening to the activity around me. I thought of the promise I had made to myself, that after I left Marseilles I would never set foot in Europe again. I wanted to leave that continent forever, even if it meant taking a chance with a ship that looked to me like a floating mausoleum.

It didn't seem like much longer before the decks were cleared, save for the crew, which was now preparing for the ship's departure. I noticed uneasily that they were all whistling. They shouldn't be doing that, I thought to myself. We've got to be very quiet about our departure. The British might have spies who could hear us and stop the boat. Whistling, I thought, comes from a happy and joyous heart; or was it motivated by inner fear? I suddenly realized that I, too, was whistling faintly, and I quickly stopped, looking around to see if anyone had noticed. I was startled to find that indeed someone had.

"Hello," said a man standing near the lifeboat. "What are you doing in there?" I eyed him warily. It seemed as though he had been standing there for some time. He didn't seem to be a member of the crew, and, more important, he didn't appear to be annoyed at finding one of the passengers sitting in a lifeboat. But no matter, I was still ready for a fight. "What kind of dirty joke do you think this is, putting all these kids in coffins?" I glared at him.

"Those aren't coffins at all; you know that," he replied calmly. Then, bracing one hand on the edge of the lifeboat and grasping a supporting rope with the other, he hopped in beside me.

"What do you think you are doing?" I snapped.

"What do you think *you* are doing?" he replied, still no trace of tension in his voice. "Do you plan to travel all the way to Haifa like this?"

"And why not? Better than that hellhole down there. I didn't survive so that I could sleep in a coffin." I was behaving like a child, I knew, but I was so tired that I couldn't seem to stop myself. If the Litvaks could only see me now; I, who had led them safely through the frontiers. I supposed I had been spoiled by the soft life in Belgium.

"Neither did I," said the man. "Neither did any of us. But we have to get as many people into Eretz Israel as we possibly can, you know that. The more we can take on this ship, the less we leave behind. And if that means sleeping in spaces so small they look like coffins, then that is what we will have to do."

I knew the man was right, and I was truly ashamed of myself. "*Slicha, ani mitstaeret,*" I apologized in Hebrew. "I'm sorry."

This was my first experience on a ship and the first time I was in a situation that did not afford me a chance to run in case of trouble, the way I had done in the past. I was trapped and at the mercy of unknown elements.

We had to face a mighty enemy, the British fleet. The British, who had fought so bravely against the Germans during the war, were now pitting their strength against the surviving victims of their former enemy. Didn't their politicians realize that we had no place to go but back to the land of our ancestors? Hadn't the Balfour Declaration of the British during the First World War given the Jewish people the right to settle in Palestine?

I turned to the man. "Do you think we will make it safely to Haifa?" I asked.

"I think so. I hope so." He reflected for a moment.

"How old are you?" he asked.

"I will be seventeen on May ninth."

"And where did you come from?"

"The orphan's school in Marquain, in Belgium," I answered. He nodded thoughtfully.

"It's a very precious cargo this ship is carrying," he said. "More than half of the passengers are children, many younger than yourself. They're only frightened now; soon they will be seasick as well. We won't be able to bring anyone up on deck during the day, either. This ship is flying under a Panamanian flag; we're supposed to be carrying a cargo of horses. Young bickering colts like yourself." He reached over and yanked playfully at my hair, and I blushed. He continued, suddenly very solemn.

"Yes, there will be hot, miserable days ahead. But no more than what many of us have already experienced. And when it's over, we will never have to run or hide again, not one of us." He smiled broadly, and the cloud of concern lifted. "What hold are you in?"

"Hold C," I said, "from Marquain."

"Oh, yes, hold C. A lot of young kids down there. And your name?"

"Alicia Jurman."

"Well, Alicia, those children are going to be hot, frightened, and very sick these next few weeks. They are going to need all the support they can get. Can I count on you?"

Suddenly I was a Brecha leader again, and I smiled, shaking my head ruefully. "Yes, of course," I said. "Well, I guess I had better get settled."

He gave my arm a squeeze. "See you around," he said, giving me a most wonderful smile of encouragement. I picked up my things, climbed from the lifeboat, and made my way down to the holds.

It was much quieter now. I found the students from Belgium and an empty space waiting for me next to little Naomi.

"I saved it for you, Alicia," she said. "I was worried. I thought you might have changed your mind."

"Me? Change my mind about going to Eretz Israel?" I shook my head. "Never."

"I am glad." She squeezed my hand gently.

That man hadn't been wrong about the days that followed; each one was truly miserable. The cooling breezes of the Mediterranean could not reach down into the hot holds of the ship, which had been renamed the *Theodor Herzl*. Because the *Theodor Herzl* was trying to pass as an ordinary freighter, it would not do for passing ships to see people, especially children, romping on the deck. Everyone but the crew had to remain below until nightfall. Even then people could be brought up only in small groups, and then for just a short time.

But most of us were too preoccupied to come up for air anyway. Those who weren't flat on their backs with seasickness were taking turns on the hand pumps, bailing, because the *Theodor Herzl*, besides being small and rickety, leaked. Not badly, but enough to keep us busy.

Most of the passengers had never before traveled by ship. Nearly everyone was sick, and the stench of vomit hung in the heavy, uncirculated air belowdecks. And the tedium was almost unbearable, especially for the younger children. But we did what we could.

I was one of the lucky few who felt well enough to move around. Perhaps it was my ancestry. On my grandfather's Swedish side my family may have included a few Viking warriors. Or perhaps it was my need to help—like nurses, who must always be well.

We had been out just a few days and I was already being constantly asked how much longer it would take to reach Haifa. If only I had had some kind of calendar to show them, those poor children. One day I thought of something—I reached down and tore away the hem of my cotton trousers. Every day after that I tore off another inch-wide strip from each pant leg. In no time at all the trousers were at mid-calf, then at my knees. Every day I walked down the narrow aisles between the stacked bunks and let the children feel the ripped hems. "See," I would say, "feel my pants. See what progress we are making." The children loved it. I was careful about letting the boys feel my "calendar," and as it turned out, I had to slap several hands before the voyage was over.

My work with the children and the story of my now very short shorts somehow reached the attention of the ship's captain, and one evening a crew member arrived at our hold, summoning me to the captain's office. As I followed the sailor through the ship's narrow corridors I tried to envision the man I had yet to see on this voyage. I pictured him as stern and elderly, perhaps with a white goatee, most certainly dressed in an impressive uniform.

I waited outside while the sailor went inside the captain's cabin. A moment later I was called in. I nearly gasped aloud; sitting there in the captain's chair was the most gorgeous young man I had ever seen. With curly brown hair and dark eyes that seemed to twinkle, he was absolutely beautiful. He was tall and was dressed in khaki pants and a

T-shirt. He flashed me a smile; even before he spoke I knew I was in love.

"So you're our calendar girl, eh?" he said pleasantly in Hebrew. I nodded dumbly. He smiled again. "What's your name?" I tried to remember it.

"Alicia," I whispered hoarsely, my voice quivering.

"Well, Alicia," he continued, "it looks like you are running out of shorts." I blushed deeply and tried to tug down the shredded hems just a little. If only he wouldn't smile so.

"I have been hearing about your good work with the children," he said. "I'm counting on you to keep an eye out for them when the going gets rough."

Rough? I thought. What could be rougher than what we'd already been through? But I nodded anyway, and he came over and shook my hand. "Shalom for now," he said. "See you in Eretz Israel."

Later that night in my claustrophobic little bunk I thought about all the things I should have said to that handsome man with the brilliant smile. If only I hadn't stared at him so openmouthed! I shuddered with embarrassment. If our captain was typical of the men I would meet in Eretz Israel, I could look forward to good prospects for finding a tall husband. Perhaps with a little luck I would even meet this captain, miraculously still single, again in a few years, when I was older.

It was about midnight on the twenty-first day of our voyage when I heard the sound of engines flying overhead. It could only have been a British airplane, flying fairly low.

"We have been spotted," said the boy standing next to me.

"Yes, so it seems," I said. "I wonder what will happen next?"

He turned and looked at me, and his silence was not the answer I had hoped for. What was I hoping for? Was I hoping that he would tell me I was just dreaming? That we had not been seen and still had a chance to slip undetected into the Haifa harbor and the safety of the crowds lining the dock?

There was no time to brood over such thoughts; a whispered command had just reached us. Quickly those of us on deck moved, collecting every able-bodied person we could find. By this time many of the twenty-four-hundred people on board had become terribly ill from the constant motion of the sea; most could hardly rise from their bunks.

Some of those passengers had to find the strength to get up; we had to stand and fight. We were grouped together on deck to coordinate our defenses, each knowing the odds of capture had been against us to begin with. "I don't think we can outrun them," one of the ship's crew said. "But if we can get close enough to the land, maybe some of us can jump ship and swim ashore. We've got to try."

Throughout the previous weeks, one of our daily chores was sorting tin cans from the garbage. These, filled with other garbage, made excellent missiles, which we saved up for use in such an emergency. This was the ammunition we planned to use to attempt to stop the British navy from boarding our ship. After all, did not David defeat Goliath with a sling?

After our initial activity, a strange calm settled over the deck of our ship as it moved ahead. We waited and waited still longer. It was three A.M. The glow in the East had become steadily brighter and more distinct; and abruptly, as though an electrical switch had been thrown, we could make out hundreds of twinkling, individual lights. For an instant all that could be heard was the sound of the water crashing along the sides of our advancing ship. Everyone stood gaping speechlessly at the sight of those lights, for a moment unable to voice their emotions.

Suddenly there was a cry. "Haifa! Haifa!" Immediately there were people leaping into the air, hugging one another, laughing, crying.

It was shortly after that that the first British frigate was spotted. Then a second frigate appeared along the horizon, and then a third. Doggedly our ship plowed forward, trying to get as close to shore as possible before the frigates surrounded us completely.

But ours was only a leaky old cargo ship; the frigates were the products of modern warfare. It didn't take long for them to bring us to a halt. I had learned enough English to understand every word suddenly coming to us from a bullhorn. I knew they were announcing their intent to board us. A few moments of silence followed the British announcement. Then we heard the voice of our captain speaking over the loudspeaker.

"This is the ship *Theodor Herzl*," he said in English. "The people on board are Jewish survivors of the Nazi concentration camps. They wish to return to the land of their ancestors. There are many children on this ship who are sick; most are orphans. They wish to rejoin their people. Let us come home."

The echo of our captain's words had barely died down, when the ship lurched sharply to one side. One of the frigates had rammed us.

The force of the jolt nearly knocked me off my feet, and I feared for the children belowdecks. Sharp lurching like that could pitch them headlong from their bunks.

For two hours the *Theodor Herzl* was thrown back and forth as it was rammed by the British frigates. For two hours we threw our garbage-filled cans and jars onto their decks. All the while the lights of Haifa twinkled on, witnessing our battle.

But when the British decided to really get down to business, we stood no chance. In a way it reminded me of the Nazis on one of their police actions. First came the tear gas, burning our eyes and throats, making it almost impossible to breathe. Then they boarded the *Theodor Herzl* from all directions, leaving us no front to protect. We were completely outmatched, but fought nevertheless.

Six of our Youth Aliyah children died from blows to the head and chest by British rifle butts. Still others found themselves sailing overboard, pitched into the sea by the invading sailors. How many drowned, or were pulled back on board to safety, I don't know. But I came close to being one of them myself when a British sailor took a firm grip of my forearm and all but lifted me off my feet. During the desperate struggle my hat came off, and my long brown hair tumbled down. It seemed to stun the sailor that I was a girl and not a boy, and his momentary surprise gave me the opportunity I was looking for. Pow! I punched him squarely in the nose with all my strength. He swore loudly, but his grip loosened, and I pulled free.

But it was all in vain; in the end we were beaten down. With the British at the controls of our ship and under British escort, the *Theodor Herzl* continued on to the port of Haifa. I looked up at the ship's bridge; what had become of our captain and the crew? Were they being kept under arrest? It was disheartening to think of such gallant men going to waste in prison. But somehow I knew that the captain was safe inside the ship somewhere and within a short time would return to Europe again to bring more people to Eretz Israel.

The journey into Haifa port, which took less than an hour, was black, filled with the heavy silence of dashed hopes. I thought about the children and the others lying belowdecks who had suffered so terribly during the past three weeks, and were suffering still; and all for nothing. I should have gone down and tried to comfort them in some way. I looked at my tattered shorts; it would never do to come off the *Theodor Herzl* in rags. I hurried to my hold and changed into the skirt and blouse that I had been keeping in my satchel. But I didn't linger belowdecks; the misery was too great down there.

As the port neared, there was virtual silence on board the *Theodor Herzl*. I looked at the Jewish flag, flying so freely in the morning breeze. The captain had raised the flag when he realized that the British would soon board our ship. I looked at it now and felt greatly comforted and proud to be a Jew.

As our ship completed its maneuvers alongside the dock, the engines that had served us so well for twenty-one days were shut down for the second time since our capture. In the quiet that followed, I realized that I could hear a faint singing coming from somewhere on board. It grew louder and stronger, a mixture of song and lamentation. It took only an instant for me to recognize the *Hatikvah*, the national anthem of Eretz Israel. I was moved to the depths of my soul and my eyes filled with tears as I hoarsely joined in singing its plaintive lyrics. As the English stood quietly by, hundreds of voices continued to sing:

> As long as the heart of the Jew beats
> And his eye is turned to the East,
> Our ancient hope still lives:
> To be a free people in Zion.

Epilogue

We were only in Eretz Israel long enough to be transferred to the military prison ships that brought us to the island of Cyprus. I still remember the name of my camp. It was called Caroalas and it was near the city of Famagusta. No matter what the British called it, although it was not a Nazi camp, it was a concentration camp and it was a prison.

I spent eight months in that camp. There were some classes, some attempt at organized normality, but mostly just heat and frustration. When I was released with other Youth Aliyah children, I was sent to an agricultural school called Mikveh Israel, near Tel Aviv.

But what I thought would be the start of a peaceful life for me was only the beginning of another nightmarish war. Arabs attacked Jewish cities and villages which at that time had a combined population of only about six hundred thousand Jews.

During the War of Independence, which lasted about two years, I served in the fledgling Israeli navy, at first in active combat and later in its welfare office.

In 1949 I met an American volunteer who stayed after the war and worked as an engineer in Haifa. We were married in 1950 and settled in Kiryat Yam "A," a small community near Haifa. In 1952, for family reasons, my husband had to return to America, and I joined him as soon as my papers could be processed. I thought of our stay in America as temporary, but I couldn't help falling in love with that beautiful country and its wonderful people.

We wanted children but had not been successful, and we wanted to find out why I couldn't conceive. My doctor told me that my sterility was due to my illnesses during the war, and especially due to typhus, which had caused a blockage in my fallopian tubes.

After four and a half years of intensive medical care, and a major and quite unusual operation to open the tubes, our miracle baby, Daniel, was born in 1958. Four years later, much to our doctor's surprise, I gave birth to our daughter, Ronit. Our third child, Zachary, was born in 1963.

For the last twenty-five years I have devoted my time to telling Alicia's story. I have spoken in grade schools, high schools, colleges, synagogues, and churches. I have spent weekends camping with youth groups and talking to them, at times choking on my tears, my anguish unbearable, but always continuing because I felt the young people, and all the people who had invited me, really wanted to know what happened during the war.

Many times I have been asked by children, "Alicia, the story you just told us . . . could you write it down in a book so that my mother and father could read it?"

It took about three years for the book *Alicia* to be written. I had to relive all my past experiences and the pain those memories brought me. There were months, especially in the last three years, when my mind was completely in the past, and I couldn't even relate to my own children. At times I felt on the brink of insanity when I wrote about my parents, brothers, all of my family and was forced to lose them and mourn all over again.

When I finally finished writing I felt as though I had come out of intensive care after a painful and very dangerous operation. I realized that my family will always continue to live inside me and through me, and that I will always be part of the six million Jewish people who were so cruelly murdered by the Germans and their collaborators.

Through the story of "Alicia" I wish to reach out, not only to survivors like myself, but to all people. I hope that it will help strengthen today's youth by imparting a better understanding of the true history of my whole lost generation. I believe that the book will teach young people what enormous reserves of strength they possess within themselves.

I pray that all its readers, Jew and non-Jew alike, may unite in the resolve that evil forces will never again be permitted to set one people against another.